Introduction to the Health Professions

Sixth Edition

Peggy S. Stanfield, MS, RD/LD, CNS
Dietetic Resources
Twin Falls, Idaho

Nanna Cross, PhD, RD/LD
Cross & Associates
Chicago, Illinois

Y.H. Hui, PhD
Science and Technology System
West Sacramento, California

JONES & BARTLETT
LEARNING

World Headquarters
Jones & Bartlett Learning
5 Wall Street
Burlington, MA 01803
978-443-5000
info@jblearning.com
www.jblearning.com

Jones & Bartlett Learning books and products are available through most bookstores and online booksellers. To contact Jones & Bartlett Learning directly, call 800-832-0034, fax 978-443-8000, or visit our website, www.jblearning.com.

Substantial discounts on bulk quantities of Jones & Bartlett Learning publications are available to corporations, professional associations, and other qualified organizations. For details and specific discount information, contact the special sales department at Jones & Bartlett Learning via the above contact information or send an email to specialsales@jblearning.com.

This publication is designed to provide accurate and authoritative information in regard to the Subject Matter covered. It is sold with the understanding that the publisher is not engaged in rendering legal, accounting, or other professional service. If legal advice or other expert assistance is required, the service of a competent professional person should be sought.

Production Credits

Publisher: David D. Cella
Managing Editor: Maro Gartside
Editorial Assistant: Teresa Reilly
Production Manager: Julie Champagne Bolduc
Production Editor: Jessica Steele Newfell
Marketing Manager: Grace Richards
Manufacturing and Inventory Control Supervisor: Amy Bacus
Composition and Project Management: Cenveo
    Publisher Services

Cover Design: Kate Ternullo
Photo Researcher: Sarah Cebulski
Cover Images: (top) © Photodisc; (bottom left) © mangostock/ShutterStock, Inc.; (bottom center) © niderlander/ShutterStock, Inc.; (bottom right) © Alexander Raths/ShutterStock, Inc.
Printing and Binding: Malloy, Inc.
Cover Printing: Malloy, Inc.

Library of Congress Cataloging-in-Publication Data
Stanfield, Peggy.
  Introduction to the health professions / Peggy S. Stanfield, Nanna Cross, Y.H. Hui. — 6th ed.
      p. ; cm.
  Includes bibliographical references and index.
  ISBN 978-1-4496-0055-6 (pbk. : alk. paper)
  1. Medicine—Vocational guidance. 2. Allied health personnel—Vocational guidance. I. Cross, Nanna. II. Hui, Y. H. (Yiu H.) III. Title.
  [DNLM: 1. Health Occupations—United States. 2. Allied Health Personnel—United States. 3. Career Choice—United States. 4. Vocational Guidance—United States. W 21]
  R690.S727 2012
  610.69—dc23
                              2011022808
6048

Printed in the United States of America
15 14 13 12 11   10 9 8 7 6 5 4 3 2

This *Sixth Edition* of *Introduction to the Health Professions* is dedicated with
appreciation and gratitude to many, but especially to:

the great teachers who channel their energies into preparing students
for health careers. We salute you.

Those dedicated and caring students who have chosen careers of service
to humanity and are sharing their talents with others.
We wish you great success.

Our dear friend, Jim Keating, who many years ago started the writing careers
of two of the authors and continues to support and encourage their endeavors.
Much love to you, Jim.

Colleagues who through the years have given help and support in so many ways.
You are greatly valued.

Contents

Preface

We are pleased to provide you with this expanded and revised *Sixth Edition* of *Introduction to the Health Professions*. We'd like to thank the teachers for their continued use of the book, and we hope this edition continues to meet their needs. As you have seen, the health field is very fluid, and in this edition we have tried to include as much new information as space would permit.

We kept the existing two major categories in place with the necessary upgrades, and we have made changes as follows.

Revisions of Chapters 1–6 cover the following:

- Changes in the demographics of the population requiring healthcare workers trained in geriatrics and health literacy to meet the needs of the elderly as well as individuals from various ethnic, racial, and socioeconomic backgrounds.
- High demand for all healthcare workers in spite of the downturn in the economy.
- Historical review of the health insurance industry in the United States.
- Expansion of the discussion of public health care—Medicaid, Medicare, and the Children's Health Insurance Program (CHIP).
- A new chapter on healthcare reform as a result of the passage of the Patient Protection and Affordable Care Act modified by the Health Care and Education Reconciliation Act of 2010.
- Details on the implementation of healthcare reform by individual states with the establishment of high-risk pools and health insurance exchanges for individuals and small employers.
- Information on educational grants and loan repayment programs as part of healthcare reform to meet the need for primary care providers—physicians, advanced nurse practitioners, and physician assistants—with more Americans having access to health care.
- Internet links to video clips of interviews of various healthcare professionals.

xii ■ PREFACE

As presented in the previous editions, the changes that have occurred in each profession are modified from the latest *Occupational Outlook* (U.S. Department of Labor, 2010–2011). A brief analysis of the changes in the chapters on health professions is as follows:

- Twenty-one chapters are completely rewritten (1–7, 9, 12, 14, 17, 19, 20–22, and 25–30), in accordance with descriptions from the latest *Occupational Outlook*. Six chapters (11, 13, 15, 18, 23, and 31) are revised with new selected data on work descriptions, education and legal requirements, employment trends, and earnings. Information has been deleted from some of these chapters because it is no longer applicable.
- In four chapters (8, 10, 16, and 24), discussion on some professions is completely rewritten while others are revised in selected areas. Information on athletic trainers is compiled into a completely new chapter (22).
- All the chapters pertaining to health information personnel, health services administration, federal and state regulators, and health education (26–29) have been updated according to the latest *Occupational Outlook*, especially information regarding educational and certification requirements, salaries, and anticipated job growth. Other revisions cover the changes in roles and responsibilities in health careers in accordance with changes in healthcare delivery systems. An example is the use of electronic medical records.

The progress of technology and the demands of the population reflect the need for more health services and additional training of health workers in many fields. Students will need to upgrade their own education to meet the requirements of the changing scene.

For a complete interactive glossary that allows you to instantly view definitions of key terms from the text and that can be easily searched by keyword, browsed alphabetically, or browsed by chapter, please visit **go.jblearning. com/IntroHP6**.

Acknowledgments

We would like to acknowledge and express our appreciation to those people who have assisted us in the production of this book and say thank you very much to Publisher Dave Cella and his colleagues for their encouragement and support. You are highly valued for your helpful suggestions and friendship.

The contents of the text material for each profession were largely obtained from government sources, especially *Occupational Outlook*, 2010–2011, the Department of Labor. We also obtained information from the organizations representing each profession, as well as various documents through the Internet and selected reports in current journals, magazines, and newspapers. We used some literature from college catalogs and other professional literature.

We appreciate the contributions of myriad groups of scientists, organizations, and others whose combined efforts provided us with national health objectives for the next 10 years (*Healthy People 2010–2020: Understanding and Improving Health*, Department of Health and Human Services). It reflects the scientific advances of the past 20 years and provides insight into trends and opportunities for improvement in the coming decades.

Last, but certainly not least, we thank the teachers and students whose expressed wishes for this kind of information has propelled us to the *Sixth Edition*. We truly hope that it will satisfy your need for information regarding the various health professions available to you and the challenges that await you.

Please let us know your thoughts and wishes so we can serve you even better with the next edition.

Reviewers

Robert S. Burlage, PhD
Professor
School of Pharmacy
Concordia University
Mequon, Wisconsin

Tamara Burton, MS, RRT
Clinical Assistant Professor
Towson University
Towson, Maryland

John Cantiello, PhD
Assistant Professor
Department of Health Administration
    and Policy
George Mason University
Fairfax, Virginia

Marie Dunstan, MS, MT in Clinical
Chemistry
Instructor
York College of Pennsylvania
York, Pennsylvania

Robert C. Miner, DBA
Professor
University of Phoenix

Tarrance Mosley, MBA
Health Sciences Advisor
Auburn University at Montgomery
Montgomery, Alabama

Gary Robinson, MS, PT, PCS
Associate Professor
PTA Program Director
Allied Health Division Chair
Murray State College
Tishomingo, Oklahoma

Anthony J. Santella, DrPH
Assistant Professor
Long Island University,
    Brooklyn Campus
Brooklyn, New York

Bonita Sasnett, EdD
Assistant Professor
Department of Health Services and
Information Management
College of Allied Health Sciences
East Carolina University
Greenville, North Carolina

Julia VanderMolen, PhD
Assistant Professor and Department
Coordinator
Allied Health and Science
Davenport University
Grand Rapids, Michigan

Susan A. Vellek, MBA, CHC, CHP
Assistant Professor
Indian River State College
Port St. Lucie, Florida

part one

The Healthcare System in the United States

chapter one

U.S. Health Care

OBJECTIVES

After studying this chapter the student should be able to:

- Discuss the changes in health problems of the population during this century.
- Identify expected future changes in the health of the population that will influence the healthcare professional.
- Identify the role of the government in the expansion of health care.

INTRODUCTION

This *Sixth Edition* differs in several respects from the first five editions for two reasons. First, Chapters 4 and 5 have been combined to form a new chapter on aging, health, and long-term care, and second, a new Chapter 5 is devoted to **healthcare reform**. The impact of major changes in the economy as well as healthcare reform legislation on health care have been incorporated into this edition.

HISTORICAL EVENTS IMPACTING HEALTH CARE

The economic downturn beginning in 2008 with a recession comparable to the depression of the 1930s resulted in job losses for many low- and middle-income workers. Many who became unemployed lost access to health insurance because the majority of Americans has health insurance through their employer. More of those having employer-sponsored health insurance were enrolled in a **high deductible health plan (HDHP)**. At the same time more children from low-income families became eligible for government-funded health insurance.[1]

Controlling healthcare costs has been a policy priority for the current White House administration,[2] with the passage of a major health reform bill signed into law by President Barack Obama on March 23, 2010.[3] Some of the reasons for the rising costs of health care are the use of expensive medical **technology** and prescription drugs, reimbursement systems that reward medical services instead of outcomes, inadequate preventive services, the aging of the population, and the increased prevalence of chronic disease, as well as high administrative costs.[2,4] Increased healthcare costs are expected to impact the government at all levels because about half of healthcare spending is covered by federal, state, and local governments through Medicare and Medicaid. Another critical issue that needs to be addressed is the inefficiencies and disparities in the current system. Comparisons with other countries and across states show large variations in spending without commensurate differences in

health outcomes.[5] Both **life expectancy** and infant mortality continue to lag behind levels in many other developed countries.[2]

The United States will need to implement healthcare reform as soon as possible. With that premise, we begin the first chapter with a look back at healthcare issues and protocols developed in the last decade. Much of the material from the fifth edition is still relevant. The succeeding chapters have been updated to reflect the anticipated changes and demographics of the twenty-first century, and the changing nature of health care and health practitioner career choices.

A LOOK BACK

Since the dawn of recorded history (and undoubtedly before), human beings have suffered sudden and devastating **epidemics** and diseases. In the United States in the second half of the nineteenth century, the most critical health problems were related to contaminated food and water, inadequate housing, and sewage disposal. A countrywide cholera epidemic and a yellow fever epidemic killed more than 30,000 people between 1853 and 1858.

By 1900, **infectious disease** epidemics had been brought under control as a result of improving environmental conditions. Cities developed systems for safeguarding the milk, food, and water supply, and health departments began to grow, applying case findings and quarantines with good results. The major epidemics that had caused deaths had been eliminated in the United States, and the pendulum swung away from **acute infectious diseases** and toward chronic conditions. Pneumonia, tuberculosis, heart disease, diarrhea, and accidents were the major conditions requiring treatment in the 1900s.

The most important factor in the decline in mortality in the twentieth century was essential hygiene, supported by home and workplace improvements and attempts to improve the environment. Better hygiene accounts for approximately one-fifth of the reduction in mortality.

Another reason for the falling death rate was the improvement of nutrition, which led to an increase in the resistance to diseases. Lack of food and the resulting malnutrition were largely responsible for the predominance of infectious diseases. Nutritional status is a critical factor in a person's response to infectious diseases, especially young children. According to the **World Health Organization (WHO)**, the best "vaccine" against common diseases is an adequate diet.

With epidemics behind them, the scientific community began working on better surgical techniques, new treatment methods, new tests to facilitate accurate diagnoses, and the treatment of individual diseases. The number of hospitals grew rapidly, and medical schools flourished.

Within a few years, medical care and patterns of disease had totally changed. The arrival of antibiotics in the 1940s signaled the end of the dominance of acute infectious disease and the ascendancy of **chronic illnesses** such as heart disease, stroke, and cancer as the conditions that accounted for two-thirds of the deaths in the United States.

Longevity and an increased number of elderly have increased the prevalence of chronic conditions associated with aging including hypertension, diabetes, end-stage renal disease, and cancer, as well as Alzheimer's disease and other forms of dementia.[6]

Medicine must now confront the diseases and health problems that are greatly influenced by the environment. **Globalization** and international travel increase the risk for infectious diseases. Newly recognized infectious agents have caused substantial public health concern and investment. These include influenza H1N1, SARS, H5N1 avian influenza, and some particularly virulent or drug-resistant bacterial strains, such as methicillin-resistant *Staphylococcus aureus* (MRSA). Influenza and pneumonia remain major causes of death, particularly among persons 65 years of age and older, and HIV/AIDS continues to spread.[7]

A LOOK FORWARD

Most diseases of today, both physical and mental, are associated with personal **lifestyle**. Individuals can take responsibility for most of them, such as physical activity, eating habits, smoking, drinking alcoholic beverages, using illicit drugs, personal hygiene, and so forth. These measures are more important for health than those that depend on society's protection from hazards and the provision of safe and essential foods.

For the future, the predominance of chronic illness as the major threat to health raises many issues. Chronic illnesses related to genetics, lifestyle, and the environment will require a reexamination of methods of intervention. It is generally accepted that the disease process begins long before the appearance of symptoms of chronic disease. This fact changes the approach to the planning and financing of health care. Because the exact date of the onset of a chronic disease cannot be pinpointed, the focus of treatment should be **prevention**. Prevention, directly related to major changes in lifestyle and personal habits, cannot be accomplished on a short-term basis. Many habits that accompany disease, such as heavy smoking, overeating, and excessive stress, are behavior patterns that cannot be changed with one-time activities, technology, or lectures. The role of medical care in preventing sickness and premature death is secondary to that of other influences, yet healthcare funding is based on the premise that it is the major role.

The public concept of health is that intervention by the doctor and early discovery of disease will prevent or cure disease, when in fact health is determined mainly by the lifestyles people choose to follow. Optimal treatment for chronic illness requires health care that is long term and continuous, while health care in the United States is primarily short term and discontinuous. Although behavioral and environmental influences are the greatest contributors to poor health, surgery and drugs are regarded as the core of health care. Although health insurance pays for treatment for acute diseases and hospitalization, the current method of financing health services emphasizes payment for specialized services, for example, surgery or cardiac care, which reinforces the concept of short-term, discontinuous service. What is needed in health care is a redistribution of resources for the prevention of disease, care of the acutely ill who require immediate treatment, and ongoing care for those with chronic diseases.

Preventive healthcare services improve health by protecting against disease, lessening the impact of disease, or detecting disease at an early stage when it is easier to treat. Although Americans use many types of clinical preventive services, utilization remains suboptimal for some services. In 2009, only 70% of children 1.5 to 3 years of age received a combined vaccination series protecting them against seven childhood infectious diseases.[7] Disparities at the poverty level remain in the use of pneumococcal vaccinations, mammography, and Pap smears.[7]

IMPACT OF TECHNOLOGY ON HEALTHCARE SERVICES

Technology has made many new procedures and methods of diagnosis and treatment possible. Clinical developments, such as infection control, less-invasive surgical techniques, advances in reproductive technology, and gene therapy for cancer treatment, continue to increase the longevity and improve the quality of life of many Americans. Advances in medical technology have improved the survival rates of trauma victims and the severely ill.

More sophisticated methods of treatment for complex conditions often require extensive care from therapists and social workers as well as other support personnel.[7] Today, organ transplants, laser-beam surgery, magnetic resonance imaging (MRI), and computerized axial tomography (CAT) are common procedures.[7] Electronic medical records, e-prescribing, and telemedicine increase both the efficiency and effectiveness of health care.

The continuing surge of technological advances is not without problems. Medical technology can also prolong life for the critically ill, unresponsive patient who has little or no chance of recovery. Services such as mechanical ventilation, kidney dialysis, parenteral (tube) feeding, and other means can keep even comatose patients alive. For the healthcare system, dying can be extremely expensive.[8]

The high cost of technology affects the financial structure of the entire healthcare system. These increased costs are visible in the form of higher health insurance costs, higher costs for hospital stays, government payments to the system, and total medical bills. This advanced technology has not only increased medical costs, but also created a social and ethical problem. Because of limits in funding, advanced treatment is not available to all people. The poor, who may need it desperately, have no access to it.

The incredible growth of technology has affected all the health professions. Students entering the health field today recognize that they must excel academically and master technical skills. Less time is spent learning personal, nontechnical aspects of care. This value system is reinforced by professionals, peers, and administrators, and by the public as well. Excellent technical performance has become a standard, at the cost of the personal, human touch.

The federal government plays an increasingly powerful role in the direction of health care. It dominates the healthcare system by virtue of its expanding monetary support of technology and services, and because it sets the rules for the provision of health care.

As health services enter the twenty-first century, it becomes apparent that the social philosophy of the twentieth century is obsolete and is moving toward a philosophy that holds society, through the government, responsible for organizing and maintaining adequate health care for all people. Health care was once considered an individual matter, but is now considered a right to which everyone should have access.

SOME HEALTH STRATEGIES FOR THE TWENTY-FIRST CENTURY

New technology and new uses for existing technology can improve the length and quality of life. However, questions remain about how much improvement is possible when resources are scarce and costs continue to increase. In addition, there is concern about whether target populations are being appropriately and equitably served. The five broad strategic objectives of the U.S. Department of Health and Human Services (USDHHS) for health care for 2010 through 2015 are to[9]

- Transform health care.
- Advance scientific knowledge and innovation.
- Advance the health, safety, and well-being of the American people.
- Increase the efficiency, transparency, and accountability of USDHHS programs.
- Strengthen the nation's health and human services infrastructure and workforce.

In the next chapter, the categories of health services currently provided and maintained by public and private funding are explored. Because there is no single "U.S. Health Care System," the many ways in which health care is delivered can be puzzling. This should not be surprising, given the historical perspective of health services, the diverse subsystems in operation in the United States, and the dynamics of social and technological changes.

SUMMARY

Health Trends

1. The five leading causes of death in 2007 were heart disease, cancer, stroke, chronic lower respiratory disease, and Alzheimer's disease.[6]

2. Mortality rates in the twentieth century show a remarkable change. Death rates from infectious diseases declined significantly. Deaths from stroke and heart disease rose to epidemic proportions in the first half of the century, but have declined dramatically since 1950. There was also a decline in lung and stomach cancer, infectious diseases such as tuberculosis and smallpox, and infant and maternal mortality.

3. By 2007, life expectancy was at the highest level ever.[8] The decline in death rates was especially notable among the young and old. The decrease in death rates among the elderly is significant. These declines were presumably a result of collaboration between medicine and public health efforts to educate the public, especially about lifestyle changes including personal hygiene, vaccinations, new treatments including medications, and social and environmental changes.

4. The most prevalent mental disorders are anxiety disorders and clinical depression. Direct costs related to medical care and indirect costs in loss of productivity total nearly $300 billion a year in the United States.[10]

5. Over 50% of the causes of death (currently) are behavioral: diet and lifestyle, lack of regular physical activity, tobacco and alcohol use, illicit use of drugs, and motor vehicle traffic fatalities.

6. Poverty is associated with poor health by its connection with inadequate nutrition, substandard housing, exposure to environmental hazards, unhealthy lifestyles, and decreased access to and use of healthcare services.[11]

7. There are racial, ethnic, and language disparities in access to health care. An example is children with special healthcare needs. Providers in family-centered care programs spent less time with Latino and African-American children compared to white children and less time with children in households in which the primary language was non-English.[12]

8. Lack of health insurance coverage is a major barrier to obtaining most healthcare services.[11]

To improve the health of all Americans, it is critical to continue collecting data on all components of health; documenting trends in risk factors, health status, and access to and utilization of healthcare services; and disseminating reliable and accurate information about the health of our population. Equally important is gaining an understanding of the healthcare needs and utilization patterns of population subgroups, especially with changes in access to health care with healthcare reform. Such insights will enable policy makers to set program priorities and allocate target resources most effectively.[7] Healthcare and population trends and healthcare reform will affect all health professionals in every career and will change the practice of medicine as we know it.

REFERENCES

1. Martinez ME, Cohen RA. Health Insurance Coverage: Early Release of Estimates from the National Health Interview Survey, January–June 2010. *National Center for Health Statistics.* 2010. Internet: http://www.cdc.gov/nchs/data/nhis/earlyrelease/insur201012.pdf

2. *The Economic Case for Health Care Reform.* Executive Office of the President. Council of Economic Advisors; 2009.

3. *Affordable Health Care for America.* Affordable Care Act. On the Floor. Internet: http://www.democraticleader.gov/floor?id=0361

4. Kimbuende E, Ranji U, Lundy J, Salganicoff A. *U.S. Healthcare Costs.* U.S. Health Care Costs. Issue Modules. Kaiser Family Foundation. 2010. Internet: http://www.kaiseredu.org/Issue-Modules/US-Health-Care-Costs/Background-Brief.aspx

5. Goodman DC, Brownlee S, Chang C-H, Fisher E. *Regional and Racial Variation in Primary Care and the Quality of Care Among Medicare Beneficiaries. A Report of the Dartmouth Atlas Project.* The Dartmouth Institute for Health Policy and Clinical Practice; 2010.

6. U.S. Department of Federal Interagency Forum on Aging-Related Statistics. *Older Americans, 2010. Key Indicators of Well-Being.* Hyattsville, MD. 2010. Internet: http://www.agingstats.gov

7. National Center for Health Statistics. Centers for Disease Control and Prevention. *Health United States, 2009: With Special Feature on Medical Technology.* Hyattsville, MD. 2010. Internet: http://www.cdc.gov/nchs/hus.htm

8. National Center for Health Statistics. Centers for Disease Control and Prevention. *Health United States, 2010: With Special Feature on Death and Dying.* Hyattsville, MD. 2010; 2011. Internet: http://www.cdc.gov/nchs/hus.htm

9. U.S. Department of Health and Human Services. *Strategic Plan and Priorities.* About the Secretary. Washington, DC; 2010. Internet: http://www.hhs.gov/secretary/about/priorities/priorities.html

10. National Institute of Mental Health. *Annual Total Direct and Indirect Costs of Serious Mental Illness (2002).* Internet: http://www.nimh.nih.gov/statistics/4COST_TOTAN.shtml

11. *The Uninsured. A Primer. Key Facts About Americans Without Health Insurance.* The Henry J. Kaiser Family Foundation. Publication no. 7451-05. Washington, DC; 2009.

12. Coker TR, Rodriguez MA, Flores G. Family-Centered Care for US Children with Special Health Care Needs: Who Gets It and Why? *Pediatrics.* 2010; 125:1159–1167.

chapter two

Categories of Health Services

OBJECTIVES

After studying this chapter, the student should be able to:

- Describe the healthcare functions of private and public facilities, inpatient and outpatient services, military facilities, and volunteer facilities.
- Identify the four major types of health services and their functions.
- Compare the functions of the two major providers of managed care.
- Name the major points of the Patient's Bill of Rights.
- Describe public health, hospital, ambulatory, and mental health services.

OVERVIEW OF THE U.S. HEALTHCARE SYSTEM

The U.S. healthcare system is extremely varied. Individual healthcare units, which at times overlap, serve a variety of people based on their economic and social status. Individuals and families receive and buy healthcare services based on what they perceive to be their immediate needs. Health care is primarily financed by personal, nongovernment funds or is paid directly by consumers through private health insurance plans. Local and state governments provide public health services.

The federal government provides very few direct health services, preferring to support new, improved services by providing money to fund expanded developments. With minor exceptions—military health care or Tricare, CHAMPVA (Civilian Health and Medical Program of the Department of Veterans Affairs), and the Indian Health Service—the federal government has no authority to provide direct services; this is a function of the private sector and the states. The federal government is involved, however, in financing research and individual health care for the elderly and indigent (via **Medicare and Medicaid**). Congress plays a key role in this federal activity by making laws, allocating funds, and doing investigative work through committees.

A wide variety of **healthcare facilities** are available. These facilities, the places where persons involved in the healthcare industry work, are broadly summarized in this chapter and are individually detailed in succeeding chapters. This discussion of the numerous healthcare fields should assist students in selecting a career and becoming knowledgeable about their chosen fields.

The healthcare industry is a complex system of diagnostic, therapeutic, and preventive services. Hospitals, clinics, government and volunteer agencies, pharmaceutical and medical equipment manufacturers, and private insurance companies provide these services. The healthcare system offers four broad types of services: health promotion, disease prevention, **diagnosis and treatment**, and **rehabilitation**.

Health promotion services help clients reduce the risk of illness, maintain optimal function, and follow healthy lifestyles. These services are provided in a variety of ways and settings. Examples include hospitals that offer consumers prenatal nutrition classes and local health departments that offer selected recipients prenatal nutrition classes plus the foods that satisfy their requirements (the Women, Infants, and Children [WIC] program). Classes at both places promote the general health of women and children. Exercise and aerobic classes offered by city recreation departments, adult education programs, and private or nonprofit gymnasiums encourage consumers to exercise and maintain cardiovascular fitness, thus promoting better health through lifestyle changes.

Illness prevention services offer a wide variety of assistance and activities. Educational efforts aimed at involving consumers in their own care include attention to and recognition of risk factors, environmental changes to reduce the threat of illness, occupational safety measures, and public health education programs and legislation. It is evident that preventive measures such as these can reduce the overall costs of health care.

Traditionally the diagnosis and treatment of illness has been the most used of the health care services. Usually people waited until they were ill to seek medical attention. However, recent advances in technology and early diagnostic techniques have greatly improved the diagnosis and treatment capacity of the healthcare delivery system—but the advances have also increased the complexity and price of health care.

Rehabilitation involves the restoration of a person to normal or near normal function after a physical or mental illness, including chemical addiction. These programs take place in many settings: homes, community centers, rehabilitation institutions, hospitals, outpatient clinics, and extended care facilities. Rehabilitation is a long process, and both the client and family require extra assistance in adjusting to a chronic disability.

HEALTHCARE FACILITIES

Expansion of the healthcare system and professional specialization has resulted in an increase in the range and types of healthcare settings. A wide variety of **healthcare facilities** are now available. The range includes inpatient, outpatient, community-based, voluntary, government, institutional, and comprehensive health maintenance agencies.

Clients not requiring hospitalization can find health care in physicians' offices, ambulatory care centers, and outpatient clinics. Immediate care clinics exist as freestanding clinics or inside a pharmacy and are staffed by physicians, nurse practitioners, or physician assistants who treat minor acute illnesses such as colds, cuts, or sprains and provide immunizations. Although physicians in office practice focus mainly on the diagnosis and treatment of specific diseases, many clinics and ambulatory centers offer health education and rehabilitation as well.

Community-based agencies provide health care to people within their defined neighborhoods. Such diverse facilities as day care centers, home health agencies, crisis intervention and drug rehabilitation centers, halfway houses, and various support groups all work in a wide variety of ways to maintain the integrity of the community.

Federally funded primary care centers serve high-need communities designated as medically underserved areas or populations, with about half being in rural areas and the other half in urban areas. The first health centers were established in 1962 for migrant and seasonal farm workers, and by 1964 two neighborhood health centers were opened in the Boston area. By 2007 there were more than 1000 health centers throughout the United States providing services to the uninsured, low-income individuals, and minorities, including 1 million homeless and 133,000 public-housing residents. In addition to primary health care, most sites offer access to oral health, mental health, and substance abuse services and pharmacy services.[1]

Privately funded free clinics are nonprofit community-based or faith-based organizations that provide health care at little or no charge to low-income individuals who are uninsured or underinsured. Referrals are made for follow-up care and health specialists as needed. Clinics may be housed in temporary physical facilities similar to those used for humanitarian relief in response to disasters such as severe weather or a toxic oil spill. Other clinics may be housed in existing physical spaces such as churches. Clinics are staffed by a variety of volunteer health professionals—doctors, dentists, nurses, optometrists, therapists, pharmacists, and others. The **National Association of Free Clinics (NAFC)** was established in 2001 to support 1200 free clinics in nearly all states within the United States. The NAFC supports free clinics through education and advocacy in Congress and with federal and state agencies. Partnerships with pharmaceutical companies and other organizations are used to obtain low-cost or free medications and medical supplies.[2]

Institutions that provide inpatient (persons admitted to a facility for diagnosis, treatment, or rehabilitation) services include hospitals, nursing homes, extended care facilities, and rehabilitation centers. Hospitals are the major agency in the healthcare system. They vary greatly in size, depending on the location. A rural hospital may have two-dozen beds; a hospital in a large city may have more than a thousand.[3]

Hospitals are either private or public. A **private hospital** is owned and operated by groups such as churches, businesses, corporations, and physicians. This type of facility is operated in such a way as to make a profit for the owners. A **public hospital** is financed and operated by a government agency, either at the local or national level. Such facilities are termed nonprofit facilities, and they admit many patients who cannot afford to pay for medical care. Patients in private hospitals have insurance, private funds, or medical assistance to pay for their care. Voluntary hospitals are usually nonprofit and often are owned and operated by religious organizations. Community hospitals are independent, nonprofit corporations consisting of local citizens interested in providing hospital care for their community.[3]

The complex hospital industry is usually categorized by three methods: function or type of service provided (from those treating a single disease such as cancer to those with multiple specialties, usually teaching hospitals); length of stay (many short term, with 5 days being the average length of stay, and fewer long term, such as psychiatric or chronic disease hospitals, where the average stay is 4 to 6 months); and ownership or source of financial support—government (or public), proprietary (private for profit), or voluntary and religious (private nonprofit) ownership.[3]

Public hospitals are owned by local, state, or federal agencies. Federally owned hospitals are generally reserved for the military, veterans, Native Americans, or other special groups. State governments usually operate chronic long-term hospitals, such as mental institutions. Local governments have city, county, or district hospitals that are primarily short term and staffed by physicians who also have private practices. These types of hospitals in small cities and towns are generally small and function as community healthcare facilities. Public hospitals in major urban areas are large and are staffed by salaried physicians and resident physicians. They take care of the economically deprived and furnish all types of services—from drug abuse treatment to family planning.[3]

Every state operates hospitals that provide long-term care (if necessary) for the treatment of the mentally ill or retarded. These state hospitals are run by state administrative agencies. At the local level, district hospitals are supported by taxes from those who live in the district. These hospitals are not involved with the governments of cities, states, or counties. Counties run county hospitals that provide services for the poor and for private patients. Municipal and county governments usually control city hospitals. Many city hospitals provide care primarily for the poor.[3]

The federal government operates hospitals and clinics for three agencies—the Veterans Administration (VA), the Indian Health Service (IHS), and military hospitals and clinics. The VA provides health care for veterans of the armed services, and each branch of the military operates hospitals for military personnel and their families. The IHS is responsible for providing health services to approximately 1.9 million American Indians and Alaska Natives belonging to more than 564 federally recognized tribes in 35 states.[4]

HOSPITALS: DEVELOPMENT AND SERVICES

The hospital is the key resource and center of the U.S. healthcare system. Hospitals not only deliver primary patient care, but also train health personnel, conduct research, and disseminate information to consumers. Since the turn of the century, hospitals have gradually become the professional heart of all medical practice. Accelerating technological advances and changing societal factors have thrust hospitals into the grasp of big business. They are the third-largest business in the United States. They employ approximately 75% of healthcare personnel, with a collective payroll that accounts for at least 40% of the nation's health expenditures. Approximately 60% of federal health monies and 40% of all state and local health monies go to hospitals.[3]

Hospitals also account for the most pressing of today's healthcare system problems, namely cost inflation. There is also widespread duplication of services, overemphasis on specialized services and diagnostic tests, and a detached manner of caring for the ill.

The major forces affecting the development of hospitals include the following: (1) advances in medical science, most notably the discovery of antiseptic techniques and sterilization processes and the use of anesthesia; (2) advances in medical education, with predominant use of scientific theory and standardization of academic training for physicians; and (3) transformation of nursing into a profession by requiring training in caring for the wounded and ill, cleanliness and sanitation procedures, dietary instruction, and simple organized care. These effective, although simple, procedures were a great boon to hospitals' growth, as the public began to see hospitals as a safe, effective place to go when they were ill. The fourth major force was the development of specialized technology such as X-rays, blood typing, and electrocardiograms, which all came into being early in the twentieth century.[3]

Hospitals have not responded quickly to the healthcare needs of an aging population. In the late 1980s they began to go into nontraditional (for hospitals) services such as outpatient care, home health care, extended care units, and rehabilitation. Their resources continue to be concentrated on acute care, short-term, curable, and special cases instead of the chronic, long-term illnesses that most often affect the elderly.

The growth of health insurance (which is discussed in Chapter 3) and of government's role in the hospital industry has had a substantial impact on hospitals. The federal government has financed hospital construction, regulated the type of construction, financed the provision of care, and set policy for the ways in which hospitals are operated. Because 54% of all hospital bills are paid by government programs, federal and state agencies are in a position to exert a great deal of control.

Proprietary hospitals are operated for the financial benefit of the persons, partnerships, or corporations that own them. The current trend is toward a buy-out of substantial numbers of these smaller hospitals by large investment firms, creating large, for-profit hospital systems. Management contracts are also on the rise, not only in for-profit hospitals but also in community hospitals. Both trends are expected to continue, as will adverse reaction to them, especially in regard to management corporations taking over community-based hospitals. Philosophy, policies, and operation change drastically under management systems—sometimes for the better, and at other times with dubious benefit. However, the proliferation of multisystem hospitals (corporation owned, leased, or managed) will probably persist. More than 50% of community hospitals are part of a corporate system, and the mergers will continue in the twenty-first century.[3]

AMBULATORY HEALTHCARE SERVICES

Care that is provided outside of institutional settings is considered **ambulatory care** and is the most frequent contact that most people have with the healthcare system. Ambulatory care can be any type of care, from simple and routine to complex and specialized. Probably the most familiar kind of ambulatory care, and the one that most people receive, is in an office of either a solo or group practice, or in a noninstitutional clinic. The type of service is primary or secondary care, and the principal health practitioners are physicians, dentists, nurses, technicians, therapists, and aides. If the community can afford an emergency transportation and immediate care system, paramedics and emergency medical technicians are also part of the ambulatory care network. Emergency advice is furnished from community hotlines and poison control centers.

Primary and secondary care is given at neighborhood health centers and migrant health centers. Psychologists and social workers staff community mental health centers. Nurses staff home health and school health services and give both primary and preventive care. Public health services, as discussed previously, include targeted programs such as family planning, immunizations, screening, maternal and child nutrition, and health education. The health practitioners in these settings are physicians, nurses, dietitians, clinical assistants, and aides. The roster may also include environmental health specialists and sanitarians who do inspections of factories, hospitals, and food establishments to ensure the safety of workers and the public. Pharmacies are ambulatory care facilities staffed by registered pharmacists who dispense drugs and health education. Optical shops with optometrists and opticians provide vision care, while medical technicians give specialized services in medical laboratories. The federal health system, previously detailed, furnishes all types of ambulatory care, as do prison services.

Many of the ambulatory care services evolve into large, highly complex organizations. For example, an executive committee may be elected to administer the operation. Designated group members may form a credentials committee to screen prospective members, or a building committee may be established. Large group practices usually have a medical director who is responsible for establishing policies regarding the scope and quality of care, as well as personnel practices.[3]

Hospitals are expanding their role to include ambulatory services. They have established fully staffed outpatient facilities and clinics. Hospital outpatient clinics include not only primary care, but also specialties such as ophthalmology, neurology, and endocrine care. Teaching hospitals operate many specialty ambulatory clinics that expose medical students and house staff to more extensive experiences. Ambulatory surgery centers and emergency medical services have both expanded, with emergency medicine becoming a specialty for physicians, and regional, hospital-based trauma centers have sprung up in many communities. Forces are at work within communities throughout the nation to enhance primary and specialized health care for all citizens.[3]

MENTAL HEALTH SERVICES

Mental health facilities in the United States were developed in the nineteenth century (as was the American Psychiatric Association), but were little more than warehouses for large numbers of poor, homeless, and social misfits. They were state hospitals whose primary purpose, instead of treating the patient, was to protect the public. The creation of the National Institute of Mental Health (NIMH) in 1946 and the development of psychopharmaceuticals in the 1950s were the major breakthroughs that led to the real treatment of mental illnesses. Psychotropic drugs enabled thousands of people to return to their communities and to be treated on an outpatient basis.[5]

As local health departments began to report successful treatment outside of institutions, federal legislation was enacted for the construction of community mental health centers. The community mental health center network was conceived in the late 1960s to discharge residents from institutions back into the community with the development of community mental health centers for providing outpatient **mental health services**. They were also provided staffing, conversion, and distress grants. The centers provide inpatient, outpatient, and day care, as well as emergency services. They are required to provide specialized services for the mental health of children and the elderly, and special prevention, treatment, and rehabilitation programs for alcoholics, drug abusers, and drug addicts. The decline of federal monies for local services has affected the comprehensiveness of the centers' services and even the survival of many of them in the places they are needed most—impoverished communities.[5]

Unfortunately, however, this network failed to care for the deinstitutionalized and there are fewer hospitals specializing in acute psychiatric illness. Between 1990 and 2004, the number of total inpatient mental health beds decreased by 35%.[6] As a result, visits to community hospital emergency rooms for acute mental health problems have increased. Also, many with severe mental illness have returned to institutions for the chronically mentally ill or live in group homes, halfway houses, or nursing homes.[6]

Mental health personnel involved in the delivery of mental health services include psychiatrists, who are MDs who make a mental diagnosis, prescribe medications, and may provide psychotherapy. Other mental health professionals include psychologists, clinical social workers, and psychiatric nurses who have advanced degrees and who provide case management and/or psychotherapy. A number of allied health fields have developed in response to the growing needs of the community and the availability of funding. These include school counselors, special education teachers, and others such as art, music, and recreational therapists.

Many problems exist within the mental health system, including a society that clings to the concept of mental illness as a stigma. One out of four Americans suffers from mental illness and substance abuse disorders every year. Mental illness and substance abuse disorders are leading causes of disability and death. Adequate and appropriate treatment for mental illness has been difficult, especially for long-term treatment. Compared to physical illness, most insurance policies have limited the number of days in the hospital and the number of outpatient visits for treating mental illness. It has been only recently that mental health services are covered by health insurance policies as a result of the Mental Health Parity and Addiction Equity Act of 2008.[7]

HEALTHCARE TEAMS

The concept of **health teams** in all types of health services has brought about changes in healthcare delivery. The health team consists of a variety of health personnel, each with a specialized function. The membership of the health team varies in accordance with the needs of the client and his or her family. There are two general types of health teams: functional and patient centered. Both depend on the kind of problem to be solved and may dissolve at any given point and regroup to meet special problems. Team members are usually doctors, nurses, dietitians, therapists, and other direct-care providers. Functional teams are formed to take care of specific problems. Examples include the mental health team or the coronary care team. Patient-centered teams include patients and their families who are involved in making healthcare decisions together with their doctor and other health care professionals. Medical technologists, radiologic technologists, and pathologists may form a backup medical care team for the patient. They are not in close contact with the patient, but deal with parts of the patient's service, such as his or her X-rays, blood samples, and cultures.

At the outside edge of the interrelated teams are the people who concentrate on the delivery, costs, quality, and availability of services. This healthcare team is composed of public health agents, hospital administrators, health educators, sanitarians, and others.

People working in the health professions must accept the changing nature of the teams and recognize that the combined skills of many professionals contribute to modern health care.

THE CONSUMER'S RIGHTS

In 1973, the American Hospital Association developed a **Patient's Bill of Rights**, which lists 12 specific rights of hospitalized patients. This bill, although not a legally binding document, states the responsibilities of the hospital and staff toward the client and his or her family. The major tenets are that the client has the right to

- Receive information pertaining to diagnosis and treatment
- Receive information on fees for services rendered
- Receive continuity of care
- Refuse diagnosis and treatment procedures

- Enjoy privacy and confidentiality from staff and physicians
- Seek a second opinion
- Change physicians and/or facilities if unsatisfied

One of the patient's most important legal rights is informed consent, that is, the physician must obtain permission from the client to perform certain actions or procedures. Informed consent must be obtained before beginning any invasive procedure, administering an experimental drug, or entering the client into any research project. Specific criteria must be adhered to for informed consent to be valid. Important factors are that the client must be rational and competent, or be represented by someone who is, and the document must be written in language the client can understand, delineate all the risks involved, state that participation is voluntary, and list the benefits of the procedure and alternatives to the procedure. The client's right to informed consent affects how the healthcare system delivers care. It usually results in increased costs from extra paperwork and other work, but it is necessary for the consumer's protection (and may reduce the care provider's vulnerability to malpractice suits).

In early 1997, President Bill Clinton appointed an Advisory Commission on consumer protection and quality in the healthcare industry that further refined the Patient's Bill of Rights. Its five care provisions were

- The right to treatment information
- The right to privacy and dignity
- The right to refuse treatment
- The right to emergency care
- The right to an advocate

Each of these rights contains additional provisions to help the consumer understand their meaning and obtain the best care.

Healthcare professionals working in such a wide variety of facilities find challenges and diversity that require them to become knowledgeable in specialized areas and to expand their range of services. The healthcare professional who prefers research may choose to work in primary research institutions such as the NIH and agencies that administer health and welfare programs. Two major agencies are the Veterans Administration Hospitals and the **Public Health Service (PHS)**. If you choose to practice in Canada, the Canada Health Care System covers medical care for all residents of Canada.

PUBLIC HEALTH SERVICES

The most important federal agency concerned with health affairs is the **U.S. Department of Health and Human Services (USDHHS)**. The agency is responsible for Medicare, Medicaid, public health, biomedical research, food and drug safety, disease control and prevention, Indian health, and mental health services. The USDHHS works closely with state and local governments and provides leadership in public health emergency preparedness in the event of severe weather, infectious disease epidemics, or biological terrorism. The USDHHS programs are administered by 11 operating divisions, including eight agencies in the U.S. Public Health Service and three human services agencies[8]:

1. Administration for Children and Families (ACF)
2. Administration on Aging (AoA)
3. Agency for Healthcare Research and Quality (AHRQ)
4. Agency for Toxic Substances and Disease Registry (ATSDR)
5. Centers for Disease Control and Prevention (CDC)
6. Centers for Medicare and Medicaid Services (CMS)
7. Food and Drug Administration (FDA)
8. Health Resources and Services Administration (HRSA)
9. Indian Health Service (IHS)
10. National Institutes of Health (NIH)
11. Substance Abuse and Mental Health Services Administration (SAMHSA)

The focus of public health is the community instead of the individual. The community may be limited to a city or may include an entire state, country, or the world. The recent outbreak of infectious diseases such as SARS, Ebola, and avian influenza, and fears about bioterrorism demonstrate the importance of global disease surveillance, pooling of research efforts to help identify pathogens, and international cooperation to develop diagnostic tests, prevention measures, and treatments.

The emphasis in public health is on prevention in contrast to medical care, in which the emphasis is treatment of disease. Public health practitioners are represented by a variety of disciplines such as nursing, medicine, veterinary medicine, dentistry, health education, and nutrition. Public health services deal primarily with four aspects of care:

1. Identifying diseases that cause death or debility
2. Assessing the factors of cause and method of transmission
3. Finding ways to control or cure diseases and methods to prevent spread
4. Educating the public to apply the findings effectively

Practitioners in public health, including epidemiologists and statisticians, study the nature of new threats and organize public measures to combat them. Because the government is usually involved in the financing and policy-making procedures, the term public health has come to include research, assessment, and control measures.

The threats to health change over time. As one set of diseases, epidemics, and conditions is brought under control or eliminated, new diseases appear. The past focus of services, as previously discussed, was to prevent or mitigate the effects of acute infectious diseases such as smallpox, bubonic plague, typhoid fever, childhood diseases, and other highly lethal maladies. With the changes in living conditions in the twentieth century, degenerative, debilitative diseases such as chronic obstructive pulmonary disease (COPD), mental and emotional dysfunction, cancer, arthritis, strokes, and coronary heart disease (CHD) have replaced infectious diseases.

The public health system requires cooperation among federal, state, and local governments. Great changes in the roles played by government agencies have occurred over time, with the most important one being the Social Security Act of 1935. This act established annual grants-in-aid from the federal government to the states, part of whose purpose was to fund full-time local health departments. These grants provided for maternal and child health services and extended the services of local public health departments according to the needs of their communities. They were matching-fund grants, in which the states matched federal money on a dollar-for-dollar basis.

Public health at the city and state level now includes such functions as licensing and accrediting health professionals and health facilities, setting standards for automobile safety devices, and supervising the quality of medical payment programs such as Medicaid.

The establishment of public health and social services in the United States has evolved over time. **Table 2-1** is a timeline of the USDHHS beginning in 1798 with an act to provide health care for sick and disabled seamen.[9]

Six basic functions were established for the Public Health Service between 1935 and 1946, and with few revisions they remain the foundation for public health agencies:

1. Vital statistics (the recording, reporting, and publication of births, deaths, and diseases)
2. Communicable disease control (any disease that is transmissible between humans)
3. Sanitation of the food, milk, water supply, and public eating places
4. Laboratory services
5. Maternal and child health
6. Health education

Strategic goals for public health put forth by the U.S. Department of Health and Human Services for 2007–2012 are to[10]

- Prevent the spread of infectious disease.
- Protect the public against injuries and environmental threats.
- Promote and encourage preventive health care, including mental health, lifelong healthy behaviors, and recovery.
- Prepare for and respond to natural and man-made disasters.

The Centers for Disease Control and Prevention (CDC) is responsible for monitoring the health of the nation. The CDC monitors the incidence of injury

TABLE 2-1 Historical Highlights of Health and Human Services in the United States

1798	Passage of an act for the relief of sick and disabled seamen, which established a federal network of hospitals for the care of merchant seamen, the forerunner of today's U.S. Public Health Service.
1862	President Lincoln appointed a chemist, Charles M. Wetherill, to serve in the new Department of Agriculture. This was the beginning of the Bureau of Chemistry, the forerunner to the Food and Drug Administration.
1871	Appointment of the first Supervising Surgeon (later called Surgeon General) for the Marine Hospital Service, which was organized the previous year.
1878	Passage of the National Quarantine Act began the transfer of quarantine functions from the states to the federal Marine Hospital Service.
1887	The federal government opened a one-room laboratory on Staten Island for research on disease, thereby planting the seed that was to grow into the National Institutes of Health.
1891	Passage of immigration legislation, assigning to the Marine Hospital Service the responsibility for the medical examination of arriving immigrants.
1902	Conversion of the Marine Hospital Service into the Public Health and Marine Hospital Service in recognition of its expanding activities in the field of public health. In 1912, the name was shortened to the Public Health Service (PHS).
1906	Congress passed the Pure Food and Drugs Act, authorizing the government to monitor the purity of foods and the safety of medicines, which is now a responsibility of the Food and Drug Administration (FDA).
1912	President Theodore Roosevelt's first White House Conference urged the creation of the Children's Bureau to combat the exploitation of children.
1921	The Bureau of Indian Affairs Health Division was created, the forerunner to the Indian Health Service.
1930	Creation of the National Institute (later Institutes) of Health, out of the Public Health Service's Hygienic Laboratory.
1935	Passage of the Social Security Act.
1938	Passage of the Federal Food, Drug, and Cosmetic Act.
1939	The Federal Security Agency was created, bringing together related federal activities in the fields of health, education, and social insurance.
1946	The Communicable Disease Center was established, forerunner of the Centers for Disease Control and Prevention (CDC).
1955	Licensing of the Salk polio vaccine. The Indian Health Service was transferred to the USDHHS from the Department of the Interior.
1961	First White House Conference on Aging.
1962	Passage of the Migrant Health Act, providing support for clinics serving agricultural workers.
1964	Release of the first Surgeon General's Report on Smoking and Health.

(continues)

TABLE 2-1 Historical Highlights of Health and Human Services in the United States (continued)

1965	Creation of the Medicare and Medicaid programs, making comprehensive health care available to millions of Americans. The Older Americans Act created nutrition and social programs administered by the USDHHS's Administration on Aging. Head Start program was created.
1966	International Smallpox Eradication program was established,—led by the U.S. Public Health Service, the worldwide eradication of smallpox was accomplished in 1977. The Community Health Center and Migrant Health Center programs were launched.
1970	Creation of the National Health Service Corps.
1971	National Cancer Act signed into law.
1975	Child Support Enforcement program established.
1977	Creation of the Health Care Financing Administration (HCFA) to manage Medicare and Medicaid separately from the Social Security Administration.
1980	Federal funding provided to states for foster care and adoption assistance.
1981	Identification of AIDS. In 1984, the Public Health Service and French scientists identified HIV. In 1985, a blood test to detect HIV was licensed.
1984	National Organ Transplantation Act signed into law.
1988	Creation of the JOBS program and federal support for child care. Passage of the McKinney Act to provide health care to the homeless.
1989	Creation of the Agency for Health Care Policy and Research (now the Agency for Healthcare Research and Quality).
1990	Human Genome Project established. Passage of the Nutrition Labeling and Education Act, authorizing the food label. Ryan White Comprehensive AIDS Resource Emergency (CARE) Act began providing support for people with AIDS.
1993	The Vaccines for Children Program was established, providing free immunizations to all children in low-income families.
1995	The Social Security Administration became an independent agency.
1996	Enactment of welfare reform under the Personal Responsibility and Work Opportunity Reconciliation Act. Enactment of the Health Insurance Portability and Accountability Act (HIPAA).
1997	Creation of the State Children's Health Insurance Program (SCHIP), enabling states to extend health coverage to more uninsured children.
1999	The Ticket to Work and Work Incentives Improvement Act of 1999 made it possible for millions of Americans with disabilities to join the workforce without fear of losing their Medicaid and Medicare coverage. Initiative on combating bioterrorism was launched.
2000	Publication of human genome sequencing.
2002	Office of Public Health Emergency Preparedness was created to coordinate efforts against bioterrorism and other emergency health threats.
2003	Enactment of the Medicare Prescription Drug Improvement and Modernization Act of 2003, the most significant expansion of Medicare since its enactment, including a prescription drug benefit.

and illness, homicide, suicide, and infectious and chronic disease such as HIV/ AIDS, H1N1 flu, heart disease, cancer, and diabetes. States conduct annual surveys of residents for behaviors that increase risk for chronic disease including diet, physical activity, smoking, and drug and alcohol use. Individual states report health statistics to the National Center for Health Statistics and the CDC compiles, analyzes, and reports data on disease prevalence. In addition, the CDC monitors air and water quality and provides support in emergencies, for example, severe weather conditions that impact health and safety.

In the United States, career opportunities in public health exist in the Commissioned Corps, an essential component of the largest public health program in the world. Corps officers are eligible for a variety of positions throughout the USDHHS and certain non-USDHHS federal agencies and programs in the areas of disease control and prevention; biomedical research; regulation of food, drugs, and medical devices; mental health and drug abuse; healthcare delivery; and international health. Opportunities are also available at the community level in public health departments and professional organizations, for example, the American Heart Association, American Diabetes Association, American Lung Association, and American Cancer Society.

The student desiring to go into public health must be aware of the political battles that are being waged over the structure of the system. New and changed roles for local, state, and federal public health agencies are apparent. The nation will continue to need public health services and leaders who keep abreast of new research and who have a grasp of modern health problems and solving problems from both a preventive and curative standpoint. These persons will also need an understanding of the political system and societal expectations and demands. The student who chooses a public health service career will be in a role with changing dynamics, while still fulfilling fundamental, long-accepted functions.

HEALTH CARE IN THE TWENTY-FIRST CENTURY

From its humble, unscientific, and often haphazard beginnings to the present multibillion-dollar industry, the private U.S. healthcare system has undergone broad and often drastic changes. Its present visibility and highly technical orientation have led to thousands of jobs, created new professions, and provided care to millions of people. It is not without the attendant problems of a giant industry, however, and in the twenty-first century the system must face and solve yet more problems. Because healthcare costs are escalating out of control, the most pressing problem of this century will be to bring health care within the reach of everyone without sacrificing quality—a very large order indeed, and one not likely to go away. Preventive health care will play an important role in achieving health care for all through federally funded primary care clinics and public health clinics funded by city and state governments. American ingenuity will face a difficult challenge in formulating a workable, affordable system for all the people.

SUMMARY

The health status of the U.S. population has improved dramatically in the last 30 years. Improvements have been made in public health measures, socioeconomic status, and medical care (especially in preventive clinical services).

Objectives for health care, as set forth in **Healthy People 2020**, are to[11]

1. Attain and promote a high quality of life for all people free of preventable disease, disability, injury, and premature death. Healthy life is defined as a full range of functional capacity at each stage of the life cycle from infancy to old age.
2. Focus on social determinants of health as well as health outcomes and risk factors. Social factors that can impact health access and risk factors are differences that occur by gender, race or ethnicity, education or income, disability, geographic location, or sexual orientation.
3. Increase the number of health professionals to meet future healthcare needs including the number of practicing primary care providers, public health workers trained in disabilities, and workers certified in geriatrics.

REFERENCES

1. Bureau of Primary Health Care. U.S. Department of Health and Human Services. *Health Centers: America's Primary Care Safety Net, Reflections on Success, 2002–2007*. Rockville, MD; 2008.
2. *What Is the NAFC?* The National Association of Free Clinics: Advocacy and Support for America's Free Clinics; 2010. Internet: http://www.freeclinics.us/index.php
3. Bureau of Labor Statistics. U.S. Department of Labor. *Career Guide to Industries 2010–2011 Edition*. 2010. Internet: http://www.bls.gov/oco/cg/cgs035.htm
4. Indian Health Service. *Indian Health Service Introduction*. 2011. Internet: http://www.ihs.gov/PublicInfo/PublicAffairs/Welcome_Info/IHSintro.asp
5. Substance Abuse and Mental Health Services Administration, U.S. Department of Health and Human Services. *Mental Health: A Report of the Surgeon General—Executive Summary*. Rockville, MD; 1999.
6. National Center for Health Statistics. Centers for Disease Control and Prevention. *Health, United States, 2010: With Special Feature on Death and Dying*. DHHS Pub. no. 2011-1232. Hyattsville, MD; 2011.
7. U.S. Department of Labor. Employee Benefits Security Administration. *Fact Sheet. The Mental Health Parity and Addiction Equity Act of 2008 (MHPAEA)*. Washington, DC; 2010.
8. U.S. Department of Health and Human Services. *Operating Divisions. Leadership Contacts*. February 14, 2011. Internet: http://www.hhs.gov/open/contacts/index.html#od
9. U.S. Department of Health and Human Services. *Health and Human Services Historical Highlights*. 2011. Internet: http://www.hhs.gov/about/hhshist.html
10. Department of Health and Human Services. *U.S. Department of Health and Human Services Strategic Plan–FY 2007–2012*. 2007. Internet: http://aspe.hhs.gov/hhsplan/2007/
11. Centers for Disease Control and Prevention. U.S. Department of Health and Human Services. *Healthy People 2020: The Road Ahead*. 2010. Internet: http://healthypeoploe.gov/HP2020/default.asp

chapter three

Paying for Health Services

OBJECTIVES

After studying this chapter, the student should be able to:

- Identify the major factors that have influenced healthcare financing.
- Explain how healthcare systems are financed.
- Describe the factors that have affected public and private health insurance.
- Explain the different methods of healthcare payment: (a) private insurance, (b) Medicare, (c) Medicaid, (d) group insurance, (e) individual insurance, (f) managed care, and (g) fee-for-service.
- Identify the role of the government in the expansion of health care.

HEALTHCARE FINANCING

Health care in the United States is funded through a variety of private payers and public programs. Public spending represents expenditures by federal, state, and local governments. Private funding is primarily through **private health insurance** with 61% of Americans having employer-sponsored health insurance. A significant portion of public health spending can be attributed to the programs administered by the **Centers for Medicare and Medicaid Services (CMS)**—Medicare, Medicaid, and the **Children's Health Insurance Program (CHIP)**.[1] The remaining portion of publicly funded health care includes expenditures for the following: the Department of Defense healthcare program for military personnel, the Department of Veterans' Affairs health program, Workers' Compensation programs, maternal and child health services, school health programs, subsidies for public hospitals and clinics, Indian healthcare services, substance abuse and mental health activities, medically related vocational rehabilitation services, medical research, and the construction of public medical facilities and the purchase of equipment.[1]

In addition to private insurance, privately funded health care includes individuals' out-of-pocket expenditures, philanthropy, and nonpatient revenues (such as revenue from gift shops and parking lots), as well as health services that are provided at employers' establishments.[1]

REIMBURSEMENT FOR HEALTHCARE SERVICES

The predominant method of reimbursement for health services has been **fee-for-service payment** or payment for each service at the time of service. The biggest problem with fee-for-service is the definition of a service and what it includes, and the fee can vary by practitioner or geographic region. In an effort to control rising healthcare costs, both public and private health insurance programs have moved to **capitation**, defined as paying the practitioner or hospital a fixed amount for a specific service. In capitation, the insurance pays a set fee to cover all the services—fee-for-service pays only for the particular service(s) rendered (itemized) at a given time. A third method is salary. Salary is used only in organizations where various other incentives are provided to the practitioner to enhance productivity.

Like healthcare practitioners, hospitals can be reimbursed through several methods. First is reimbursement for specific services (same as fee-for-service). Second is the capitation method. The hospital may also be reimbursed by the number of days of care. Many hospitals average payments among patients instead of individualizing costs.

GOVERNMENT-FUNDED HEALTH INSURANCE

Medicare and Medicaid are government or public health insurance programs designed to pay for the treatment of medically diagnosed conditions. The Medicare program is a federal insurance program for people aged 65 years and older, certain disabled people younger than 65 years, and any adult with permanent kidney failure (end-stage renal disease). Patients on Medicare are entitled to the same benefits and care as those with private insurance. The main difference is that the government pays the hospital bills instead of the individual or private insurance. The Medicare program is administered by CMS of the U.S. Department of Health and Human Services (USDHHS).[2]

Medicaid is the federal–state cooperative health insurance plan for the indigent. People with incomes below the poverty level established by a state can use this government-sponsored health insurance program. Only certain low-income individuals are eligible: U.S. citizens or legal immigrants, pregnant women, children, parents of low-income children, seniors, and those with disabilities. Medicaid also provides coverage for people with chronic illnesses or disabilities who are excluded from private health insurance that is designed primarily for the healthy.[3]

Individual states administer Medicaid programs, and each state sets its own guidelines regarding eligibility and services. States receive matching funds from the federal government to help pay for Medicaid coverage. The matching rate ranges from 50% to 76% depending on a state's per-capita income; wealthier states receive lower federal matches and poorer states receive higher matches.

Medicaid includes the same services as private insurance, with primary care through federally qualified health centers plus dental and vision care, transportation, and translation services.[2] Medicaid is the primary source of health insurance for more than 30% of all children and over 56% of low-income children. Medicaid finances over one-third of all births (41%) and is the largest source of public funding for family planning services.[3] Although women and children account for 75% of the total Medicaid beneficiaries, the majority of Medicaid spending (67%) is for the elderly and for children and adults with disabilities. Medicaid is also the source of funding for treating those with mental illness.[4] In 2009, 62% of Medicaid expenditures were for acute care and 33% were for nursing home and long-term care, including community-based and home-based care.[5]

The Children's Health Insurance Program (CHIP), known from its inception until March 2009 as the State Children's Health Insurance Program (SCHIP), received federal funding through fiscal year 2007 to provide healthcare coverage for low-income children—generally those below 200% of the federal poverty level who do not qualify for Medicaid and would otherwise be uninsured. Subsequent legislation, including the Children's Health Insurance Program Reauthorization Act (CHIPRA) of 2009 extended CHIP funding through fiscal year 2013.

Federal and state governments jointly finance CHIPRA very similarly to Medicaid. States may elect to provide coverage to qualifying children by expanding their Medicaid programs or through a state program separate from Medicaid. A number of states have also been granted waivers to cover parents of children enrolled in CHIP. Before CHIPRA, states were not allowed to use federal funds to cover legal immigrants during the first five years of living in the United States. Thirty-five million children are covered by both Medicaid and CHIP.[6]

HISTORY OF HEALTH INSURANCE IN THE UNITED STATES

Health insurance coverage has been a hotly debated topic in the United States since the early 1900s. From the beginning, the main issue has been whether health insurance should be publicly or privately financed. Government-sponsored healthcare efforts were initiated between 1915 and 1920 at the state level and in the 1930s at the federal level. However, the only outcome of these efforts was limited financial support for public health, and healthcare services for mothers and children. Congress enacted legislation to improve access to medical care for those on public assistance in the 1950s and for the needy elderly in the 1960s.[1]

The most significant change in government **healthcare financing** was when Congress approved Medicare and Medicaid with the passage of Title XVIII and Title XIX, respectively, of the Social Security Act of 1965. Medicare funded health care for all elderly regardless of income, and Medicaid was established for those on public aid. In 1973, Medicare was expanded to include those with certain disabilities and chronic kidney disease. Congress has expanded Medicaid for those living at or near the poverty level including working and jobless families and individuals with diverse physical and mental conditions, and low-income seniors. Further expansion of health care for children came with the passage of Title XXI of the Social Security Act, a program initiated by the Balanced Budget Act of 1997.[1]

Private health insurance started with hospital coverage in the 1920s because of increased consumer demand and increased costs for hospital care.

The first private hospital insurance plan was developed in 1929 when a group of Dallas teachers contracted with Baylor University Hospital to provide 21 days of hospitalization for a fixed $6.00 payment. The contract ensured that teachers had access to hospital care and that the hospital was paid. Community hospitals later joined together to develop prepaid hospital plans to avoid competition among hospitals. These plans eventually combined under the name of Blue Cross and allowed subscribers a free choice of physician and hospital. Expanding medical services became a reality after World War II when the federal government began subsidizing hospital construction and medical research.[7]

Physicians began to organize prepaid plans for physician services with the development of **Blue Cross and Blue Shield**, when in 1939 the California Physicians' Service began the first prepayment plan to cover physicians' services. Employees with incomes less than $3000 annually were eligible for a fee of $1.70 per month. Later the **American Medical Association (AMA)** encouraged state and local medical societies to form their own prepayment plans. In 1946 these physician-sponsored plans affiliated and became known as Blue Shield. These plans offered medical and surgical benefits for hospitalized members, and some plans covered outpatient doctors' visits. Doctors charged patients the difference between their actual charges and the amount for which they were reimbursed by Blue Shield. This allowed doctors to maintain control and to price discriminate by charging different prices to different patients.[7]

Other private insurance companies began offering health insurance after Blue Shield demonstrated that financial loss could be prevented by offering health insurance only to the young and healthy who were employed. The government aided the expansion of private insurance companies by excluding employers' contributions to health insurance from taxable income. During World War II private health insurance coverage grew rapidly as an employee **fringe benefit** because the government limited direct wage increases. Demand for health insurance increased as medical technology advanced.[7]

The first managed care insurance programs were started with **health maintenance organizations (HMOs)**, Kaiser Permanente in California, and Group Health Cooperative in Washington State. Kaiser Permanente started in California during the depression of the 1930s and expanded to mostly the Western states—Washington, Oregon, Hawaii, and Colorado.[8] Group Health Cooperative began in 1947 and expanded into Idaho.[9] Kaiser evolved from healthcare programs to cover on-the-job injuries of workers constructing the Los Angeles Aqueduct and the Grand Coulee Dam. The HMO started with one physician, Stanley Garfield, MD, in the small town of Desert Center in an effort to receive payment for treating sick and injured workers during the building of the aqueduct. Later, Dr. Garfield established health care for workers of the Kaiser Shipyards in the San Francisco Bay area during World War II. Thereafter, the HMO expanded through efforts of unions, and the Kaiser HMO became available to the public on October 1, 1945.[8]

By the mid-1970s, the United States entered a new stage in the history of health insurance. Fee-for-service payment was no longer appropriate or sufficient for managing medical expenses. As one of the four most inflationary sectors of the economy (energy, food, and housing being the top three), medical care logically became a target of anti-inflationary measures. Attempts to slow the increasing costs of health care included industry-wide wage and price controls initiated in 1971, followed by Medicare policies to slow price increases by doctors and hospitals and to decrease the unnecessary use of hospital services. During the 1980s there was another radical change in the way health care was financed. The term managed care came into common usage and remains a significant aspect of the current evolution.

In 1983, Congress passed a prospective payment bill, under which hospitals are paid a set amount for each patient in any of the established disease categories and **diagnosis-related groups (DRGs)**. This means that Medicare will not pay beyond the set fees for the identified type of illness, no matter how long the patient is hospitalized or what services he or she receives. As a result, Medicare hospital admissions dropped and the lengths of stay were shorter, but Medicare payments continued to rise. In 1985, Congress began to regulate direct Medicare payments to physicians by a resource-based relative value scale for payment and established the Physician Payment Review Commission. In 1988, the Commission replaced the CPR (customary, prevailing, and reasonable) system with a fee schedule that was implemented in 1992 in an effort to control healthcare costs.[10]

A shift in the balance of power between unions and management is another dramatic change that has radically altered health care. The 1980s saw a weakening of union bargaining power and a high unemployment rate. These two factors enabled management to decrease employee benefits. Prior to this time, fringe benefits, especially in the areas of health care, had been escalating with the same intensity as healthcare costs. Employees had come to expect more free health benefits with each ensuing contract. Now employers were able to restrain costs by requiring employees to pay higher deductibles and copayments. Many companies went to managed care health plans, which direct patients to the most cost-effective source of care.

The oversupply of physicians led to competition, the reorganization of medical practice, advertising for clients, and increased medical costs. The government directly intervened in medical education more than 30 years ago to ensure that there would be enough physicians to keep up with the demands of Medicare. This was accomplished with grants, scholarships, low-interest or no-interest loans, and other incentives, making access to a medical education easy for qualified individuals.

Medical care has shifted from the hospital into the community because revolutionary advances in medical technology created a new dimension in healthcare delivery. Examples of recent advances are portable, mobile units for diagnosing almost every known disease without hospital admission—magnetic resonance imaging (MRI), mammography, ultrasound, telemedicine, and other technological advances are available in doctors' offices and outpatient clinics and can even be taken into homes. Freestanding surgical centers and outpatient surgery are thriving, facilitated especially by advances made in fiber optics and lasers. These factors have led to what is called distributive health care, which is changing the healthcare system as well as creating different ways of paying for health care.[11]

MANAGED CARE: HMOs AND PPOs

Managed care organizations (MCOs) are divided primarily into health maintenance organizations (HMOs) and **preferred provider organizations (PPOs)**. The term managed care means a system in which employers and health insurers channel patients to the most cost-effective site of care. An umbrella label, health maintenance organization was coined in the 1970s to describe independent plans that offer benefits to an enrolled group of subscribers. HMOs are a form of prepaid health insurance, and about 570 such organizations existed in the United States in 2008.[12]

Physicians and other providers agree to provide certain services for a specified cost often with a cap on total patient visits or procedures during a benefit period. HMOs are a common form of supplementary health insurance for those on Medicare as well as Medicaid. An HMO provides basic and supplemental health maintenance and treatment services to enrollees who pay a fixed fee. The range of health services delivered depends on the voluntary contractual agreement between the enrollee and the plan. The focus of HMOs is health maintenance, and these agencies employ a large number of healthcare professionals. People belonging to an HMO must use the agency's designated facilities instead of choosing their own, but the services rendered are all prepaid. The consumer's cost is generally less than that in other facilities.

The major characteristic of the HMO is that it combines the insurance with a broad range of health services. It must compete with commercial insurers and Blue Cross/Blue Shield. Therefore, it has a strong incentive to operate in a cost-effective, efficient manner. The HMO has been seen as a model for encouraging the regulation of healthcare costs through competition. On average, prepaid group practice is less expensive, for the same benefit package, than traditional underwriting.

The greatest drawback of the HMO lies in the fact that the enrollee must find a physician within the HMO group for services. This often entails geographic problems, because HMO group physicians tend to practice in large, metropolitan medical centers. If enrollees go outside the HMO for health care, no benefits are available to them.

PPOs are another option open to the consumer for the delivery of health care. PPOs comprise groups of physicians or a hospital that provides companies with comprehensive health services at a discount. The majority of Americans with private health insurance (69%) receive their care through a PPO.[12] The benefits of a PPO are choice of provider and hospital, and cost control.

PPOs are either a group of providers who have voluntarily joined together to render health care on a contractual basis, or a group of providers who have been organized by a payer through contractual arrangement for a particular delivery system. The providers can be hospitals, physicians, other healthcare services, or any combination of these. PPOs are fee-for-service systems, as opposed to HMOs, which are capitated (that is, insurance pays providers a set fee in advance to cover all required services that the insured person needs). Patients subscribing to a PPO have the freedom to go wherever they want, including outside the PPO system. From an economic standpoint, however, the incentive to use PPO contract providers is that they are less expensive. Under a PPO contract, standard fee-for-service charges are generally discounted. These discounts range from 10% to 20% for hospital services performed by a physician in a hospital environment. The essential elements of a PPO, then, are as follows: fee-for-service, contractual arrangements, organization of providers, discounts, free choice, and economic incentives. PPOs are an emerging trend. Currently the majority of Americans with private health insurance receive medical care through a PPO healthcare delivery system.

The biggest impact on healthcare delivery caused by the managed care explosion is a substantial reduction in hospital use. As more and more people are covered by managed care plans, incentives to cut hospital use will continue to bring the number of hospital days down. As this trend continues, it is probable that marginal providers will leave the market and the remainder will compete based on convenience, price, and quality.

HEALTHCARE COSTS

The United States spends more on health per capita than any other country. Costs have gradually increased since the implementation of Medicare in 1965. In 2007, healthcare expenditures totaled $2.2 trillion and Medicare, Medicaid, and CHIP accounted for $769.6 billion.[1] The portion of the gross national product (GNP) attributable to health care increased from 5.9% to 16.2% between 1965 and 2007 because of the huge surge in medical, hospital, and nursing home costs during this period.[1] Costs continue to rise because of the complexity of health care and the number of elderly requiring care.

Public funds are increasingly being used to finance health care because of the rising cost of private health insurance. For the years 1974 to 1991, private funds paid for 58% to 59% of all healthcare costs. By 1995, however, the private share of health costs had declined further to 54% of the country's total healthcare expenditures, primarily because of the falling share of out-of-pocket spending, and then remained relatively stable at 55% to 56% between 1997 and 2005. The share of health care provided by public spending increased correspondingly during the 1992 to 1996 period and stabilized during the period 1997 to 2005.[1] After 2006, there was a slight increase in the share of healthcare spending paid for by public programs as the implementation of Medicare Part D caused shifts in the sources of funds that pay for prescription drugs.[1]

Some major problems plague the healthcare system in the United States. First, the cost of health care is exorbitant and continues to rise. Health insurance premiums continue to increase. Hospitals are finding it more difficult to maintain profit margins. Nationwide, hospital costs exceeded the amount reimbursed by Medicare and Medicaid by $32 billion for approximately 50% of hospitals in the United States in 2008.[13]

More hospitals, more specialist doctors, more growth in medical science and healthcare technology, greatly expanded research, and expanded insurance coverage have contributed to this phenomenal rise in costs. Second, health care is fragmented. Patients with multiple health problems, especially the elderly, often see a battery of specialists who only rarely coordinate care or provide clear instructions for disease management by patients and/or their family. Third, the many technological changes taking place can quickly outdate the knowledge and skills of the health practitioner. Fourth, the elderly population is expanding rapidly, increasing the need for special care and technology for this group. Services provided to low-income and racial minorities are inadequate. Last, there is an uneven distribution of health services. Although rural areas and towns usually build small clinics or hospitals, the number of rural health workers is low when compared to the number in cities. Overall life expectancy has improved, yet racial, geographic, and socioeconomic disparities in mortality and health status are widening. Geographic areas differ dramatically in the use of the hospital as a site of care for the exacerbation of chronic disease when outpatient care would be more cost-effective. Recent findings from the Dartmouth project emphasize the importance of identifying reasons for differences in the quality and cost of healthcare services based on race, socioeconomic status, and geographic region.[14]

Support personnel in medicine, dentistry, and physical and occupational therapy are becoming more available as the demand for health care increases. Nurse practitioners and physician assistants practice independently in clinics affiliated with pharmacies or freestanding immediate-care clinics. Walk-in patients are seen without appointments, and healthcare costs are less than physician visits. Dental technicians and physical and occupational therapy assistants expand services while lowering healthcare costs.

HEALTHCARE EXPENDITURES

The largest category of expenditures for personal health care is for hospital care (31%). Physicians' services rank second in monies spent for health care, at about 21% of the total health service budget; the remainder of the health dollar is divided among other professional services, nursing home and home care, and prescription drugs.[15] Healthcare expenditures fall unevenly on the population. If age 65 years is the lower limit for the elderly segment of the population, then this group's expenditures are three times higher than the per-capita expenditures for younger people, and the expenditures for those 85 years or older are two times higher than for those 65 to 74 years of age.[15]

The elderly are likely to have one or more chronic diseases that account for a large portion of Medicare spending. For example, the 15% of Medicare beneficiaries who have heart failure account for 45% of Medicare spending, and the 18% with diabetes account for 32% of Medicare spending. Spending for health care also varies across geographic regions, with higher spending in areas where the quantity of services (number of hospital beds, number of physician specialists) is available.[14]

Different approaches to delivering high-quality health care for the lowest cost are being evaluated. The Institute for Health Care Improvement provides support to medical groups and hospitals to research current practices and develop innovative methods to reduce healthcare costs. The goal is to improve the quality of care with the appropriate use of physician specialists, coordination of care, and patient and family support, and the appropriate use of resources at the end of life.[16] Chronic care coordination for the elderly with more than one chronic condition is also being used with this population.[17]

HEALTH INSURANCE COVERAGE IN THE UNITED STATES

Most Americans with private health insurance belong to a group plan financed through their employer. Of those with employer-based health insurance, the majority (58%) are enrolled in a PPO, HMO (19%), or high-deductible health plan with a savings option (HDHP/SO) (13%).[18] The availability of employer-sponsored coverage has been declining with a drop from 69% to 63% between 2000 and 2008, with most decreases in businesses with fewer than 200 employees. Even for those who do have access to insurance through their employer, the cost shared by the employee continues to increase out-of-pocket expenses with higher costs for premiums and higher deductibles that now average more than 10% of the family income for 1 out of 5 middle-class families. Employers with fewer than 200 employees are less likely to offer health insurance to their employees, while nearly all unionized workers have access to health insurance. Differences in health coverage vary by industry, with low-wage and part-time workers and those in agriculture, construction, and service industries being less likely to have coverage. When insurance is offered, it is becoming increasingly unaffordable for many. In 2010 the share of the total premium for a single employee was 19%, and for a family was 30%.[18]

Job losses that accompanied the recession in 2009 left 15% of middle-income Americans without health insurance, even though most live in families with at least one full-time worker. The economic downturn coupled with rapidly rising insurance premiums decreased employer-sponsored health insurance by 7% between 2000 and 2008. The biggest impact was on the middle class with only 66% of families earning $45,000 to $85,000 having medical insurance through their employer. The impact on low-income workers has been less severe because those with lower incomes have greater access to government-sponsored health care such as Medicaid.[14]

Fewer of the unemployed are able to afford to pay for premiums through the Consolidated Omnibus Budget Reconciliation Act (COBRA) and often have limited access to nongroup coverage because of high deductibles, costly premiums, and coverage limitations as a result of preexisting medical conditions.

The most important trends that account for the deterioration of health coverage are the following:

- Rising cost of premiums for employer-sponsored health insurance. In 2010 the annual premium for employer-based health insurance for a family of four was $13,770 and for an individual was $5049. The cost of health insurance premiums for a family increased 114% between 2000 and 2010.[18]
- Employers eliminating coverage because of escalating costs of premiums or shifting more costs to employees by choosing those plans with the highest out-of-pocket payments.
- The trend toward temporary and part-time work, which seldom includes health coverage. In 2006, 11% of working Americans had part-time jobs, and another 10% were independent contractors.
- Stricter requirements for new immigrants. Since July 2006, the application and renewal of Medicaid benefits requires proof of citizenship status.

As a result of these trends, lack of insurance and underinsurance are becoming widespread problems. Great disparities in access to health insurance are seen between ethnic groups and within the general population.

- Only 13% of residents in the Midwest lacked coverage compared to 20% of residents in the South; 32% of Hispanics were uninsured compared to 16% of whites and 21% of blacks.[19]
- More of those with annual incomes less than $25,000 lacked health insurance (27%) compared to those with incomes at or above $75,000 (9%).[19] The foreign-born population was more likely to be without health insurance than natives—34% compared to 14% in 2009. In addition, 46% of noncitizens were without health insurance.[19]
- In the general population, 37% of poor full-time workers were uninsured in 2006 and of these, 71% were in families with at least one full-time worker and 11% in families with a part-time worker.
- The key factors influencing lack of insurance coverage were age, race, educational attainment, and work experience.
- People aged 18 to 34 years were more likely than other groups to lack coverage. The elderly, because of Medicare, are at the other extreme (1.8% without coverage).[19]
- Among all adults, the likelihood of being uninsured declines as education level increases.

EFFECT ON HEALTHCARE PROVIDERS

According to the U.S. Department of Labor's most recent statistics, more than 14 million working Americans are employed in health care with 35% working in hospitals, 23% in nursing or personal care facilities, and 43% working in ambulatory care settings, primarily in offices of physicians, dentists, and other healthcare professionals.[20] Predicted growth in employment in the healthcare professions is twice that of non–health care because of the aging of the population. Age demographics are predicted to change in 2020 with a 54% increase in those 65 years and older and a 57% increase in those 85 years and older, with almost no increase in those in the age range of typical workers, 18 to 64 years.

There are some winners in the job redistribution. Demands for primary care (family physicians, physician's assistants, and nurses with advanced degrees, such as nurse practitioners or nurse midwives) are increasing. More procedures performed outside of hospitals means jobs for skilled laboratory personnel. The government mandate to require all medical records to be in an electronic format by 2014 will expand opportunities in health information technology and records management. It is expected that easy access to patient data through electronic medical records will be used for research to evaluate the effectiveness of diagnostic and treatment protocols to improve the quality of care and control costs. This will increase the demand for health professionals with additional training in statistics and business. There is an increased need for many rehabilitation specialties, such as physical, occupational, and speech therapists; home health workers; and geriatric personnel. Healthcare reform with greater numbers of individuals eligible for health insurance is expected to increase the demand for health care and healthcare workers. Shortages of all healthcare workers are anticipated in the next decade because of greater demand with an aging population and increased access with healthcare reform.

The health field of the future remains full of challenges for health personnel. Other issues are discussed in later chapters. Health care as it is known will not disappear, but may change considerably.

REFERENCES

1. Klees BS, Wolfe CJ, Curtis, CA. *Medicare & Medicaid. Title XVIII and Title XIX of the Social Security Act.* Baltimore, MD: Office of the Actuary Centers for Medicare and Medicaid Services, DHHS; 2009.
2. Department of Health and Human Services. Centers for Medicare and Medicaid Services. *Your Medicare Benefits.* CMS Product no. 10116. Baltimore, MD: DHHS; 2009.
3. *Medicaid. A Primer: Key Information on Our Nation's Health Coverage Program for Low Income People.* The Kaiser Commission on Medicaid and the Uninsured. Washington, DC: Kaiser Family Foundation; 2010.
4. *Top 4 Things to Know About Medicaid.* The Kaiser Commission on Medicaid and the Uninsured. Chartpack. Publication no. 8162. Washington, DC: Kaiser Family Foundation; February 2011.

5. *Distribution of Medicaid Spending by Service, FY2009.* Medicare and CHIP. Kaiser Family Foundation/Statehealthfacts.org. February 25, 2011. Internet: http://www.statehealthfacts.org/comparetable.jsp?ind=178&cat=4&sort=188

6. *State Adoption of Coverage and Enrollment Options in the Children's Health Insurance Reauthorization Act of 2009.* Kaiser Commission on Medicaid and the Uninsured. Key Facts. Publication no. 8146. Washington, DC: Kaiser Family Foundation; February 2011.

7. Thomasson M. *Health Insurance in the United States.* Economic History Association. 2010. Internet: http://eh.net/encyclopedia/article/thomasson.insurance.health.us

8. *Kaiser Permanente—More than 60 Years of Quality.* News Center. News and Perspectives from Kaiser Permanente. 2010. Internet: http://www.kp.org/newscenter

9. *About Group Health.* Group Health Cooperative. 2010. Internet: http://www.ghc.org/index.jhtml

10. Oliver, TR. Analysis, Advice and Congressional Leadership: The Physician Payment Review Commission and the Politics of Medicare. *Journal of Health Politics, Policy and Law.* 1993; 18:113–174.

11. National Center for Health Statistics. Centers for Disease Control and Prevention. *Health, United States, 2009: With Special Feature on Technology.* Hyattsville, MD. 2010.

12. *PPO Resources.* The American Association of Preferred Provider Organizations. 2011. http://www.aappo.org/index.cfm?pageid=10

13. *Underpayment by Medicare and Medicaid Fact Sheet.* American Hospital Association. 2009.

14. Rowland D, Hoffman C, McGinn-Shapiro M. *Health Care and the Middle Class: More Costs and Less Coverage.* Menlo Park, CA: Kaiser Family Foundation; 2009.

15. Federal Interagency Forum on Aging-Related Statistics. *Older Americans 2010. Key Indicators of Well-Being.* Washington, DC: U.S. Government Printing Office; 2010.

16. *About IHI.* Institute for Healthcare Improvement. 2011. Internet: http://www.ihi.org/ihi

17. Berenson R, Howell J. *Structuring, Financing and Paying for Effective Chronic Care Coordination.* A Report Commissioned by the National Coalition on Care Coordination (N3C); 2009.

18. *Employer Health Benefits 2010 Summary of Findings.* Kaiser Family Foundation. Health Research & Educational Trust. Publication no. 8086. 2010. Internet: http://ehbs.kff.org/pdf/2010/8086.pdf

19. DeNavas-Walt C, Proctor BD, Smith JC. *Income, Poverty, and Health Insurance Coverage in the United States: 2008.* U.S. Census Bureau, Current Population Reports, P60-236. Washington, DC: U.S. Government Printing Office; 2009.

20. Bureau of Labor Statistics. Department of Labor. *Career Guide to Industries, 2010-11 Edition.* February 2010. Internet: http://www.bls.gov/oco/cg/cgs035.htm

chapter four

Aging, Health, and Long-Term Care

KEY TERMS

Alzheimer's disease
Assisted living care
Community-based care
Continuing care
Demographic
Frail elderly
Geriatrics
Health literacy
Home health agencies
  (HHAs)

Hospice
Intermediate care
  facility (ICF)
Long-term health care
  (LTC)
Meals on Wheels
Program of All-Inclusive
  Care for the Elderly
  (PACE)

Proprietary nursing
  homes
Self-directed home
  care
Shelter care
Skilled nursing facility
  (SNF)
Voluntary nursing
  homes

OBJECTIVES

After studying this chapter, the student should be able to:

- List at least three benefits for the elderly provided by Medicaid that are not provided by Medicare.
- Differentiate between skilled nursing and intermediate care facilities.
- Describe the services provided by assisted living facilities.
- Describe the services provided by each of the following: (a) home health, (b) hospice, and (c) shelter care homes and workshops.
- Discuss the role of health literacy in delivering quality health care.
- Explain how shifts in demographics will impact the skills and training needs of healthcare workers.
- Discuss future trends in long-term health care including community-based care.

THE IMPACT OF FUTURE DEMOGRAPHIC CHANGES ON HEALTHCARE NEEDS

In Chapter 1, we summarized recent trends in U.S. health care and the need for new strategies to address inequities in access to health care and rising healthcare costs. This chapter briefly explores the role of **demographic** changes in determining the nation's future healthcare needs. Because the population 65 years of age and older will continue to increase rapidly through the year 2020 and beyond, this chapter focuses on the need for various health services for the elderly, as well as the need for qualified practitioners to carry out these services. The discussion covers nursing homes, community-based health services such as home health agencies and **hospice**, personnel needs, and trends in the needs for long-term care.

The aging of the population has important implications for health care, public health, and human service systems. As the older fraction of the population increases, more services will be required for the treatment and management of chronic and acute health conditions and disabilities. In addition, Medicare beneficiaries with multiple chronic conditions, especially the **frail elderly** with functional or cognitive impairments in addition to chronic medical illness, will need care coordination.[1]

According to projections from the U.S. Census Bureau, after the first Baby Boomers turn 65 years old in 2011, the number of older people will substantially increase. In 2050, the age group 65 years and older is anticipated to be twice as large as in 2010, and will represent nearly 20% of the total U.S. population. The segment that is 85 years old and older (the "old-old") will also experience rapid growth from 5.8 million in 2010 to 19 million in 2050.[2]

In recent years, the old-old have been the fastest growing segment of the population. Furthermore, life expectancy at this advanced age is increasing. Sixty-one percent of this group is female, mainly widows.[2]

COMMON HEALTH PROBLEMS IN AN AGING POPULATION

Chronic diseases, arising from both emotional and physical causes, will be the most important of the future disabilities. Chronic disease, which is managed rather than cured, will require continuing services from physicians and other healthcare personnel. Conditions range from relatively minor to very severe. The minor problems require little care from others, but the severe ones require increasing amounts of care and professional help. Chronic conditions tend to be cumulative, so the elderly, especially the old-old, often experience multiple problems and require a substantial number of services.

The most prevalent chronic conditions in 2007 among the elderly living in the community were, in order of prevalence, hypertension, arthritis, heart disease, cancer, and diabetes. Limitations associated with aging increase dramatically after age 85 years; 60% have a hearing impairment and 28% are visually impaired.[3] The most debilitating conditions producing functional impairment among the elderly are dementia, stroke, and hip fractures. Those 85 years of age or older are five times more likely to have dementia and 10 to 15 times more likely to have a hip fracture than someone 60 to 65 years of age.[4] Dementia is estimated to affect over 20% of this age group and accounts for 40% of nursing home residents.[5]

It is noteworthy, however, that of the oldest-old living in the community, at least 40% report no limits in their daily activities, and 66% of them perceive their health to be good to excellent. Physicians' visits are no more frequent for them than for the young-old. Hospital stays and nursing home residence, however, are much more prevalent than for the young-old. About 1.6 million elderly age 65 years and older are in institutional settings, with 1.4 million living in nursing homes, of which about two-thirds are age 85 and older. These nursing home residents often have a great need for care with activities of daily living and/or have severe cognitive impairment as a result of **Alzheimer's disease** or other dementia.[6]

MEDICARE FOR THE ELDERLY

The Centers for Medicare and Medicaid Services (CMS) oversee the Medicare program. Medicare-covered benefits apply mostly to the treatment of patients with acute illnesses who require hospitalization and short-term skilled nursing care in rehabilitation centers or nursing homes, or home health care. Medicare is divided into four parts. Part A is hospital insurance, and all elderly beneficiaries are automatically enrolled. Part B is supplemental medical insurance and is voluntary, although the majority of the elderly purchase Part B. Part C is supplemental hospital and medical insurance, and Part D is medication insurance. All have deductibles and coinsurance. Under Part A, Medicare pays for all reasonable hospital expenses minus a deductible for the first 60 days of each benefit period. Part B pays for doctors' services and outpatient hospital services, including emergency room visits; ambulatory services; diagnostic and laboratory tests; durable medical equipment; physical therapy; occupational therapy; speech pathology; medical nutrition therapy; preventive services including screening for diabetes, cardiovascular disease, and certain cancers; bone density measurements; and certain immunizations. It does not pay for dental, vision, podiatry, or routine physical examinations. Medicare B pays 80% of the approved amount according to a fee schedule for covered services, in excess of the annual deductible. Many elderly purchase Part C, also called Medicare Advantage, from a private insurance company. Medicare Advantage Plans provide all of Part A (hospital insurance) and Part B (medical insurance) coverage, and may offer extra coverage such as vision, hearing, dental, and/or health and wellness programs. Most also include Medicare prescription drug coverage or Part D. Medicare pays a fixed amount to the private insurance company offering Medicare Advantage Plans to cover the cost of Medicare Part B premiums and additional services.[7]

MEDICAID FOR THE ELDERLY

Other than being administered by CMS, Medicaid and Medicare structures have little in common. Medicaid covers a broad range of services not covered by Medicare, acting as a supplemental insurance for the elderly and disabled. It also pays their Medicare premiums, includes cost-sharing requirements, and covers prescription drugs. However, a large number of the elderly do not take advantage of Medicaid coverage because of the inability to navigate the publicly run system.

The Medicaid program is the primary payer and the only safety-net program for **long-term health care (LTC)**. However, those who need LTC qualify for Medicaid only if they are also low income. Long-term care in a nursing home can cost $70,000 per year, and few families have unlimited funds to cover this cost. Many elderly deplete their savings and then are eligible for LTC through Medicaid.[8]

Medicaid operates under tight budget constraints, and provider payment rates are substantially below market rates. This is a problem for the managed care organizations (MCOs), to whom many Medicaid recipients are referred, causing a substantial number of organizations that do not bid on contracts or choose to opt out of the system entirely. Many physicians in private practice do not accept Medicaid patients for the same reason. Both factors decrease access to care by the elderly population.

LONG-TERM CARE

Long-term health care is defined as the help needed by people of any age who are unable to care for themselves because of physical and/or mental impairment. As the term implies, this care is for extended periods, ranging from months to years to a lifetime. Long-term care is provided in institutions or the community, or it can be home based. An estimated 1.4 million people reside in nearly 16,000 nursing homes in the United States. People tend to regard long-term care as being only for the aged, but the fact is that approximately 4 million impaired children and adults younger than 65 years of age need long-term care support in addition to 6 million elderly.[9] However, with the dramatic increase in the population that is older than 65 years, and especially those older than 80 years, the need for long-term care is increasing and costs are escalating. Cost containment is a major issue that the aging population is addressing with vigor. (This is discussed at length in Chapter 3.) Adequate personnel to provide long-term care is another critical health issue.

Although families, friends, and neighbors may be able to help the disabled, family units have become smaller over the years and most able people are working. Frequently, no one is around to take care of the disabled or elderly who cannot manage the tasks of daily living. For some of these people, community-based services are an alternative to institutional care, but for many others such services are not enough. These individuals include the vast numbers of chronically and/or mentally ill, the frail elderly, impaired children, and the permanently disabled.

Long-term care facilities include more than just nursing homes, although these account for around 70% of care provided in long-term facilities. Other long-term care establishments include psychiatric and mental retardation hospitals, chronic disease hospitals, and rehabilitation hospitals. Types of long-term care within the system are assisted living facilities, home health services, **community-based care** (shelter homes and workshops), and hospice programs.

NURSING HOMES

Nursing homes originated with county poor houses (alms-houses). They were first established in the nineteenth century to care for the poor and provide food, shelter, and clothing. Over time, they became community dumps for castoff unfortunates. The conditions in these places were atrocious. Society gets what it pays for; many accounts of starving, beating, and murder erupted from time to time, creating scandals. This prompted states to set up regulations governing nursing home care, but most states were unwilling to close the proprietary or **voluntary nursing homes** because they would then be responsible for the occupants. Instead, they chose to look the other way.[10]

In the twenty-first century, nursing homes that have developed under other sponsorship such as church groups, fraternal organizations, and volunteer groups are proliferating. Many such organizations have started homes to care for their members. It is widely acknowledged that the quality of service in these types of nursing homes is high. The shortcomings of government and **proprietary nursing homes** continue, however, as do periodic reports of scandal. Homes that cheat patients, physically and mentally abuse patients, neglect care, provide inadequate medical and nursing care, or are firetraps frequently make the news. To make matters worse, the number of people who need good long-term care is growing, and the available beds are insufficient.[10]

Of the available nursing home beds, the proprietary sector clearly led in number, commanding 70% to 80% of the market until the late 1990s. The poor and chronically ill who needed nursing home care the most were at the bottom of the list for proprietary nursing homes. Many of these homes also restricted the types of patients they would admit, preferring not to have persons who required a great amount of care or who might damage the property. Long waiting lists for the admission of Medicare/Medicaid patients resulted from these restrictions, prompting Congress to enact legislation to construct nonprofit nursing homes. With the rising costs of nursing home care, most of the private paying patients needed to convert to Medicaid as soon as their funds were depleted. Medicare/Medicaid patients are now welcomed at most proprietary institutions.

With the advent of Medicare and Medicaid came federal stipulations governing eligibility. There are now two types of recognized homes: *skilled nursing facilities* and *intermediate care facilities*. A **skilled nursing facility (SNF)** is a nursing home that provides the level of care closest to hospital care. Twenty-four-hour nursing services, medical supervision, rehabilitation, physical therapy, pharmacy and dietetic services, and occupational and recreational therapy are provided in accordance with federal guidelines. Skilled homes are for convalescents and patients with long-term illnesses.

An **intermediate care facility (ICF)** provides less extensive care and services. People in intermediate facilities usually need daily personal care because they are not able to care for themselves or live alone, but they do not need 24-hour care. Although nursing care is provided, it does not need to be around the clock. The emphasis in an ICF is on personal care and social services. Some also employ rehabilitation and occupational therapists. These homes must meet federal guidelines to receive government funding.[10] Many general hospitals also have extended care, skilled nursing units within their facilities. With fewer acute care beds occupied, the units can generate income that allows the hospital to remain open.

Assisted living facilities are home to 1 million elderly adults in one of more than 36,000 facilities in the United States. Residents or their families typically pay the cost, but Medicaid finances care for 12%. Costs are generally lower than those for nursing home care. Adults eligible for **assisted living care** are those who require assistance with activities of daily living (ADLs) including dressing, bathing, eating, or using the bathroom, but do not require 24-hour care or medical care. Assisted living may be part of a retirement community, nursing home, senior housing complex, or a stand-alone facility. Licensing requirements vary by state and are known by different names such as residential care, board and care, congregate care, and personal care. Some assisted living facilities are part of a retirement community, known as a **continuing care** community that allows residents to move from independent living to assisted living to a skilled nursing facility as their needs change.[11]

The Omnibus Budget Reconciliation Act of 1987 (OBRA 87) was enacted in response to concerns about the poor quality of care and inadequate regulation in nursing homes in the United States. A change brought about by OBRA 87 required Medicare and Medicaid standards and certification procedures regarding long-term care facilities to merge, and intermediate-care facilities' standards were upgraded to correspond to those for skilled care facilities.[10]

The federal government, through CMS, is responsible for nursing home standards, while individual states are responsible for monitoring facilities to ensure that standards are met. A new requirement for state surveys of facilities stated that surveys were to be unannounced and include resident interviews and direct observation. The OBRA 87 created minimum standards of care, including staffing requirements and rights for residents. These standards emphasized quality of life issues and the prevention of abuse, mistreatment, and neglect, including the use of physical and chemical restraints. Rights of residents included the following:

- Freedom from abuse, mistreatment, and neglect
- Freedom from physical restraints
- Right to privacy
- Accommodation of medical, physical, psychological, and social needs
- Participation in resident and family groups
- Treatment with dignity
- Exercise of self-determination
- Free communication
- Participation in the review of one's care plan
- Advance notice regarding any changes in care, treatment, or change of status in the facility
- Ability to voice grievances without discrimination or reprisal

In the 20 years since OBRA 87, there have been some improvements in the quality of care for residents, but there continue to be problems. An ongoing problem in LTC is the shortage of certified nursing assistants, which is associated with a low level of training and a high level of job turnover, ranging from 70% to over 100% turnover in 1 year. Low wages, lack of benefits, and difficult working conditions account for much of the high staff turnover.[12,13]

Many of the elderly who make up 85% of the population of nursing homes would not need this type of care if more long-term services were available in the community. Community-based long-term care services should continue to grow as the government liberalizes its policies for alternatives to nursing homes. Another reason for the growth of community services is the fact that most people and their families prefer to avoid institutionalization whenever possible.

COMMUNITY SERVICES

Findings of a National Institutes of Health (NIH) committee on personnel needs clearly established that the older population will require the expansion of a wide range of health services, including preventive, primary, long-term, hospice, and rehabilitative care. Expanded services can help many older people maintain functional independence and remain at home for longer periods. More options are now available for meeting the long-term care needs of the elderly who prefer living at home. Examples are home care and community care funded by both Medicare and Medicaid and by private foundations. Recent legislation as part of healthcare reform established a long-term insurance choice for Americans. It is self-funded and voluntary. Workers will pay premiums in order to receive a daily cash benefit if they develop a disability. The benefit is flexible and could be used for a range of community support services, from respite care to home care.[8]

There are 7 million low-income disabled or elderly Americans eligible for both Medicare and Medicaid. Healthcare costs for these individuals are twice that for other adults on Medicare and are eight times higher than that for children on Medicaid. Coordination of care is difficult because Medicare is a federal program and Medicaid is managed by individual states. Combined Medicare/Medicaid programs allow for the coordination of care, for example, the PACE program described in the following.

The **Program of All-Inclusive Care for the Elderly (PACE)** provides comprehensive preventive, primary, acute, and long-term care services so older individuals with chronic care needs can continue living in the community.[14] The PACE model of care began in the 1970s in the Chinatown–North Beach area of San Francisco to meet the long-term care needs of elderly immigrants. PACE has expanded to 72 sites in urban and rural areas in 30 states across the United States.[15] Services include adult day care with physical, occupational, and recreational therapy; nutrition counseling; personal care; social services; meals; and medical care. As needs change, participants may receive home, hospital, or nursing home care. PACE programs receive Medicare and Medicaid capitation payments. PACE is available to individuals 55 years of age or older who are certified by their state to need nursing home care but are able to live safely in the community. A typical PACE participant is very similar to the average nursing home resident. She is 80 years old, has 7.9 medical conditions, is limited in three activities of daily living, and has a 50% chance of having dementia. Even though PACE participants require high levels of care, more than 90% are able to continue living in the community.[14]

COMMUNITY HEALTH AGENCIES

Home Health

Home health agencies (HHAs) provide part-time nursing and medical care in patients' homes, as well as other services such as physical, speech, and occupational therapy; social services; and sometimes medical supplies and equipment such as wheelchairs, walkers, and so forth. Homemaker services may also be part of the package. Physicians, physician assistants, and nurse practitioners provide medical care at home. The agency may be independently operated or managed by a public health department or hospital. Patient fees, government grants, private insurance, or Medicare and Medicaid may finance agency services. Variations of HHAs include the well-known Visiting Nurse Association, which most often employs Public Health Service (PHS) nurses. These nurses go to patients' homes and change dressings, give injections, and request other types of services as needed.

A new development in home and community-based care is consumer-directed or **self-directed home care** where the consumer rather than an agency is responsible for hiring home care workers. The federal CMS, under the *Real Choice System Change* and *Independence Plus* grants, has provided funds to assist states in implementing these programs.[16,17]

Meals on Wheels is another HHA variation. This agency supplies one hot meal a day (usually lunch) to shut-ins. It may also add a snack for dinner to go along with other foods the patient may have in the house. Patients on therapeutic diets for special conditions can be accommodated. Contracts are made with various agencies, usually hospitals, to provide the meals, which are typically delivered by volunteers.

Hospice

In 1967, the hospice movement was resurrected from its beginnings during the medieval era in England. Whereas the first hospices cared for the wounded, sick, and dying, modern hospices care only for the dying. Hospices are operated on the principle that the dying have special needs and wants that hospital personnel are too busy to handle. Hospice care helps manage pain and other symptoms associated with dying when conventional treatment is no longer of value. It allows the dying to spend their last days in their homes among people who are sensitive to their needs and wishes. Hospice seeks to improve the quality of the last days of life. Most hospices offer only home services, although some have added bed care facilities, because they are more likely to be funded by Medicare—this funding comes not as a humanitarian measure, but as an effort to reduce the cost of hospital inpatient care for the terminally ill. Medicare hospice benefits will achieve significant cost savings as well as serve the needs of the terminally ill elderly more appropriately and humanely.

Supportive Housing

The U.S. Department of Housing and Urban Development provides supportive housing, such as shelters, for the homeless with disabilities, primarily those with severe mental illness, or chronic problems with alcohol or drug abuse. Both **shelter care** homes and sheltered workshops are available to long-term care recipients. If a person needs only to be maintained so that he or she receives the basics—food, shelter, clothing, companionship—and has no major physical problems that require nursing care, then a carefully chosen shelter home may be sufficient. Since 1984 there have been federal regulations in effect that govern shelter home operations. These include, but are not limited to, an adequate, balanced diet; acceptable sanitation and safety features; and some consulting services from professionals. Sheltered workshops exist for the physically and mentally challenged. These are places where the person can learn a repetitive skill and be sheltered from the normal work world. The work and production schedules are not geared to commercial output. The capabilities of the worker are taken into account.

DEMOGRAPHIC TRENDS AND PROJECTIONS

The staggering statistics of the aging U.S. population emphasize the trend that will occur in future health care as well as concerns regarding how and where that care will be delivered. By the mid-twenty-first century, because of the rapidly increasing population that is older than age 65, the number of elderly individuals will triple. The need for LTC (home and nursing home care) and the associated costs will increase tenfold. All of this will put extraordinary demands on the LTC system.

Changes in the racial and ethnic composition of the U.S. population have important consequences for the nation's health because many of the measures of disease and disability differ significantly by race and ethnicity. Racial and ethnic minority groups account for 25% of the U.S. population. In recent decades, the percentage of the population that is of Hispanic or Asian origin has more than doubled. In 2008, 20% of the population aged 65 years or older identified themselves as Black or African American, Asian, American Indian or Alaska Native, Native Hawaiian, or Other Pacific Islander.[3] Shifts in the U.S. population is expected to change with a decease in whites and an increase in all other racial groups between 2010 and 2050.[2]

These shifts in the racial and ethnic makeup of the United States require health professionals and organizations to achieve cultural competence and to ensure that they utilize appropriate and tailored approaches in working with these population groups. A Healthy People 2020 recommendation is to increase the proportion of all degrees awarded to members of underrepresented racial and ethnic groups among the health professions to meet the needs of all patients, regardless of their background.[18]

Limited **health literacy** affects people of all ages, races, incomes, and education levels, but the impact of limited health literacy disproportionately affects lower socioeconomic and minority groups. Research over the past 2 decades has shown that health information is often presented in a way that is not usable to the majority of Americans. Health literacy is the degree to which individuals have the capacity to obtain, process, and understand basic health information and services needed to make appropriate health decisions. Examples of health literacy are the ability to understand instructions on prescription drug bottles, appointment slips, medical education brochures, doctors' directions, and consent forms, and the ability to negotiate complex healthcare systems. Health literacy is not simply the ability to read. It requires a complex group of reading, listening, analytical, and decision-making skills, and the ability to apply these skills to health situations. It affects people's ability to search for and use health information, adopt healthy behaviors, and act on important public health alerts. Limited health literacy is also associated with worse health outcomes and higher costs.[19,20]

POTENTIAL HEALTHCARE NEEDS

Future healthcare needs will depend in large part on the health and functional status of the growing elderly population. The potential needs discussed here may assist students in determining where future personnel needs might be greatest and how they might best serve in health care. In the future, the majority of older individuals are likely to be healthy and able to function independently. More than 90% of elderly people continue to live in the community, and more than two-thirds of them perceive their health to be good to excellent.

Health Service Needs

A very broad range of services is required to address the healthcare needs of the older population. Necessary services include prevention activities, as well as primary, acute, postacute, rehabilitative, long-term, and hospice care. Because the old-old population is the one increasing most rapidly, services needed in the twenty-first century will be focused on maintaining the functional capacities of persons of advanced age and on providing long-term care to the frail elderly. After the year 2011, a more rapid expansion will occur in the young-old group. These persons will need more preventive, primary, and acute care services.

Many of the health and related care services for the elderly will take place in community settings. The vast majority of disabled elderly now receive all their care in community settings, and this trend is expected to continue. The workplace of some healthcare personnel, therefore, will shift. New sites for health care will need to evolve, such as new residential and living arrangements, and the expansion of integrated care systems, involving institutional and community facilities, case management, and cost-sharing arrangements. More emphasis will be placed on rehabilitation and self-care.

Other prospective changes in the health field include increased technology to detect and treat diseases, increased availability of health insurance benefits, more professional and public interest in community-based services, a concentration of the sickest patients in hospitals, new health programs for low-income groups, and a large supply of physicians and other health personnel. These factors will increase the utilization of health services.

PERSONNEL NEEDS

Requirements for personnel specifically prepared to serve older people will greatly exceed the current supply. Healthcare practitioners will routinely serve older people in the future as part of their regular duties. This care will make up approximately one-third to two-thirds of the workload of physicians and other healthcare personnel. Although attention to aging and **geriatrics** has expanded in recent years, most health education programs give little emphasis to these issues. Greatly expanded training programs are required to prepare personnel to provide services in homes, hospices, nursing homes, and other community settings.

Personnel need to ensure the adequacy and availability of health care for older persons should be monitored and modifications made in healthcare delivery and financing as needed. To provide responsive care to older persons, greater emphasis on the special needs and conditions of older persons should be included in the education of all health and human service personnel. Government funding sources at all levels should support ongoing study and research into the special psychological and physiological characteristics of the elderly.

Future Education for the Health Professions

Today's healthcare workforce lacks much of the training required to provide appropriate care to today's older adults and is thus unprepared for the projected increase in the number of older Americans over the next 20 years. Equally important, the healthcare workforce is older than in the past. The healthcare personnel of tomorrow need to begin now to develop some special skills to deal with future changes. First, curricula must include the requirements and care of the elderly population. A second requisite is the need to assume an active role in developing acceptable health policies. Health professionals must be able to assess needs accurately and teach at all levels. Because healthcare providers will have to address new health issues, policies, technologies, and practice guidelines over the course of their careers, continuing education programs will need to be updated periodically.

Interdisciplinary respect and understanding will be critical for future health professionals. An ideal mechanism to achieve this would be shared educational experiences, with a health science core of studies and laboratories that allow students from many disciplines to interact and jointly provide care. Would-be healthcare professionals must learn to establish strong, effective, collegial relationships with practitioners of all healthcare disciplines. In this way, the student of today can prepare for a leadership role in clinical care, the political process, and national healthcare planning and research.

Shifts in Training Health Personnel

Health personnel in the coming years will need to develop a broader understanding and competence in geriatrics. An extended curriculum to encompass these goals should be established. It likely will include a variety of clinical settings and short-term, intensive courses to bring practitioners up to current knowledge levels. Healthcare providers will need to address new health issues, policies, technologies, and practice guidelines over the course of their careers.

Physicians direct the work of other health personnel, and therefore will need to develop additional competencies and leadership roles for the practice of geriatric medicine. All physicians should receive education and training in geriatric medicine as part of their professional preparation. Care of chronically ill, frail elderly persons should be emphasized. Special attention should be focused on clinical pharmacology, especially for patients on multiple medications, and on the impact of sensory loss and dental health on nutritional status.

Dentists, dental hygienists, and dental assistants will be serving substantially larger numbers of elderly. Like nurses, they should receive education concerning the special needs and conditions of the elderly as part of their basic preparation. Professional nursing students in the past have had limited curricular content focused on the care of the elderly. Innovative educational preparation with a focus on the needs and care of the elderly must be emphasized. Nursing personnel need expanded knowledge and skills, with stress on health promotion and nutrition for the elderly. They should be encouraged to go into geriatric nursing or to specialize in advanced gerontology education.

Social work personnel must be prepared to meet the diverse social services needs of the elderly. They will require a specialized knowledge of the aging process and the interpersonal dynamics of the aging and their families.

A large number of other types of health personnel are increasingly involved in the care of older persons, both at the community level and in institutions. Many different occupations and specialties make critical contributions to the care and well-being of the elderly. Often the care of the elderly calls for multidisciplinary and interdisciplinary activities. Diverse competencies and skills are required to respond effectively to the challenge of caring for the aged population; the appropriate use of well-prepared allied health professionals and supporting health personnel will be critical to maintaining such a large elderly population at their optimum potential.

Health professionals need to be knowledgeable about the health problems of different ethnic, racial, and socioeconomic groups including recent immigrants. Training in factors related to health literacy and approaches to simplify patient education are needed. Health literacy is critical in ensuring the delivery of quality health care and reducing hospital and emergency room readmissions and healthcare costs.

Part II of this book describes the work of many health professionals and supporting personnel in great detail. The Bureau of Labor Statistics identified more than 14 million health workers in 200 occupations in 2008, and the projected number for 2018 was 17 million in 250 occupations. More than 400,000 additional jobs are expected in physicians' offices. The most rapid growth, however, is expected to be in offices other than doctors', such as those of physical therapists, outpatient facilities, nurse practitioners, and home health agencies. Each of the professions will need expanded personnel to take care of the aging population. Students considering a career in the health field are encouraged to continue—their services will be greatly needed.

SUMMARY

Although the need for health services will increase dramatically in future decades because of the drastic increase in the elderly population, the exact nature and scope of our future healthcare system remain uncertain. Changes in the structure of the healthcare system and uncertainty about how to finance future health care make it difficult to project career situations precisely. Under any conditions, however, the trends indicate a need for substantial increases in the number of health personnel specifically prepared to provide services to older persons.

The use of health services will be concentrated among older and very old persons. This fact has important implications for the education and training of all healthcare personnel. The impact of these changes will have an increasing role in the delivery of health care and on the economy of the United States.

REFERENCES

1. Berenson R, Howell J. *Structuring, Financing and Paying for Effective Chronic Care Coordination*. A Report Commissioned by the National Coalition on Care Coordination (N3C). 2009.
2. Vincent GK, Velkoff VA. *The Older Population in the United States 2010 to 2050. Population Estimates and Projections*. U.S. Department of Commerce Economics and Statistics Administration. U.S. Census Bureau. 2010.
3. Federal Interagency Forum on Aging-Related Statistics. *Older Americans 2010: Key Indicators of Well-Being*. Washington, DC: U.S. Government Printing Office; July 2010.
4. Centers for Disease Control and Prevention. *Hip Fractures Among Older Adults*. 2008. Internet: http://www.cdc.gov/ncipc/factsheets/adulthipfx.htm
5. National Institute on Aging. *One in Seven Americans Age 71 and Older Has Some Type of Dementia, NIH Funded Study Estimates*. 2007. Internet: http://www.nia.nih.gov/NewsAndEvents/PressReleases/PR20071030ADAMS.htm
6. Administration on Aging. U.S. Department of Health and Human Services. *A Profile of Older Americans: 2010*. Aging Statistics. February 25, 2011. Internet: http://www.aoa.gov/aoaroot/aging_statistics/Profile/2010/6.asp
7. Centers for Medicare and Medicaid Services. *National Medicare Handbook*. CMS Product no. 10050. February 2011. Internet: http://www.medicare.gov/Publications/Pubs/pdf/10050.pdf
8. *The Community Living Assistance Services and Supports (CLASS) Act*. Focus on Health Care Reform. Robert Woods Johnson Foundation. 2009.
9. *Medicaid and Long-Term Care Services and Supports*. Medicaid Facts. Kaiser Commission on Medicaid and the Uninsured. Publication no. 2186-08. Washington, DC: Kaiser Family Foundation; March 2011. Internet: http://www.kff.org/medicaid/upload/2186-08.pdf
10. *The Evolution of Nursing Home Care in the United States*. Today's Nursing Homes. Health Spotlight. Online News Hour. Internet: http://www.pbs.org/newshour/health/nursinghomes/timeline.html

11. *What Is Assisted Living?* About ALFA. Assisted Living Federation of America. Alexandria, VA. 2009. Internet: http://www.alfa.org/alfa/What_is_Assisted_Living1.asp?SnID=724251500

12. Decker FH, Gruhn P, Matthew-Martin L, Dollard KJ, Tucker AM, Bizette L. *2002 AHCA Survey of Nursing: Staff Vacancy and Turnover in Nursing Homes.* Washington, DC: American Health Care Association; 2003.

13. Stone RI, Wiener JM. *Who Will Care for Us? Addressing the Long-Term Care Workforce Crisis.* Washington, DC: The Urban Institute; 2001.

14. Centers for Medicare and Medicaid Services. *Quick Facts About Programs of All-Inclusive Care for the Elderly (PACE).* CMS Publication no. 11341. 2008. Internet: http://www.cms.gov/PACE/Downloads/externalfactsheet.pdf

15. What Is Pace? National Pace Association. Alexandria, VA. 2002. Internet: http://www.npaonline.org/website/article.asp?id=12

16. Weiner JM, Siebenaler K. *Increasing Options for Self-Directed Services. Initiatives of the FY 2003 Independence Plus Grantees.* Baltimore, MD: Centers for Medicare and Medicaid Services; 2007.

17. O'Keeffe J, O'Keeffe C, Weiner JM, Siebenaler K. *Increasing Options for Self-Directed Services. Initiatives of the FY 2003 Independence Plus of the FY 2003 Independence Plus Grantees.* Baltimore, MD: Centers for Medicare and Medicaid Services; 2007.

18. Centers for Disease Control and Prevention. U.S. Department of Health and Human Services. *Healthy People 2020: The Road Ahead.* 2009. Internet: http://healthypeople.gov/HP2020/default.asp

19. U.S. Department of Health and Human Services. Office of Disease Prevention and Health Promotion. *National Action Plan to Improve Health Literacy.* Washington, DC; 2010.

20. National Network of Libraries of Medicine. *Health Literacy. Consumer Health Manual.* Bethesda, MD. 2010. Internet: http://nnlm.gov/outreach/consumer/hlthlit.html

chapter five

Healthcare Reform

KEY TERMS

Affordable Care Act
  (ACA)
American Health Benefit
  Exchanges
Catastrophic health plan
Early Retiree Reinsurance
Hardship waiver
Health Care and
  Education
  Reconciliation
  Act of 2010

Health Savings Account
  (HSA)
Healthcare workforce
High deductible health
  plan
High-risk pools
Lifetime limits
National Conference of
  State Legislation
  (NCSL)

Preexisting medical
  condition
Small Business Options
  Program Exchange
  (SHOP)

OBJECTIVES

After studying this chapter, the student should be able to:

- Describe the expansion of healthcare insurance under healthcare reform through (a) Medicaid, (b) the Children's Health Care Program (CHIP), (c) Health Insurance Exchanges, (d) high-risk pools, and (e) Early Retiree Reinsurance programs.

- Describe sources of funding the healthcare reform law.

- Explain the role of the states in implementing healthcare reform.

- Discuss the impact of healthcare reform on the healthcare workforce.

OVERVIEW OF HEALTHCARE REFORM

Previous chapters in this text discussed the need for healthcare reform—the number of Americans without health insurance and the increasing cost of health care. This chapter highlights the components of healthcare reform including the timeline for implementation. Healthcare reform is very complex and will require many entities for implementation: the federal government, state governments, private insurance companies, and primary healthcare providers. Healthcare reform will have a direct impact on how health insurance is made available to the uninsured and will increase access to health care for many Americans.

Healthcare reform will expand access to healthcare insurance for an estimated 30 million uninsured individuals in the United States. The majority of Americans obtain health insurance through an employer; however, not all employers, especially small businesses, offer health insurance. The self-employed and unemployed often lack health insurance because of the high cost of premiums. Even those who are employed often choose to opt out of health insurance because of the cost of the employee's share of premiums. Private health insurance carriers can drop individuals with health insurance when the cost of care reaches the **lifetime limits** for healthcare costs after a serious accident or illness such as cancer.

HEALTHCARE REFORM LEGISLATION

President Obama signed healthcare reform legislation into law in March 2010. The Patient Protection and Affordable Care Act (H.R. 3590) modified by the **Health Care and Education Reconciliation Act of 2010** (H.R. 4872) are collectively called the **Affordable Care Act (ACA)**.[1] Previous attempts by Democratic U.S. presidents to expand healthcare coverage failed.[2]

The sweeping changes under the ACA are comparable in scope to changes brought about by the Social Security Act of 1965 when Medicare was made available to the elderly. However, the Social Security Act had bipartisan support, whereas the current ACA was passed by a Democratic majority in the House of Representatives.

There is a possibility that parts of the healthcare reform legislation will be repealed as a result of the November 2010 mid-term elections that changed the balance of power in the House of Representatives with a loss of a Democratic majority. Those who voted for Republican candidates reported an unfavorable view of the healthcare reform law (56%) and would like the entire law repealed (54%) or part of the law repealed (30%).[3]

Because regulation of health insurance is the responsibility of the states, implementation of many aspects of healthcare reform will be done at the state level. Many states, however, have opposed healthcare reform; some states have filed a federal lawsuit in response to the ACA, and some members of state legislatures proposed legislation to limit, alter, or oppose selected state or federal actions.[4] The most unpopular mandate is the requirement for individuals to buy health insurance if they lack coverage through an employer.

Although the law is not likely to be repealed, federal funds for implementing health reform could be withheld, and states may not have the money to implement health reform. The economic downturn of 2009 has seriously impacted state budgets. Federal funds from the American Recovery and Reinvestment Act (ARRA) of 2009 allowed states to expand the number of residents on Medicaid. However, by 2011 many states were experiencing severe budget deficits and may not be able to expand Medicaid as outlined by healthcare reform.[5] Another concern is the ongoing costs for individual states to implement healthcare reform including the administration of Health Exchanges and the expansion of Medicaid and CHIP. Although physician members of the American Medical Association (AMA) supported health-system reform, the AMA had recommended additional policy changes, for example, changes in medical liability to reduce the cost of medical malpractice insurance and changes in physician reimbursement for patients on Medicare.[6]

Health insurance will be expanded through a variety of mechanisms. First, all U.S. citizens and legal residents will be required to have health insurance. To help bring costs under control for all Americans and cover all Americans with preexisting conditions, all Americans who can afford insurance will have the responsibility to purchase it. Those who are uninsured add over $1000 to the average premium of families with insurance. This added cost covers emergency room care for Americans without insurance. Those without health insurance can obtain insurance through state-based **American Health Benefit Exchanges**. Second, employers with more than 200 employees will be required to offer health insurance to all employees. Small businesses with more than 100 employees will be able to purchase insurance through the **Small Business Health Options Program Exchange (SHOP)**. Third, Medicaid will be expanded to include parents of young children and childless adults younger than 65 years of age with incomes up to 133% of the Federal Poverty Level (FPL). Fourth, CHIP will be expanded with financial support from the federal government.

Last, temporary **Early Retiree Reinsurance** programs will be available to those 55 to 64 years of age who are without health insurance. Healthcare reform will be implemented in increments from 2010 through 2014.[7] Healthcare reform mandated the following changes in 2010[8]:

- Eliminate annual and lifetime limits imposed by private insurance companies.
- Cover preexisting conditions (adults will be able to purchase insurance through federal high-risk pools, and children with preexisting conditions are eligible for health insurance through private insurance).
- Extend coverage (children up to 26 years of age can obtain coverage through their parents' health insurance policy).
- Eliminate co-payments and deductibles for preventive services such as mammograms or colonoscopies.
- Prohibit the discrimination against low-salary workers for coverage by group health plans.

HIGH-RISK POOLS

Individuals who have a **preexisting medical condition**, for example, cancer, heart disease, or diabetes, are considered "high risk" by insurance carriers because the cost of health care will be higher than for someone who does not have a health condition requiring ongoing medical care. Private insurance carriers historically have denied coverage for preexisting medical conditions for new enrollees. The ACA requires the establishment of a temporary national high-risk pool to supplement **high-risk pools** offered at the state level. Each state may choose to operate high-risk pools or allow the U.S. Department of Health and Human Services (USDHHS) to do so. The Government Employees Health Association, which administers health insurance for federal employees, will administer high-risk pools for states that have chosen the federal option. Individuals who have been uninsured for at least six months and have proof of being denied coverage because of a preexisting condition are eligible to purchase health insurance through high-risk pools. Beginning in 2014, private insurance carriers will no longer be allowed to deny coverage or charge higher premiums based on preexisting conditions or gender.[9]

EXEMPTIONS TO REQUIRED HEALTHCARE COVERAGE

Individuals and families are eligible for a waiver from the requirement to purchase health insurance, called a **hardship waiver**, if coverage is unaffordable based on a percentage of income. In addition, exceptions are made for religious objectors and taxpayers with incomes below the tax-filing threshold ($9350 for a single individual or $18,700 for a married couple in 2009). Americans under the age of 30 years and other Americans exempt from the requirement to purchase insurance are eligible for a low-cost **catastrophic**

health plan or a **high deductible health plan** that only covers serious illness and injury. Others who are exempt are those who already have health insurance through government programs—federal employees covered by the Federal Employees Health Benefits Plan, veterans covered by the Department of Veteran Affairs, those in the military, and members of Indian tribes. Those that have health insurance through Medicaid, Medicare, and CHIP are also exempt from obtaining health insurance through Health Exchanges. Undocumented immigrants and the incarcerated are not eligible to purchase insurance through ACA Health Exchanges or high-risk pools.[7]

HEALTH INSURANCE EXCHANGES

The Exchange will serve as a point of access for health coverage for individuals and small employers as they shop for, select, and enroll in high-quality, affordable private health plans that fit their needs at competitive prices. Exchanges will provide assistance for eligible individuals to receive premium tax credits for health insurance or to obtain coverage through federal or state healthcare programs, for example, Medicare, Medicaid, and CHIP. By providing one-stop shopping, Exchanges will make purchasing health insurance easier and more understandable. Individuals will be able to apply for and enroll in Medicaid or CHIP through streamlined, easy-to-use, state-by-state websites. These programs will coordinate procedures to provide seamless enrollment, save time, and lower administrative costs.[9]

Another responsibility of Exchanges is to plan and implement an aggressive outreach and education campaign to reach the uninsured who need information on health insurance options and individual responsibility to obtain health insurance. The first individuals to provide outreach and education could be Exchange employees and state employees working for social service agencies. These individuals could then use a variety of avenues for outreach: schools, community groups, private employers, health insurers, hospitals, physicians and other healthcare workers, community health centers, the media, and public service announcements.[10]

Implementing healthcare reform will require collaboration between states and the federal government, across state agencies and throughout the health insurance industry. The USDHHS will provide guidance to the states for the implementation of Exchanges. In addition, the **National Conference of State Legislators (NCSL)** is a bipartisan organization with many resources for individual states including training on healthcare reform for legislators and governments at the state level. The USDHHS is required to establish and operate an Exchange for states that are unable to demonstrate before 2013 that an Exchange will be operational by January 2014. Two or more adjoining states are allowed to form an Exchange as a way to combine resources for administering the Exchange; for example, Wyoming and Montana, which have a combined population of less than 2 million people, could benefit from a joint Exchange.

The federal government is financing startup funds to the states for establishing Exchanges. The USDHHS made available an initial allotment of grant funds up to $1 million for each state and the District of Columbia in September 2010. The grants were for planning purposes, and the next round of grants will be for the purpose of establishing an Exchange. Necessary Exchange costs will be fully funded by the USDHHS until 2015. After January 1, 2015, Exchanges must be funded by individual states.[10]

Health plans offered through Health Exchanges will be available at five different levels based on the percentage of the medical claims that would be paid by the plan. The health plans are based on the percentage of medical claims that will be covered by the health plan with annual out-of-pocket expenses equal to the current **Health Savings Account (HSA)** limit of $5950 for individuals and $11,900 for families.[10] The cost of the premium to individuals and families will be based on income related to the FPL and shared by subsidies from the federal government. For example, the cost of premiums for those with incomes up to 133% of the FPL would be 2%, and for those with incomes 300% to 400% of the FPL, the cost of the premium would be 9.5%. Individuals with incomes up to 400% of poverty will be eligible to purchase coverage through the state-based Exchanges if insurance is not available through an employer. Monthly premiums will range from $115 to $1735, depending on the enrollee's age and state of residence, with most being between $140 and $900. Small-business owners will not only be able to choose insurance coverage through this exchange, but will receive a new tax credit to help offset the cost of covering their employees.

The USDHHS will specify the "essential health benefits" included in the "essential health benefits package" that Qualified Health Plans (QHPs) will be required to cover (effective beginning 2014). Essential health benefits will include at least the following general categories[11]:

- Ambulatory patient services
- Emergency services
- Hospitalization
- Maternity and newborn care
- Mental health and substance use disorder services, including behavioral health treatment
- Prescription drugs
- Rehabilitative and habilitative services and devices
- Laboratory services
- Preventive and wellness care, and chronic disease management
- Pediatric services, including oral and vision care

Medical services that are not covered by the ACA are cosmetic surgery, elective abortions, in vitro fertilization, and custodial care or long-term care. Also, dental and vision care are not considered "essential health benefits" for adults.

The federal requirements for Exchanges are certifying and monitoring the performance of QHPs. The core functions of an Exchange are[12]

- Certification, recertification, and decertification of plans; operation of a toll-free hotline
- Maintenance of a website for providing information on plans to current and prospective enrollees
- Assignment of a price and quality rating to plans
- Presentation of plan benefit options in a standardized format
- Provision of information on Medicaid and CHIP eligibility, and determination of eligibility for individuals in these programs
- Provision of an electronic calculator to determine the actual cost of coverage
- Certification of individuals exempt from the individual responsibility requirement

Health insurance companies (not the Exchanges) will be responsible for billing and collecting premiums and coordinating with the federal government for the advance payment of tax credits for individuals and small businesses eligible for subsidized health insurance. This will add to the administrative workload of individual insurance carriers within each state.[10]

FINANCING HEALTHCARE REFORM

The estimated cost of healthcare reform is $828 billion for fiscal years 2010 through 2019. An estimated one-half of the cost ($410 billion) will come from expanding Medicaid with an additional $29 billion to fund CHIP. An estimated $31 billion of the costs will come from funding tax credits and subsidies for small businesses, and $507 billion to fund subsidies for low- to middle-income individuals buying health insurance through Health Insurance Exchanges.[13] Financing healthcare reform is planned through changes in Medicare and Medicaid, and additional revenue from new taxes and penalties on individuals and businesses failing to implement the mandates of the ACA.

Savings in Medicare and Medicaid spending will come from lower payments to hospitals for patients on Medicaid and Medicare because the prediction is that nearly everyone will have health insurance with implementation of the ACA. Thus, there will be fewer uninsured patients receiving hospital care, and the dollar amount of uncompensated care by hospitals is expected to decrease.[13] The ACA will also reduce payments for Medicare Advantage Plans with an expected savings of $136 billion over the next decade.[14] Medicare Advantage Plans—"Part C" or "MA" Plans—are funded by the federal government but administered by private insurance companies. MA plans provide Part A (hospital insurance) and Part B (medical insurance) and have cost the federal government an average of $1000 more per person than traditional Medicare. Savings are expected because the ACA prohibits MA plans from charging seniors more than they would pay for services under the traditional Medicare program.[15]

INDIVIDUAL RESPONSIBILITY

Taxes to fund healthcare reform that will impact individuals beginning in 2013 are an increase in the Medicare Hospital Insurance (HI) payroll tax and an increase in the amount of medical expenses that can be counted as a deduction on income taxes. HI payroll tax will increase from 1.45% to 2.35% for individuals with incomes above $200,000 and for families with incomes above $250,000.[13] Another change is that medical expenses will need to be 10% of income (instead of the current 7.5%) in order to be used as a deduction when filing individual income tax returns.[7]

PHARMACEUTICAL AND PRIVATE INSURANCE RESPONSIBILITY

Taxes will also impact the pharmaceutical and health insurance industries. Annual fees will be imposed on the pharmaceutical manufacturing industry beginning in 2012 and on private insurance companies beginning in 2014. In addition, the ACA establishes an excise tax on non-personal-use retail sales by manufacturers and importers of medical devices. Fees would be assessed on the specified industry as a whole; the share of the fee payable by any given firm in that industry would be determined based on sales (for manufacturers and importers of drugs) and on net premiums (in the case of insurers). The excise tax on medical device sales will be effective in 2011. It is likely that the fees and excise taxes will be passed on to health consumers in the form of higher drug and device prices and higher insurance premiums, with an associated increase in overall national health expenditures.[13]

PENALTIES

Beginning in 2014 the penalties for individuals who fail to purchase health insurance are $695 per year up to a maximum of $2085 per year. The penalty for large employers (those with more than 50 employees) that do not provide coverage is $2000 multiplied by the number of workers in the business in excess of 30 workers. Other penalties can be imposed on insurance carriers if the coverage does not have an actuarial value of at least 60%—meaning that on average it covers at least 60% of the cost of covered services for a typical population—or if the premium for coverage would exceed 9.5% of a worker's income.[7] However, the employer may lack the motivation to provide insurance coverage for employees because the penalty of $2000 per employee is less than the cost of health insurance premiums—an average of $5049 for an individual in 2010.[16]

PREDICTING THE SUCCESS OF HEALTHCARE REFORM

A review of healthcare reform in the state of Massachusetts can predict outcomes on the national level because the ACA is modeled after the Massachusetts program. In terms of the number of residents now having health insurance, the program can be considered successful with over 97% of the residents having health insurance.[17] In terms of limiting a rise in healthcare costs the program has been unsuccessful. More adult residents have seen doctors and other healthcare providers and are receiving preventive care and prescription medications. Reform has lowered out-of-pocket expenses for those with low incomes and chronic disease, and fewer residents report going without needed care because of cost. Compliance to the mandate for individuals to purchase health insurance is high with only 1% being fined by the Massachusetts Department of Revenue for lacking health insurance.[17] Adults rate the quality of health care under reform to be very good or excellent. The majority of physicians (70%) support health reform and 75% want health reform to continue. Two gaps in health reform were an inadequate supply of primary care providers and rising costs of health care. The gap in providers was exacerbated by a swell in the number of individuals with health insurance. Massachusetts is managing this crisis with the recruitment of primary physicians, increasing enrollment in medical schools, and providing financial incentives for medical students choosing primary care.[17] The net cost of healthcare reform to the state of Massachusetts is budgeted at 1% of the annual 2011 budget.[18] The costs of expanding state coverage is partly offset by lower expenses for uncompensated care. As before healthcare reform in the state, the majority of employers offer health insurance for employees instead of relying on the state to provide insurance.[17]

MEETING NEEDS FOR HEALTHCARE WORKERS

Part of the ACA addresses predicted gaps in access to primary care in anticipation of greater demand with more individuals having healthcare coverage. Mechanisms for increasing the supply of primary care providers will be funding for scholarships and loan repayment through the National Health Service Corps. The ACA also increases the loan repayment amount and enables additional flexibility for providers to meet their service requirements. By funding scholarships and loan repayment programs, the number of primary care physicians, nurses, physician assistants, mental health providers, and dentists will increase in the areas of the country that need them most. Grant programs will support the training of primary care providers, including family medicine, pediatrics, general internal medicine, and physician assistants. The ACA will also award competitive grants to nursing schools to strengthen nurse education and training programs and to improve nurse retention throughout the country. It increases the student loan amounts for nursing students and addresses critical nurse faculty shortages by making nursing faculty eligible for loan repayment and scholarship programs. Healthcare reform addresses critical public **healthcare workforce** shortages by supporting training in public health and preventive medicine, and it supports education and training grants to meet the critical needs of Americans who require mental and behavioral health care. It also creates scholarships and loan repayment programs for allied health professionals, including radiology technicians and physical therapists. It increases funding for geriatric education and training. It establishes a Ready Reserve Corps to respond in times of national emergency, and it supports fellowship training in public health as well as grants to promote the community health workforce.[19]

SUMMARY

Healthcare reform was designed to reduce the number of uninsured individuals in the United States. The law provides funds for subsidizing the purchase of health insurance to lower the cost of premiums for low- to middle-income individuals to improve the affordability of health insurance and access to health care. Individual states will have the burden of implementing healthcare reform, from establishing high-risk pools and Health Exchanges to evaluating the quality of health plans offered by local insurance carriers. Expected challenges to implementing and administering healthcare reform are increased costs and an inadequate supply of healthcare workers, especially primary care providers. Healthcare reform is expected to create greater opportunities for students interested in health careers in primary care and nursing and to expand the number of healthcare workers in underserved areas through grants, scholarships, and other financial incentives.

REFERENCES

1. *Affordable Health Care for America.* Affordable Care Act. On the Floor. Internet: http://www.democraticleader.gov/floor?id=0361
2. *Health Care Reform.* Overview. Updated Feb. 23, 2011. Times Topics. *The New York Times.* Internet: http://topics.nytimes.com/top/news/health/diseasesconditionsandhealthtopics/health_insurance_and_managed_care/health_care_reform/index.html
3. *Public Opinion on Health Care Issues. Kaiser Health Tracking Poll—November 2010.* Public Opinion and Survey Research Program. Publication no. 8120. Menlo Park, CA: Kaiser Family Foundation; November 9, 2010.
4. Cauchi R. *State Legislation and Actions Challenging Certain Health Reforms, 2010–11.* Issues and Research. Health. National Conference of State Legislators. Washington, DC. February 22, 2011. Internet: http://www.ncsl.org/default.aspx?tabid=18906
5. *Medicaid's Continuing Crunch in a Recession: A Mid-Year Update for State FY 2010 and Preview for FY 2011.* Issue Paper. Publication no. 8049. Kaiser Commission on Medicaid and the Uninsured. Washington, DC: Kaiser Family Foundation; February 2010.
6. *Our Vision for Health System Reform.* Health System Reform. American Medical Association. 2011. Internet: http://www.ama-assn.org/ama/pub/health-system-reform/about-us.shtml
7. *Summary of New Health Reform Law.* Focus on Health Reform. Publication no. 8061. Menlo Park, CA: Kaiser Family Foundation; March 26, 2010. Internet: http://www.kff.org/healthreform/upload/8061.pdf
8. *Health Reform Implementation: Immediate Issues & Research.* Health. National Conference of State Legislators. Washington, DC. Internet: http://www.ncsl.org/documents/health/HlthRefImp923.pdf
9. Cassidy A. Pre-Existing Condition Insurance Plan. *Health Affairs.* Robert Wood Johnson Foundation. August 10, 2010.

10. Carey R. *Health Insurance Exchanges: Key Issues for State Implementation.* State Coverage Initiatives. Robert Wood Johnson Foundation. September 2010.

11. *Essential Health Benefits.* Glossary. Resources. U.S. Department of Health and Human Services. Washington, DC. Internet: http://www.healthcare.gov/glossary/e/essential.html

12. *American Health Benefit Exchange Model Act.* 2010 National Association of Insurance Commissioners. November 22, 2010. Internet: http://www.naic.org/documents/committees_b_exchanges_adopted_health_benefit_exchanges.pdf

13. Foster RS. *Estimated Financial Effects of the "Patient Protection and Affordable Care Act," as Amended.* Department of Health and Human Services. Centers for Medicare and Medicaid Services, Office of the Actuary. April 22, 2010.

14. Potetz L, Cubanski J, Neuman T. *Medicare Spending and Financing. A Primer.* Publication no. 7731-03. Menlo Park, CA: Kaiser Family Foundation; February 2011. Internet: http://www.kff.org/medicare/upload/7731-03.pdf

15. *The Affordable Care Act—Implementation Timeline.* Timeline. Putting Americans in Control of their Healthcare. The Administration. Internet: http://www.whitehouse.gov/healthreform/timeline

16. *Employer Health Benefits. 2010 Summary of Findings.* Publication no. 8086. Menlo Park, CA, and Chicago, IL: Kaiser Family Foundation and Health Research and Educational Trust; 2010. Internet: http://ehbs.kff.org/pdf/2010/8086.pdf

17. Long SK. *What Is the Evidence on Health Reform in Massachusetts and How Might the Lessons Apply to National Health Reform? Timely Analysis of Immediate Health Policy Issues.* The Urban Institute. Robert Wood Johnson Foundation. June 2010.

18. Patrick DL, Murray TP. *FY 2011 House 2 Budget Recommendation: Issues in Brief. Health Care Reform. Quality, Affordable Health Care for All.* Governor's Budget FY 2011. 2010. Internet: http://www.mass.gov/bb/h1/fy11h1/exec_11/hbudbrief17.htm

19. *Title V. Health Care Workforce.* Putting Americans in Control of their Healthcare. The Administration. 2010. Internet: http://www.whitehouse.gov/health-care-meeting/proposal/titlev

chapter six

Health Career Planning

OBJECTIVES

After studying this chapter, the student should be able to:

- Obtain all facts pertinent to careers in health services.
- Recognize the specialized knowledge and skills necessary for a given profession.
- Evaluate employment opportunities.
- Find an appropriate health career.
- Select the appropriate school for training.

INTRODUCTION

Because health care has developed from a small concern into a multibillion-dollar industry and the largest employer in the United States, it is appropriate that this book assists students in obtaining facts that will steer them toward satisfying careers in health services. The first five chapters in this book were devoted to the development of healthcare services, healthcare delivery, and many of the issues involved in meeting the goals set for health care. This chapter focuses on the personnel issues—where and why health professionals are needed.

As one of the largest industries in 2008, health care provided 14.3 million jobs for wage and salary workers. Ten of the twenty fastest-growing occupations are health-care related. Health care will generate 3.2 million new wage and salary jobs between 2008 and 2018, more than any other industry, largely in response to rapid growth in the elderly population. The economic downturn beginning in 2008 resulted in job losses in all parts of the economy except for the hospital industry.[1]

Many opportunities are anticipated for students pursuing a health career. Most important is the projected shortages in healthcare professionals beginning in 2020. The aging of the population will increase the number of older people needing health care. At the same time many health professionals will reach retirement age while the number of younger workers is expected to remain static. Tougher immigration rules that are slowing the numbers of foreign healthcare workers entering the United States should make it easier to get a job in this industry. The U.S. Bureau of Labor Statistics projects major growth in healthcare occupations with a critical shortage of nurses and significant shortages of **primary care physicians** and public health workers.[1] In many cases, it may be easier for job seekers with health-specific training to obtain jobs and advance in their careers. Specialized clinical training is a requirement for many jobs in health care and is an asset even for many administrative jobs that do not specifically require it.[1]

A vast amount of knowledge has accumulated since 1900. One result of the knowledge explosion has been a necessary increase in medical personnel who can be grouped by their specialized knowledge and skills important to healthcare activities. The techniques and instruments developed in response to the new knowledge are extremely important; they have affected the staffing patterns and content of educational programs of many of the health services and precipitated the development of new health occupations. Both medicine and dentistry have developed subspecialties, and both are becoming more dependent on the services of additional personnel in the diagnosis and treatment of disease.

Advances in medical technology have improved the survival rates of trauma victims who need extensive care from therapists and social workers and other supportive personnel. In addition, advances in information technology continue to improve patient care and worker efficiency; for example, bedside computer terminals and handheld computers that record notes on each patient. Information on vital signs and orders for tests are transferred electronically to a main database; this process eliminates the need for paper and reduces record-keeping errors.[2]

Many careers in health care involve direct contact with clients or patients. Desirable traits for those careers are a strong desire to help others, a genuine concern for the welfare of patients and clients, and an ability to deal with people of diverse backgrounds in stressful situations. Many of the healthcare jobs that are regulated by state **licensure** require healthcare professionals to complete continuing education at regular intervals to maintain valid licensure.[1]

Health care has grown into a complex system with many important links, which are examined briefly in this chapter. Understanding where the system is and where it might be going should give students important clues to career opportunities. This understanding will help in evaluating where the jobs are likely to be and discerning where a particular health career fits into the entire picture.

EMPLOYERS OF HEALTH PROFESSIONALS AND HEALTH-RELATED PERSONNEL

The healthcare industry includes establishments ranging from small-town private practices of physicians who employ only one medical assistant to busy inner-city hospitals that provide thousands of diverse jobs. In 2008, around 48% of nonhospital healthcare establishments employed fewer than five workers. In contrast, 72% of hospital employees were in establishments with more than 1000 workers. About 595,800 establishments make up the healthcare industry; they vary greatly in terms of size, staffing patterns, and organizational structures. About 76% of healthcare establishments are offices of physicians, dentists, or other health practitioners. Although hospitals constitute only 1% of all healthcare establishments, they employ 35% of all workers. Another 21% are employed in nursing and residential care facilities. Each segment of the healthcare industry provides a different mix of wage and salary health-related jobs.[1]

Healthcare jobs are found throughout the country, but they are concentrated in metropolitan areas. The healthcare industry consists of the following segments.

Hospitals

As a group, hospitals are the best-known and largest single employer of health workers. As discussed in Chapter 2, the general hospital cares for patients with various medical conditions requiring diagnosis and surgical/medical treatment. This is the hospital people are most likely to see in their own community and to visit if they have medical problems. General hospitals represent 87% of hospitals. Patients in these hospitals generally stay a short time—a few days to a few weeks.[1]

In specialty hospitals, patients are usually limited to those who have a specific illness or condition. Specialty hospitals may be for psychiatric illness, chronic disease, and rehabilitation of patients, for example, for patients after a severe accident, stroke, heart attack, or surgery. Specialty hospitals are identified as "long term" because their patients are usually hospitalized for several months before they are well enough to return to their homes.[1]

The mix of workers needed varies, depending on the size, geographic location, goals, philosophy, funding, organization, and management style of the institution. Hospitals employ workers with all levels of education and training, thereby providing a wider variety of opportunities than is offered by other segments of the healthcare industry. About 28% of hospital workers are registered nurses. Hospitals also employ many physicians and surgeons, therapists, and social workers. About 21% of hospital jobs are in a service occupation, such as nursing, and psychiatric and home health aides. Hospitals also employ large numbers of office and administrative support workers. Hospitals will be the slowest growing segment within the healthcare industry because of efforts to control hospital costs and the increasing use of outpatient clinics and other alternative-care sites.[1]

Nursing Homes and Community-Based Care

Nursing homes were almost unknown before the 1930s but have grown rapidly in number since then. By 2008, there were approximately 1.4 million persons residing in 16,000 nursing homes. An additional 1 million individuals reside in assisted living facilities. Home and community-based care is also expanding, especially for the elderly.[3]

Nursing care facilities provide inpatient nursing, rehabilitation, and health-related personal care to those who need continuous nursing care, but do not require hospital services. Residential care facilities provide around-the-clock social and personal care to children, the elderly, and others who have a limited ability to care for themselves. The services offered vary from skilled bedside nursing to simple personal care (bathing, dressing, providing meals, and so forth).[1]

Skilled nursing or medical care is sometimes provided in the home, under a physician's supervision. Home healthcare services are provided mainly to the elderly. The development of in-home medical technologies, substantial cost savings, and patients' preference for care in the home has helped change this once-small segment of the industry into one of the fastest-growing health-care services. Employment in home health care and nursing and residential care should increase rapidly as life expectancies rise and families are less able to care for their elder family members and rely more on long-term care facilities. About 59% of jobs in this segment are in service occupations, mostly home health aides and personal and home care aides. Nursing and therapist jobs also account for substantial shares of employment in this segment.[1]

Other Inpatient Facilities

In addition to nursing homes, there are more than 5000 other residential health facilities for persons who do not need hospitalization or nursing home care. These include alcohol and drug rehabilitation centers, group homes, and halfway houses. About half of these facilities are for the mentally retarded and emotionally disturbed; these employ three-quarters of the 250,000 workers engaged in inpatient care.[1]

Outpatient and Other Health Facilities or Services

About 36% of all healthcare establishments fall into this industry segment. Physicians and surgeons practice privately or in groups of practitioners who have the same or different specialties. Many physicians and surgeons prefer to join group practices because they afford backup coverage, reduce overhead expenses, and facilitate consultation with peers. Physicians and surgeons are increasingly working as salaried employees of group medical practices, clinics, or integrated health systems. Many of the jobs in offices of physicians are in professional and related occupations, primarily physicians, surgeons, and registered nurses. About 37% of all jobs, however, are in office and administrative support occupations, such as receptionists and information clerks.[1]

About 20% of healthcare establishments are dentists' offices. Most employ only a few workers, who provide preventative, cosmetic, or emergency care. Some offices specialize in a single field of dentistry, such as orthodontics or periodontics. Roughly 35% of all jobs in this segment are in service occupations, mostly dental assistants. The typical staffing pattern in dentists' offices consists of one dentist with a support staff of dental hygienists and dental assistants. Larger practices are more likely to employ office managers and administrative support workers. Demand for dental care will rise due to the greater retention of natural teeth by middle-aged and older persons, a greater awareness of the importance of dental care, and an increased ability to pay for services.[1]

Nearly 500,000 health workers are employed in vital types of settings or services that are often overlooked as part of the health industry when career opportunities in the health fields are being evaluated. The following list describes some of them.

- Ambulance services transport patients and frequently provide emergency medical services.
- Blood banks draw, process, store, and distribute human whole blood and its derivatives.
- Clinical (medical) laboratories test samples of tissues or fluids to determine the absence or presence and extent of diseases and thereby help physicians diagnose or treat illness.
- Dental laboratories provide services to dentists by making and repairing artificial teeth and other dental appliances.
- Family planning services provide physical examinations, laboratory tests, consultations, education, treatments, and the issuance of drugs and contraceptives related to reproduction.
- Home health services provide health care and supportive services to sick or disabled persons at their place of residence when their illnesses do not require hospital or nursing home care or when their disabilities do not allow them to travel to an outpatient facility.
- Opticians' establishments sell and/or make eyeglasses according to the prescription of an optometrist or an ophthalmologist.
- Poison control centers provide comprehensive services to the population regarding the effects of toxic substances and the antidotes available.
- Community mental health centers provide comprehensive services to people with physical, mental, or social disabilities to help them return to satisfying jobs and lifestyles. Certain centers might work with special problems only—rehabilitation of the blind, deaf, or mentally retarded, for example. Certain centers also provide inpatient/outpatient care, day care, and 24-hour emergency, consultation, and educational services for problems related to mental health.
- Migrant health programs provide health services to migrant and seasonal farm workers who would not qualify for health services available to permanent residents of a particular state.
- Neighborhood health centers provide medical, dental, laboratory, radiological, and pharmaceutical services for people living in a particular geographic area within a city.
- Health maintenance organizations (HMOs) provide consumers with comprehensive health services, including hospitalization, office visits, preventive health checkups, and immunizations. Instead of the traditional pay-as-you-go system, consumers and/or their employers pay a fixed monthly fee that covers all these services, no matter how often they are used.

- Health practitioners' offices employ health professionals of various kinds, depending on the size of the practice and the patients who are being served. Some practitioners work alone in private practice, while others share office space and services in a group practice. Practitioners who commonly operate their own offices include chiropractors, podiatrists, optometrists, occupational and physical therapists, audiologists, speech-language pathologists, psychologists, licensed clinical social workers, dietitians, nutritionists, and veterinarians. Demand for the services of this segment is related to the ability of patients to pay, either directly or through health insurance. Hospitals and nursing facilities may contract out for these services. This segment also includes the offices of practitioners of alternative medicine, such as acupuncturists, homeopaths, hypnotherapists, and naturopaths. About 42% of jobs in this industry segment are professional and related occupations.
- Voluntary health agencies at the national, state, and local levels are concerned with specific health problems or health services. Some of their activities include raising funds for medical research, alerting the public to specific health problems, providing health education programs, and making health services more available at the community level. The American Cancer Society, American Heart Association, and National Foundation–March of Dimes are examples of voluntary health agencies.
- Professional health associations at the national, state, and local levels represent the members of a particular health profession or of a particular type of health facility such as an association of hospitals or community health centers. Their activities often include improving the professional education of their members, establishing standards of practice or operations for their fields, and carrying out research of interest to their members. The American Medical Association, American Hospital Association, American Dietetic Association, and the National Association of Community Health Centers are some examples.

Government

At the federal, state, and local levels, the government offers numerous opportunities for health professionals. State and local governments operate health departments that help to control the spread of communicable disease, safeguard the purity of food and water supplies, and promote health education and health measures such as inoculations. At the federal level, the U.S. Department of Health and Human Services' Public Health Service (PHS) is concerned with the health of all citizens.[4]

Other branches of the government also offer opportunities for health-related employment. The U.S. Department of Labor's Occupational Safety and Health Administration (OSHA) enforces standards related to job health and safety. The U.S. Department of Agriculture's state-sponsored programs ensure that meat, poultry, and eggs are disease-free and meet sanitary conditions. The Food and Drug Administration (FDA) monitors the safety of food, prescription drugs, and medical devices. The U.S. Army, Navy, and Air Force and the Veterans Administration offer employment opportunities in practically every health occupation described in this book.

Industry

Industries not only manufacture prescription drugs and numerous over-the-counter medications, but also produce common household health supplies as well as supplies used by hospitals and other health facilities. Medical devices such as hearing aids, cardiac pacemakers, artificial limbs, and braces are made by industry, as is the sophisticated diagnostic and treatment equipment used in health care today. In addition to producing such items, industrial health care employs thousands of people in research and development to discover new health products and technology.

Many large corporations, for example, automobile manufacturing plants and food processing plants, have started health clinics manned by health professionals within their own companies. Their employees can receive immediate, in-house health care and health checkups. The occupational health and safety of workers is a vital concern, and industry employs special health personnel to ensure that employees will not be exposed to unnecessary job hazards.

EMPLOYMENT OPPORTUNITIES

Health care continually moves in new and different directions. This movement may alter what health workers will be doing, where they will be working, and how many will be employed in a particular occupation. Opportunities may expand in some areas and diminish in others, as has already happened in the case of many careers and will continue to happen as technology and the population change and greater access to health care with health care reform is achieved.

No one can predict with absolute certainty the employment outlook for a particular career. The following discussion of current trends gives some clues as to where one might find especially good opportunities today and in the future.

Changing Opportunities from New Technology

Advances in technology are frequently responsible for changes in career opportunities. Research is conducted constantly to discover methods of preventing disease and improving ways to diagnose and treat illness. This often results in the development and introduction of a complex machine or a sophisticated medical technique into health care. When this happens, health workers must be trained to operate the machine or to perform the technique correctly and safely.

The first persons selected for training are usually people who are already employed in health and work in a related area. They receive on-the-job training. However, as a new service becomes better known and is widely used by hospitals and other health facilities, more workers are needed. On-the-job training is often no longer practical, and formal education programs in hospitals or colleges are created. Qualified students—not just healthcare workers—then have the opportunity for training. As the number of these newly trained workers increases, a separate and distinct occupation may emerge.

New Opportunities Through Expanded Functions

People in several health professions require additional training and knowledge and are certified or licensed to perform many tasks that were previously done only by a physician or dentist. Some examples include the dental hygienist, the nurse practitioner, and the **physician assistant**. These professions are described in later chapters in more detail.

Opportunities in Rural and Inner-City Communities

In some parts of the country, new health workers are finding it difficult to obtain jobs, while in other places communities cannot find enough workers to fill existing healthcare jobs. This national problem is often referred to as the **maldistribution of health personnel**. Healthcare workers are not distributed according to the population or health needs in many geographic areas. Low-income and overpopulated inner-city areas and underpopulated rural areas are hardest hit by this maldistribution.

Shortage areas need health professionals of all kinds. This might mean relocation to find the best future opportunities. **Health Professional Shortage Areas (HPSAs)** for providers of primary care, dental care, and mental health care have been designated for each of the 50 states and territories of the United States. More than 6000 U.S. communities are primary medical care HPSAs; 4000 are dental HPSAs; and 3000 are mental health HPSAs.[5]

Primary Care

Most Americans need **primary health care** that focuses on prevention, early detection and treatment, and a **medical home** for both preventive and follow-up care. Primary care can often reduce health costs, because it is generally easier and less expensive to prevent problems or treat them in their earliest stages. Although the number of primary care physicians is growing, physicians who practice this kind of basic medicine are still outnumbered three to one by doctors who specialize in other fields.

Primary care physicians or generalists include **family practice physicians** and physicians in general pediatric practice or general internal medicine practice. Family practice physicians deliver comprehensive, primary healthcare services for all family members; pediatricians provide primary care to infants, children, and adolescents; and internists care for adults. This increased emphasis on primary care affects not only the career of the physician, but also most other health workers who assist or support the physician. The places in which people work are also affected. Facilities that emphasize primary care, such as HMOs and neighborhood health centers, will probably increase in number.

The **Health Care and Education Reconciliation Act** (also known as the Affordable Care Act [ACA]) signed into law on March 30, 2010, provided funds for strengthening the healthcare workforce. The Prevention and Public Health Fund of the ACA funded primary residency programs, physician assistant training programs, nurse practitioner and nurse midwifery programs, and nurse-managed health clinics.[6] Other grants were awarded to support **Area Health Education Centers (AHECs)** for interdisciplinary training and **Geriatric Academic Career Awards (GACAs)** for training in geriatric care. In addition, grants were awarded for Nursing Assistant and Home Health Aide Program training. The Health Resources and Services Administration (HRSA) within the Department of Health and Human Services (USDHHS) administers the grants. These grant programs include funds to cover tuition and other educational expenses for medical students preparing to be physicians in primary care, students of **advanced practice nursing**, and students in geriatric training programs.[7]

Expanding Opportunities in Outpatient Health Facilities

In 1978 the United States spent $39 billion on health care. Twelve years later the figure was more than $139 billion. In 2007, health spending reached $2.2 trillion, or $7421 per person. Containing costs will be perhaps the most important priority of the health field during the coming years. Because the cost of inpatient care in hospitals and nursing homes represents a large part of the nation's healthcare bill, new strategies have been launched to keep this cost down. Outpatient and community-based alternatives to hospitals or nursing homes are becoming successful. Home care services now enable many ill or aged people to remain in their own homes rather than live as patients in nursing homes. With a growing elderly population, home care services should become increasingly more important, and more workers will be needed to deliver these services.

Ambulatory or "walk-in" patient care in private practitioners' offices, hospital outpatient departments, community health centers, or other health facilities is helping to reduce hospitalization. In the past, many medical procedures, including certain diagnostic tests and simple surgery, were done only on an inpatient hospital basis. Now these same procedures are safely and routinely performed on an outpatient basis in an office setting. This greater emphasis on ambulatory care may shift employment opportunities from hospitals to other kinds of health facilities. (See Chapter 2 for details on ambulatory facilities.)

Opportunities for Women and Minorities

The number of women and minorities is increasing in professions where these groups have been traditionally underrepresented, such as dentistry, veterinary medicine, optometry, podiatry, and health services administration. Congress, federal and state agencies, and professional associations in the health field are making special efforts to create new educational and professional opportunities for women and minorities in these fields. As discussed in Chapter 4, the U.S. Department of Health and Human Services has addressed the need to increase the quality of health services by recommending that an increased proportion of all degrees be awarded to members of underrepresented racial and ethnic groups.

The trends discussed here are not the only ones in health care today, but the discussion may make you more aware of the dynamics of the health field. So as you look into your future as a health worker, watch the healthcare system carefully. Be alert to changes and advances reported in the media. They may affect how and where you become involved in the health field and may help to guide your future.

HEALTH CAREERS: SOMETHING FOR EVERYONE

The health field, perhaps more than any other career area, offers wide-ranging opportunities to match almost any interest.

- Do you like to work with your hands? Dental technicians, optical mechanics, biomedical equipment technicians, prosthetists, and many other health professionals work with their hands.
- Are you interested in working with machines? Respiratory therapists, electroencephalograph (EEG) technologists, and radiologic technologists are a few of the professionals who work with patients and medical machines.
- Are you fascinated by photography or the fine arts? Art, music, or dance therapist or biological photographer is among the health careers in which you can use these talents.
- Do you enjoy working with people? Nursing, medicine, dentistry, dietetics, optometry, social work, rehabilitation, and mental health are some health career areas that will give you the opportunity to work with and help people of all ages.

These careers only begin to enumerate the possibilities. Health careers do offer something for everyone, but too often students say "no" to health careers simply because they do not have the facts. Some common assumptions students make when talking about health careers include such statements as the following.

I couldn't work around sick people in a hospital. That's depressing. Besides, I can't stand the sight of blood.

A health career does not automatically mean a hospital job or care of the sick. Health careers have many facets. You can work in health care in research, health planning and administration, health education, disease prevention, environmental protection, and other important areas. Jobs are not just in hospitals. Private doctors' offices, schools, government, industry, and many other places also need and employ health workers.

But don't judge hospital work until you try it, either as a hospital volunteer or as a part-time employee. You may discover by working there and observing trained health professionals that you too can learn to accept the less pleasant parts of helping people get well. You will also find that even in hospitals many jobs are "behind-the-scenes," with little or no direct contact with patients.

You need science and math for health careers. That's not for me.

Science and mathematics are required for some healthcare jobs, but many others do not emphasize these subjects. Health education, social services, and mental health are just a few areas where psychology, social studies, and other subjects are stressed. However, even when science and math are needed, different levels of skills are required. Some occupations such as optometrist and scientist require in-depth knowledge, while many other careers require just good basic skills and working knowledge of science and math.

Training takes too long.

Some careers do take 7 or more years of preparation. Professional occupations, such as *physicians and surgeons*, *dentists*, *registered nurses*, *social workers*, and *physical therapists*, usually require at least a Bachelor degree in a specialized field or higher education in a specific health field. Professional workers often have high levels of responsibility and complex duties. In addition to providing services, these workers may supervise other workers or conduct research. Most health occupations require only 2 to 4 years' preparation. For example, *registered nurses* may enter through Associate degree or diploma programs.

Training costs too much.

In one sense, the cost of training is only relative. It must be balanced against what one can earn. Figures show that lifetime earnings generally increase with years of education. On the other hand, if you don't think you can afford training, you are not alone. Most students today need and can find financial aid for training. Scholarships and loan repayment programs are available to students who are willing to make a commitment to working in underserved areas or in the armed services. The National Health Service Corps (NHSC)[8] and the Indian Health Services (IHS)[9] provide financial assistance in the form of scholarships and loan repayment for students who agree to serve in the designated HPSA or with the IHS. The National Health Service Corps places physicians, dentists, and mental health workers in HPSA underserved rural and urban areas.[8] The IHS hires health professionals of all kinds for their hospitals and clinics.[9] As part of healthcare reform the ACA provides funds to support students pursuing careers in primary medical care—pediatrics, family practice, and internal medicine. Funds are also available to support the training of physician assistants and advanced nurse practitioners to meet primary care needs.[7]

Training is too hard.

Don't sell yourself short. Many students who felt the same way are now working as doctors, nurses, therapists, technologists, or other health professionals. If you fear that training may be too hard for you, then think twice. A change of attitude, a special remedial program, or additional study may be all you need to succeed. Most community colleges and educational centers offer the special studies needed to prepare you for education in a health career.

Each year many interested, qualified students give up on a health career simply because they did not explore alternatives when their first career choice was not possible. A prime example is the aspiring physician who is not admitted to a medical or osteopathic school and drops out of the health field entirely.

The health field is vast; in it you will find many related careers where you can contribute and find personal satisfaction. Your talents are definitely needed in the health field.

EXPLORING HEALTH CAREERS

Career exploration can be a learning experience as you make new discoveries about the world of work and yourself. The reality of the work world is always different from what you learn in school or from research in books. One good way to gain firsthand information is to visit several facilities. Make appointments and visit several departments within the facilities. Compare different types of facilities and what people with the same job titles are doing in each one.

If you have a particular interest, set up interviews with a health worker in that discipline. This is usually very rewarding for you both. Most health professionals enjoy talking to students and answering questions about their particular fields.

Visit laboratories, both private and hospital based. Visit practitioners in private practice and those in salaried positions. Learn all you can about community-based programs and special services offered by clinics and hospitals.

Ask about the philosophy of each facility you visit. Does it provide in-service education for its employees and offer continuing education programs? Does it subscribe to patient education concepts? What are the general amenities offered to workers in different kinds of facilities?

Before you go exploring, do your homework. View video clips of health professionals available on the websites listed at the end of this chapter. Visit the websites of professional organizations listed in certain chapters of this book.

Do some more reading in the library. Be prepared to ask pertinent questions that will help you make decisions.

Visit schools that offer majors in the health services. You can find out much about the professions by talking to students and instructors and by spending some time on campus and possibly in classes (most schools permit such visits). Another way to learn more about health careers is to join student health profession organizations in high school or community college.

Some professions stipulate that students have some experience in the field before they are considered for admission to an academic program. Experience can be obtained by summer work, part-time jobs, or volunteer work in a facility. The firsthand experience you gain from such an endeavor will not only help you make decisions about your career, but may also help you get into the school of your choice.

As you explore, keep an open mind. Investigate many careers, not just those with which you are familiar. The more information you have, the easier your career decisions will be.

SELECTING A SCHOOL

Next to choosing a career, selecting the right school for training is the most important career decision you will need to make. As you read the job requirements for the many careers detailed in Part II of this book, you will discover that health career training is available in many kinds of schools: 2-year and 4-year colleges and universities; technical institutes; medical, dental, and other professional schools; hospitals; private, vocational, and trade schools; and the military. The secret to selecting the right school lies in answering one important question: Will the school you are interested in prepare you for the career you want? Before you seek the answer to this question, you should understand three basic terms related to employment in the health field: licensure, **professional certification**, and **professional registration**.

LICENSURE

Before you can work in many health professions, a state license is required. The qualifications for licensure vary. In general, a student must graduate from a school whose program is approved by the state licensing agency, and then prove that he or she is qualified to give health services by passing a special licensing examination. Licensure is the state's way of protecting the public from unqualified health practitioners.

The health professions that are licensed vary with each state. Some professions, such as registered nurse, practical nurse, physician, dentist, optometrist, podiatrist, pharmacist, social worker, and veterinarian, are licensed in all states. Individual state licensing agencies also vary. The state's Education Department, Department of Higher Education, and Department of Health are usually the responsible agencies. A state agency and a specialty board such as the Board of Nursing or the Board of Dentistry may also grant licenses jointly.

Professional Certification

Professional certification ensures that health professionals meet established levels of competency. Certification is granted by national health professionals' organizations, not by the individual states, so it has national recognition. In health professions in which there is no state licensure, professional certification may be required for employment. However, even when certification is not required, it is a strong asset. Most employers prefer to hire certified professionals, and in a tight job market, certification may be the key to getting a job.

In general, to qualify for certification, a student must first complete a program of training recognized by the profession. Usually this means graduating from an accredited (approved by the professional organization) program. Some organizations accredit programs jointly with the AMA. After graduation, the student must pass a special certification examination.

Professional Registration

Technically, professional registration means the listing of certified health professionals on an official roster kept by a state agency or health professionals' organization. In practical terms, some health professionals' organizations use the term registration interchangeably with certification.

USING THIS BOOK TO SELECT AND PLAN A HEALTH CAREER

Part II of this book describes in detail the requirements, including registration, licensure, and certification of the well-known health professions. In addition to information about requirements, each of the following chapters describes the work and the work environment, employment opportunities and trends, and earnings for a specific category of patient care career. The chapters also discuss related occupations and additional sources of information about the particular career. Taken together, the career descriptions present a practical, detailed "road map" of the vast healthcare field.

Appendix B has an extensive list of places to begin collecting information on careers and job opportunities. Appendix C will help you with job hunting, writing résumés, and successful interviewing.

Additional Information

The U.S. government and professional organizations involved in education and training programs in the health professions are excellent resources for students exploring health careers. General information on health careers is available from

- American Medical Association/Health Professions Career and Education Directory, 515 N. State St., Chicago, IL 60654. Internet: http://www.ama-assn.org/go/alliedhealth
- Bureau of Health Professions, Room 8A-09, 5600 Fishers Ln., Rockville, MD 20857. Internet: http://bhpr.hrsa.gov

Video clips describing a variety of health careers are available from government and nonprofit websites:

- Career Videos for Health Science. One-Stop Career System Multimedia Career Video Library. U.S. Department of Labor. Employment and Training Administration. Internet: http://www.careerinfonet.org/videos/COS_videos_by_cluster.asp?id=27&nodeid=28
- ExploreHealthCareers.org. American Dental Education Association. 2010. Internet: http://explorehealthcareers.org

Students interested in pursuing a medical career should contact

- Association of American Medical Colleges, 2450 N St. NW, Washington, DC 20037. Internet: http://www.aamc.org/students

For a list of accredited programs in allied health fields, contact

- Commission on Accreditation of Allied Health Education Programs, 1361 Park St., Clearwater, FL 33756. Internet: http://www.caahep.org

Financial aid in the form of loan repayments for healthcare workers in underserved areas is listed as follows:

- Indian Health Service. Internet: http://www.ihs.gov
- National Health Service Corps. Internet: http://www.nhsc.bhpr.hrsa.gov

REFERENCES

1. Bureau of Labor Statistics. U.S. Department of Labor. *Career Guide to Industries, 2010–11 Edition, Healthcare.* Internet: http://www.bls.gov/oco/cg/cgs035.htm
2. National Center for Health Statistics. *Health United States, 2009: With Special Feature on Medical Technology.* Hyattsville, MD; 2010. Internet: http://www.cdc.gov/nchs/hus.htm
3. Administration on Aging. U.S. Department of Health and Human Services. *A Profile of Older Americans: 2010.* Aging Statistics. February 25, 2011. Internet: http://www.aoa.gov/aoaroot/aging_statistics/Profile/2010/6.asp
4. Operating Divisions. Leadership Contacts. HHS.gov/Open. February 14, 2011. Internet: http://www.hhs.gov/open/contacts/index.html#od
5. HRSA Health Professions. U.S. Department of Health and Human Services. *Shortage Designation: HPSAs, MUAs, and MUPs.* 2010.
6. HRSA Health Professions. U.S. Department of Health and Human Services. *HRSA Awards $17 Million to Boost Community Primary Care Training.* September 30, 2010.
7. *Affordable Care Act Bolsters the Primary Care Workforce in Medically Underserved Communities.* News. U.S. Department of Health and Human Services. Washington, DC. January 3, 2011. Internet: http://www.hhs.gov/news/press/2010pres/11/20101122b.html
8. National Health Service Corps. U.S. Department of Health and Human Services. *National Health Service Corps Scholarship.* 2011. Internet: http://nhsc.hrsa.gov/scholarship
9. Indian Health Services. U.S. Department of Health and Human Services. *Jobs and Student Opportunities.* Rockville, MD. 2011. Internet: http://www.ihs.gov/index.cfm?module=Jobs

part two

Health Professions Involving Patient Care

chapter seven

Medicine*

KEY TERMS

Allergists
Allopathic physicians
Anesthesiologists
Cardiologists
Cost of training
DO
Dermatologists
Emergency physicians
Group practice

Gynecologists
Internists
MD
Obstetricians
Ophthalmologists
Otolaryngology
Pathologists
Pediatricians
Preventive medicine

Primary care specialists
Psychiatrists
Radiologists
Rotations
Solo practitioners
Surgeons
Wage-and-salary
 physicians

*All information in this chapter, unless otherwise indicated, was obtained from Bureau of Labor Statistics. U.S. Department of Labor. *Occupational Outlook Handbook 2010–2011 Edition.* 2010.

OBJECTIVES

The following objectives are for all chapters in Part II. After studying the chapters in this part the student should be able to:

- Describe the responsibilities and work of each profession.

- Classify the types of specialties in each profession.

- Discuss the environment in which the work takes place.

- Identify any adjunct personnel who assist the professionals with their work.

- Compare and contrast the following factors among the professions: educational requirements, employment trends, opportunities for advancement, salary potential, and career ladders.

- Describe the differences in licensing, certification, and registration for careers of interest.

- Identify the professionals who do similar tasks or have similar responsibilities.

- Discuss the advantages of the national organizations to which professionals belong.

- Explain the concept and functions of interdisciplinary teams.

DOCTORS: THE PERCEPTIONS

SIGNIFICANT POINTS

- Many physicians and surgeons work long, irregular hours.

- Acceptance to medical school is highly competitive.

- Formal education and training requirements—typically 4 years of undergraduate school, 4 years of medical school, and 3 to 8 years of internship and residency—are among the most demanding of any occupation, but earnings are among the highest.

- Job opportunities should be very good, particularly in rural and low-income areas.

Although it is only one of many career paths available to those with the interest and aptitude for a career involving patient care, the profession of physician is one that most readily comes to mind when one thinks of medicine. The title "Dr." traditionally inspires respect—and perhaps envy. Media portrayals through the years have contributed to a popular perception of doctors as public servants of rare intelligence, compassion, and skill; encounters with the medical system have left some consumers convinced that doctors have feet of clay that are shod in gold-plated boots.

Although public perceptions of physicians will undoubtedly persist despite demonstrations of their inapplicability, individuals approaching a career choice should be guided by realities rather than perceptions. The **cost of training** is a serious consideration for would-be physicians, and, like other healthcare professionals, physicians must adjust to changes in the healthcare system, some of which are potentially constraining to autonomy and earning power.

DOCTORS: THE REALITIES

Work Description

Physicians and **surgeons** diagnose illnesses and prescribe and administer treatment for people suffering from injury or disease. Physicians examine patients, obtain medical histories, and order, perform, and interpret diagnostic tests. They counsel patients on diet, hygiene, and preventive health care.

There are two types of physicians: **MD** (*Medical Doctor*) and **DO** (*Doctor of Osteopathic Medicine*). MDs also are known as **allopathic physicians**. Although both MDs and DOs may use all accepted methods of treatment, including drugs and surgery, DOs place special emphasis on the body's musculoskeletal system, **preventive medicine**, and holistic patient care. DOs are most likely to be **primary care specialists**, although they can be found in all specialties. About half of DOs practice general or family medicine, general internal medicine, or general pediatrics.

Physicians work in one or more of several specialties, including, but not limited to, anesthesiology, family and general medicine, general internal medicine, general pediatrics, obstetrics and gynecology, psychiatry, and surgery.

Anesthesiologists focus on the care of surgical patients and pain relief. Like other physicians, they evaluate and treat patients and direct the efforts of their staffs. Through continual monitoring and assessment, these critical care specialists are responsible for the maintenance of the patient's vital life functions—heart rate, body temperature, blood pressure, and breathing—during surgery. They also work outside of the operating room, providing pain relief in the intensive care unit, during labor and delivery, and for those who suffer from chronic pain. Anesthesiologists confer with other physicians and surgeons about appropriate treatments and procedures before, during, and after operations.

Family and general physicians often provide the first point of contact for people seeking health care, by acting as the traditional family physician. They assess and treat a wide range of conditions, from sinus and respiratory infections to broken bones. Family and general physicians typically have a base of regular, long-term patients. These doctors refer patients with more serious conditions to specialists or other healthcare facilities for more intensive care.

General **internists** diagnose and provide nonsurgical treatment for a wide range of problems that affect internal organ systems, such as the stomach, kidneys, liver, and digestive tract. Internists use a variety of diagnostic techniques to treat patients through medication or hospitalization. Like general practitioners, general internists commonly act as primary care specialists. They treat patients referred from other specialists and, in turn, they refer patients to other specialists when more complex care is required.

General **pediatricians** care for the health of infants, children, teenagers, and young adults. They specialize in the diagnosis and treatment of a variety of ailments specific to young people and track patients' growth to adulthood. Like most physicians, pediatricians work with different healthcare workers, such as nurses and other physicians, to assess and treat children with various ailments. Most of the work of pediatricians involves treating day-to-day illnesses—minor injuries, infectious diseases, and immunizations—that are common to children, much as a general practitioner treats adults. Some pediatricians specialize in pediatric surgery or serious medical conditions, such as autoimmune disorders or serious chronic ailments.

Obstetricians and **gynecologists** (*OB/GYNs*) specialize in women's health. They are responsible for women's general medical care, and they also provide care related to pregnancy and the reproductive system. Like general practitioners, OB/GYNs attempt to prevent, diagnose, and treat general health problems, but they focus on ailments specific to the female anatomy, such as cancers of the breast or cervix, urinary tract and pelvic disorders, and hormonal disorders. OB/GYNs also specialize in childbirth, which includes treating and counseling women throughout their pregnancy, from giving prenatal diagnoses to assisting with delivery and providing postpartum care.

Psychiatrists are the primary mental healthcare givers. They assess and treat mental illnesses through a combination of psychotherapy, psychoanalysis, hospitalization, and medication. Psychotherapy involves regular discussions with patients about their problems; the psychiatrist helps them find solutions through changes in their behavioral patterns, the exploration of their past experiences, or group and family therapy sessions. Psychoanalysis involves long-term psychotherapy and counseling for patients. In many cases, medications are administered to correct chemical imbalances that cause emotional problems.

Surgeons specialize in the treatment of injury, disease, and deformity through operations. Using a variety of instruments, and with patients under anesthesia, a surgeon corrects physical deformities, repairs bone and tissue after injuries, or performs preventive surgeries on patients with debilitating diseases or disorders. Although a large number perform general surgery, many surgeons choose to specialize in a specific area. One of the most prevalent specialties is orthopedic surgery: the treatment of the musculoskeletal system. Others include neurological surgery (treatment of the brain and nervous system), cardiovascular surgery, **otolaryngology** (treatment of the ear, nose, and throat), and plastic or reconstructive surgery. Like other physicians, surgeons also examine patients, perform and interpret diagnostic tests, and counsel patients on preventive health care.

Other physicians and surgeons work as a variety of other medical and surgical specialists, including **allergists**, **cardiologists**, **dermatologists**, **emergency physicians**, gastroenterologists, **ophthalmologists**, **pathologists**, and **radiologists**.

Work Environment

Many physicians—primarily general and family practitioners, general internists, pediatricians, OB/GYNs, and psychiatrists—work in small, private offices or clinics, often assisted by a small staff of nurses and other administrative personnel. Increasingly, physicians are practicing in groups or healthcare organizations that provide backup coverage and allow for more time off. Physicians in a **group practice** or healthcare organization often work as part of a team that coordinates care for a number of patients; they are less independent than the **solo practitioners** of the past. Surgeons and anesthesiologists usually work in well-lighted, sterile environments while performing surgery and often stand for long periods. Most work in hospitals or in surgical outpatient centers.

Many physicians and surgeons work long, irregular hours. In 2008, 43% of all physicians and surgeons worked 50 or more hours a week. Nine percent of all physicians and surgeons worked part time. Physicians and surgeons travel between an office and a hospital to care for their patients. While on call, a physician will deal with many patients' concerns over the phone and make emergency visits to hospitals or nursing homes.

Employment Opportunities

Physicians and surgeons held about 661,400 jobs in 2008; approximately 12% were self-employed. About 53% of **wage-and-salary physicians** and surgeons worked in offices of physicians, and 19% were employed by hospitals. Others practiced in federal, state, and local governments, educational services, and outpatient care centers.

According to medical board of different states in 2009, 45% of physicians in patient care were in primary care, with 55% in specialties (see **Table 7-1**).

A growing number of physicians are partners or wage-and-salary employees of group practices. Organized as clinics or as associations of physicians, medical groups can more easily afford expensive medical equipment, share support staff, and benefit from other business advantages.

According to state medical boards, the New England and middle Atlantic states have the highest ratios of physicians to the population; the South Central and Mountain states have the lowest. Physicians tend to locate in

TABLE 7-1 Distribution of Practicing Physicians in the Major Industrial States in the United States in 2006 (Data Compiled by the Medical Boards of Those States)

Medical Fields	Percentage Distribution	
Primary care	45	
Family medicine/general practice		12.4
Pediatrics		9.1
Internal medicine		18.9
Obstetrics and gynecology		4.6
Specialties	55	
Anesthesiology		5.5
Psychiatry		5.2
General surgery		5.0
Emergency medicine		4.1
Others		35.2

urban areas, close to hospitals and education centers. Similar data showed that in 2009, about 75% to 80% of physicians in patient care were located in metropolitan areas, while the remaining 20% to 25% were located in rural areas.

Educational and Legal Requirements

The common path to practicing as a physician requires 8 years of education beyond high school and 3 to 8 additional years of internship and residency. All states, the District of Columbia, and U.S. territories license physicians.

Formal education and training requirements for physicians are among the most demanding of any occupation—4 years of undergraduate school, 4 years of medical school, and 3 to 8 years of internship and residency, depending on the specialty selected. A few medical schools offer combined undergraduate and medical school programs that last 6 or 7 years rather than the customary 8 years.

Premedical students must complete undergraduate work in physics, biology, mathematics, English, and inorganic and organic chemistry. Students also take courses in the humanities and the social sciences. Some students volunteer at local hospitals or clinics to gain practical experience in the health professions.

The minimum educational requirement for entry into medical school is 3 years of college; most applicants, however, have at least a Bachelor degree, and many have advanced degrees. In 2008, there were 129 medical schools accredited by the Liaison Committee on Medical Education (LCME). The LCME is the national accrediting body for MD medical education programs.

The American Osteopathic Association accredits schools that award a DO degree; there were 25 schools accredited in 31 locations in 2008.

Acceptance to medical school is highly competitive. Most applicants must submit transcripts, scores from the Medical College Admission Test, and letters of recommendation. Schools also consider an applicant's character, personality, leadership qualities, and participation in extracurricular activities. Most schools require an interview with members of the admissions committee.

Students spend most of the first 2 years of medical school in laboratories and classrooms, taking courses such as anatomy, biochemistry, physiology, pharmacology, psychology, microbiology, pathology, medical ethics, and laws governing medicine. They also learn to take medical histories, examine patients, and diagnose illnesses. During their last 2 years, students work with patients under the supervision of experienced physicians in hospitals and clinics, learning acute, chronic, preventive, and rehabilitative care. Through **rotations** in internal medicine, family practice, obstetrics and gynecology, pediatrics, psychiatry, and surgery, they gain experience in the diagnosis and treatment of illness.

Following medical school, almost all MDs enter a residency—graduate medical education in a specialty that takes the form of paid on-the-job training, usually in a hospital. Most DOs serve a 12-month rotating internship after graduation and before entering a residency, which may last 2 to 6 years.

A physician's training is costly. According to the Association of American Medical Colleges, in 2007, 85% of public medical school graduates and 86% of private medical school graduates were in debt for educational expenses.

- *Licensure and certification.* To practice medicine as a physician, all states, the District of Columbia, and U.S. territories require licensing. All physicians and surgeons practicing in the United States must pass the United States Medical Licensing Examination (USMLE). To be eligible to take the USMLE in its entirety, physicians must graduate from an accredited medical school. Although physicians licensed in one state usually can get a license to practice in another without further examination, some states limit reciprocity. Graduates of foreign medical schools generally can qualify for licensure after passing an examination and completing a U.S. residency. For specific information on licensing in a given state, contact that state's medical board. MDs and DOs seeking board certification in a specialty may spend up to 7 years in residency training, depending on the specialty. A final examination immediately after residency or after 1 or 2 years of practice is also necessary for certification by a member board of the American Board of Medical Specialists (ABMS) or the American Osteopathic Association (AOA). The ABMS represents 24 boards related to medical specialties ranging from allergy and immunology to urology. The AOA has approved 18 specialty boards, ranging from anesthesiology to surgery. For certification in a subspecialty, physicians usually need another 1 to 2 years of residency.

- *Other qualifications.* People who wish to become physicians must have a desire to serve patients, be self-motivated, and be able to survive the pressures and long hours of medical education and practice. Physicians also must have a good bedside manner, emotional stability, and the ability to make decisions in emergencies. Prospective physicians must be willing to study throughout their career to keep up with medical advances.
- *Advancement.* Some physicians and surgeons advance by gaining expertise in specialties and subspecialties, and by developing a reputation for excellence among their peers and patients. Physicians and surgeons may also start their own practice or join a group practice. Others teach residents and other new doctors, and some advance to supervisory and managerial roles in hospitals, clinics, and other settings.

Employment Trends

Employment is expected to grow much faster than the average for all occupations. Job opportunities should be very good, particularly in rural and low-income areas.

Employment Change

Employment of physicians and surgeons is projected to grow 22% from 2008 to 2018, much faster than the average for all occupations. Job growth will occur because of the continued expansion of healthcare-related industries. The growing and aging population will drive overall growth in the demand for physician services, as consumers continue to demand high levels of care using the latest technologies, diagnostic tests, and therapies. Many medical schools are increasing their enrollments based on a perceived new demand for physicians.

Despite growing demand for physicians and surgeons, some factors will temper growth. For example, new technologies allow physicians to be more productive. This means physicians can diagnose and treat more patients in the same amount of time. The rising cost of health care can dramatically affect the demand for physicians' services. Physician assistants and nurse practitioners, who can perform many of the routine duties of physicians at a fraction of the cost, may be increasingly used. Furthermore, the demand for physicians' services is highly sensitive to changes in healthcare reimbursement policies. If changes to health coverage result in higher out-of-pocket costs for consumers, they may demand fewer physician services.

Job Prospects

Opportunities for individuals interested in becoming physicians and surgeons are expected to be very good. In addition to job openings from employment growth, openings will result from the need to replace the relatively high number of physicians and surgeons expected to retire over the 2008–2018 decade.

Job prospects should be particularly good for physicians willing to practice in rural and low-income areas because these medically underserved areas typically have difficulty attracting these workers. Job prospects will also be especially good for physicians in specialties that afflict the rapidly growing elderly population. Examples of such specialties are cardiology and radiology because the risks for heart disease and cancer increase as people age. Most experts expect that the number of physicians and surgeons will increase from ~65,000 in 2008 to 800,000 in 2018.

Earnings

Earnings of physicians and surgeons are among the highest of any occupation. In 2009, physicians practicing primary care had a total median annual compensation of $200,000, and physicians practicing in medical specialties earned about $400,000. More information on the latest data on salaries of individual categories of practicing physicians (surgery, pediatrics, and so on) is available from the additional sources of information presented in the following.

Self-employed physicians—those who own or are part owners of their medical practice—generally have higher median incomes than salaried physicians. Earnings vary according to number of years in practice, geographic region, hours worked, skill, personality, and professional reputation. Self-employed physicians and surgeons must provide for their own health insurance and retirement.

RELATED OCCUPATIONS

Physicians work to prevent, diagnose, and treat diseases, disorders, and injuries. Other healthcare practitioners who need similar skills and who exercise critical judgment include chiropractors, dentists, optometrists, physician assistants, podiatrists, registered nurses, and veterinarians.

ADDITIONAL INFORMATION

For a list of medical schools and residency programs, as well as general information on premedical education, financial aid, and medicine as a career, contact

- Association of American Medical Colleges, Section for Student Services, 2450 N St. NW, Washington, DC 20037. Internet: http://www.aamc.org/students

  For information on licensing, contact

- Federation of State Medical Boards, P.O. Box 619850, Dallas, TX 75261-9850. Internet: http://www.fsmb.org

For general information on physicians, contact

- American Medical Association, 515 N. State St., Chicago, IL 60654. Internet: http://www.ama-assn.org/go/becominganmd
- American Osteopathic Association, Department of Communications, 142 East Ontario St., Chicago, IL 60611. Internet: http://www.osteopathic.org

For information about various medical specialties, contact

- American Academy of Family Physicians, Resident Student Activities Department, P.O. Box 11210, Shawnee Mission, KS 66207-1210. Internet: http://fmignet.aafp.org
- American Board of Medical Specialties, 222 N. LaSalle St., Suite 1500, Chicago, IL 60601. Internet: http://www.abms.org
- American College of Obstetricians and Gynecologists, P.O. Box 96920, Washington, DC 20090. Internet: http://www.acog.org
- American College of Surgeons, Division of Education, 633 North Saint Clair St., Chicago, IL 60611. Internet: http://www.facs.org
- American Psychiatric Association, 1000 Wilson Blvd., Suite 1825, Arlington, VA 22209. Internet: http://www.psych.org
- American Society of Anesthesiologists, 520 N. Northwest Hwy., Park Ridge, IL 60068. Internet: http://www.asahq.org/career/homepage.htm

Information on federal scholarships and loans is available from the directors of student financial aid at schools of medicine. Information on licensing is available from state boards of examiners.

chapter eight

Dentists*

KEY TERMS

ADA
ADHA
DAT
Dental assistants
Dental hygienists
Dental public health
  specialist

Endodontists
Fissure sealants
Oral pathologists
Oral and maxillofacial
  surgeons

Orthodontists
Pediatric dentists
Periodontists
Prosthodontists

---

*All information in this chapter, unless otherwise indicated, was obtained from Bureau of Labor Statistics. U.S. Department of Labor. *Occupational Outlook Handbook 2010–2011 Edition*. 2010.

DENTISTS

SIGNIFICANT POINTS

- About 3 out of 4 dentists are solo practitioners.
- Dentists must graduate from an accredited dental school and pass written and practical examinations; competition for admission to dental school is keen.
- Faster than average employment growth is projected.
- Job prospects should be good, reflecting the need to replace the large number of dentists expected to retire.

Work Description

Dentists diagnose and treat problems with teeth and tissues in the mouth, along with giving advice and administering care to help prevent future problems. They provide instruction on diet, brushing, flossing, the use of fluorides, and other aspects of dental care. They remove tooth decay, fill cavities, examine X-rays, place protective plastic sealants on children's teeth, straighten teeth, and repair fractured teeth. They also perform corrective surgery on gums and supporting bones to treat gum diseases. Dentists extract teeth and make models and measurements for dentures to replace missing teeth. They also administer anesthetics and write prescriptions for antibiotics and other medications.

Dentists use a variety of equipment, including X-ray machines, drills, mouth mirrors, probes, forceps, brushes, and scalpels. Lasers, digital scanners, and other computer technologies also may be used. Dentists wear masks, gloves, and safety glasses to protect themselves and their patients from infectious diseases.

Dentists in private practice oversee a variety of administrative tasks, including bookkeeping and the buying of equipment and supplies. They may employ and supervise **dental hygienists**, **dental assistants**, dental laboratory technicians, and receptionists.

Most dentists are general practitioners, handling a variety of dental needs. Other dentists practice in any of nine specialty areas. **Orthodontists**, the largest group of specialists, straighten teeth by applying pressure to the teeth with braces or other appliances. The next largest group, **oral and maxillofacial surgeons**, operates on the mouth, jaws, teeth, gums, neck, and head. The remainder may specialize as pediatric dentists (focusing on dentistry for children and special-needs patients); **periodontists** (treating gums and bone supporting the teeth); **prosthodontists** (replacing missing teeth with permanent fixtures, such as crowns and bridges, or with removable fixtures such as dentures); **endodontists** (performing root-canal therapy); **oral pathologists** (diagnosing oral diseases); oral and maxillofacial radiologists (diagnosing diseases in the head and neck through the use of imaging technologies); or **dental public health specialists** (promoting good dental health and preventing dental diseases within the community).

Work Environment

Most dentists are solo practitioners, meaning that they own their own businesses and work alone or with a small staff. Some dentists have partners, and a few work for other dentists as associate dentists.

Most dentists work 4 or 5 days a week. Some work evenings and weekends to meet their patients' needs. The number of hours worked varies greatly among dentists. Most full-time dentists work between 35 and 40 hours a week. However, others, especially those who are trying to establish a new practice, work more. Also, experienced dentists often work fewer hours. It is common for dentists to continue in part-time practice well beyond the usual retirement age.

Dentists usually work in the safety of an office environment. However, work-related injuries can occur, such as those resulting from the use of hand-held tools when performing dental work on patients.

Employment Opportunities

Dentists held about 141,900 jobs in 2008. Employment was distributed among general practitioners and specialists, as shown in **Table 8-1**. Approximately 15% of all dentists were specialists. About 28% of dentists were self-employed and not incorporated. Very few salaried dentists worked in hospitals and offices of physicians. Almost all dentists work in private practice. According to the American Dental Association (**ADA**), about three out of four dentists in private practice are solo proprietors, and almost 15% belong to a partnership.

Educational and Legal Requirements

All 50 states and the District of Columbia require dentists to be licensed. To qualify for a license in most states, candidates must graduate from an accredited dental school and pass written and practical examinations.

Education and Training

In 2008, there were 57 dental schools in the United States accredited by the ADA's Commission on Dental Accreditation. Dental schools require a

TABLE 8-1 Employment Distribution Among General Practitioners and Specialists

Specialties	Distribution
Dentists, general	120,200
Orthodontists	700
Oral and maxillofacial surgeons	6700
Prosthodontists	500
Dentists, all other specialists	6900

minimum of 2 years of college-level predental education prior to admittance. Most dental students have at least a Bachelor degree before entering dental school, although a few applicants are accepted to dental school after 2 or 3 years of college and complete their Bachelor degree while attending dental school. According to the ADA, 85% of dental students had a Bachelor degree prior to beginning their dental program in the 2006–2007 academic year.

High school and college students who want to become dentists should take courses in biology, chemistry, physics, health, and mathematics. College undergraduates planning on applying to dental school are required to take many science courses. Because of this, some choose a major in a science, such as biology or chemistry, whereas others take the required science coursework while pursuing a major in another subject.

All dental schools require applicants to take the Dental Admissions Test **(DAT)**. When selecting students, schools consider scores earned on the DAT, applicants' grade point averages, and information gathered through recommendations and interviews. Competition for admission to dental school is keen.

Dental school usually lasts 4 academic years. Studies begin with classroom instruction and laboratory work in science, including anatomy, microbiology, biochemistry, and physiology. Beginning courses in clinical sciences, including laboratory techniques, are also completed. During the last 2 years, students treat patients, usually in dental clinics, under the supervision of licensed dentists. Most dental schools award the degree of Doctor of Dental Surgery (DDS). Others award an equivalent degree, Doctor of Dental Medicine (DMD).

Licensure

Licensing is required to practice as a dentist. In most states, licensure requires passing written and practical examinations in addition to having a degree from an accredited dental school. Candidates may fulfill the written part of the state licensing requirements by passing the National Board Dental Examinations. Individual states or regional testing agencies administer the written or practical examinations.

Individuals can be licensed to practice any of the nine recognized specialties in all 50 states and the District of Columbia. Requirements include 2 to 4 years of postgraduate education and, in some cases, the completion of a special state examination. A postgraduate residency term also may be required, usually lasting up to 2 years. Most state licenses permit dentists to engage in both general and specialized practice.

Other Qualifications

Dentistry requires diagnostic ability and manual skills. Dentists should have good visual memory; excellent judgment regarding space, shape, and color; a high degree of manual dexterity; and scientific ability. Good business sense, self-discipline, and good communication skills are helpful for success in private practice.

Advancement

Dentists and aspiring dentists who want to teach or conduct research full time usually spend an additional 2 to 5 years in advanced dental training, in programs operated by dental schools or hospitals. Many private practitioners also teach part time, including supervising students in dental school clinics.

Some dental school graduates work for established dentists as associates for 1 to 2 years to gain experience and save money to equip an office of their own. Most dental school graduates, however, purchase an established practice or open a new one immediately after graduation.

Employment Opportunities

Employment is projected to grow faster than average. Job prospects should be good, reflecting the need to replace the large number of dentists expected to retire.

Employment Change

The employment of dentists is projected to grow by 16% through 2018, which is faster than the average for all occupations. The demand for dental services is expected to continue to increase. The overall U.S. population is growing, and the elderly segment of the population is growing even faster; these phenomena will increase the demand for dental care. Many members of the baby-boom generation will need complicated dental work. In addition, elderly people are more likely to retain their teeth than were their predecessors, so they will require much more care than in the past. The younger generation will continue to need preventive checkups despite an overall increase in the dental health of the public over the last few decades. Recently, some private insurance providers have increased their dental coverage. If this trend continues, people with new or expanded dental insurance will be more likely to visit a dentist than in the past. Also, although they are currently a small proportion of dental expenditures, cosmetic dental services, such as providing teeth-whitening treatments, will become increasingly popular. This trend is expected to continue as new technologies allow these procedures to take less time and be much less invasive.

However, the employment of dentists is not expected to keep pace with the increased demand for dental services. Productivity increases from new technology, as well as the tendency to assign more tasks to dental hygienists and assistants, will allow dentists to perform more work than they have in the past. As their practices expand, dentists are likely to hire more hygienists and dental assistants to handle routine services.

Dentists will increasingly provide care and instruction aimed at preventing the loss of teeth, rather than simply providing treatments such as fillings. Improvements in dental technology also will allow dentists to offer more effective and less painful treatment to their patients.

Job Prospects

As an increasing number of dentists from the baby-boom generation reach retirement age, many of them will retire or work fewer hours and stop taking on new patients. Furthermore, the number of applicants to, and graduates from, dental schools has increased in recent years. Job prospects should be good, because younger dentists will be able to take over the work of older dentists who retire or cut back on hours, as well as provide dental services to accommodate the growing demand.

Demand for dental services tends to follow the business cycle, primarily because these services usually are paid for either by the patient or by private insurance companies. As a result, during slow times in the economy, demand for dental services can decrease; consequently, dentists may have difficulty finding employment, or if already in an established practice, they may work fewer hours because of reduced demand. **Table 8-2** shows some projection data provided by the Department of Labor.

Earnings

Median annual wages of salaried general dentists were $142,870 in May 2008. Earnings vary according to number of years in practice, location, hours worked, and specialty. Self-employed dentists in private practice tend to earn more than salaried dentists.

Dentists who are salaried often receive benefits paid by their employer, with health insurance and malpractice insurance being among the most common. However, like other business owners, self-employed dentists must provide their own health insurance, life insurance, retirement plans, and other benefits.

TABLE 8-2   Some Projection Data from the Department of Labor for Dentists

Occupational Title	Employment, 2008	Projected Employment, 2018	Change, 2008–2018	
			Number	Percentage
Dentists	141,900	164,000	22,100	16
Dentists, general	120,200	138,600	18,400	15
Oral and maxillofacial surgeons	6700	7700	1000	15
Orthodontists	7700	9200	1500	20
Prosthodontists	500	700	100	28
Dentists, all other specialists	6900	7900	1000	15

Related Occupations

Dentists examine, diagnose, prevent, and treat diseases and abnormalities. Other workers who perform similar tasks include chiropractors, optometrists, physicians and surgeons, podiatrists, and veterinarians.

Additional Information

For information on dentistry as a career, a list of accredited dental schools, and a list of state boards of dental examiners, contact

* American Dental Association, Commission on Dental Accreditation, 211 E. Chicago Ave., Chicago, IL 60611. Internet: http://www.ada.org

For information on admission to dental schools, contact

* American Dental Education Association, 1400 K St. NW, Suite 1100, Washington, DC 20005. Internet: http://www.adea.org

For more information on general dentistry or on a specific dental specialty, contact

* Academy of General Dentistry, 211 East Chicago Ave., Suite 900, Chicago, IL 60611. Internet: http://www.agd.org
* American Association of Orthodontists, 401 North Lindbergh Blvd., St. Louis, MO 63141. Internet: http://www.braces.org
* American Association of Oral and Maxillofacial Surgeons, 9700 West Bryn Mawr Ave., Rosemont, IL 60018. Internet: http://www.aaoms.org
* American Academy of Pediatric Dentistry, 211 East Chicago Ave., Suite 1700, Chicago, IL 60611. Internet: http://www.aapd.org
* American Academy of Periodontology, 737 North Michigan Ave., Suite 800, Chicago, IL 60611. Internet: http://www.perio.org
* American Academy of Prosthodontists, 211 East Chicago Ave., Suite 1000, Chicago, IL 60611. Internet: http://www.prosthodontics.org
* American Association of Endodontists, 211 East Chicago Ave., Suite 1100, Chicago, IL 60611. Internet: http://www.aae.org
* American Academy of Oral and Maxillofacial Radiology, P.O. Box 1010, Evans, GA 30809. Internet: http://www.aaomr.org/
* American Association of Public Health Dentistry, 3085 Stevenson Dr., Suite 200, Springfield, IL 62703. Internet: http://www.aaphd.org

People interested in practicing dentistry should obtain the requirements for licensure from the board of dental examiners of the state in which they plan to work.

To obtain information on scholarships, grants, and loans, including federal financial aid, prospective dental students should contact the office of student financial aid at the schools to which they apply.

DENTAL HYGIENISTS

SIGNIFICANT POINTS

- A degree from an accredited dental hygiene school and a state license are required for this job.
- Dental hygienist ranks among the fastest-growing occupations.
- Job prospects are expected to be favorable in most areas, but strong competition for jobs is likely in some areas.
- About half of all dental hygienists work part time, and flexible scheduling is a distinctive feature of this job.

Work Description

Dental hygienists clean teeth and provide other preventive dental care; they also teach patients how to practice good oral hygiene. Hygienists examine patients' teeth and gums, recording the presence of diseases or abnormalities. They remove calculus, stains, and plaque from teeth; take and develop dental X-rays; and apply cavity preventive agents such as fluorides and pit and **fissure sealants**. In some states, hygienists administer local anesthetics and anesthetic gas; place and carve filling materials, temporary fillings, and periodontal dressings; remove sutures; and smooth and polish metal restorations.

Dental hygienists also help patients develop and maintain good oral health. For example, they may explain the relationship between diet and oral health, inform patients how to select toothbrushes, and show patients how to brush and floss their teeth. Dental hygienists use hand and rotary instruments, lasers, and ultrasonics to clean teeth; X-ray machines to take dental pictures; syringes with needles to administer local anesthetics; and models of teeth to explain oral hygiene.

The nature of the work may vary by practice setting. In schools, for example, hygienists may assist the dentist in examining children's teeth to determine the dental treatment required. Hygienists who have advanced training may teach or conduct research.

Work Environment

Dental hygienists usually work in clean, well-lighted offices. Important health safeguards for persons in this occupation include regular medical checkups, strict adherence to proper radiologic procedures, compliance with required infection control procedures, including the latest safety precautions, and the use of appropriate protective devices when administering nitrous oxide/oxygen analgesia. The occupation is one of several covered by the Consumer-Patient Radiation Health and Safety Board, which sets uniform standards for the training and certification of individuals who perform medical and dental radiologic procedures.

Most hygienists work 30 to 35 hours per week in jobs that may include Saturday or evening hours. Flexible scheduling is a distinctive feature of this job.

Employment Opportunities

Dental hygienists held about 174,100 jobs in 2008. Because multiple job holding is common in this field, the number of jobs exceeds the number of hygienists. About 51% of dental hygienists worked part time. Almost all jobs for dental hygienists—about 96%—were in offices of dentists. A very small number worked for employment services, in physicians' offices, or in other industries.

Educational and Legal Requirements

Prospective dental hygienists must become licensed in the state in which they wish to practice. A degree from an accredited dental hygiene school is required along with licensure examinations.

Education and Training

A high school diploma and college entrance test scores are usually required for admission to a dental hygiene program. High school students interested in becoming a dental hygienist should take courses in biology, chemistry, and mathematics. Also, some dental hygiene programs require applicants to have completed at least 1 year of college. Specific entrance requirements vary from one school to another.

In 2008, there were 301 dental hygiene programs accredited by the Commission on Dental Accreditation. Most dental hygiene programs grant an Associate degree, although some also offer a certificate, a Bachelor degree, or a Master degree. A minimum of an Associate degree or certificate in dental hygiene is generally required for practice in a private dental office. A Bachelor or Master degree usually is required for research, teaching, or clinical practice in public or school health programs.

Schools offer laboratory, clinical, and classroom instruction in subjects such as anatomy, physiology, chemistry, microbiology, pharmacology, nutrition, radiography, histology (the study of tissue structure), periodontology (the study of gum diseases), pathology, dental materials, clinical dental hygiene, and social and behavioral sciences.

Licensure

Dental hygienists must be licensed by the state in which they practice. Nearly all states require candidates to graduate from an accredited dental hygiene school and pass both a written and clinical examination. The American Dental Association's Joint Commission on National Dental Examinations administers the written examination, which is accepted by all states and the District of Columbia. State or regional testing agencies administer the clinical examination. In addition, most states require an examination on the legal aspects of dental hygiene practice. Alabama is the only state that allows licensure candidates to take its examinations if they have been trained through a state-regulated on-the-job program in a dentist's office.

Other Qualifications

Dental hygienists should work well with others because they work closely with dentists and dental assistants as well as deal directly with patients. Hygienists also need good manual dexterity, because they use dental instruments within a patient's mouth, with little room for error.

Advancement

Advancement opportunities usually come from working outside a typical dentist's office, and usually require a Bachelor or Master degree in dental hygiene. Some dental hygienists may choose to pursue a career teaching in a dental hygiene program, working in public health, or working in a corporate setting.

Employment Trends

Dental hygienist ranks among the fastest-growing occupations, and job prospects are expected to be favorable in most areas, but competition for jobs is likely in some areas.

Employment Change

Employment of dental hygienists is expected to grow 36% through 2018, which is much faster than the average for all occupations. This projected growth ranks dental hygienist among the fastest-growing occupations, in response to increasing demand for dental care and the greater use of hygienists.

The demand for dental services will grow because of population growth, older people increasingly retaining more teeth, and a growing focus on preventive dental care. To meet this demand, facilities that provide dental care, particularly dentists' offices, will increasingly employ dental hygienists, and more hygienists per office, to perform services that have been performed by dentists in the past. Ongoing research indicating a link between oral health and general health also will spur the demand for preventive dental services, which are typically provided by dental hygienists.

Job Prospects

Job prospects are expected to be favorable in most areas, but will vary by geographical location. Because graduates are permitted to practice only in the state in which they are licensed, hygienists wishing to practice in areas that have an abundance of dental hygiene programs may experience strong

TABLE 8-3 Projections Data from the National Employment Matrix for Dental Hygienists

Occupational Title	Employment, 2008	Projected Employment, 2018	Change, 2008–2019	
			Number	Percentage
Dental hygienists	174,100	237,000	62,900	36

competition for jobs. Older dentists, who have been less likely to employ dental hygienists, are leaving the occupation and will be replaced by recent graduates, who are more likely to employ one or more hygienists. In addition, as dentists' workloads increase, they are expected to hire more hygienists to perform preventive dental care, such as cleaning, so that they may devote their own time to more complex procedures. **Table 8-3** shows some projection data provided by the Department of Labor.

Earnings

Median annual wages of dental hygienists were $66,570 in May 2008. The middle 50% earned between $55,220 and $78,990. The lowest 10% earned less than $44,180, and the highest 10% earned more than $91,470.

Earnings vary by geographic location, employment setting, and years of experience. Dental hygienists may be paid on an hourly, daily, salary, or commission basis. Benefits vary substantially by practice setting and may be contingent upon full-time employment. According to a 2009 survey conducted by the American Dental Hygienist Association, about half of all hygienists reported receiving some form of employment benefits. Of those receiving benefits, paid vacation, sick leave, and retirement plans were the most common.

Related Occupations

Other workers supporting health practitioners in an office setting include dental assistants, medical assistants, occupational therapist assistants and aides, physical therapist assistants and aides, physician assistants, and registered nurses. Dental hygienists sometimes work with radiation technology, as do radiation therapists.

Additional Information

For information on a career in dental hygiene, including educational requirements, contact

- American Dental Hygienists Association (**ADHA**), 444 N. Michigan Ave., Suite 3400, Chicago, IL 60611. Internet: http://www.adha.org

For information about accredited programs and educational requirements, contact

- Commission on Dental Accreditation, American Dental Association, 211 E. Chicago Ave., Chicago, IL 60611. Internet: http://www.ada.org/prof/ed/accred/commission/index.asp

The State Board of Dental Examiners in each state can supply information on licensing requirements.

DENTAL ASSISTANTS

SIGNIFICANT POINTS

- Job prospects should be excellent.
- Dentists are expected to hire more assistants to perform routine tasks so dentists may devote their time to more complex procedures.
- Many assistants learn their skills on the job, although an increasing number are trained in dental-assisting programs; most programs take 1 year or less to complete.
- More than one-third of dental assistants worked part time in 2008.

Work Description

Dental assistants perform a variety of patient care, office, and laboratory duties. They work chairside as dentists examine and treat patients. They make patients as comfortable as possible in the dental chair, prepare them for treatment, and obtain dental records. Assistants hand instruments and materials to dentists, and keep patients' mouths dry and clear by using suction or other devices. They also sterilize and disinfect instruments and equipment, prepare tray setups for dental procedures, and instruct patients on postoperative and general oral health care.

Some dental assistants prepare materials for making impressions and restorations, expose radiographs, and process dental X-ray film as directed by the dentist. State law determines which clinical tasks a dental assistant may perform, but in most states they may remove sutures, apply anesthetic and caries-preventive agents to the teeth and oral tissue, remove excess cement used in the filling process, and place rubber dams on the teeth to isolate them for individual treatment. Many states are expanding dental assistants' duties to include tasks such as coronal polishing and restorative dentistry functions for those assistants who meet specific training and experience requirements.

Those with laboratory duties make casts of the teeth and mouth from impressions taken by dentists, clean and polish removable appliances, and make temporary crowns. Dental assistants with office duties arrange and confirm appointments, receive patients, keep treatment records, send bills, receive payments, and order dental supplies and materials. Dental assistants should not be confused with dental hygienists, who are licensed to perform a wider variety of clinical tasks.

Work Environment

Dental assistants work in a well-lighted, clean environment. Their work area is usually near the dental chair, so they can arrange instruments, materials, and medication and hand them to the dentist when needed. Dental assistants wear gloves and masks to protect themselves from infectious diseases. Following safety procedures minimizes the risks of handling radiographic equipment.

Almost half of dental assistants had a 35- to 40-hour workweek in 2008. More than one-third worked part time, or fewer than 35 hours per week, and many others had variable schedules. Depending on the hours of the dental office where they work, assistants may have to work on Saturdays or evenings. Some dental assistants hold multiple jobs by working at dental offices that are open on different days or by scheduling their work at a second office around the hours they work at their primary office.

Employment Opportunities

Dental assistants held about 295,300 jobs in 2008. About 93% of all jobs for dental assistants were in offices of dentists. A small number of jobs were in the federal, state, and local governments or in offices of physicians. Some dental assistants worked part time, sometimes in more than one dental office.

Educational and Legal Requirements

Many assistants learn their skills on the job, although an increasing number are trained in dental-assisting programs offered by community and junior colleges, trade schools, technical institutes, or the armed forces. Most programs take 1 year to complete. For assistants to perform more advanced functions, or to have the ability to complete radiological procedures, many states require assistants to obtain a license or certification.

Education and Training

In most states, there are no formal education or training requirements to become an entry-level dental assistant. High school students interested in a career as a dental assistant should take courses in biology, chemistry, health, and office practices. For those wishing to pursue further education, the Commission on Dental Accreditation (CODA) approved 281 dental-assisting training programs in 2009. Programs include classroom, laboratory, and preclinical instruction in dental-assisting skills and related theory. In addition, students gain practical experience in dental schools, clinics, or dental offices. Most programs take 1 year or less to complete and lead to a certificate or diploma. Two-year programs offered in community and junior colleges lead to an Associate degree. All programs require a high school diploma or its equivalent, and some require science or computer-related courses for admission. A number of private vocational schools offer 4- to 6-month courses in dental assisting, but the Commission on Dental Accreditation does not accredit these programs.

A large number of dental assistants learn through on-the-job training. In these situations, the employing dentist or other dental assistants in the dental office teach the new assistant dental terminology, the names of the instruments, how to perform daily duties, how to interact with patients, and other things necessary to help keep the dental office running smoothly. Although some things can be picked up easily, it may be a few months before new dental assistants are completely knowledgeable about their duties and comfortable doing all of their tasks without assistance.

A period of on-the-job training is often required even for those who have completed a dental-assisting program or have some previous experience. Different dentists may have their own styles of doing things that need to be learned before an assistant can be comfortable working with them. Office-specific information, such as where files are kept, will need to be learned at each new job. Also, as dental technology changes, dental assistants need to stay familiar with the tools and procedures that they will be using or helping dentists to use. On-the-job training is often sufficient to keep assistants up to date on these matters.

Licensure

Most states regulate the duties that dental assistants are allowed to perform. Some states require licensure or registration to perform expanded functions or to perform radiological procedures within a dentist's office. Licensure may include attending an accredited dental-assisting program and passing a written or practical examination. There are a variety of schools offering courses—approximately 10 to 12 months in length—that meet their state's requirements. Other states require dental assistants to complete state-approved education courses of 4 to 12 hours in length. Some states offer the registration of other dental-assisting credentials with little or no education required. Some states require continuing education to maintain licensure or registration. A few states allow dental assistants to perform any function delegated to them by the dentist.

Individual states have adopted different standards for dental assistants who perform certain advanced duties. In some states, for example, dental assistants who perform radiological procedures must complete additional training. Completion of the Radiation Health and Safety examination offered by Dental Assisting National Board (DANB) meets the standards in more than 30 states. Some states require the completion of a state-approved course in radiology as well. Twelve states have no formal requirements to perform radiological procedures.

Certification and Other Qualifications

Certification is available through the DANB and is recognized or required in 37 states. Certification is an acknowledgment of an assistant's qualifications and professional competence and may be an asset when one is seeking employment. Candidates may qualify to take the DANB certification examination by graduating from an ADA-accredited dental assisting education program or by having 2 years of full-time, or 4 years of part-time, experience as a dental assistant. In addition, applicants must have current certification in cardiopulmonary resuscitation. For annual recertification, individuals must earn continuing education credits. Other organizations offer registration, most often at the state level. Dental assistants must be a second pair of hands for a dentist; therefore, dentists look for people who are reliable, work well with others, and have good manual dexterity.

Advancement

Without further education, advancement opportunities are limited. Some dental assistants become office managers, dental-assisting instructors, dental product sales representatives, or insurance claims processors for dental insurance companies. Others go back to school to become dental hygienists. For many, this entry-level occupation provides basic training and experience and serves as a stepping-stone to more highly skilled and higher paying jobs. Assistants wishing to take on expanded functions or perform radiological procedures may choose to complete coursework in those functions allowed under state regulation or, if required, obtain a state-issued license.

Employment Trends

Employment is expected to increase much faster than average; job prospects are expected to be excellent.

Employment Change

Employment is expected to grow 36% from 2008 to 2018, which is much faster than the average for all occupations. In fact, dental assistant is expected to be among the fastest growing occupations over the 2008–2018 projection period.

Population growth, greater retention of natural teeth by middle-aged and older people, and an increased focus on preventive dental care for younger generations will fuel demand for dental services. Older dentists, who have been less likely to employ assistants or have employed fewer, are leaving the occupation and will be replaced by recent graduates, who are more likely to use one or more assistants. In addition, as dentists' workloads increase, they are expected to hire more assistants to perform routine tasks, so that they may devote their own time to more complex procedures.

TABLE 8-4   Projections Data from the National Employment Matrix for Dental Assistants

Occupational Title	Employment, 2008	Projected Employment, 2018	Change, 2008–2019	
			Number	Percentage
Dental assistants	295,300	400,900	105,600	36

Job Prospects

Job prospects for dental assistants should be excellent, as dentists continue to need the aid of qualified dental assistants. There will be many opportunities for entry-level positions, which may offer on-the-job training, but some dentists prefer to hire experienced assistants, those who have completed a dental-assisting program, or those who have met state requirements to take on expanded functions within the office. In addition to job openings due to employment growth, numerous job openings will arise out of the need to replace assistants who transfer to other occupations, retire, or leave for other reasons. **Table 8-4** shows some projection data provided by the Department of Labor.

Earnings

Median annual wages of dental assistants were $32,380 in May 2008. The middle 50% earned between $26,980 and $38,960. The lowest 10% earned less than $22,270, and the highest 10% earned more than $46,150.

Benefits vary substantially by practice setting and may be contingent upon full-time employment. According to a 2008 survey by the Dental Assisting National Board, 86% of Certified Dental Assistants (CDAs) reported receiving paid vacation from their employers, and more than half of CDAs received health benefits.

Related Occupations

Other workers supporting health practitioners include dental hygienists, medical assistants, surgical technologists, pharmacy aides, pharmacy technicians, occupational therapist assistants and aides, and physical therapist assistants and aides.

Additional Information

Information about career opportunities and accredited dental assistant programs is available from

- Commission on Dental Accreditation, American Dental Association, 211 East Chicago Ave., Suite 1900, Chicago, IL 60611. Internet: http://www.ada.org/prof/ed/accred/commission/index.asp

For information on becoming a Certified Dental Assistant and a list of state boards of dentistry, contact

- Dental Assisting National Board, Inc., 444 N. Michigan Ave., Suite 900, Chicago, IL 60611. Internet: http://www.danb.org

For more information on a career as a dental assistant and general information about continuing education, contact

- American Dental Assistants Association, 35 East Wacker Dr., Suite 1730, Chicago, IL 60601. Internet: http://www.dentalassistant.org

chapter nine

Nursing*

*All information in this chapter, unless otherwise indicated, was obtained from Bureau of Labor Statistics. U.S. Department of Labor. *Occupational Outlook Handbook 2010–2011 Edition*. 2010.

REGISTERED NURSES

SIGNIFICANT POINTS

- Registered nurse (RN) constitutes the largest healthcare occupation, with 2.6 million jobs.
- About 60% of RN jobs are in hospitals.
- The three typical educational paths to registered nursing are a Bachelor degree, an Associate degree, and a diploma from an approved nursing program; advanced practice nurses—**clinical nurse specialists, nurse anesthetists, nurse-midwives,** and nurse practitioners—need a Master degree.
- Overall job opportunities are expected to be excellent, but may vary by employment and geographic setting; some employers report difficulty in attracting and retaining an adequate number of RNs.

Work Description

Registered nurses (RNs), regardless of specialty or work setting, treat patients, educate patients and the public about various medical conditions, and provide advice and emotional support to patients' family members. RNs record patients' medical histories and symptoms, help perform diagnostic tests and analyze results, operate medical machinery, administer treatment and medications, and help with patient follow-up and rehabilitation.

RNs teach patients and their families how to manage their illnesses or injuries, explaining posttreatment home care needs; diet, nutrition, and exercise programs; and self-administration of medication and physical therapy. Some RNs may work to promote general health by educating the public on warning signs and symptoms of disease. RNs also might run general health screening or immunization clinics, blood drives, and public seminars on various conditions.

When caring for patients, RNs establish a care plan or contribute to an existing plan. Plans may include numerous activities, such as administering medication, including careful checking of dosages and avoiding interactions; starting, maintaining, and discontinuing intravenous (IV) lines for fluid, medication, blood, and blood products; administering therapies and treatments; observing the patient and recording those observations; and consulting with physicians and other healthcare clinicians. Some RNs provide direction to licensed practical nurses and nursing aides regarding patient care. RNs with advanced educational preparation and training may perform diagnostic and therapeutic procedures and may have prescriptive authority.

Specific work responsibilities will vary from one RN to the next. RNs' duties and titles are often determined by their work setting or patient population served. RNs can specialize in one or more areas of patient care. There generally are four ways to specialize. RNs may work a particular setting or type of treatment, such as perioperative nurses, who work in operating rooms and assist surgeons. RNs may specialize in specific health conditions, as do diabetes management nurses, who assist patients to manage diabetes. Other RNs specialize in working with one or more organs or body system types, such as dermatology nurses, who work with patients who have skin disorders. RNs may also specialize with a well-defined population, such as geriatric nurses, who work with the elderly. Some RNs may combine specialties. For example, **pediatric oncology** nurses deal with children and adolescents who have cancer. The opportunities for specialization in registered nursing are extensive and are often determined on the job.

There are many options for RNs who specialize in a work setting or type of treatment. Ambulatory care nurses provide preventive care and treat patients with a variety of illnesses and injuries in physicians' offices or in clinics. Some ambulatory care nurses are involved in telehealth, providing care and advice through electronic communications media such as videoconferencing, the Internet, or by telephone. Critical care nurses provide care to patients with serious, complex, and acute illnesses or injuries that require very close monitoring and extensive medication protocols and therapies. Critical care nurses often work in critical or intensive care hospital units. Emergency, or trauma, nurses work in hospital or stand-alone emergency departments, providing initial assessments and care for patients with life-threatening conditions. Some emergency nurses may become qualified to serve as transport nurses, who provide medical care to patients who are transported by helicopter or airplane to the nearest medical facility. Holistic nurses provide care such as acupuncture, massage and aromatherapy, and biofeedback, which are meant to treat patients' mental and spiritual health in addition to their physical health. **Home healthcare nurses** provide at-home nursing care for patients, often as follow-up care after discharge from a hospital or from a rehabilitation, long-term care, or skilled nursing facility. Hospice and palliative care nurses provide care, most often in home or hospice settings, focused on maintaining quality of life for terminally ill patients. Infusion nurses administer medications, fluids, and blood to patients through injections into patients' veins. Long-term care nurses provide healthcare services on a recurring basis to patients with chronic physical or mental disorders, often in long-term care or skilled nursing facilities. Medical-surgical nurses provide health promotion and basic medical care to patients with various medical and surgical diagnoses. Occupational health nurses seek to prevent job-related injuries and illnesses, provide monitoring and emergency care services, and help employers implement health and safety standards. Peri-anesthesia nurses provide preoperative and postoperative care to patients undergoing anesthesia during surgery or other procedures. Perioperative nurses assist surgeons by selecting and handling instruments, controlling bleeding, and suturing incisions. Some of these nurses also can specialize in plastic and reconstructive surgery. Psychiatric–mental health nurses treat patients with personality and mood disorders. Radiology nurses provide care to patients undergoing diagnostic radiation procedures such as ultrasounds, **magnetic resonance imaging**, and radiation therapy for oncology diagnoses.

Rehabilitation nurses care for patients with temporary and permanent disabilities. Transplant nurses care for both transplant recipients and living donors, and monitor signs of organ rejection.

RNs specializing in a particular disease, ailment, or healthcare condition are employed in virtually all work settings, including physicians' offices, outpatient treatment facilities, home healthcare agencies, and hospitals. Addictions nurses care for patients seeking help with alcohol, drug, tobacco, and other addictions. Intellectual and developmental disabilities nurses provide care for patients with physical, mental, or behavioral disabilities; care may include help with feeding, controlling bodily functions, sitting or standing independently, and speaking or other communication. Diabetes management nurses help diabetics to manage their disease by teaching them proper nutrition and showing them how to test blood sugar levels and administer insulin injections. Genetics nurses provide early detection screenings, counseling, and treatment of patients with genetic disorders, including cystic fibrosis and Huntington's disease. HIV/AIDS nurses care for patients diagnosed with HIV and AIDS. Oncology nurses care for patients with various types of cancer and may assist in the administration of radiation and chemotherapies and follow-up monitoring. Wound, ostomy, and continence nurses treat patients with wounds caused by traumatic injury, ulcers, or arterial disease; provide postoperative care for patients with openings that allow for alternative methods of bodily waste elimination; and treat patients with urinary and fecal incontinence.

RNs specializing in the treatment of a particular organ or body system usually are employed in hospital specialty or critical care units, specialty clinics, and outpatient care facilities. Cardiovascular nurses treat patients with coronary heart disease and those who have had heart surgery, providing services such as postoperative rehabilitation. Dermatology nurses treat patients with disorders of the skin, such as skin cancer and psoriasis. Gastroenterology nurses treat patients with digestive and intestinal disorders, including ulcers, acid reflux disease, and abdominal bleeding. Some nurses in this field also assist in specialized procedures such as endoscopies, which look inside the gastrointestinal tract using a tube equipped with a light and a camera that can capture images of diseased tissue. Gynecology nurses provide care to women with disorders of the reproductive system, including endometriosis, cancer, and sexually transmitted diseases. Nephrology nurses care for patients with kidney disease caused by diabetes, hypertension, or substance abuse. Neuroscience nurses care for patients with dysfunctions of the nervous system, including brain and spinal cord injuries and seizures. Ophthalmic nurses provide care to patients with disorders of the eyes, including blindness and glaucoma, and to patients undergoing eye surgery. Orthopedic nurses care for patients with muscular and skeletal problems, including arthritis, bone fractures, and muscular dystrophy. **Otorhinolaryngology nurses** care for patients with ear, nose, and throat disorders, such as cleft palates, allergies, and sinus disorders. Respiratory nurses provide care to patients with respiratory disorders such as asthma, tuberculosis, and cystic fibrosis. Urology nurses care for patients with disorders of the kidneys, urinary tract, and male reproductive organs, including infections, kidney and bladder stones, and cancers.

RNs who specialize by population provide preventive and acute care in all healthcare settings to the segment of the population in which they specialize, including newborns (neonatology), children and adolescents (pediatrics), adults, and the elderly (gerontology or geriatrics). RNs also may provide basic health care to patients outside of healthcare settings in such venues as correctional facilities, schools, summer camps, and the military. Some RNs travel around the United States and throughout the world providing care to patients in areas with shortages of healthcare workers.

Most RNs work as staff nurses as members of a team providing critical health care. However, some RNs choose to become advanced practice nurses, who work independently or in collaboration with physicians, and may focus on the provision of primary care services. Clinical nurse specialists provide direct patient care and expert consultations in one of many nursing specialties, such as psychiatric–mental health. Nurse anesthetists provide anesthesia and related care before and after surgical, therapeutic, diagnostic, and obstetrical procedures. They also provide pain management and emergency services, such as airway management. Nurse-midwives provide primary care to women, including gynecological exams, family planning advice, prenatal care, assistance in labor and delivery, and neonatal care. **Nurse practitioners** serve as primary and specialty care providers, providing a blend of nursing and healthcare services to patients and families. The most common specialty areas for nurse practitioners are family practice, adult practice, women's health, pediatrics, acute care, and geriatrics. However, there are a variety of other specialties that nurse practitioners can choose, including neonatology and mental health. Advanced practice nurses can prescribe medications in all states and in the District of Columbia.

Some nurses have jobs that require little or no direct patient care, but still require an active RN license. Forensics nurses participate in the scientific investigation and treatment of abuse victims, violence, criminal activity, and traumatic accident. Infection control nurses identify, track, and control infectious outbreaks in healthcare facilities and develop programs for outbreak prevention and response to biological terrorism. Nurse educators plan, develop, implement, and evaluate educational programs and curricula for the professional development of student nurses and RNs. Nurse informaticists manage and communicate nursing data and information to improve decision making by consumers, patients, nurses, and other healthcare providers. RNs also may work as healthcare consultants, public policy advisors, pharmaceutical and medical supply researchers and salespersons, and medical writers and editors.

Work Environment

Most RNs work in well-lit, comfortable healthcare facilities. Home health and public health nurses travel to patients' homes, schools, community centers, and other sites. RNs may spend considerable time walking, bending, stretching, and standing. Patients in hospitals and **nursing care facilities** require 24-hour care; consequently, nurses in these institutions may work nights, weekends, and holidays. RNs also may be on call—available to work on short notice. Nurses who work in offices, schools, and other settings that do not provide 24-hour care are more likely to work regular business hours. About 20% of RNs worked part time in 2008.

RNs may be in close contact with individuals who have infectious diseases and with toxic, harmful, or potentially hazardous compounds, solutions, and medications. RNs must observe rigid, standardized guidelines to guard against disease and other dangers, such as those posed by radiation, accidental needle sticks, chemicals used to sterilize instruments, and anesthetics. In addition, they are vulnerable to back injury when moving patients.

Employment Opportunities

As the largest healthcare occupation, registered nurses held about 2.6 million jobs in 2008. Hospitals employed the majority of RNs, with 60% of such jobs. About 8% of jobs were in offices of physicians, 5% in home healthcare services, 5% in nursing care facilities, and 3% in employment services. The remainder worked mostly in government agencies, social assistance agencies, and educational services.

Educational and Legal Requirements

The three typical educational paths to registered nursing are a Bachelor degree, an Associate degree, and a diploma from an approved nursing program. Nurses most commonly enter the occupation by completing an Associate degree or Bachelor degree program. Individuals then must complete a national licensing examination in order to obtain a nursing license. Advanced practice nurses—clinical nurse specialists, nurse anesthetists, nurse-midwives, and nurse practitioners—need a Master degree.

Education and Training

There are three typical educational paths to registered nursing—a Bachelor of science degree in nursing **(BSN)**, an Associate degree in nursing **(ADN)**, and a diploma. BSN programs, offered by colleges and universities, take about 4 years to complete. ADN programs, offered by community and junior colleges, take about 2 to 3 years to complete. Diploma programs, administered in hospitals, last about 3 years. Generally, licensed graduates of any of the three types of educational programs qualify for entry-level positions as staff nurses. There are hundreds of registered nursing programs that result in an ADN or BSN; however, there are relatively few diploma programs.

Individuals considering a career in nursing should carefully weigh the advantages and disadvantages of enrolling in each type of education program. Advancement opportunities may be more limited for ADN and diploma holders compared to RNs who obtain a BSN or higher. Individuals who complete a Bachelor degree receive more training in areas such as communication, leadership, and critical thinking, all of which are becoming more important as nursing practice becomes more complex. Additionally, Bachelor degree programs offer more clinical experience in nonhospital settings. A Bachelor or higher degree is often necessary for administrative positions, research, consulting, and teaching.

Many RNs with an ADN or diploma later enter Bachelor degree programs to prepare for a broader scope of nursing practice. Often, they can find an entry-level position and then take advantage of tuition reimbursement benefits to work toward a BSN by completing an **RN-to-BSN** program. Accelerated Master degree in nursing **(MSN)** programs also are available. They typically take 3 to 4 years to complete full time and result in the award of both the BSN and MSN.

There are education programs available for people interested in switching to a career in nursing as well. Individuals who already hold a Bachelor degree in another field may enroll in an accelerated BSN program. Accelerated BSN programs last 12 to 18 months and provide the fastest route to a BSN for individuals who already hold a degree. MSN programs also are available for individuals who hold a Bachelor or higher degree in another field; Master degree programs usually last 2 years.

All nursing education programs include classroom instruction and supervised clinical experience in hospitals and other healthcare facilities. Students take courses in anatomy, physiology, microbiology, chemistry, nutrition, psychology and other behavioral sciences, and nursing. Coursework also includes the liberal arts for ADN and BSN students.

Supervised clinical experience is provided in hospital departments such as pediatrics, psychiatry, maternity, and surgery. A number of programs include clinical experience in nursing care facilities, public health departments, home health agencies, and ambulatory clinics.

Licensure and Certification

In all states, the District of Columbia, and U.S. territories, students must graduate from an approved nursing program and pass a national licensing examination, known as the National Council Licensure Examination, or **NCLEX**-RN, in order to obtain a nursing license. Other eligibility requirements for licensure vary by state. Contact your state's board of nursing for details.

Other Qualifications

Nurses should be caring, sympathetic, responsible, and detail oriented. They must be able to direct or supervise others, correctly assess patients' conditions, and determine when consultation is required. They need emotional stability to cope with human suffering, emergencies, and other stresses.

RNs should enjoy learning because some states and/or employers require continuing education credits at regular intervals. Career-long learning is a distinct reality for RNs.

Some nurses may become credentialed in specialties such as ambulatory care, gerontology, informatics, pediatrics, and many others. Credentialing for RNs is available from the American Nursing Credentialing Center, the National League for Nursing, and many others. Although credentialing is usually voluntary, it demonstrates adherence to a higher standard and some employers may require it.

Advancement

Most RNs begin as staff nurses in hospitals and, with experience and good performance, often move to other settings or are promoted to positions with more responsibility. In management, nurses can advance from assistant unit manager or head nurse to more senior-level administrative roles of assistant director, director, vice president, or chief of nursing. Increasingly, management-level nursing positions require a graduate or an advanced degree in nursing or health services administration. Administrative positions require leadership, communication and negotiation skills, and good judgment.

Some RNs choose to become advanced practice nurses, who work independently or in collaboration with physicians, and may focus on providing primary care services. There are four types of **advanced practice nurses (APNs)**: clinical nurse specialists, nurse anesthetists, nurse-midwives, and nurse practitioners. Clinical nurse specialists provide direct patient care and expert consultations in one of many nursing specialties, such as psychiatric–mental health. Nurse anesthetists provide anesthesia and related care before and after surgical, therapeutic, diagnostic, and obstetrical procedures. They also provide pain management and emergency services, such as airway management. Nurse-midwives provide primary care to women, including gynecological exams, family planning advice, prenatal care, assistance in labor and delivery, and neonatal care. Nurse practitioners serve as primary and specialty care providers, providing a blend of nursing and healthcare services to patients and families.

All four types of advanced practice nurses require at least a Master degree. In addition, all states specifically define requirements for registered nurses in advanced practice roles. Advanced practice nurses may prescribe medicine, but the authority to prescribe varies by state. Contact your state's board of nursing for specific regulations regarding advanced practice nurses.

Some nurses move into the business side of health care. Their nursing expertise and experience on a healthcare team equip them to manage ambulatory, acute, home-based, and chronic care businesses. Employers—including hospitals, insurance companies, pharmaceutical manufacturers, and managed care organizations, among others—need RNs for health planning and development, marketing, consulting, policy development, and quality assurance. Other nurses work as college and university faculty or conduct research.

Employment Trends

Overall job opportunities for registered nurses are expected to be excellent, but may vary by employment and geographic setting. Some employers report difficulty in attracting and retaining an adequate number of RNs. Employment of RNs is expected to grow much faster than average and, because the occupation is very large, 581,500 new jobs will result, among the largest number of new jobs for any occupation. Additionally, hundreds of thousands of job openings will result from the need to replace experienced nurses who leave the occupation.

Employment Change

Employment of registered nurses is expected to grow by 22% from 2008 to 2018, much faster than the average for all occupations. Growth will be driven by technological advances in patient care, which permit a greater number of health problems to be treated, and by an increasing emphasis on preventive care. In addition, the number of older people, who are much more likely than younger people to need nursing care, is projected to grow rapidly.

However, employment of RNs will not grow at the same rate in every industry. The projected growth rates for RNs in the industries with the highest employment of these workers are shown in **Table 9-1**. Employment is expected to grow more slowly in hospitals—health care's largest industry—than in most other healthcare industries. Although the intensity of nursing care is likely to increase, requiring more nurses per patient, the number of inpatients (those who remain in the hospital for more than 24 hours) is not likely to grow by much. Patients are being discharged earlier, and more procedures are being done on an outpatient basis, both inside and outside hospitals. Rapid growth is expected in hospital outpatient facilities, such as those providing same-day surgery, rehabilitation, and chemotherapy.

More and more sophisticated procedures, once performed only in hospitals, are being performed in physicians' offices and in outpatient care centers, such as freestanding ambulatory surgical and emergency centers. Accordingly, employment is expected to grow fast in these places as health care in general expands.

Employment in nursing care facilities is expected to grow because of increases in the number of older persons, many of whom require long-term care. Many elderly patients want to be treated at home or in residential care

TABLE 9-1 Projected Growth Rates of RNs in Industries

Industry	Percentage
Offices of physicians	48
Home healthcare services	33
Nursing care facilities	25
Employment services	24
Hospitals, public and private	17

facilities, which will drive demand for RNs in those settings. The financial pressure on hospitals to discharge patients as soon as possible should produce more admissions to nursing and residential care facilities and referrals to home health care. Job growth also is expected in units that provide specialized long-term rehabilitation for stroke and head injury patients, as well as units that treat Alzheimer's victims.

Employment in home health care is expected to increase in response to the growing number of older persons with functional disabilities, consumer preference for care in the home, and technological advances that make it possible to bring increasingly complex treatments into the home. The type of care demanded will require nurses who are able to perform complex procedures.

Job Prospects

Overall job opportunities are expected to be excellent for registered nurses. Employers in some parts of the country and in certain employment settings report difficulty in attracting and retaining an adequate number of RNs, primarily because of an aging RN workforce and a lack of younger workers to fill positions. Qualified applicants to nursing schools are being turned away because of a shortage of nursing faculty. The need for nursing faculty will only increase as many instructors near retirement. Despite the slower employment growth in hospitals, job opportunities should still be excellent because of the relatively high turnover of **hospital nurses**. To attract and retain qualified nurses, hospitals may offer signing bonuses, family-friendly work schedules, or subsidized training. Although faster employment growth is projected in physicians' offices and outpatient care centers, RNs may face greater competition for these positions because they generally offer regular working hours and more comfortable working environments. Generally, RNs with at least a Bachelor degree will have better job prospects than those without a Bachelor degree. In addition, all four advanced practice specialties—clinical nurse specialists, nurse practitioners, nurse-midwives, and nurse anesthetists—will be in high demand, particularly in medically underserved areas such as inner cities and rural areas. Relative to physicians, these RNs increasingly serve as lower-cost primary care providers. **Table 9-2** shows the projections data from the national employment matrix.

Earnings

Median annual wages of registered nurses were $62,450 in May 2008. The middle 50% earned between $51,640 and $76,570. The lowest 10% earned

TABLE 9-2   Projections Data from the National Employment Matrix for Registered Nurses

Occupational Title	Employment, 2008	Projected Employment, 2018	Change, 2008–2018	
			Number	Percentage
Registered nurses	2,618,700	3,200,200	581,500	22

TABLE 9-3 Median Annual Wages in the Industries Employing the Largest Numbers of Registered Nurses in May 2008

Employment services	$68,160
General medical and surgical hospitals	63,880
Offices of physicians	59,210
Home healthcare services	58,740
Nursing care facilities	57,060

less than $43,410, and the highest 10% earned more than $92,240. Median annual wages in the industries employing the largest numbers of registered nurses in May 2008 are shown in **Table 9-3**.

Many employers offer flexible work schedules, child care, educational benefits, and bonuses. About 21% of registered nurses are union members or covered by a union contract.

Related Occupations

Because of the number of specialties for registered nurses, and the variety of responsibilities and duties, many other healthcare occupations are similar in some aspects of their job. Some healthcare occupations with similar levels of responsibility that work under the direction of physicians or dentists are dental hygienists, diagnostic medical sonographers, emergency medical technicians and paramedics, licensed practical and licensed vocational nurses, and physician assistants.

Additional Information

For information on a career as a registered nurse and nursing education, contact

- National League for Nursing, 61 Broadway, 33rd Floor, New York, NY 10006. Internet: http://www.nln.org/

For information on baccalaureate and graduate nursing education, nursing career options, and financial aid, contact

- American Association of Colleges of Nursing, 1 Dupont Cir. NW, Suite 530, Washington, DC 20036. Internet: http://www.aacn.nche.edu/

For additional information on registered nurses, including credentialing, contact

- American Nurses Association, 8515 Georgia Ave., Suite 400, Silver Spring, MD 20910. Internet: http://nursingworld.org/

For information on the National Council Licensure Examination (NCLEX-RN) and a list of individual state boards of nursing, contact

- National Council of State Boards of Nursing, 111 E. Wacker Dr., Suite 2900, Chicago, IL 60601. Internet: http://www.ncsbn.org/

  For a list of accredited clinical nurse specialist programs, contact

- National Association of Clinical Nurse Specialists, 2090 Linglestown Rd., Suite 107, Harrisburg, PA 17110. Internet: http://www.nacns.org/

  For information on nurse anesthetists, including a list of accredited programs, contact

- American Association of Nurse Anesthetists, 222 S. Prospect Ave., Park Ridge, IL 60068. Internet: http://www.aana.com/

  For information on nurse-midwives, including a list of accredited programs, contact

- American College of Nurse-Midwives, 8403 Colesville Rd., Suite 1550, Silver Spring, MD 20910. Internet: http://www.midwife.org/

  For information on nurse practitioners, including a list of accredited programs, contact

- American Academy of Nurse Practitioners, P.O. Box 12846, Austin, TX 78711. Internet: http://www.aanp.org/

  For additional information on registered nurses in all fields and specialties, contact

- American Society of Registered Nurses, 1001 Bridgeway, Suite 233, Sausalito, CA 94965. Internet: http://www.asrn.org/

LICENSED PRACTICAL AND LICENSED VOCATIONAL NURSES
SIGNIFICANT POINTS

- Most training programs last about 1 year and are offered by vocational or technical schools, or community or junior colleges.
- Overall job prospects are expected to be very good, but job outlook varies by industry.
- Replacement needs will be a major source of job openings, as many workers leave the occupation permanently.

Work Description

Licensed practical nurses (LPNs), or **licensed vocational nurses (LVNs)**, care for people who are sick, injured, convalescent, or disabled under the direction of physicians and registered nurses. The nature of the direction and supervision required varies by state and job setting.

LPNs care for patients in many ways. Often, they provide basic bedside care. Many LPNs measure and record patients' vital signs such as height, weight, temperature, blood pressure, pulse, and respiration. They also prepare and give injections and enemas, monitor catheters, dress wounds, and give alcohol rubs and massages. To help keep patients comfortable, they assist with bathing, dressing, and personal hygiene, moving in bed, standing, and walking. They might also feed patients who need help eating. Experienced LPNs may supervise nursing assistants and aides.

As part of their work, LPNs collect samples for testing, perform routine laboratory tests, and record food and fluid intake and output. They clean and monitor medical equipment. Sometimes, they help physicians and registered nurses perform tests and procedures. Some LPNs help to deliver, care for, and feed infants.

LPNs also monitor their patients and report adverse reactions to medications or treatments. LPNs gather information from patients, including their health history and how they are currently feeling. They may use this information to complete insurance forms, preauthorizations, and referrals, and they share information with registered nurses and doctors to help determine the best course of care for a patient. LPNs often teach family members how to care for a relative or teach patients about good health habits.

Most LPNs are generalists and will work in any area of health care. However, some work in a specialized setting, such as a nursing home, a doctor's office, or in home health care. LPNs in nursing care facilities help to evaluate residents' needs, develop care plans, and supervise the care provided by nursing aides. In doctors' offices and clinics, they may be responsible for making appointments, keeping records, and performing other clerical duties. LPNs who work in home health care may prepare meals and teach family members simple nursing tasks. In some states, LPNs are permitted to administer prescribed medicines, start intravenous fluids, and provide care to ventilator-dependent patients.

Work Environment

Most licensed practical nurses work a 40-hour week. In some work settings where patients need around-the-clock care, LPNs may have to work nights, weekends, and holidays. About 18% of LPNs and LVNs worked part time in 2008. They often stand for long periods and help patients move in bed, stand, or walk.

LPNs may face hazards from caustic chemicals, radiation, and infectious diseases. They are subject to back injuries when moving patients. They often must deal with the stress of heavy workloads. In addition, the patients they care for may be confused, agitated, or uncooperative.

Employment Opportunities

Licensed practical and licensed vocational nurses held about 753,600 jobs in 2008. About 25% of LPNs worked in hospitals, 28% in nursing care facilities, and another 12% in offices of physicians. Others worked for home healthcare services; employment services; residential care facilities; community care facilities for the elderly; outpatient care centers; and federal, state, and local government agencies.

Educational and Legal Requirements

Most practical nursing training programs last about 1 year and are offered by vocational and technical schools, or community or junior colleges. LPNs must be licensed to practice.

Education and Training

LPNs must complete a state-approved training program in practical nursing to be eligible for licensure. Contact your state's board of nursing for a list of approved programs. Most training programs are available from technical and vocational schools, or community and junior colleges. Other programs are available through high schools, hospitals, and colleges and universities. A high school diploma or its equivalent usually is required for entry, although some programs accept candidates without a diploma, and some programs are part of a high school curriculum.

Most year-long practical nursing programs include both classroom study and supervised clinical practice (patient care). Classroom study covers basic nursing concepts and subjects related to patient care, including anatomy, physiology, medical-surgical nursing, pediatrics, obstetrics nursing, pharmacology, nutrition, and first aid. Clinical practice usually is in a hospital but sometimes includes other settings.

Licensure

The National Council Licensure Examination, or NCLEX-PN, is required in order to obtain licensure as an LPN. The exam is developed and administered by the National Council of State Boards of Nursing. The NCLEX-PN is a computer-based exam and varies in length. The exam covers four major client needs categories: safe and effective care environment, health promotion and maintenance, psychosocial integrity, and physiological integrity. Eligibility for licensure may vary by state; for details, contact your state's board of nursing.

Other Qualifications

LPNs should have a caring, sympathetic nature. They should be emotionally stable because working with the sick and injured can be stressful. They also need to be observant and have good decision-making and communication skills. As part of a healthcare team, they must be able to follow orders and work under close supervision.

LPNs should enjoy learning because some states and/or employers require continuing education credits at regular intervals. Career-long learning is a distinct reality for LPNs.

Advancement

In some employment settings, such as nursing homes, LPNs can advance to become charge nurses who oversee the work of other LPNs and nursing aides.

LPNs may become credentialed in specialties like IV therapy, gerontology, long-term care, and pharmacology. Some LPNs also choose to become registered nurses through LPN-to-RN training programs.

Employment Trends

Employment of LPNs is projected to grow much faster than average. Overall job prospects are expected to be very good, but job outlook varies by industry. The best job opportunities will occur in nursing care facilities and home healthcare services.

Employment Change

Employment of LPNs is expected to grow by 21% between 2008 and 2018, much faster than the average for all occupations, in response to the long-term care needs of an increasing elderly population and the general increase in demand for healthcare services.

Demand for LPNs will be driven by the increase in the share of the older population. Older persons have an increased incidence of injury and illness, which will increase their demand for healthcare services. In addition, with better medical technology, people are living longer, increasing the demand for long-term health care. Job growth will occur over all healthcare settings, but especially those that service the geriatric population like nursing care facilities, community care facilities, and home healthcare services.

In order to contain healthcare costs, many procedures once performed only in hospitals are being performed in physicians' offices and in outpatient care centers, largely because of advances in technology. As a result, the number of LPNs should increase faster in these facilities than in hospitals. Nevertheless, hospitals will continue to demand the services of LPNs and will remain one of the largest employers of these workers.

Job Prospects

In addition to projected job growth, job openings will result from replacement needs, as many workers leave the occupation permanently. Very good

TABLE 9-4 Projections Data from the National Employment Matrix for Licensed Practical and Licensed Vocational Nurses

Occupational Title	Employment, 2008	Projected Employment, 2018	Change, 2008–2018	
			Number	Percentage
Licensed practical and licensed vocational nurses	753,600	909,200	155,600	21

job opportunities are expected. Rapid employment growth is projected in most healthcare industries, with the best job opportunities occurring in nursing care facilities and in home healthcare services. There is a perceived inadequacy of available health care in many rural areas, so LPNs willing to locate in rural areas should have good job prospects. Projections data from the National Employment Matrix are shown in **Table 9-4**.

Earnings

Median annual wages of licensed practical and licensed vocational nurses were $39,030 in May 2008. The middle 50% earned between $33,360 and $46,710. The lowest 10% earned less than $28,260, and the highest 10% earned more than $53,580. Median annual wages in the industries employing the largest numbers of licensed practical and licensed vocational nurses in May 2008 are shown in **Table 9-5**.

Related Occupations

LPNs work closely with people while helping them. Other healthcare occupations that work closely with patients include athletic trainers, emergency medical technicians and paramedics, home health aides and personal and home care aides, medical assistants, nursing and psychiatric aides, and registered nurses.

TABLE 9-5 Median Annual Wages in the Industries Employing the Largest Numbers of Licensed Practical and Licensed Vocational Nurses in May 2008

Employment services	$44,690
Nursing care facilities	40,580
Home healthcare services	39,510
General medical and surgical hospitals	38,080
Offices of physicians	35,020

Additional Information

For information about practical nursing and specialty credentialing, contact the following organizations:

- National Association for Practical Nurse Education and Service, Inc., 1940 Duke St., Suite 200, Alexandria, VA 22314. Internet: http://www. napnes.org
- National Federation of Licensed Practical Nurses, Inc., 605 Poole Dr., Garner, NC 27529. Internet: http://www.nflpn.org
- National League for Nursing, 61 Broadway, 33rd Floor, New York, NY 10006. Internet: http://www.nln.org

Information on the NCLEX-PN licensing exam is available from

- National Council of State Boards of Nursing, 111 East Wacker Dr., Suite 2900, Chicago, IL 60601. Internet: http://www.ncsbn.org

chapter ten

Pharmacy*

---

*All information in this chapter, unless otherwise indicated, was obtained from Bureau of Labor Statistics. U.S. Department of Labor. *Occupational Outlook Handbook 2010–2011 Edition.* 2010.

PHARMACEUTICAL PARTNERS

One of the main tools of physicians treating patients is medication. Although doctors prescribe **pharmaceuticals**, the professionals who actually dispense the medication are pharmacists. The details of the pharmacist's profession follow in the rest of this chapter.

PHARMACISTS

SIGNIFICANT POINTS

- Excellent job opportunities are expected.
- Earnings are relatively high, but some pharmacists are required to work nights, weekends, and holidays.
- Pharmacists are becoming more involved in counseling patients and planning drug therapy programs.
- Pharmacists must graduate from an accredited college of pharmacy and pass a series of examinations to be licensed.

Work Description

Pharmacists advise health professionals and the public on the proper selection and use of medicines. The special knowledge of the pharmacist is needed because of the complexity and potential **side effects** of the large and growing number of pharmaceutical products on the market.

In addition to providing information, pharmacists dispense drugs and medicines prescribed by physicians, dentists, and other health professionals. Pharmacists must understand the use, composition, and effects of drugs and how they are tested for purity and strength. **Compounding**—the actual mixing of ingredients to form powders, tablets, capsules, ointments, and solutions—is now only a small part of a pharmacist's practice, as most medicines are produced by pharmaceutical companies in the dosage and form used by the patient.

Pharmacists practicing in community or retail pharmacies may have other duties. Pharmacists in community or retail pharmacies counsel patients as well as answer questions about prescription drugs, such as those regarding possible adverse reactions or interactions. They provide information about over-the-counter drugs and make recommendations after asking a series of health questions, such as whether the customer is taking any other medications. Such pharmacists also give advice about durable medical equipment and home healthcare supplies. Those who own or manage community pharmacies may sell non-health-related merchandise, hire and supervise personnel, and oversee the general operation of the pharmacy. Some community pharmacists provide specialized services to help patients manage conditions such as diabetes, asthma, smoking cessation, or high blood pressure.

The widespread use of computers in retail stores allows pharmacists to create medication profiles for their customers. A **medication profile** is a computerized record of the customer's drug therapy. Pharmacists use these profiles to ensure that harmful drug interactions do not occur and to monitor a patient's compliance with the doctor's instructions—by comparing how long it takes the patient to finish the drug against the recommended daily dosage.

Pharmacists in hospitals and clinics dispense medications and advise the medical staff on the selection and side effects of drugs. They may make sterile solutions, buy medical supplies, teach students majoring in health-related disciplines, and perform administrative duties. They also may be involved in patient education, monitoring of drug regimens, and drug use evaluation. In addition, pharmacists work as consultants to the medical team on drug therapy and patient care. In some hospitals they make hospital rounds with physicians, talking to patients and monitoring pharmaceutical use. Their role is crucial to safe, efficient, and proper therapeutic care.

Pharmacists who work in home health care monitor drug therapy and prepare *infusions*—solutions that are injected into patients—and other medications for use in the home.

Pharmacotherapists specialize in drug therapy and work closely with physicians. They may make hospital rounds with physicians, talking to patients and monitoring pharmaceutical use.

Nutrition support pharmacists help determine and prepare the drugs needed for nutrition. Some pharmacists work in oncology (cancer) and psychiatric drug treatment.

Some pharmacists prepare and dispense *radioactive pharmaceuticals.* Called **radiopharmacists** or **nuclear pharmacists**, they apply the principles and practices of pharmacy and radiochemistry to produce radioactive drugs that are used for diagnosis and therapy.

Pharmacists use their basic educational backgrounds in a host of federal and state positions. At the federal level, pharmacists hold staff and supervisory posts in the U.S. Public Health Service, the Veterans Administration, the Food and Drug Administration, and in all branches of the armed services. Certain of these posts provide commissioned officer status; others come under the heading of civil service.

State and federal boards are boards charged with regulating the practice of pharmacy to preserve and protect public health. These legal boards governing pharmacy practice usually employ pharmacists as full-time executive officers. One or more inspectors, frequently also pharmacists, serve each state. As state health agencies consolidate their purchases, pharmacists are often engaged as purchasers of medical and pharmaceutical supplies on a mass scale.

Nearly every state has an active pharmaceutical association that employs a full-time executive officer. This officer is usually a graduate of a college of pharmacy. Several national professional associations are also guided by pharmacists with an interest and special talent in organizational work.

Other pharmacists are engaged in highly specialized tasks. There are pharmacists in advertising, packaging, technical writing, magazine editing, and science reporting. Pharmacists with legal training serve as patent law-yers or as experts in pharmaceutical law. Pharmacists are found in U.S. space laboratories, aboard ships such as the S.S. Hope, and directing giant manufacturing firms.

Work Environment

Pharmacists usually work in clean, well-lighted, and well-ventilated areas that resemble small laboratories. Shelves are lined with hundreds of differ-ent drug products. In addition, some items are refrigerated, and many sub-stances (narcotics, depressants, and stimulants) are kept under lock and key. Pharmacists spend much time on their feet. When working with dangerous pharmaceutical products, pharmacists must take the proper safety precau-tions, such as wearing gloves and masks and working with special protec-tive equipment. Because pharmacies in many communities and hospitals are open around the clock, pharmacists in those settings may have to work eve-nings, nights, weekends, and holidays.

Most full-time salaried pharmacists work approximately 40 hours a week, and about 12% worked more than 50 hours per week in 2008. Many community and hospital pharmacies are open for extended hours, so phar-macists may be required to work nights, weekends, and holidays. *Consul-tant pharmacists* may travel to nursing homes or other facilities to monitor patients' drug therapy. About 19% of pharmacists worked part time in 2008.

Employment Opportunities

Pharmacists held about 269,900 jobs in 2008. About 65% worked in retail settings, which include community pharmacies that were either indepen-dently owned or part of a drugstore chain, grocery store, department store, or mass merchandiser. Most of these community pharmacists were salaried employees, but some were self-employed owners. About 22% of pharmacists worked in hospitals. A small proportion worked in mail order and Internet pharmacies, pharmaceutical wholesalers, offices of physicians, and the fed-eral government.

Educational and Legal Requirements

A license is required in all states, the District of Columbia, and all U.S. territo-ries. In order to obtain a license, pharmacists must earn a Doctor of Pharmacy (PharmD) degree from a college of pharmacy and pass several examinations.

Education and Training

Pharmacists must earn a PharmD degree from an accredited college or school of pharmacy. The PharmD degree has replaced the Bachelor of Pharmacy degree, which is no longer being awarded. To be admitted to a PharmD program, an applicant must have completed at least 2 years of specific professional study. This requirement generally includes courses in mathematics and natural sciences, such as chemistry, biology, and physics, as well as courses in the humanities and social sciences. In addition, most applicants have completed 3 or more years at a college or university before moving on to a PharmD program, although this is not specifically required. Most PharmD programs require applicants to take the Pharmacy College Admissions Test (PCAT). PharmD programs generally take 4 years to complete.

Courses offered at colleges of pharmacy are designed to teach students about all aspects of drug therapy. In addition, students learn how to communicate with patients and other healthcare providers about drug information and patient care. Students also learn professional ethics, concepts of public health, and medication distribution systems management. In addition to receiving classroom instruction, students in PharmD programs spend about one-fourth of their time in a variety of pharmacy practice settings under the supervision of licensed pharmacists.

Some colleges of pharmacy also award the Master of Science degree or the PhD degree. Both degrees are awarded after the completion of a PharmD and are designed for those who want additional clinical, laboratory, and research experience. Areas of graduate study include *pharmaceutics* and **pharmaceutical chemistry** (physical and chemical properties of drugs and dosage forms), *pharmacology* (effects of drugs on the body), and *pharmacy administration*. Many Master and PhD degree holders go on to do research for a drug company or teach at a university.

Other options for pharmacy graduates who are interested in further training include 1 or 2-year residency programs or fellowships. Pharmacy residencies are postgraduate training programs in pharmacy practice and usually require the completion of a research project. These programs are often mandatory for pharmacists who wish to work in hospitals. Pharmacy fellowships are highly individualized programs designed to prepare participants to work in a specialized area of pharmacy, such as clinical practice or research laboratories. Some pharmacists who own their own pharmacy obtain a Master degree in business administration (MBA). Others may obtain a degree in public administration or public health.

Licensure

A license to practice pharmacy is required in all states, the District of Columbia, and all U.S. territories. To obtain a license, a prospective pharmacist must graduate from a college of pharmacy that is accredited by the ACPE and pass a series of examinations. All states, U.S. territories, and the District of Columbia require the North American Pharmacist Licensure Exam (NAPLEX), which tests pharmacy skills and knowledge. Forty-four states and the District of Columbia also require the Multistate Pharmacy Jurisprudence Exam (MPJE), which tests pharmacy law. Both exams are administered by the National Association of Boards of Pharmacy **(NABP)**. Of the eight states and territories that do not require the **MPJE**, each has its own pharmacy law exam. In addition to the NAPLEX and MPJE, some states and territories require additional exams that are unique to their jurisdiction.

All jurisdictions except California currently grant license transfers to qualified pharmacists who already are licensed by another jurisdiction. Many pharmacists are licensed to practice in more than one jurisdiction. Most jurisdictions require continuing education for license renewal. Persons interested in a career as a pharmacist should check with individual jurisdiction boards of pharmacy for details on license renewal requirements and license transfer procedures.

Graduates of foreign pharmacy schools may also qualify for licensure in some U.S. states and territories. These individuals must apply for certification from the Foreign Pharmacy Graduate Examination Committee (FPGEC). Once certified, they must pass the Foreign Pharmacy Graduate Equivalency Examination (FPGEE), Test of English as a Foreign Language (TOEFL) exam, and Test of Spoken English (TSE) exam. They then must pass all of the exams required by the licensing jurisdiction, such as the NAPLEX and MPJE. Applicants who graduated from programs accredited by the Canadian Council for Accreditation of Pharmacy Programs (CCAPP) between 1993 and 2004 are exempt from FPGEC certification and examination requirements.

Other Qualifications

Prospective pharmacists should possess scientific aptitude, good interpersonal skills, and a desire to help others. They also must be conscientious and pay close attention to detail, because the decisions they make affect human lives.

Advancement

In community pharmacies, pharmacists usually begin at the staff level. Pharmacists in chain drugstores may be promoted to pharmacy supervisor or manager at the store level, then to manager at the district or regional level, and later to an executive position within the chain's headquarters. Hospital pharmacists may advance to supervisory or administrative positions. After they gain experience and secure the necessary capital, some pharmacists become owners or part owners of independent pharmacies. Pharmacists in the pharmaceutical industry may advance into marketing, sales, research, quality control, production, or other areas.

Employment Trends

Employment is expected to increase much faster than the average through 2018. As a result of job growth, the replacement of workers leaving the occupation, and the limited capacity of training programs, job prospects should be excellent.

Employment Change

Employment of pharmacists is expected to grow by 17% between 2008 and 2018, which is much faster than the average for all occupations. The increasing numbers of middle-aged and elderly people—who use more prescription drugs than younger people—will continue to spur demand for pharmacists throughout the projection period. Other factors likely to increase the demand for pharmacists include scientific advances that will make more pharmaceutical products available and increasing coverage of prescription drugs by health insurance plans and Medicare.

As the use of prescription drugs increases, demand for pharmacists will grow in most practice settings, such as community pharmacies, hospital pharmacies, and mail-order pharmacies. As the population ages, assisted living facilities and home care organizations should see particularly rapid growth. Demand will also increase as cost-conscious insurers, in an attempt to improve preventive care, use pharmacists in areas such as patient education and the administration of vaccines.

Demand is also increasing in managed care organizations where pharmacists analyze trends and patterns in medication use, and in *pharmacoeconomics*—the cost and benefit analysis of different drug therapies. New jobs also are being created in disease management—the development of new methods for curing and controlling diseases—and in sales and marketing. Rapid growth is also expected in *pharmacy informatics*—the use of information technology to improve patient care.

Job Prospects

Excellent opportunities are expected for pharmacists over the 2008 to 2018 period. Employers in many parts of the country report difficulty in attracting and retaining adequate numbers of pharmacists—primarily the result of the limited training capacity of PharmD programs. In addition, as a larger percentage of pharmacists elect to work part time, more individuals will be needed to fill the same number of prescriptions. Job openings will also result from faster-than-average employment growth and from the need to replace workers who retire or leave the occupation for other reasons. **Table 10-1** shows some projection data provided by the Department of Labor.

TABLE 10-1 Projections Data from the National Employment Matrix for Pharmacists

Occupational Title	Employment, 2008	Projected Employment, 2018	Change, 2008–2018	
			Number	Percentage
Pharmacists	243,000	296,000	53,000	22

Earnings

The median annual wage and salary of pharmacists in May 2008 was $106,410. The middle 50% earned between $92,670 and $121,310 a year. The lowest 10% earned less than $77,390, and the highest 10% earned more than $131,440 a year.

Related Occupations

Pharmacy technicians and **pharmacy aides** also work in pharmacies. Persons in other professions who may work with pharmaceutical compounds include biological scientists, medical scientists, chemists, and materials scientists. Increasingly, pharmacists are involved in patient care and therapy, work that they have in common with physicians and surgeons.

Additional Information

For information on pharmacy as a career, preprofessional and professional requirements, programs offered by colleges of pharmacy, and student financial aid, contact

- American Association of Colleges of Pharmacy, 1727 King St., Alexandria, VA 22314. Internet: http://www.aacp.org

General information on careers in pharmacy is available from

- American Society of Health-System Pharmacists, 7272 Wisconsin Ave., Bethesda, MD 20814. Internet: http://www.ashp.org
- National Association of Chain Drug Stores, 413 N. Lee St., Alexandria, VA 22313. Internet: http://www.nacds.org
- Academy of Managed Care Pharmacy, 100 North Pitt St., Suite 400, Alexandria, VA 22314. Internet: http://www.amcp.org
- American Pharmacists Association, Constitution Ave. NW, Washington, DC 20037. Internet: http://www.pharmacist.com

Information on the North American Pharmacist Licensure Exam (NAPLEX) and the Multistate Pharmacy Jurisprudence Exam (MPJE) is available from

- National Association of Boards of Pharmacy, 1600 Feehanville Dr., Mount Prospect, IL 60056. http://www.nabp.net

State licensure requirements are available from each state's board of pharmacy. Information on specific college entrance requirements, curricula, and financial aid is available from any college of pharmacy.

PHARMACY TECHNICIANS AND AIDES
SIGNIFICANT POINTS

- Job opportunities are expected to be good, especially for those with certification or previous work experience.
- Many technicians and aides work evenings, weekends, and holidays.
- About 75% of jobs were in a retail setting.

Work Description

Pharmacy technicians and aides help licensed pharmacists prepare prescription medications, provide customer service, and perform administrative duties within a pharmacy setting. *Pharmacy technicians* generally are responsible for receiving prescription requests, counting tablets, and labeling bottles, while *pharmacy aides* perform administrative functions such as answering phones, stocking shelves, and operating cash registers. In organizations that do not have aides, however, pharmacy technicians may be responsible for these clerical duties.

Pharmacy technicians who work in retail or mail-order pharmacies have various responsibilities, depending on state rules and regulations. Technicians receive written prescription requests from patients. They also may receive prescriptions sent electronically from doctors' offices, and in some states they are permitted to process requests by phone. They must verify that the information on the prescription is complete and accurate. To prepare the prescription, technicians retrieve, count, pour, weigh, measure, and sometimes mix the medication. Then they prepare the prescription labels, select the type of container, and affix the prescription and auxiliary labels to the container. Once the prescription is filled, technicians price and file the prescription, which must be checked by a pharmacist before it is given to the patient. Technicians may establish and maintain patient profiles, as well as prepare insurance claim forms. Technicians always refer any questions regarding prescriptions, drug information, or health matters to a pharmacist.

In hospitals, nursing homes, and assisted-living facilities, technicians have added responsibilities, including preparing sterile solutions and delivering medications to nurses or physicians. Technicians may also record the information about the prescribed medication onto the patient's profile.

Pharmacy aides work closely with pharmacy technicians. They primarily perform administrative duties such as answering telephones, stocking shelves, and operating cash registers. They also may prepare insurance forms and maintain patient profiles. Unlike pharmacy technicians, pharmacy aides do not prepare prescriptions or mix medications.

Work Environment

Pharmacy technicians and aides work in clean, organized, well-lighted, and well-ventilated areas. Most of their workday is spent on their feet. They may be required to lift heavy boxes or to use stepladders to retrieve supplies from high shelves.

Technicians and aides often have varying schedules that include nights, weekends, and holidays. In facilities that are open 24 hours a day, such as hospital pharmacies, technicians and aides may be required to work nights. Many technicians and aides work part time.

Employment Opportunities

Pharmacy technicians and aides held about 381,200 jobs in 2008. Of these, about 326,300 were pharmacy technicians and about 54,900 were pharmacy aides. About 75% of jobs were in a retail setting, and about 16% were in hospitals.

Educational and Legal Requirements

There is no national training standard for pharmacy technicians, but employers favor applicants who have formal training, certification, or previous experience. There also are no formal training requirements for pharmacy aides, but a high school diploma may increase an applicant's prospects for employment.

Education and Training

There are no standard training requirements for pharmacy technicians, but some states require a high school diploma or its equivalent. Although most pharmacy technicians receive informal on-the-job training, employers favor those who have completed formal training and certification. On-the-job training generally ranges between 3 and 12 months.

Formal technician education programs are available through a variety of organizations, including community colleges, vocational schools, hospitals, and the military. These programs range from 6 months to 2 years and include classroom and laboratory work. They cover a variety of subject areas, such as medical and pharmaceutical terminology, pharmaceutical calculations, pharmacy record keeping, pharmaceutical techniques, and pharmacy law and ethics. Technicians also are required to learn the names, actions, uses, and doses of the medications with which they work. Many training programs include **internships**, in which students gain hands-on experience in actual pharmacies. After completion, students receive a diploma, a certificate, or an Associate degree, depending on the program.

There are no formal education requirements for pharmacy aides, but employers may favor applicants with a high school diploma or its equivalent. Experience operating a cash register, interacting with customers, managing inventory, and using computers may be helpful. Pharmacy aides also receive informal on-the-job training that generally lasts less than 3 months.

Certification and Other Qualifications

In most states, pharmacy technicians must be registered with the state board of pharmacy. Eligibility requirements vary, but in some states applicants must possess a high school diploma or its equivalent and pay an application fee.

Most states do not require technicians to be certified, but voluntary certification is available through several private organizations. The Pharmacy Technician Certification Board (PTCB) and the Institute for the Certification of Pharmacy Technicians (ICPT) administer national certification examinations. Certification through such programs may enhance an applicant's prospects for employment and is required by some states and employers. To be eligible for either exam, candidates must have a high school diploma or its equivalent and no felony convictions of any kind. In addition, applicants for the PTCB exam must not have had any drug-related or pharmacy-related convictions, including misdemeanors. Many employers will reimburse the cost of the exams.

Under these programs, technicians must be recertified every 2 years. Recertification requires 20 hours of continuing education within the 2-year certification period. Continuing education hours can be earned from several different sources, including colleges, pharmacy associations, and pharmacy technician training programs. Up to 10 hours of continuing education also can be earned on the job under the direct supervision and instruction of a pharmacist.

Good customer service and communication skills are needed because pharmacy technicians and aides interact with patients, coworkers, and healthcare professionals. Basic mathematics, spelling, and reading skills also are important, as technicians must interpret prescription orders and verify drug doses. Technicians also must be precise: details are sometimes a matter of life and death.

Advancement

Advancement opportunities generally are limited, but in large pharmacies and health systems, pharmacy technicians and aides with significant training or experience can be promoted to supervisory positions. Some may advance into specialty positions such as chemotherapy technician or nuclear pharmacy technician. Others may move into sales. With a substantial amount of formal training, some technicians and aides go on to become pharmacists.

Employment Trends

Employment is expected to increase much faster than average, and job opportunities are expected to be good.

Employment Change

Employment of pharmacy technicians and aides is expected to increase by 25% from 2008 to 2018, which is much faster than the average for all occupations. The increased number of middle-aged and elderly people—who use more prescription drugs than younger people—will spur demand for pharmacy workers throughout the projection period. In addition, as scientific advances lead to new drugs, and as more people obtain prescription drug coverage, pharmacy workers will be needed in growing numbers.

Employment of pharmacy technicians is expected to increase by 31%. As cost-conscious insurers begin to use pharmacies as patient-care centers and pharmacists become more involved in patient care, pharmacy technicians will continue to see an expansion of their role in the pharmacy. In addition, they will increasingly adopt some of the administrative duties that were previously performed by pharmacy aides, such as answering phones and stocking shelves. As a result of this development, demand for pharmacy aides should decrease, and employment is expected to decline moderately, decreasing by 6% over the projection period.

Job Prospects

Job opportunities for pharmacy technicians are expected to be good, especially for those with previous experience, formal training, or certification. Job openings will result from employment growth as well as the need to replace workers who transfer to other occupations or leave the labor force.

Despite declining employment, job prospects for pharmacy aides also are expected to be good. As people leave this occupation, new applicants will be needed to fill the positions that remain (see **Table 10-2**).

Earnings

Median hourly wages of wage and salary pharmacy technicians in May 2008 were $13.32. The middle 50% earned between $10.95 and $15.88. The lowest 10% earned less than $9.27, and the highest 10% earned more than $18.98.

TABLE 10-2 Projected Employment Data from the National Employment Matrix for Pharmacy Technicians and Aides

Occupational Title	Projected Employment, 2018	Change, 2008–2018	
		Number	Percentage
Pharmacy technicians and aides	477,500	96,300	25
Pharmacy technicians	426,000	99,800	31
Pharmacy aides	51,500	−3500	−6

Median hourly wages of wage and salary pharmacy aides were $9.66 in May 2008. The middle 50% earned between $8.47 and $11.62. The lowest 10% earned less than $7.69, and the highest 10% earned more than $14.26.

Certified technicians may earn more than noncertified technicians. Some technicians and aides belong to unions representing hospital or grocery store workers.

Related Occupations

Other occupations related to health care include dental assistants, medical assistants, medical records and health information technicians, medical transcriptionists, and pharmacists.

Additional Information

For information on pharmacy technician certification programs, contact

- Pharmacy Technician Certification Board, 2215 Constitution Ave. NW, Washington DC 20037-2985. Internet: http://www.ptcb.org
- Institute for the Certification of Pharmacy Technicians, 2536 S. Old Hwy. 94, Suite 224, St. Charles, MO 63303. Internet: http://www.nationaltechexam. org

For a list of accredited pharmacy technician training programs, contact

- American Society of Health-System Pharmacists, 7272 Wisconsin Ave., Bethesda, MD 20814. Internet: http://www.ashp.org

For pharmacy technician career information, contact

- National Pharmacy Technician Association, P.O. Box 683148, Houston, TX 77268. Internet: http://www.pharmacytechnician.org

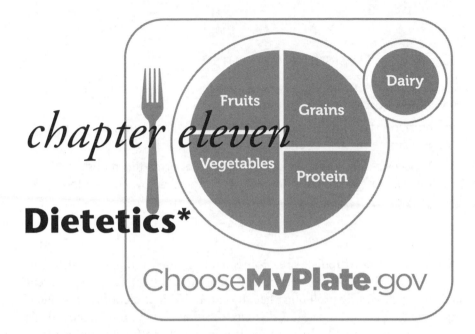

chapter eleven

Dietetics*

ChooseMyPlate.gov

KEY TERMS

American Dietetic
  Association (ADA)
Business dietitian
Clinical dietitians
Community dietitians

Consultant dietitians
Dietetic assistant
Dietetic technician,
  registered (DTR)
Educator dietitian

Internships
Management dietitians
Nutritionists
Registration
Research dietitians

---

*All information in this chapter, unless otherwise indicated, was obtained from Bureau of Labor Statistics. U.S. Department of Labor. *Occupational Outlook Handbook 2010–2011 Edition*. 2010.

DIETITIANS

SIGNIFICANT POINTS

- Most jobs are in hospitals, nursing care facilities, outpatient care centers, and offices of physicians or other health practitioners.
- Dietitians and nutritionists need at least a Bachelor degree; licensure, certification, or registration requirements vary by state.
- Applicants with specialized training, an advanced degree, or certifications beyond the particular state's minimum requirement should enjoy the best job opportunities.

Work Description

Dietitians and **nutritionists** are professionals trained in applying the principles of nutrition to food selection and meal preparation. They help prevent and treat illnesses by promoting healthy eating habits, scientifically evaluating clients' diets, and suggesting diet modifications. They counsel individuals and groups; set up and supervise food service systems for institutions such as schools, hospitals, and prisons; promote sound eating habits through education; and conduct research. Major areas of specialization include clinical, management, community, business and industry, and consultant dietetics. Dietitians also work as educators and researchers.

Clinical dietitians provide nutritional services for patients in hospitals, nursing homes, clinics, or doctors' offices. They assess patients' nutritional needs, develop and implement nutrition programs, and evaluate and report the results. Clinical dietitians confer with doctors and nurses about each patient so as to coordinate nutritional and medical needs.

Expanding knowledge in medical science has led to practice specialties in dietetics. Increasingly, clinical dietitians specialize in such areas as management of obese patients, care of the critically ill, renal care, and diabetes care. Those who care for critically ill patients oversee the preparation of custom-mixed, high-nutrition formulas for patients who require tube or intravenous feedings. Dietitians who specialize in renal dietetics treat dialysis patients and other individuals with kidney problems; those who work with diabetics are responsible for establishing long-term nutritional care programs and a system for close monitoring.

Aside from assessing nutritional needs and developing a plan of treatment for individual patients, clinical dietitians may also perform administrative and managerial duties. In a nursing home or small hospital, the dietitian may also manage the food service department.

Consulting has become a significant specialty in dietetics. It has appeal for dietitians who need flexible work time and have a desire to be autonomous. **Consultant dietitians** work under contract with healthcare facilities or in their own private practices. They perform nutrition screenings for their clients, and they offer advice on diet-related concerns such as weight loss or cholesterol reduction. Some work for wellness programs, sports teams, supermarkets, and other nutrition-related businesses. They may consult with food service managers, providing expertise in sanitation, safety procedures, menu development, budgeting, and planning. They advise food and pharmaceutical industries; speak at professional seminars; author food, nutrition, and diet books; counsel patients in nursing homes and medical and dental centers; plan food service systems; and tailor nutrition regimens within fitness programs for athletes, dancers, and others.

Community dietitians counsel individuals and groups on sound nutrition practices to prevent disease and to promote good health. Employed in such places as home health agencies, HMOs, and human service agencies that provide group and home-delivered meals, their job is to evaluate individual needs, establish nutritional care plans, and communicate the principles of good nutrition in a way that individuals and their families can understand. Many community dietitians counsel on food selection in relation to lifestyle. They coordinate nutrition awareness and disease prevention programs in settings such as public health agencies, day care centers, and health clubs.

In addition to evaluating clients, dietitians working in a home health setting may provide informal instruction on nutrition, grocery shopping, or preparation of special infant formulas. In HMOs, dietitians provide nutritional counseling on a range of topics, from weight control to menu planning for diabetics. The dietitian may also collaborate with other HMO staff in conducting information sessions on such subjects as alcoholism, smoking, or hypertension.

Practice opportunities for clinical and community dietitians are becoming more diverse because of increased interest in nutrition and fitness on the part of the public and the medical profession alike. This new awareness has resulted in opportunities for private practitioners in areas such as manufacturing, advertising, and marketing food. Dietitians who work for food manufacturers or grocery store chains may analyze the nutritional content of foods for labeling purposes or marketing efforts. They may also prepare literature for distribution to customers, students, or other interested parties. Dietitians employed by magazines may determine the nutritional content of new recipes, analyze and report on the effectiveness of new diets, or report on important topics in nutrition, such as the importance of dietary fiber or the value of vitamin supplements.

Dietitians are becoming increasingly visible in business. As businesses become more cognizant of the public's desire for accurate nutrition information, they are eager to hire experts. The **business dietitian** works as a professional resource for corporations in product development, food styling, and menu design; as the sales professional or purchasing agent representing food, equipment, or nutrition product accounts; and as a food, nutrition, or marketing expert in public relations and media.

Management dietitians are responsible for large-scale food services in such places as hospitals, company cafeterias, prisons, schools, and colleges and universities. They supervise the planning, preparation, and service of meals; select, train, and direct food service supervisors and workers; budget for and purchase food, equipment, and supplies; enforce sanitary and safety regulations; and prepare records and reports. Increasingly, dietitians use computer programs to plan meals that satisfy nutrition requirements and are economical at the same time. Dietitians who are directors of dietetic departments also decide on departmental policy, coordinate dietetic services with the activities of other departments, and are responsible for the dietetic department's budget, which in large organizations may amount to millions of dollars annually.

Research dietitians usually are employed in academic medical centers or educational institutions, although some work in community health programs. Using established research methods and analytical techniques, they conduct studies in areas that range from basic science to practical applications. Research dietitians may examine changes in the way the body uses food over the course of a lifetime, for example, or the interaction of drugs and diet. They may investigate the nutritional needs of persons with particular diseases, behavior modification as it relates to diet and nutrition, or applied topics such as food service systems and equipment. Often research dietitians collaborate with life scientists, physicians, nurses, biomedical engineers, and researchers from other disciplines.

Dietitians have always recognized the need to teach, whether in clinical practice, community settings, or corporations, and some are specifically interested in pursuing careers as health educators. The **educator dietitian** teaches the science of nutrition and food service systems management in colleges, universities, and hospitals; conducts nutrition and food service systems research; and author's articles and books on nutrition and food service systems. Dietitians in education usually hold advanced degrees and have considerable experience.

Work Environment

Most dietitians work 40 hours per week. About 19% worked part time in 2008. Those employed in hospitals sometimes work on weekends, while those in commercial food services tend to have irregular hours. Dietitians and nutritionists spend much of their time in clean, well-lighted, and well-ventilated areas such as research laboratories, classrooms, or offices near food preparation areas. However, they may spend time in kitchens and serving areas that are often hot and steamy and where some light lifting may be required. Dietitians and nutritionists in clinical settings may be on their feet for most of the workday. Those involved in consulting spend a significant amount of time traveling.

Employment Opportunities

Dietitians and nutritionists held about 60,300 jobs in 2008. More than half of all jobs were in hospitals, nursing care facilities, outpatient care centers, or offices of physicians and other health practitioners. State and local government agencies provided additional jobs—mostly in correctional facilities, health departments, and other public-health-related areas. Some dietitians and nutritionists were employed in special food services, an industry made up of firms providing food services on contract to facilities such as colleges and universities, airlines, correctional facilities, and company cafeterias.

Other jobs were in public and private educational services, community care facilities for the elderly (which includes assisted-living facilities), individual and family services, home healthcare services, and the federal government—mostly in the U.S. Department of Veterans Affairs. Some dietitians were self-employed, working as consultants to facilities such as hospitals and nursing care facilities, or providing dietary counseling to individuals.

Experienced dietitians may advance to assistant, associate, or director of a dietetic department, or they may become self-employed. Some dietitians specialize in areas such as renal or pediatric dietetics. Others may leave the occupation to become sales representatives for equipment, pharmaceutical, or food manufacturers. Advancement to higher-level positions in teaching and research requires graduate education; public health nutritionists usually must earn a graduate degree. Graduate study in institutional or business administration is valuable to those interested in management dietetics.

Clinical specialization offers another path to career advancement. Specialty areas for clinical dietitians include kidney disease, diabetes, cancer, heart disease, pediatrics, and gerontology.

Educational and Legal Requirements

Dictitians and nutritionists need at least a Bachelor degree. Licensure, certification, or **registration** requirements vary by state.

Education and Training

Becoming a dietitian or nutritionist usually requires at least a Bachelor degree in dietetics, foods and nutrition, food service systems management, or a related area. Graduate degrees also are available. College students in these majors take courses in foods, nutrition, institution management, chemistry, biochemistry, biology, microbiology, and physiology. Other suggested courses include business, mathematics, statistics, computer science, psychology, sociology, and economics. High school students interested in becoming a dietitian or nutritionist should take courses in biology, chemistry, mathematics, health, and communications.

As of 2008, there were 279 Bachelor degree programs and 18 Master degree programs approved by the **American Dietetic Association**'s **(ADA)** Commission on Accreditation for Dietetics Education.

Licensure

Of the 48 states and jurisdictions with laws governing dietetics, 35 require licensure, 12 require statutory certification, and 1 requires registration. Requirements vary by state. As a result, interested candidates should determine the requirements of the state in which they want to work before sitting for any exam.

In states that require licensure, only people who are licensed can work as dietitians and nutritionists. States that require statutory certification limit the use of occupational titles to people who meet certain requirements; individuals without certification can still practice as a dietitian or nutritionist but without using certain titles. Registration is the least restrictive form of state regulation of dietitians and nutritionists. Unregistered people are permitted to practice as dietitians or nutritionists.

Certification and Other Qualifications

Although not required, the Commission on Dietetic Registration of the American Dietetic Association awards the Registered Dietitian credential to those who pass an exam after completing academic coursework and a supervised internship. This certification is different from the statutory certification regulated by some states and is discussed in the previous section. To maintain a Registered Dietitian status, workers must complete at least 75 credit hours in approved continuing education classes every 5 years.

A supervised internship, required for certification, can be completed in one of two ways. The first requires the completion of a program accredited by the Commission on Dietetic Registration. As of 2009, there were 51 accredited programs that combined academic and supervised practice experience and generally lasted 4 to 5 years. The second option requires the completion of 900 hours of supervised practice experience in any of the 243 accredited **internships**. These internships may be full-time programs lasting 6 to 12 months or part-time programs lasting 2 years.

Advancement

Experienced dietitians may advance to management positions, such as assistant director, associate director, or director of a dietetic department, or may become self-employed. Some dietitians specialize in areas such as renal, diabetic, cardiovascular, or pediatric dietetics. Others leave the occupation to become sales representatives for equipment, pharmaceutical, or food manufacturers. A Master degree can help some workers to advance their careers, particularly in career paths related to research, advanced clinical positions, or public health.

Employment Trends

Average employment growth is projected. Good job opportunities are expected, especially for dietitians with specialized training, an advanced degree, or certifications beyond the particular state's minimum requirement.

Employment Change

Employment of dietitians and nutritionists is expected to increase 9% during the 2008–2018 projection decade, about as fast as the average for all occupations. Job growth will result from an increasing emphasis on disease prevention through improved dietary habits. A growing and aging population will boost demand for nutritional counseling and treatment in hospitals, residential care facilities, schools, prisons, community health programs, and home healthcare agencies. Public interest in nutrition and increased emphasis on health education and prudent lifestyles also will spur demand, especially in food service management.

Employment growth, however, may be constrained if some employers substitute other workers, such as health educators, food service managers, and dietetic technicians, to do work related to nutrition. Also, demand for nutritional therapy services is related to the ability of patients to pay, either out-of-pocket or through health insurance, and although more insurance plans now cover nutritional therapy services, the extent of such coverage varies among plans. Growth may be curbed by limitations on insurance reimbursement for dietetic services.

Hospitals will continue to employ a large number of dietitians and nutritionists to provide medical nutritional therapy and plan meals. Hospitals also will continue, however, to contract with outside agencies for food service and move medical nutritional therapy to outpatient care facilities, slowing job growth related to food service in hospitals and outpatient facilities, and with other employers.

The number of dietitian positions in nursing care facilities is expected to decline, as these establishments continue to contract with outside agencies for food services. However, employment is expected to grow rapidly in contract providers of food services, in outpatient care centers, and in offices of physicians and other health practitioners.

Finally, with increased public awareness of obesity and diabetes, Medicare coverage may be expanded to include medical nutrition therapy for renal and diabetic patients, creating job growth for dietitians and nutritionists specializing in those diseases.

Job Prospects

In addition to employment growth, job openings will result from the need to replace experienced workers who retire or leave the occupation for other reasons. Overall job opportunities will be good for dietitians and nutritionists, particularly for licensed and registered dietitians. Job opportunities should be particularly good in outpatient care facilities, offices of physicians, and food service management. Dietitians and nutritionists without a Bachelor degree will face keen competition for jobs.

Dietitians with specialized training, an advanced degree, or certifications beyond the particular state's minimum requirement will experience the best job opportunities. Those specializing in renal and diabetic nutrition or

TABLE 11-1 Projections Data from the National Employment Matrix for Dietitians and Nutritionists

Occupational Title	Employment 2008	Projected Employment 2018	Change 2008–2018	
			Number	Percentage
Dietitians and nutritionists	60,300	65,800	5600	9

gerontological nutrition will benefit from the growing number of diabetics and the aging of the population. **Table 11-1** shows some projection data provided by the Department of Labor.

Earnings

Median annual wages of dietitians and nutritionists were $50,590 in May 2008. The middle 50% earned between $41,060 and $61,790. The lowest 10% earned less than $31,460, and the highest 10% earned more than $73,410. Median annual wages in the industries employing the largest numbers of dietitians and nutritionists in May 2008 are shown in **Table 11-2**.

According to the American Dietetic Association, median annualized wages for registered dietitians in 2007 varied by practice area as follows: $60,008 in consultation and business; $64,002 in food and nutrition management; $66,061 in education and research; $52,000 in clinical nutrition/ambulatory care; $53,997 in clinical nutrition/long-term care; $48,006 in community nutrition; and $48,984 in clinical nutrition/acute care. Salaries also vary by years in practice, education level, and geographic region.

Related Occupations

Workers in other occupations who may apply the principles of dietetics include food service managers, health educators, dietetic technicians, and registered nurses.

TABLE 11-2 Median Annual Wages in the Industries Employing the Largest Numbers of Dietitians and Nutritionists in May 2008

Outpatient care centers	$52,120
General medical and surgical hospitals	51,390
Nursing care facilities	51,110
Local government	47,390
Special food services	45,410

Additional Information

For a list of academic programs, scholarships, and other information about dietetics, contact

- The American Dietetic Association, 120 South Riverside Plaza, Suite 2000, Chicago, IL 60606-6995. Internet: http://www.eatright.org

For information on the Registered Dietitian exam and other specialty credentials, contact

- The Commission on Dietetic Registration, 120 South Riverside Plaza, Suite 2000, Chicago, IL 60606-6995. Internet: http://www.cdrnet.org

DIETETIC TECHNICIANS

Work Description

A **dietetic technician, registered (DTR)** works as a member of the food service, management, and healthcare team, independently or in consultation with a registered dietitian. The dietetic technician supervises support staff, monitors cost-control procedures, interprets and implements quality assurance procedures, counsels individuals or small groups, screens patients/clients for nutritional status, and develops nutrition care plans. The dietetic technician helps to supervise food production and service; plans menus; tests new products for use in the facility; and selects, schedules, and conducts orientation programs for personnel. The technician may also be involved in selecting personnel and providing on-the-job training. The dietetic technician obtains, evaluates, and uses dietary histories to plan nutritional care for patients. Using this information, the technician guides families and individuals in selecting food, preparing it, and planning menus based on nutritional needs. The dietetic technician has an active part in calculating nutrient intakes and dietary patterns.

Work Environment

Most dietetic technicians work 40 hours per week. They may work weekends as well as early or late shifts, depending on the facility in which they are employed. They spend some of their time in clean, well-lighted, ventilated areas and some time in hot, steamy kitchens and serving areas. They may be on their feet for most of their working day, and may be required to do some lifting.

Employment Opportunities

Job opportunities for dietetic technicians vary depending on the geographic area and the number of hospitals within that area. Job opportunities are available in hospitals, clinics, day care centers, restaurants, health clubs,

WIC (Women, Infants, and Children) programs, Meals on Wheels programs, community health programs, and nursing homes. Dietetic technicians also work in university food service operations, some commercial food establishments, correctional facilities, public schools, health clubs, weight management clinics, food companies, and contract food management companies.

Educational and Legal Requirements

Individuals interested in becoming a dietetic technician, registered, should expect to study a wide variety of topics focusing on food, nutrition, and management. These areas of study are supported by communication, and by the sciences: biological, physiological, behavioral, and social. Becoming a dietetic technician involves a combination of academic preparation and supervised practice culminating in a minimum of an Associate degree from an institution sponsoring a program accredited or approved by the Commission on Accreditation for Dietetics Education (CADE) of the American Dietetic Association.

DTRs are trained in food and nutrition and are an integral part of healthcare and food service management teams. They must meet met the following criteria to earn the DTR credential:

1. Achieve at least a 2-year Associate degree at a U.S. regionally accredited college or university.
2. Complete a dietetic technician program approved by the Commission on Accreditation for Dietetics Education of the ADA, including 450 hours of supervised practice experience in various community programs, healthcare, and food service facilities.
3. Pass a national, written examination administered by the Commission on Dietetic Registration.
4. Complete continuing professional educational requirements to maintain registration.

Employment Trends

The job market for DTRs is assumed to be similar to that for dietitians and nutritionists. According to the U.S. Bureau of Labor Statistics, employment of dietitians and nutritionists is expected to grow faster than the average for all occupations through the year 2018 because of increased emphasis on disease prevention, a growing and aging population, and public interest in nutrition. Employment in hospitals is expected to show little change because of anticipated slow growth and reduced lengths of hospital stay. In contrast, faster growth is anticipated in nursing homes, residential care facilities, and physician clinics. In 2010, about 25,000 persons were employed in this occupation. Potential employers are

1. General medical and surgical hospitals
2. Nursing care facilities

3. Community care facilities for the elderly
4. Offices of other health practitioners
5. State and local government
6. Elementary and secondary schools
7. Community food and housing, and emergency and other relief services
8. Grocery stores
9. Corporations and other private sector institutions

Earnings

The salary levels of DTRs vary with region, employment setting, geographical location, scope of responsibility, and so on. The range in 2008 was $16,000 to $35,000, with an average hourly wage of $11 to $15.

Related Occupations

Workers with duties similar to those of dietetic technicians include Associate-degree nurses, licensed practical nurses, and dietary managers.

Additional Information

The ADA's website (http://www.eatright.org) includes additional information about careers in dietetics. Access this information directly at http://www.eatright.org/join/careers.html.

Names, addresses, and directors' names of educational programs that are accredited or approved by the Commission on Accreditation for Dietetics Education of the ADA are online at http://www.eatright.org/cade/. For additional information, such as a course catalog or list of required nutrition classes, contact the CADE-accredited/approved programs that you are interested in attending. For other career guidance information, search the ADA's website.

DIETETIC ASSISTANTS

The **dietetic assistant** is the third level among personnel involved in the provision of nutritional care. The amount of involvement in patient care depends on education, training, and work experience.

The dietetic assistant, under direct supervision from a food service manager, dietetic technician, or dietitian, works in the preparation and serving areas of hospitals and other healthcare facilities. The government, community agencies, restaurants, schools, universities, and the military also offer opportunities.

Dietetic assistant positions have no educational requirements. Assistants frequently receive on-the-job training only, although it is now common practice in accredited facilities to send the worker to a minimum of 45 clock hours of formal classroom/laboratory classes. These classes are often held at junior and community or technical colleges and taught by a registered dietitian.

After having passed the course, the student receives a certificate. The assistant must be employed by a health or community agency such as Head Start, school lunch program, or extended care facility to be eligible to take these courses.

Most dietetic assistants are assigned a preceptor who observes and assists them with assigned tasks or projects at the workplace. The assistant performs routine duties as assigned by the manager, dietetic technician, or dietitian according to the job specification.

Others who perform similar tasks are nursing assistants and home health aides. Salaries vary widely within and among geographic locations.

Because requirements for employment vary widely in this job, prospective employees are advised to ask the agency to which they apply if certification will be an expected part of obtaining the job. Employers who want certified dietetic assistants are often willing to pay all or a part of the student's fees.

Dietetic assistants may progress up the career ladder by completing additional coursework and becoming eligible to take an entrance examination given by the Dietary Managers Association to be promoted to dietary manager of a food service. Those who do not belong to the association may take the additional approved courses and obtain jobs as food service supervisors. Accredited healthcare facilities are required to have a person with one or more advanced courses as the head of the dietary department.

chapter twelve

Optometry*

KEY TERMS		
Apprenticeship programs	Health and visual sciences	Ophthalmic laboratory technicians
Corrective lenses	Laser surgery	Ophthalmologists
Dispensing opticians	Low-vision rehabilitation	Optics
Doctor of Optometry	OAT	Optometrists
Franchises	Ocular disease	Vision therapy

*All information in this chapter, unless otherwise indicated, was obtained from Bureau of Labor Statistics. U.S. Department of Labor. *Occupational Outlook Handbook 2010–2011 Edition*. 2010.

OPTOMETRISTS

SIGNIFICANT POINTS

- Admission to optometry school is competitive; only about 1 out of 3 applicants was accepted in 2007.
- Graduation from an accredited college of optometry and a state license administered by the National Board of Examiners in Optometry are required.
- Employment is expected to grow much faster than the average in response to the vision care needs of a growing and aging population.
- Job opportunities are likely to be excellent.

Work Description

Optometrists, also known as doctors of optometry, or ODs, are the main providers of vision care. They examine people's eyes to diagnose vision problems, such as nearsightedness and farsightedness, and they test patients' depth and color perception and ability to focus and coordinate the eyes. Optometrists may prescribe eyeglasses or contact lenses, or they may provide other treatments, such as **vision therapy** or **low-vision rehabilitation**.

Optometrists also test for glaucoma and other eye diseases and diagnose conditions caused by systemic diseases such as diabetes and high blood pressure, referring patients to other health practitioners as needed. They prescribe medication to treat vision problems or eye diseases, and some provide preoperative and postoperative care to cataract patients, as well as to patients who have had corrective **laser surgery**. Like other physicians, optometrists encourage preventive measures by promoting nutrition and hygiene education to their patients to minimize the risk of eye disease.

Although most work in a general practice as a primary care optometrist, some optometrists prefer to specialize in a particular field, such as contact lenses, geriatrics, pediatrics, or vision therapy. As a result, an increasing number of optometrists are forming group practices in which each group member specializes in a specific area while still remaining a full-scope practitioner. For example, an expert in low-vision rehabilitation may help legally blind patients by custom fitting them with a magnifying device that will enable them to read. Some may specialize in occupational vision, developing ways to protect workers' eyes from on-the-job strain or injury. Others may focus on sports vision, head trauma, or **ocular disease** and special testing. A few optometrists teach optometry, perform research, or consult.

Most optometrists are private practitioners who also handle the business aspects of running an office, such as developing a patient base, hiring employees, keeping paper and electronic records, and ordering equipment and supplies. Optometrists who operate franchise optical stores also may have some of these duties.

Optometrists should not be confused with **ophthalmologists** or **dispensing opticians**. Ophthalmologists are physicians who perform eye surgery, as well as diagnose and treat eye diseases and injuries. Like optometrists, they also examine eyes and prescribe eyeglasses and contact lenses. Dispensing opticians fit and adjust eyeglasses and, in some states, may fit contact lenses according to prescriptions written by ophthalmologists or optometrists.

Work Environment

Optometrists usually work in their own offices, which are clean, well lighted, and comfortable. Although most full-time optometrists work standard business hours, some work weekends and evenings to suit the needs of patients. Emergency calls, once uncommon, have increased with the passage of therapeutic-drug laws expanding optometrists' ability to prescribe medications.

Employment Opportunities

Optometrists held about 34,800 jobs in 2008. Salaried jobs for optometrists were primarily in offices of optometrists; offices of physicians, including ophthalmologists; and health and personal care stores, including optical goods stores. A few salaried jobs for optometrists were in hospitals, the federal government, or outpatient care centers, including health maintenance organizations. About 25% of optometrists are self-employed. According to a 2008 survey by the American Optometric Association, most self-employed optometrists worked in private practice or in partnership with other health-care professionals. A small number worked for optical chains or **franchises** or as independent contractors.

Educational and Legal Requirements

The **Doctor of Optometry** degree requires the completion of a 4-year program at an accredited school of optometry, preceded by at least 3 years of pre-optometric study at an accredited college or university. All states require optometrists to be licensed.

Education and Training

Optometrists need a Doctor of Optometry degree, which requires the completion of a 4-year program at an accredited school of optometry. In 2009, there were 19 colleges of optometry in the United States and 1 in Puerto Rico that offered programs accredited by the Accreditation Council on Optometric Education of the American Optometric Association. Requirements for admission to optometry schools include college courses in English, mathematics, physics, chemistry, and biology. Because a strong background in science is important, many applicants to optometry school major in a science, such as biology or chemistry, as undergraduates. Other applicants major in another subject and take many science courses offering laboratory experience.

Admission to optometry school is competitive; about 1 out of 3 applicants was accepted in 2007. All applicants must take the Optometry Admissions Test (**OAT**), a standardized exam that measures academic ability and scientific comprehension. The OAT consists of four tests: survey of the natural sciences, such as biology, general chemistry, and organic chemistry; reading comprehension; physics; and quantitative reasoning. As a result, most applicants take the test after their sophomore or junior year in college, allowing them an opportunity to take the test again and raise their score. A few applicants are accepted to optometry school after 3 years of college and complete their Bachelor degree while attending optometry school. However, most students accepted by a school or college of optometry have completed an undergraduate degree. Each institution has its own undergraduate prerequisites, so applicants should contact the school or college of their choice for specific requirements.

Optometry programs include classroom and laboratory study of **health and visual sciences** and clinical training in the diagnosis and treatment of eye disorders. Courses in pharmacology, **optics**, vision science, biochemistry, and systemic diseases are included.

One-year postgraduate clinical residency programs are available for optometrists who wish to obtain advanced clinical competence within a particular area of optometry. Specialty areas for residency programs include family practice optometry, pediatric optometry, geriatric optometry, vision therapy and rehabilitation, low-vision rehabilitation, cornea and contact lenses, refractive and ocular surgery, primary eye care optometry, and ocular disease.

Licensure

All states and the District of Columbia require that optometrists be licensed. Applicants for a license must have a Doctor of Optometry degree from an accredited optometry school and must pass both a written national board examination and a national, regional, or state clinical examination. The written and clinical examinations of the National Board of Examiners in Optometry usually are taken during the student's academic career. Many states also require applicants to pass an examination on relevant state laws. Licenses must be renewed every 1 to 3 years and, in all states, continuing education credits are needed for renewal.

Other Qualifications

Business acumen, self-discipline, and the ability to deal tactfully with patients are important for success. The work of optometrists also requires attention to detail and manual dexterity.

Advancement

Optometrists who wish to teach or conduct research may study for a Master degree or PhD in visual science, physiological optics, neurophysiology, public health, health administration, health information and communication, or health education.

Employment Trends

Employment of optometrists is expected to grow much faster than the average for all occupations through 2018, in response to the vision care needs of a growing and aging population. Excellent job opportunities are expected.

Employment Change

Employment of optometrists is projected to grow 24% between 2008 and 2018. A growing population that recognizes the importance of good eye care will increase demand for optometrists. Also, an increasing number of health insurance plans that include vision care should generate more job growth.

As the population ages, there will likely be more visits to optometrists and ophthalmologists because of the onset of vision problems that occur at older ages, such as cataracts, glaucoma, and macular degeneration. In addition, increased incidences of diabetes and hypertension in the general population as well as in the elderly will generate greater demand for optometric services as these diseases often affect eyesight.

Employment of optometrists would grow more rapidly if not for productivity gains that are expected to allow each optometrist to see more patients. These expected gains stem from the greater use of optometric assistants and other support personnel, who can reduce the amount of time optometrists need with each patient.

The increasing popularity of laser surgery to correct some vision problems was previously thought to have an adverse effect on the demand for optometrists as patients often do not require eyeglasses afterward. However, optometrists will still be needed to provide preoperative and postoperative care for laser surgery patients; therefore, laser eye surgery will likely have little to no impact on the employment of optometrists.

Job Prospects

Excellent job opportunities are expected over the next decade because there are only 19 schools of optometry in the United States, resulting in a limited number of graduates—about 1200—each year. This number is not expected to keep pace with demand. However, admission to optometry school is competitive.

In addition to job growth, the need to replace optometrists who retire will also create many employment opportunities. According to the American Optometric Association, nearly one-quarter of practicing optometrists are approaching retirement age. As they begin to retire, many opportunities will arise, particularly in individual and group practices. **Table 12-1** shows some projection for job growth for optometrists.

TABLE 12-1 Projections Data from the National Employment Matrix for Optometrists

Occupational Title	Employment, 2008	Projected Employment, 2018	Change, 2008–2018 Number	Percentage
Optometrists	34,800	43,200	8500	24

Earnings

Median annual wages of salaried optometrists were $96,320 in May 2008. The middle 50% earned between $70,140 and $125,460. Median annual wages of salaried optometrists in offices of optometrists were $92,670. Salaried optometrists tend to earn more initially than do optometrists who set up their own practices. In the long run, however, those in private practice usually earn more.

According to the American Optometric Association, the average annual income for self-employed optometrists was $175,329 in 2007.

Self-employed optometrists, including those in individual, partnerships, and group practice, continue to earn higher income than those in other settings. Earnings also vary by group size. For example, practitioners in large groups (six or more people) earn $159,300; practitioners in mid-sized groups (three to five people) earn $179,205; those in small practices (two people) earn $176,944; and individual practitioners earn an average of $134,094. Self-employed optometrists must also provide their own benefits. Practitioners associated with optical chains earn $100,704 on average. However, they typically enjoy paid vacation, sick leave, and pension contributions.

Related Occupations

Other workers who apply scientific knowledge to prevent, diagnose, and treat disorders and injuries include chiropractors, dentists, physicians and surgeons, podiatrists, psychologists, and veterinarians

Additional Information

For information on optometry as a career and a list of accredited optometric institutions of education, contact

- Association of Schools and Colleges of Optometry, 6110 Executive Blvd., Suite 420, Rockville, MD 20852. Internet: http://www.opted.org

  Additional career information is available from

- American Optometric Association, Educational Services, 243 N. Lindbergh Blvd., St. Louis, MO 63141. Internet: http://www.aoa.org

The board of optometry in each state can supply information on licensing requirements. For information on specific admission requirements and sources of financial aid, contact the admissions officers of individual optometry schools.

OPTICIAN, DISPENSING
SIGNIFICANT POINTS

- Employers increasingly prefer dispensing opticians to complete certification or graduate from an accredited 2-year Associate degree program in opticianry; some large employers may provide an apprenticeship.
- Twenty-two states require a license to practice.
- Employment growth is projected to be average and reflect the steady demand for corrective lenses and fashionable eyeglass frames.
- Job opportunities are likely to be very good.

Work Description

Helping people see better and look good at the same time is the job of a dispensing optician. Dispensing opticians help select and fit eyeglasses and contact lenses for people with eye problems, following prescriptions written by ophthalmologists or optometrists. Dispensing opticians recommend eyeglass frames, lenses, and lens coatings after considering the prescription and the customer's occupation, habits, and facial features. When fitting new eyeglasses, opticians use sophisticated diagnostic instruments to measure various characteristics of a client's eyes, including the thickness, width, curvature, and surface topography of the cornea. They also obtain a customer's prescription history to remake eyeglasses or contact lenses, or they may verify a prescription with the examining optometrist or ophthalmologist.

Dispensing opticians prepare work orders that give **ophthalmic laboratory technicians** the information they need to grind and insert lenses into a frame. The work order includes prescriptions for lenses and information on their size, material, color, and style. Some dispensing opticians grind and insert lenses themselves. They may also apply tint to lenses. After the glasses are made, dispensing opticians verify that the lenses meet the specifications, and then they may reshape or bend the frames with pliers for a custom fit.

Many opticians also spend time fixing and refitting broken frames, as well as instructing clients about wearing or caring for eyeglasses. Additionally, administrative duties have become a major part of their work, including keeping records on customers' prescriptions, work orders, and payments, and tracking inventory and sales.

Some dispensing opticians, after additional education and training, specialize in fitting contacts, artificial eyes, or cosmetic shells to cover blemished eyes. To fit contact lenses, dispensing opticians measure the shape and size of the eye, select the type of contact lens material, and prepare work orders specifying the prescription and lens size. Dispensing opticians observe customers' eyes, corneas, lids, and contact lenses with sophisticated instruments and microscopes. During several follow-up visits, opticians teach the proper insertion, removal, and care of contact lenses.

Work Environment

Dispensing opticians work indoors, mainly in medical offices, optical stores, or in large department or club stores. Opticians spend a fair amount of time on their feet. If they prepare lenses, they need to take precautions against the hazards of glass cutting, chemicals, and machinery. Although most dispensing opticians work during regular business hours, those in retail stores may work evenings and weekends. Some work part time.

Employment Opportunities

Dispensing opticians held about 59,800 jobs in 2008. About 40% worked in offices of optometrists. Another 33% worked in health and personal care stores, including optical goods stores. Many of these stores offer one-stop shopping where customers can have their eyes examined, choose frames, and have glasses made on the spot. Some opticians work in optical departments of department stores or other general merchandise stores, such as warehouse clubs and superstores. About 13% worked in offices of physicians, primarily ophthalmologists, who sell glasses directly to patients. One percent were self-employed and ran their own unincorporated businesses.

Educational and Legal Requirements

Many employers increasingly prefer dispensing opticians to complete certification or graduate from an accredited 2-year Associate degree program in opticianry; some large employers may provide an apprenticeship that may last 2 years or longer.

Education and Training

Although a high school diploma is all that is required to get into this occupation, most workers have completed at least some college courses or a degree. Classes in physics, basic anatomy, algebra, and trigonometry, as well as experience with computers are particularly valuable. These classes prepare dispensing opticians to learn job skills, including optical mathematics, optical physics, and the use of precision measuring instruments and other machinery and tools.

Structured **apprenticeship programs** are more commonly available in states where licensing is not mandatory, and these programs are usually offered by large employers. Apprentices receive technical instruction along with training in office management and sales. Under the supervision of an experienced optician, optometrist, or ophthalmologist, apprentices work directly with patients, fitting eyeglasses and contact lenses.

Formal training in the field is offered in community colleges and in a few 4-year colleges and universities. As of 2008, the Commission on Opticianry Accreditation accredited 22 Associate degree programs in 13 states. Graduation from an accredited program in opticianry can be advantageous as it provides a nationally recognized credential.

Licensure

As of 2009, 22 states require dispensing opticians to be licensed. States may require individuals to pass one or more of the following for licensure: a state practical examination, a state written examination, and certification examinations offered by the American Board of Opticianry (ABO) and the National Contact Lens Examiners (NCLE). To qualify for the examinations, states often require applicants to complete postsecondary training or work as apprentices for 2 to 4 years.

Some states allow graduates of opticianry programs to take the licensure exam immediately upon graduation; others require a few months to a year of experience. Continuing education is commonly required for licensure renewal. Information about specific licensing requirements is available from the state board of occupational licensing.

Certification

Any optician can apply to the ABO and the NCLE for certification of their skills. Certification signifies to customers and employers that an optician has a certain level of expertise. Certification must be renewed every 3 years through continuing education. The State of Texas offers voluntary registration for the occupation.

Other Qualifications

Dispensing opticians deal directly with the public, so they should be tactful, pleasant, and able to communicate well. Fitting contact lenses requires considerable skill, care, and patience, so manual dexterity and the ability to do precision work are essential.

Advancement

Some experienced dispensing opticians open their own optical stores. Others become managers of optical stores or sales representatives for wholesalers or manufacturers of eyeglasses or lenses.

Employment Trends

Employment of dispensing opticians is expected to grow about as fast as average for all occupations through 2018, as the population ages and demand for **corrective lenses** increases. Very good job prospects are expected.

Employment Change

Employment in this occupation is expected to rise 13% over the 2008–2018 decade. Middle age is a time when many individuals use corrective lenses for the first time, and elderly persons generally require more vision care than others. As the share of the population in these older age groups increases and as people live longer, more opticians will be needed to provide service to them. In addition, awareness of the importance of regular eye exams is increasing across all age groups, especially children and those older than 65 years of age. Recent trends indicate a movement toward a "low vision" society, where a growing number of people view things that are closer in distance, such as computer monitors, over the course of an average day. This trend is expected to increase the need for eye care services. Fashion also influences demand. Frames come in a growing variety of styles, colors, and sizes, encouraging people to buy more than one pair.

Somewhat moderating the need for optician services is the increasing use of laser surgery to correct vision problems. Although the surgery remains relatively more expensive than eyewear, patients who successfully undergo this surgery may not require glasses or contact lenses for several years. Also, new technology is allowing workers to make the measurements needed to fit glasses, therefore allowing dispensing opticians to work faster and limiting the need for more workers.

Job Prospects

Overall, the need to replace dispensing opticians who retire or leave the occupation will result in very good job prospects. Employment opportunities for opticians in offices of optometrists—the largest employer—will be particularly good as an increasing number of ophthalmologists are expected to utilize better-trained opticians to handle more tasks, allowing ophthalmologists to see more patients.

Job opportunities also will be good at general merchandise stores because this segment is expected to experience much faster than average growth, as well as high turnover because of less favorable working conditions, such as long hours and mandatory weekend shifts.

Nonetheless, the number of job openings overall will be somewhat limited because the occupation is small. Also, dispensing opticians are vulnerable to changes in the business cycle because eyewear purchases often can be deferred for a time. Job prospects will be best for those who have certification and those who have completed a formal opticianry program. Job candidates with extensive knowledge of new technology, including new refraction systems, framing materials, and edging techniques, should also experience favorable conditions. **Table 12-2** shows some projections for employment.

Earnings

Median annual wages of dispensing opticians were $32,810 in May 2008. The middle 50% earned between $26,170 and $41,930. The lowest 10% earned less than $21,250, and the highest 10% earned more than $50,580.

TABLE 12-2   Projections Data from the National Employment Matrix for Dispensing Opticians

Occupational Title	Employment, 2008	Projected Employment, 2018	Change, 2008–2018	
			Number	Percentage
Opticians, dispensing	59,800	67,800	8000	13

TABLE 12-3 Median Annual Earnings in the Industries Employing the Largest Numbers of Dispensing Opticians in May 2008

Other general merchandise stores	$40,080
Health and personal care stores	34,700
Offices of physicians	34,090
Department stores	33,750
Offices of optometrists	30,460

Median annual wages in the industries employing the largest numbers of dispensing opticians in May 2008 are shown in **Table 12-3**.

Benefits for opticians are generally determined by the industries in which they are employed. In general, those who work part time or in small retail shops have fewer benefits than those who may work for large optical chains or department stores. Self-employed opticians must provide their own benefits.

Related Occupations

Other workers who deal with customers and perform delicate work include jewelers and precious stone and metal workers, ophthalmic laboratory technicians, and orthotists and prosthetists.

Additional Information

To learn about apprenticeship programs and state licensing requirements, contact

- Opticians Association of America, 4064 E. Fir Hill Dr., Lakeland, TN 38002. Internet: http://www.oaa.org

To learn about voluntary certification for opticians who fit eyeglasses, as well as a list of state licensing boards for opticians, contact

- American Board of Opticianry, 6506 Loisdale Rd., Suite 209, Springfield, VA 22150. Internet: http://www.abo.org/

For information on voluntary certification for dispensing opticians who fit contact lenses, contact

- National Contact Lens Examiners, 6506 Loisdale Rd., Suite 209, Springfield, VA 22150. Internet: http://www.abo-ncle.org

For a list of the 22 Associate degree programs accredited by the Commission on Opticianry Accreditation, contact

- National Federation of Opticianry Schools, 2800 Springport Rd., Jackson, MI 49202. Internet: http://www.nfos.org

chapter thirteen

Physician Assistant*

KEY TERMS

Emergency medicine	Internal medicine	Primary care
Family practice	Middle-level health	Psychiatry
Geriatrics	workers	Surgery
Gynecology	NCCPA	Telemedicine
Healthcare workers	Pediatrics	

---

*All information in this chapter, unless otherwise indicated, was obtained from Bureau of Labor Statistics. U.S. Department of Labor. *Occupational Outlook Handbook 2010–2011 Edition.* 2010.

A RELATIVELY NEW PROFESSION

The occupation of physician assistant (PA) came into being during the mid-1960s in response to a shortage of primary care physicians. The purpose of the PA in **primary care** is to help physicians provide personal health services to patients under their care. PAs are skilled health practitioners, qualified through academic and clinical training to serve patients with and under the supervision of a doctor of medicine (MD) or osteopathy (DO), who is responsible for the performance of that particular assistant. PAs are also responsible for their own actions. They are **middle-level health workers** with skills beyond those of a registered nurse and short those of a licensed physician.

PHYSICIAN ASSISTANT

SIGNIFICANT POINTS

- Requirements for admission to training programs vary; most applicants have a college degree and some health-related work experience.
- Physician assistants must complete an accredited education program and pass a national exam in order to obtain a license.
- Employment is projected to grow much faster than average.
- Job opportunities should be good, particularly in rural and inner-city healthcare facilities.

Work Description

Physician assistants are formally trained to provide routine diagnostic, therapeutic, and preventive healthcare services under the direction and supervision of a physician. They take medical histories, examine patients, order and interpret laboratory tests and X-rays, and make preliminary diagnoses. They also treat minor injuries by suturing, splinting, and casting. PAs record progress notes, instruct and counsel patients, and order or carry out therapy. In 46 states and the District of Columbia, physician assistants may prescribe medications. PAs may have managerial duties, too. Some order medical and laboratory supplies and equipment; others supervise technicians and assistants.

Physician assistants always work under the supervision of a physician. The extent of supervision, however, depends on the work setting. For example, PAs working in rural or inner-city clinics, where a physician may be available just 1 or 2 days each week, may provide most of the health care for patients and consult with the supervising physician and other medical professionals as needed or required by law. Other PAs may make house calls or go to hospitals and nursing homes to check on patients and report to the physician.

Physician assistants assist physicians in a variety of practice settings and specialty areas. The most important practice settings are hospitals, clinics, and physicians' offices. Leading medical specialties using PAs are

family practice, internal medicine, general **surgery, emergency medicine, pediatrics**, orthopedic surgery, thoracic surgery, and **geriatrics**.

The duties of physician assistants are determined by the supervising physician and by state law. Aspiring PAs should investigate the laws and regulations in the states where they wish to practice.

Work Environment

Although PAs generally work in a comfortable, well-lighted environment, they often must stand for long periods and do considerable walking. The workweek and schedule vary according to practice setting. Some emergency room PAs work 24-hour shifts twice weekly, and others work three 12-hour shifts each week. The workweek of PAs who work in physicians' offices may include weekends, night hours, or early morning hospital rounds to visit patients. PAs in clinics usually work a 5-day, 40-hour week.

Employment Opportunities

Physician assistants held about 74,800 jobs in 2008. The number of jobs is greater than the number of practicing PAs because some hold two or more jobs. For example, some PAs work with a supervising physician, but also work in another practice, clinic, or hospital. According to the American Academy of Physician Assistants, about 15% of actively practicing PAs worked in more than one clinical job concurrently in 2008.

More than 53% of jobs for PAs were in the offices of physicians. About 24% were in public or private hospitals. The rest were mostly in outpatient care centers, including health maintenance organizations, the federal government, and public or private colleges, universities, and professional schools. Very few PAs were self-employed.

Educational and Legal Requirements

Physician assistant programs usually last at least 2 years. Admission requirements vary by program, but many require at least 2 years of college and some healthcare experience. All states require that PAs complete an accredited, formal education program and pass a national exam to obtain a license.

Education and Training

Physician assistant education programs usually last at least 2 years and are full time. Most programs are in schools of allied health, academic health centers, medical schools, or 4-year colleges; a few are in community colleges, the military, or hospitals. Many accredited PA programs have clinical teaching affiliations with medical schools.

In 2008, 142 education programs for physician assistants were accredited or provisionally accredited by the American Academy of Physician Assistants. Eighty percent or 113 of these programs offered the option of a

Master degree, 21 of them offered a Bachelor degree, 3 awarded an Associate degree, and 5 awarded a certificate.

Admission requirements vary, but many programs require 2 years of college and some work experience in the healthcare field. Students should take courses in biology, English, chemistry, mathematics, psychology, and the social sciences. Many PAs have prior experience as registered nurses, and others come from varied backgrounds, including military corpsmen or medics, and allied health occupations, such as respiratory therapists, physical therapists, and emergency medical technicians and paramedics.

PA education includes classroom instruction in biochemistry, pathology, human anatomy, physiology, microbiology, clinical pharmacology, clinical medicine, geriatric and home health care, disease prevention, and medical ethics. Students obtain supervised clinical training in several areas, including family medicine, internal medicine, surgery, prenatal care and **gynecology**, geriatrics, emergency medicine, **psychiatry**, and pediatrics. Sometimes, PA students serve one or more of these rotations under the supervision of a physician who is seeking to hire a PA. The rotations often lead to permanent employment.

Licensure

All states and the District of Columbia have legislation governing the qualifications or practice of physician assistants. All jurisdictions require physician assistants to pass the Physician Assistant National Certifying Examination, administered by the National Commission on Certification of Physician Assistants (**NCCPA**) and open only to graduates of accredited PA education programs. Only those successfully completing the examination may use the credential "Physician Assistant–Certified." To remain certified, PAs must complete 100 hours of continuing medical education every 2 years. Every 6 years, they must pass a recertification examination or complete an alternative program combining learning experiences and a take-home examination.

Other Qualifications

Physician assistants must have a desire to serve patients and be self-motivated. PAs also must have a good bedside manner, emotional stability, and the ability to make decisions in emergencies. Physician assistants must be willing to study throughout their career to keep up with medical advances.

Certification and Advancement

Some PAs pursue additional education in a specialty such as surgery, neonatology, or emergency medicine. PA postgraduate educational programs are available in areas such as internal medicine, rural primary care, emergency medicine, surgery, pediatrics, neonatology, and occupational medicine. Candidates must be graduates of an accredited program and be certified by the NCCPA.

As they attain greater clinical knowledge and experience, PAs can advance to added responsibilities and higher earnings. However, by the very nature of the profession, clinically practicing PAs always are supervised by physicians.

Employment Trends

Employment is expected to grow much faster than average as healthcare establishments increasingly use physician assistants to contain costs. Job opportunities for PAs should be good, particularly in rural and inner-city clinics, as these settings typically have difficulty attracting physicians.

Employment Change

Employment of physician assistants is expected to grow 39% from 2008 to 2018, much faster than the average for all occupations. Projected rapid job growth reflects the expansion of healthcare industries and an emphasis on cost containment, which results in the increasing use of PAs by healthcare establishments.

Physicians and institutions are expected to employ more PAs to provide primary care and to assist with medical and surgical procedures because PAs are cost-effective and productive members of the healthcare team. Physician assistants can relieve physicians of routine duties and procedures. **Telemedicine**—using technology to facilitate interactive consultations between physicians and physician assistants—also will expand the use of physician assistants.

Besides working in traditional office-based settings, PAs should find a growing number of jobs in institutional settings such as hospitals, academic medical centers, public clinics, and prisons. PAs also may be needed to augment medical staffing in inpatient teaching hospital settings as the number of hours physician residents are permitted to work is reduced, encouraging hospitals to use PAs to supply some physician resident services.

Job Prospects

Job opportunities for PAs should be good, particularly in rural and inner-city clinics because those settings have difficulty attracting physicians. In addition to job openings from employment growth, openings will result from the need to replace physician assistants who retire or leave the occupation permanently. Opportunities will be best in states that allow PAs a wider scope of practice. **Table 13-1** shows some projection data provided by the Department of Labor.

TABLE 13-1 Projection Data from the National Employment Matrix for Physician Assistants

Occupational Title	Employment, 2008	Projected Employment, 2018	Change, 2008–2018	
			Number	Percentage
Physician assistants	74,800	103,900	29,200	39

TABLE 13-2   Median Annual Earnings in the Industries Employing the Largest Numbers of Physician Assistants in May 2008

General medical and surgical hospitals	$84,550
Outpatient care centers	84,390
Offices of physicians	80,440
Federal executive branch	78,200
Colleges, universities, and professional schools	74,200

Earnings

Median annual earnings of wage-and-salary physician assistants were $81,230 in May 2008. The middle 50% earned between $68,210 and $97,070. The lowest 10% earned less than $51,360, and the highest 10% earned more than $110,350. Median annual wages in the industries employing the largest numbers of physician assistants in May 2008 are shown in **Table 13-2**.

According to the American Academy of Physician Assistants' 2008 Census Report, median income for physician assistants in full-time clinical practice was $85,710 in 2008; median income for first-year graduates was $74,470. Income varies by specialty, practice setting, geographic location, and years of experience. Employers often pay for their employees' liability insurance, registration fees with the Drug Enforcement Administration, state licensing fees, and credentialing fees.

Related Occupations

Other **healthcare workers** who provide direct patient care that requires a similar level of skill and training include audiologists, occupational therapists, physical therapists, registered nurses, and speech-language pathologists.

Additional Information

For information on a career as a physician assistant, including a list of accredited programs, contact

- American Academy of Physician Assistants Information Center, 950 North Washington St., Alexandria, VA 22314. Internet: http://www.aapa.org

For a list of accredited physician assistant, programs, contact

- Accreditation Review Commission on Education for the Physician Assistants, 12000 Findley Rd., Suite 240, Johns Creek, GA 30097. Internet: http://www.arc-pa.org

For eligibility requirements and a description of the Physician Assistant National Certifying Examination, contact

- National Commission on Certification of Physician Assistants, Inc., 12000 Findley Rd., Suite 200, Duluth, GA 30097. Internet: http://www.nccpa.net

chapter fourteen

Communication Impairments*

*All information in this chapter, unless otherwise indicated, was obtained from Bureau of Labor Statistics. U.S. Department of Labor. *Occupational Outlook Handbook 2010–2011 Edition.* 2010.

SPEECH, LANGUAGE, AND HEARING IMPAIRMENTS: AN OVERVIEW

Speech, language, and **hearing impairments** hinder communication and can cause problems throughout life. Children who have difficulty speaking, hearing, or understanding language, for instance, cannot participate fully with others in play or classroom activities. Sometimes these children are thought to have mental or emotional problems, when in fact the problem is one of language or hearing. Adults with speech, language, or hearing impairments may have problems on the job and may withdraw socially to avoid frustration and embarrassment. The aging process almost invariably brings some degree of hearing loss. Severe loss, if not treated, can result in diminished pleasure in everyday activities, social isolation, and, even worse, wrongful labeling of elderly people as demented or "confused."

A **language disorder** is defined as an inability to use the symbols of language through appropriate **grammatical patterns**, proper use of words and their meanings, and the correct use of speech sounds. A **speech disorder** is identified by an individual's difficulty in producing speech sounds, controlling voice production, and maintaining speech rhythm. Individuals with speech and language disorders also include those with physical conditions such as a stroke or head injury, cleft palate, or cerebral palsy. Other causes of speech and language disorders are hearing loss, viral diseases, certain drugs, poor speech and language models in the home, or a short attention span.

Hearing impairment can take many forms. It can be an inability to hear speech and other sounds clearly, even though the sounds are sufficiently loud. It can be an inability to understand and use speech in communication, although speech is sufficiently loud and can be heard clearly. It can be the inability to hear speech and other sounds loudly enough, which is considered a loss of hearing sensitivity. A person can experience these three types of hearing impairments in combination. Thus, hearing impairment is more complex than simply the inability to hear speech or other sounds well enough. Some hearing impairments can be subtle and difficult to recognize. Hearing impairment can be a serious problem because the ability to communicate is our most human characteristic. Many individuals with hearing impairments experience social, emotional, and educational isolation. Viral infections, head injury, birth defects, excessively loud noises, drugs, tumors, heredity, and the aging process can cause hearing impairments. Hearing impairment is the disorder most frequently reported to physicians. Approximately half of the people in the United States who have hearing impairments are 65 year of age or older.

SPEECH-LANGUAGE PATHOLOGISTS

SIGNIFICANT POINTS

- About 48% worked in educational services; most others were employed by healthcare and social assistance facilities.

- A Master degree in speech-language pathology is the standard educational requirement; almost all states regulate these workers, and licensing requirements vary.
- Favorable job opportunities are expected.

Work Description

Speech-language pathologists, sometimes called speech therapists, assess, diagnose, treat, and help to prevent disorders related to speech, language, cognitive communication, voice, swallowing, and fluency.

Speech-language pathologists work with people who cannot produce speech sounds or cannot produce them clearly; those with speech rhythm and fluency problems, such as stuttering; people with voice disorders, such as inappropriate pitch or harsh voice; those with problems understanding and producing language; those who wish to improve their communication skills by modifying an accent; and those with cognitive communication impairments, such as attention, memory, and problem-solving disorders. They also work with people who have swallowing difficulties.

Speech, language, and swallowing difficulties can result from a variety of causes including stroke, brain injury or deterioration, developmental delays or disorders, learning disabilities, cerebral palsy, cleft palate, voice pathology, mental retardation, hearing loss, or emotional problems. Problems can be congenital, developmental, or acquired. Speech-language pathologists use special instruments and qualitative and quantitative assessment methods, including standardized tests, to analyze and diagnose the nature and extent of impairments.

Speech-language pathologists develop an individualized plan of care tailored to each patient's needs. For individuals with little or no speech capability, speech-language pathologists may select augmentative or alternative communication methods, including automated devices and sign language, and teach their use. They teach patients how to make sounds, improve their voices, or increase their oral or written language skills to communicate more effectively. They also teach individuals how to strengthen muscles or use compensatory strategies to swallow without choking or inhaling food or liquid. Speech-language pathologists help patients develop, or recover, reliable communication and swallowing skills so patients can fulfill their educational, vocational, and social roles.

Speech-language pathologists keep records on the initial evaluation, progress, and discharge of clients. This helps pinpoint problems, tracks client progress, and justifies the cost of treatment when applying for reimbursement. They counsel individuals and their families concerning **communication disorders** and how to cope with the stress and misunderstanding that often accompany them. They also work with family members to recognize and change behavior patterns that impede communication and treatment, and show them communication-enhancing techniques to use at home.

Most speech-language pathologists provide direct clinical services to individuals with communication or swallowing disorders. In medical facilities, they may perform their job in conjunction with physicians, social workers, psychologists, and other therapists. Speech-language pathologists in schools collaborate with teachers, special educators, interpreters, other school personnel, and parents to develop and implement individual or group programs, provide counseling, and support classroom activities.

Some speech-language pathologists conduct research on how people communicate. Others design and develop equipment or techniques for diagnosing and treating speech problems.

Work Environment

Speech-language pathologists usually work at a desk or table in clean, comfortable surroundings. In medical settings, they may work at the patient's bedside and assist in positioning the patient. In schools, they may work with students in an office or classroom. Some work in clients' homes.

Although the work is not physically demanding, it requires attention to detail and intense concentration. The emotional needs of clients and their families may be demanding. Most full-time speech-language pathologists work 40 hours per week. About 20% of speech-language pathologists worked part time in 2008. Those who work on a contract basis may spend a substantial amount of time traveling between facilities.

Employment Opportunities

Speech-language pathologists held about 119,300 jobs in 2008. About 48% were employed in educational services. Others were employed in hospitals; offices of other health practitioners, including speech-language pathologists; nursing care facilities; home healthcare services; individual and family services; outpatient care centers; and child day care centers.

Nine percent of speech-language pathologists were self-employed in 2008. They contract to provide services in schools, offices of physicians, hospitals, or nursing care facilities, or work as **consultants** to industry.

Educational and Legal Requirements

A Master degree is the most common level of education among speech-language pathologists. Licensure or certification requirements also exist, but vary by state.

Education and Training

Most speech-language pathologist jobs require a Master degree. The Council on Academic Accreditation is an entity of the American Speech-Language-Hearing Association; it accredits postsecondary academic programs in speech-language pathology. Although graduation from an accredited program is not always required, it is required by some states for licensure and is mandatory for professional credentialing from the American Speech-Language-Hearing Association. In 2009, about 240 colleges and universities offered graduate programs, at both the master's and doctoral levels, in speech-language pathology accredited by the Council on Academic Accreditation. Speech-language pathology courses cover anatomy, physiology, and the development of the areas of the body involved in speech, language, and swallowing; the nature of disorders; principles of acoustics; and psychological aspects of communication. Graduate students may also learn to evaluate and treat speech, language, and swallowing disorders as part of curriculum in supervised clinical practicum.

Licensure and Certification

In 2009, 47 states regulated speech-language pathologists. Typical licensing requirements are a Master degree from an accredited college or university; a passing score on the national examination on speech-language pathology, offered through the Praxis Series of the Educational Testing Service; 300 to 375 hours of supervised clinical experience; and 9 months of postgraduate professional clinical experience. Most states have continuing education requirements for licensure renewal. Medicaid, Medicare, and private health insurers generally require a practitioner to be licensed to qualify for reimbursement. For specific regulation and eligibility requirements contact your state's regulatory board.

State regulation of speech language pathologists may differ for pathologists practicing in schools. For information on the state regulation of speech-language pathologists in public schools contact your state's Department of Education. The **Certificate of Clinical Competence in Speech-Language Pathology (CCC-SLP)** credential offered by the American Speech-Language-Hearing Association is a voluntary credential; however, the CCC-SLP meets some or all of the requirements for licensure in some states. To earn a CCC, a person must have a graduate degree from an accredited university, which typically includes a 400-hour supervised clinical practicum; complete a 36-week full-time postgraduate clinical fellowship; and pass the Praxis Series examination in speech-language pathology administered by the Educational Testing Service.

Other Qualifications

Speech-language pathologists should be able to effectively communicate diagnostic test results, diagnoses, and proposed treatment in a manner easily understood by their patients and their families. They must be able to approach problems objectively and be supportive. Because a patient's progress may be slow, patience, compassion, and good listening skills are necessary.

Advancement

As speech-language pathologists gain clinical experience and engage in continuing professional education, many develop expertise with certain populations, such as preschoolers and adolescents, or disorders, such as aphasia and learning disabilities. Some may obtain board recognition in a specialty area, such as child language, fluency, or feeding and swallowing. Experienced clinicians may become mentors or supervisors of other therapists or be promoted to administrative positions.

Employment Trends

Faster-than-average employment growth is projected. Job opportunities are expected to be favorable.

Employment Change

Employment of speech-language pathologists is expected to grow by 19% from 2008 to 2018, faster than the average for all occupations. As the members of the baby-boom generation continue to age, the possibility of neurological disorders and associated speech, language, and swallowing impairments increases. Medical advances also are improving the survival rate of premature infants and trauma and stroke victims, who then need assessment and sometimes treatment.

Employment in educational services will increase with the growth in elementary and secondary school enrollments, including enrollment of special education students. The 2004 Individuals with Disabilities Education Act is a federal law that guarantees special education and related services to all eligible children with disabilities. Greater awareness of the importance of the early identification and diagnosis of speech and language disorders in young children will also increase employment.

In healthcare facilities, restrictions on reimbursement for therapy services may limit the growth of speech-language pathologist jobs in the near term. However, the long-run demand for therapists should continue to rise as growth in the number of individuals with disabilities or limited function spurs demand for therapy services.

The number of speech-language pathologists in private practice should increase because hospitals, schools, and nursing care facilities will contain costs by increasingly contracting out for these services.

Job Prospects

In addition to job growth, a number of job openings in speech-language pathology will be a result of retirements. Opportunities should be favorable, particularly for those with the ability to speak a second language, such as Spanish. Demand for speech-language pathologists can be regional, so job prospects are expected to be favorable for those who are willing to relocate,

TABLE 14-1 Projection Data from the National Employment Matrix for Speech-Language Pathologists

Occupational Title	Employment, 2008	Projected Employment, 2018	Change, 2008–2018	
			Number	Percentage
Speech-language pathologists	119,300	141,400	22,100	19

particularly to areas experiencing difficulty in attracting and hiring speech-language pathologists. **Table 14-1** shows some projection data provided by the Department of Labor.

Earnings

Median annual wages of speech-language pathologists were $62,930 in May 2008. The middle 50% earned between $50,330 and $79,620. The lowest 10% earned less than $41,240, and the highest 10% earned more than $99,220. Median annual wages in the industries employing the largest numbers of speech-language pathologists in 2008 are shown in **Table 14-2**.

Some employers may reimburse speech-language pathologists for their required continuing education credits. About 40% of speech-language pathologists were union members or covered by union contract in 2008.

Related Occupations

Speech-language pathologists specialize in the prevention, diagnosis, and treatment of speech and language problems. Workers who treat other physical and mental health problems include **audiologists**, occupational therapists, physical therapists, psychologists, and recreational therapists.

Additional Information

State licensing boards can provide information on licensure requirements. State departments of education can supply information on certification requirements for those who wish to work in public schools.

TABLE 14-2 Median Annual Wages in the Industries Employing the Largest Numbers of Speech-Language Pathologists in 2008

Nursing care facilities	$79,120
Home healthcare services	77,030
General medical and surgical hospitals	68,430
Offices of other health practitioners	67,910
Elementary and secondary schools	58,140

For information on careers in speech-language pathology, a description of the CCC-SLP credential, and a listing of accredited graduate programs in speech-language pathology, contact

- American Speech-Language-Hearing Association, 2200 Research Blvd., Rockville, MD 20850. Internet: http://www.asha.org

AUDIOLOGISTS

SIGNIFICANT POINTS

- About 64% worked in healthcare facilities; many others were employed by educational services.
- All states regulate licensure of audiologists; requirements vary by state.
- A Master degree in audiology (hearing) is the standard level of education required; however, a doctoral degree is becoming more common for new entrants.
- Job prospects will be favorable for those possessing the doctoral (**AuD**) degree.

Work Description

Audiologists work with people who have hearing, balance, and related ear problems. They examine individuals of all ages and identify those with the symptoms of hearing loss and other auditory, balance, and related sensory and neural problems. They then assess the nature and extent of the problems and help the individuals manage them. Using audiometers, computers, and other testing devices, they measure the loudness at which a person begins to hear sounds, the ability to distinguish between sounds, and the impact of hearing loss on an individual's daily life. In addition, audiologists use computer equipment to evaluate and diagnose balance disorders. Audiologists interpret these results and may coordinate them with medical, educational, and psychological information to make a diagnosis and determine a course of treatment.

Hearing disorders can result from a variety of causes including trauma at birth, viral infections, genetic disorders, exposure to loud noise, certain medications, or aging. Treatment may include examining and cleaning the ear canal, fitting and dispensing hearing aids, and fitting and programming cochlear implants. Audiologic treatment also includes counseling on adjusting to hearing loss, training on the use of hearing instruments, and teaching communication strategies for use in a variety of environments. For example, they may provide instruction in listening strategies. Audiologists also may recommend, fit, and dispense personal or large-area amplification systems and alerting devices.

In audiology clinics, audiologists may independently develop and carry out treatment programs. They keep records on the initial evaluation, progress, and discharge of patients. In other settings, audiologists may work with other health and education providers as part of a team in planning and implementing services for children and adults. Audiologists who diagnose and treat balance disorders often work in collaboration with physicians, and physical and occupational therapists.

Some audiologists specialize in work with the elderly, children, or hearing-impaired individuals who need special treatment programs. Others develop and implement ways to protect workers' hearing from on-the-job injuries. They measure noise levels in workplaces and conduct hearing protection programs in factories and in schools and communities.

Audiologists who work in private practice also manage the business aspects of running an office, such as developing a patient base, hiring employees, keeping records, and ordering equipment and supplies.

Some audiologists conduct research on types of, and treatment for, hearing, balance, and related disorders. Others design and develop equipment or techniques for diagnosing and treating these disorders.

Work Environment

Audiologists usually work at a desk or table in clean, comfortable surroundings. The job is not physically demanding but does require attention to detail and intense concentration. The emotional needs of patients and their families may be demanding. Most full-time audiologists work about 40 hours per week, which may include weekends and evenings to meet the needs of patients. Those who work on a contract basis may spend a substantial amount of time traveling between facilities.

Employment Opportunities

Audiologists held about 12,800 jobs in 2008. About 64% of all jobs were in healthcare facilities—offices of physicians or other health practitioners, including audiologists; hospitals; and outpatient care centers. About 14% of jobs were in educational services. Other jobs for audiologists were in health and personal care stores and in state and local governments.

Educational and Legal Requirements

All states regulate the licensure of audiologists; requirements vary by state. At least a Master degree in audiology is required, but a doctoral degree is increasingly necessary.

Education and Training

Individuals pursuing a career will need to earn a doctoral degree. In 2009, 18 states required a doctoral degree or its equivalent for new applicants to practice audiology. The doctoral degree in audiology is a graduate program typically lasting 4 years and resulting in the AuD designation.

The Council on Academic Accreditation (CAA) is an entity of the American Speech-Language-Hearing Association (ASHA) that accredits education programs in audiology. In 2009, the CAA accredited 70 doctoral programs in audiology. Graduation from an accredited program may be required to obtain a license in some states, and professional credentialing.

Requirements for admission to programs in audiology include courses in English, mathematics, physics, chemistry, biology, psychology, and communication. Graduate coursework in audiology includes anatomy; physiology; physics; genetics; normal and abnormal communication development; auditory, balance, and neural systems assessment and treatment; diagnosis and treatment; pharmacology; and ethics. Graduate curriculums also include supervised clinical practicum and externships.

Licensure and Certification

Audiologists are regulated by licensure in all 50 states. Eighteen of those states require a doctoral degree for licensure. Some states regulate the practice of audiology and the dispensing of hearing aids separately, meaning some states will require an additional license called a **Hearing Aid Dispenser license**. Many states require that audiologists complete continuing education for license renewal. Eligibility requirements, hearing aid dispensing requirements, and continuing education requirements vary from state to state. For specific requirements, contact your state's medical or health board.

Audiologists can earn the **Certificate of Clinical Competence in Audiology (CCC-A)** offered by the American Speech-Language-Hearing Association; they may also be credentialed through the American Board of Audiology. Professional credentialing may satisfy some or all of the requirements for state licensure.

Other Qualifications

Audiologists should be able to effectively communicate diagnostic test results, diagnoses, and proposed treatments in a manner easily understood by their patients. They must be able to approach problems objectively and provide support to patients and their families. Because a patient's progress may be slow, patience, compassion, and good listening skills are necessary.

It is important for audiologists to be aware of new diagnostic and treatment technologies. Most audiologists participate in continuing education courses to learn new methods and technologies.

Advancement

With experience, audiologists can advance to open their own private practice. Audiologists working in hospitals and clinics can advance to management or supervisory positions.

Employment Trends

The projection is that much faster than average employment growth is expected. However, because of the small size of the occupation, few job openings are expected. Job prospects will be favorable for those possessing the AuD degree.

Employment Change

Employment of audiologists is expected to grow 25% from 2008 to 2018, much faster than the average for all occupations. Hearing loss is strongly associated with aging, so the increased growth of older population groups will cause the number of people with hearing and balance impairments to increase markedly.

Medical advances also are improving the survival rate of premature infants and trauma victims, who then need assessment and sometimes treatment. Greater awareness of the importance of the early identification and diagnosis of hearing disorders in infants also will increase employment. In addition to medical advances, technological advances in hearing aids may drive demand. Digital hearing aids have become smaller in size and also have quality-improving technologies like reducing feedback. Demand may be spurred by those who switch from analog to digital hearing aids, as well as those who will desire new or first-time hearing aids because they are becoming less visible.

Employment in educational services will increase along with growth in elementary and secondary school enrollments, including the enrollment of special education students. Growth in the employment of audiologists will be moderated by limitations on reimbursements made by third-party payers for the tests and services they provide.

Job Prospects

Job prospects will be favorable for those possessing the AuD degree. Only a few job openings for audiologists will arise from the need to replace those who leave the occupation, because the occupation is relatively small and workers tend to stay in this occupation until they retire. Demand may be greater in areas with large numbers of retirees, so audiologists who are willing to relocate may have the best job prospects. **Table 14-3** shows some projection data from the Department of Labor.

TABLE 14-3   Projection Data from the National Employment Matrix for Audiologists

Occupational Title	Employment, 2008	Projected Employment, 2018	Change, 2008–2018	
			Number	Percentage
Audiologists	12,800	16,000	3200	25

Earnings

Median annual wages of audiologists were $62,030 in May 2008. The middle 50% earned between $50,470 and $78,380. The lowest 10% earned less than $40,360, and the highest 10% earned more than $98,880. Some employers may pay for continuing education courses. About 15% of audiologists were union members or were covered under union contracts in 2008.

Related Occupations

Audiologists specialize in the prevention, diagnosis, and treatment of hearing problems. Workers who treat other problems related to physical or mental health include occupational therapists, optometrists, physical therapists, psychologists, and speech-language pathologists.

Additional Information

State licensing boards can provide information on licensure requirements. State departments of education can supply information on certification requirements for those who wish to work in public schools.

For information on the specific requirements of your state, contact that state's licensing board. Career information, a description of the CCC-A credential, and information on state licensure is available from

- American Speech-Language-Hearing Association, 2200 Research Blvd., Rockville, MD 20850. Internet: http://www.asha.org

For information on the AuD degree, contact

- Audiology Foundation of America, 8 N. 3rd St., Suite 301, Lafayette, IN 47901. Internet: http://www.audfound.org

chapter fifteen

Emergency Medical Technicians and Paramedics*

KEY TERMS

Advanced airway
  devices
EKGs
Emergency equipment
Emergency medical
  services

Emergency skills
EMT-Basic
EMT-Intermediate
EMT-Paramedic
Endotracheal
  intubations

First Responder
National Registry of
  Emergency Medical
  Technicians (NREMT)
Trauma centers
Volunteer EMTs

---

*All information in this chapter, unless otherwise indicated, was obtained from Bureau of Labor Statistics. U.S. Department of Labor. *Occupational Outlook Handbook 2010–2011 Edition*. 2010.

HIGH DRAMA IN HEALTH CARE

Paramedics, or emergency medical technicians (EMTs), have a career that is often very dramatic, calling for immediate, calm application of the EMT's skills amid sometimes dangerous conditions. The September 11, 2001, attack on the World Trade Center was the most dramatic and deadly situation that paramedics, along with teams of firefighters and police, have ever faced, and they lived up to their potential and training with great heroism. If you watched the terrible events unfolding at that scene, you saw many of them in action as their ambulances drove through dangerous smoke, fire, and rubble to help rescue and transport the critically injured to hospitals. Their bravery in the face of peril speaks well of the crucial role played by paramedics in times of crisis, as well as in everyday life.

Although not every call received by a paramedic team is a life-or-death situation, the potential for drama always exists. The remainder of this chapter details the dramatic as well as the mundane aspects of this healthcare profession.

EMT-PARAMEDICS

SIGNIFICANT POINTS

- Employment is projected to grow as fast as the average for all occupations.
- Emergency medical technicians and paramedics need formal training and certification or licensure, but requirements vary by state.
- Emergency services function 24 hours a day, so emergency medical technicians and paramedics have irregular working hours.
- Opportunities will be best for those who have earned advanced certifications.

Work Description

People's lives often depend on the quick reaction and competent care of emergency medical technicians (EMTs) and paramedics. Incidents as varied as automobile accidents, heart attacks, slip and falls, childbirth, and gunshot wounds all require immediate medical attention. EMTs and paramedics provide this vital service as they care for and transport the sick or injured to a medical facility.

In an emergency, EMTs and paramedics are typically dispatched by a 911 operator to the scene, where they often work with police and firefighters. Once they arrive, EMTs and paramedics assess the nature of the patient's condition while trying to determine whether the patient has any preexisting medical conditions. Following medical protocols and guidelines, they provide appropriate emergency care and, when necessary, transport the patient. Some paramedics are trained to treat patients with minor injuries on the scene of an accident, or they may treat them at their home, without transporting them to a medical facility. Emergency treatment is carried out under the medical direction of physicians.

EMTs and paramedics may use special equipment, such as backboards, to immobilize patients before placing them on stretchers and securing them in the ambulance for transport to a medical facility. These healthcare workers generally go out in teams. During the transport of a patient, one EMT or paramedic drives while the other monitors the patient's vital signs and gives additional care as needed. Some paramedics work as part of a helicopter's flight crew to transport critically ill or injured patients to hospital **trauma centers**.

At the medical facility, EMTs and paramedics help transfer patients to the emergency department, report their observations and actions to emergency department staff, and may provide additional emergency treatment. After each run, EMTs and paramedics replace used supplies and check equipment. If a transported patient had a contagious disease, EMTs and paramedics decontaminate the interior of the ambulance and report cases to the proper authorities.

EMTs and paramedics also provide transportation for patients from one medical facility to another, particularly if they work for private ambulance services. Patients often need to be transferred to a hospital that specializes in their injury or illness or to a nursing home.

Beyond these general duties, the specific responsibilities of EMTs and paramedics depend on their level of qualification and training. The **National Registry of Emergency Medical Technicians (NREMT)** certifies emergency medical service providers at five levels: **First Responder**; **EMT-Basic**; **EMT-Intermediate**, which has two levels called 1985 and 1999; and Paramedic. Some states, however, have their own certification programs and use distinct names and titles.

The EMT-Basic represents the first component of the emergency medical technician system. An EMT trained at this level is prepared to care for patients at the scene of an accident and while transporting patients by ambulance to the hospital under medical direction. The EMT-Basic has the **emergency skills** to assess a patient's condition and manage respiratory, cardiac, and trauma emergencies.

The EMT-Intermediate has more advanced training. However, the specific tasks that those certified at this level are allowed to perform vary greatly from one state to another. **EMT-Paramedics** provide the most extensive prehospital care. In addition to carrying out the procedures of the other levels, paramedics may administer drugs orally and intravenously, interpret electrocardiograms (**EKGs**), perform **endotracheal intubations**, and use monitors and other complex equipment. However, as with EMT-Intermediate, what paramedics are permitted to do varies by state.

Work Environment

EMTs and paramedics work both indoors and out, in all types of weather. They are required to do considerable kneeling, bending, and heavy lifting. These workers risk noise-induced hearing loss from sirens and back injuries from lifting patients. In addition, EMTs and paramedics may be exposed to diseases such as hepatitis-B and AIDS, as well as violence from mentally unstable patients. The work is not only physically strenuous but can be stressful, sometimes involving life-or-death situations and suffering patients. Nonetheless, many people find the work exciting and challenging and enjoy the opportunity to help others.

EMTs and paramedics employed by fire departments work about 50 hours a week. Those employed by hospitals frequently work between 45 and 60 hours a week, and those in private ambulance services, between 45 and 50 hours. Some of these workers, especially those in police and fire departments, are on call for extended periods. Because emergency services function 24 hours a day, EMTs and paramedics have irregular working hours.

Employment Opportunities

EMTs and paramedics held about 210,700 jobs in 2008. Most career EMTs and paramedics work in metropolitan areas. **Volunteer EMTs** and paramedics are more common in small cities, towns, and rural areas. These individuals volunteer for fire departments, **emergency medical services**, or hospitals and may respond to only a few calls per month.

Paid EMTs and paramedics were employed in a number of industries. About 45% worked as employees of private ambulance services. About 29% worked in local government. Another 20% worked in hospitals. The type of work or responsibility within each employment service is as follows:

1. Private ambulance services are usually contracted by private or public organizations for emergency situations.
2. Local government is usually required to provide ambulance emergency medical services associated with the fire and police departments.
3. Hospitals obviously are required to provide the same services for patients in emergency situations.

Educational and Legal Requirements

Generally, a high school diploma is required to enter a training program to become an EMT or paramedic. Workers must complete a formal training and certification process.

Education and Training

A high school diploma usually is required to enroll in a formal emergency medical technician training program. Training is offered at progressive levels: EMT-Basic, EMT-Intermediate, and EMT-Paramedic.

At the EMT-Basic level, coursework emphasizes emergency skills, such as managing respiratory, trauma, and cardiac emergencies, and patient assessment. Formal courses are often combined with time in an emergency room or ambulance. The program provides instruction and practice in dealing with bleeding, fractures, airway obstruction, cardiac arrest, and emergency childbirth. Students learn how to use and maintain common **emergency equipment**, such as backboards, suction devices, splints, oxygen delivery systems, and stretchers. Graduates of approved EMT-Basic training programs must pass a written and practical examination administered by the state certifying agency or the NREMT.

At the EMT-Intermediate level, training requirements vary by state. The nationally defined levels (EMT-Intermediate 1985 and EMT-Intermediate 1999) typically require 30 to 350 hours of training based on the scope of practice. Students learn advanced skills, such as the use of **advanced airway devices**, intravenous fluids, and some medications.

The most advanced level of training for this occupation is EMT-Paramedic. At this level, the caregiver receives training in anatomy and physiology as well as advanced medical skills. Most commonly, the training is conducted in community colleges and technical schools over 1 to 2 years and may result in an Associate degree. Such education prepares the graduate to take the NREMT examination and become certified as a paramedic. Extensive related coursework and clinical and field experience is required. Refresher courses and continuing education are available for EMTs and paramedics at all levels.

Licensure

All 50 states require certification for each of the EMT levels. In most states and the District of Columbia registration with the NREMT is required at some or all levels of certification. Other states administer their own certification examination or provide the option of taking either the NREMT or state examination. To maintain certification, EMTs and paramedics must recertify, usually every 2 years. Generally, they must be working as an EMT or paramedic and meet a continuing education requirement.

Other Qualifications

EMTs and paramedics should be emotionally stable; have good dexterity, agility, and physical coordination; and be able to lift and carry heavy loads. They also need good eyesight—corrective lenses may be used—with accurate color vision.

Advancement

Paramedics can become supervisors, operations managers, administrative directors, or executive directors of emergency services. Some EMTs and paramedics become instructors, dispatchers, or physician assistants; others move into sales or marketing of emergency medical equipment. A number of people become EMTs and paramedics to test their interest in health care before training as registered nurses, physicians, or other health workers.

Employment Trends

Employment for EMTs and paramedics is expected to grow about as fast as the average for all occupations through 2018. Job prospects should be good, particularly in cities and private ambulance services.

Employment Change

Employment of emergency medical technicians and paramedics is expected to grow by 19% between 2008 and 2018, which is about as fast as the average for all occupations. Full-time, paid EMTs and paramedics will be needed to replace unpaid volunteers. It is becoming increasingly difficult for emergency medical services to recruit and retain unpaid volunteers because of the amount of training and the large time commitment these positions require. As a result, more paid EMTs and paramedics are needed. Furthermore, as a large segment of the population—aging members of the baby-boom generation becomes more likely to have medical emergencies, demand will increase for EMTs and paramedics. Demand for part-time, volunteer EMTs and paramedics will continue in rural areas and smaller metropolitan areas.

Job Prospects

Job prospects should be favorable. Many job openings will arise from growth and from the need to replace workers who leave the occupation because of the limited potential for advancement, as well as the modest pay and benefits in private-sector jobs.

Job opportunities should be best in private ambulance services. Competition will be greater for jobs in local government, including fire, police, and independent third-service rescue squad departments, which tend to have better salaries and benefits. As clients and patients expect and demand higher levels of care before arriving at the hospital, EMTs and paramedics who have advanced education and certifications, such as paramedic-level certification, should enjoy the most favorable job prospects. **Table 15-1** shows some projections data provided by the Department of Labor.

Earnings

Earnings of EMTs and paramedics depend on the employment setting and geographic location of their jobs, as well as their training and experience.

TABLE 15-1   Projections Data from the National Employment Matrix for Emergency Medical Technicians and Paramedics

Occupational Title	Employment, 2008	Projected Employment, 2018	Change, 2008–2018	
			Number	Percentage
Emergency medical technicians and paramedics	210,700	229,700	19,000	9

Median hourly wages of EMTs and paramedics were $14.10 in May 2008. The middle 50% earned between $11.13 and $18.28. The lowest 10% earned less than $9.08, and the highest 10% earned more than $23.77. Median hourly wages in the industries employing the largest numbers of EMTs and paramedics in May 2008 were $12.99 in other ambulatory health-care services and $15.45 in local government.

In 2008, about 27% of EMTs and paramedics belonged to a union or were covered by a union contract.

Related Occupations

Other workers in occupations that require quick and level-headed reactions to life-or-death situations are air traffic controllers, firefighters, physician assistants, police and detectives, and registered nurses.

Additional Information

General information about emergency medical technicians and paramedics is available from

- National Association of Emergency Medical Technicians, P.O. Box 1400, Clinton, MS 39060-1400. Internet: http://www.naemt.org
- National Highway Traffic Safety Administration, Office of Emergency Medical Services, 1200 New Jersey Ave. SE, NTI-140, Washington, DC 20590. Internet: http://www.ems.gov
- National Registry of Emergency Medical Technicians, Rocco V. Morando Bldg., 6610 Busch Blvd., P.O. Box 29233, Columbus, OH 43229. Internet: http://www.nremt.org

chapter sixteen

Imaging Modalities*

KEY TERMS		
American Registry for Diagnostic Medical Sonographers (ARDMS)	Dosimetrists	Positron emission scanners
American Registry of Radiologic Technologists (ARRT)	Fluoroscopies	Radiation therapy
	High-frequency transducers	Radiographers
	Ionizing radiation	Radiologic technicians
Beam modification devices	Magnetic resonance imaging (MRI)	Radiologist
Computed tomography (CT)	Magnetic resonance scanners	Registered Diagnostic Medical Sonographers (RDMS)
CT technologists	MRI technologist	Sonographers
Diagnostic imaging	Obstetric and gynecologic sonographers	Ultrasound machines
Diagnostic medical sonography		

*All information in this chapter, unless otherwise indicated, was obtained from Bureau of Labor Statistics. U.S. Department of Labor. *Occupational Outlook Handbook 2010–2011 Edition*. 2010.

X-RAYS AND BEYOND

Perhaps the most familiar use of the X-ray is the diagnosis of broken bones. Although this remains a major use, medical uses of radiation go far beyond that. Today, radiation is used not only to produce images of the interior of the body, but also to treat disease. The rapidly growing use of imaging techniques that do not involve X-rays has transformed the field, and the term **diagnostic imaging** embraces procedures such as ultrasound and magnetic resonance scans in addition to the familiar X-ray.

With the application of computer technology to radiology, the field has been revolutionized. Computer-enhanced equipment produces amazingly clear and sharp images. Thanks in part to the speed with which computerized scanners can read and organize the millions of messages involved in a single test, it is now possible to view soft tissues and organs such as the heart and brain, parts of the body that until quite recently could be examined only through invasive techniques such as exploratory surgery.

Remarkable strides have occurred in the development of imaging equipment that does not involve the use of radiation, thereby reducing the risk of adverse side effects. Examples include **ultrasound machines**, which use sound waves; **magnetic resonance scanners**, which use radio waves; and **positron emission scanners**. Although discovered many years ago, some of these imaging techniques became clinically practical only during the 1990s, as a result of improvements in electronic circuitry that enable computers to handle the vast amount of data involved.

Future generations of imaging equipment are certain to be even more sophisticated than machines in use today. Physicians seeking to confirm a diagnosis or monitor a patient's condition will obtain better information, and patients will be subjected to less risk or discomfort. There is ample reason to believe that technological advances in this field will continue to occur very rapidly, and that the clinical benefits will spur even more extensive use of diagnostic imaging procedures.

RADIOLOGIC TECHNOLOGISTS AND TECHNICIANS
SIGNIFICANT POINTS

- Employment is projected to grow faster than average; those with knowledge of more than one diagnostic imaging procedure will have the best employment opportunities.

- Formal training programs in radiography are offered in hospitals or colleges and universities and lead to a certificate, an Associate degree, or a Bachelor degree.

- Most states require licensure, and requirements vary.

- Although hospitals will remain the primary employers, a number of new jobs will be found in physicians' offices and diagnostic imaging centers.

Work Description

Radiologic technologists and technicians perform diagnostic imaging examinations. Radiologic technicians perform imaging examinations like X-rays, while technologists use other imaging modalities such as **computed tomography (CT), magnetic resonance imaging (MRI)**, and mammography.

Radiologic technicians, sometimes referred to as **radiographers**, produce X-ray films (radiographs) of parts of the human body for use in diagnosing medical problems. They prepare patients for radiologic examinations by explaining the procedure, removing jewelry and other articles through which X-rays cannot pass, and positioning patients so that the parts of the body can be appropriately radiographed. To prevent unnecessary exposure to radiation, these workers surround the exposed area with radiation protection devices, such as lead shields, or limit the size of the X-ray beam. Radiographers position radiographic equipment at the correct angle and height over the appropriate area of a patient's body. Using instruments similar to a measuring tape they may measure the thickness of the section to be radiographed and set controls on the X-ray machine to produce radiographs of the appropriate density, detail, and contrast.

Radiologic technologists and technicians must follow physicians' orders precisely and conform to regulations concerning the use of radiation to protect themselves, their patients, and their coworkers from unnecessary exposure.

In addition to preparing patients and operating equipment, radiologic technologists and technicians keep patient records and adjust and maintain equipment. They also may prepare work schedules, evaluate purchases of equipment, or manage a radiology department.

Radiologic technologists perform more complex imaging procedures. When performing **fluoroscopies**, for example, radiologic technologists prepare a solution for the patient to drink, allowing the **radiologist** (a physician who interprets radiographs) to see soft tissues in the body.

Some radiologic technologists specialize in CT as **CT technologists**. CT scans produce a substantial number of cross-sectional X-rays of an area of the body. From those cross-sectional X-rays, a three-dimensional image is made. The CT uses **ionizing radiation**; therefore, it requires the same precautionary measures that are used with X-rays.

Radiologic technologists also can specialize in magnetic resonance imaging (MRI) as **MRI technologists**. MRI, like CT, produces multiple cross-sectional images to create a three-dimensional image. Unlike CT and X-rays, MRI uses nonionizing radio frequencies to generate image contrast.

Radiologic technologists might also specialize in mammography. Mammographers use low-dose X-ray systems to produce images of the breast.

In addition to radiologic technologists, others who conduct diagnostic imaging procedures include cardiovascular technologists and technicians, diagnostic medical **sonographers**, and nuclear medicine technologists.

Work Environment

Physical stamina is important in this occupation because technologists and technicians are on their feet for long periods and may lift or turn disabled patients. Technologists and technicians work at diagnostic machines, but also may perform some procedures at patients' bedsides. Some travel to patients in large vans equipped with sophisticated diagnostic equipment.

Although radiation hazards exist in this occupation, they are minimized by the use of lead aprons, gloves, and other shielding devices, and by instruments monitoring exposure to radiation. Technologists and technicians wear badges measuring radiation levels in the radiation area, and detailed records are kept on their cumulative lifetime dose.

Most full-time radiologic technologists and technicians work about 40 hours a week. They may, however, have evening, weekend, or on-call hours. Some radiologic technologists and technicians work part time for more than one employer; for those, travel to and from facilities must be considered.

Employment Opportunities

Radiologic technologists held about 214,700 jobs in 2008. About 61% of all jobs were in hospitals. Most other jobs were in offices of physicians; medical and diagnostic laboratories, including diagnostic imaging centers; and outpatient care centers.

Educational and Legal Requirements

There are multiple paths to entry into this profession offered in hospitals or colleges and universities. Most states require licensure, and requirements vary.

Education and Training

Formal training programs in radiography lead to a certificate, an Associate degree, or a Bachelor degree. An Associate degree is the most prevalent level of educational attainment among radiologic technologists and technicians. Some may receive a certificate. Certificate programs typically last around 21 to 24 months.

The Joint Review Committee on Education in Radiologic Technology accredits formal training programs in radiography. The committee accredited 213 programs resulting in a certificate, 397 programs resulting in an Associate degree, and 35 resulting in a Bachelor degree in 2009. The programs provide both classroom and clinical instruction in anatomy and physiology, patient care procedures, radiation physics, radiation protection, principles of imaging, medical terminology, positioning of patients, medical ethics, radiobiology, and pathology.

Students interested in radiologic technology should take high school courses in mathematics, physics, chemistry, and biology.

Licensure

Federal legislation protects the public from the hazards of unnecessary exposure to medical and dental radiation by ensuring that operators of radiologic equipment are properly trained. However, it is up to each state to require the licensure of radiologic technologists. Most states require licensure for practicing radiologic technologists. Licensing requirements vary by state—for specific requirements contact your state's health board.

Certification

The **American Registry of Radiologic Technologists (ARRT)** offers voluntary certification for radiologic technologists. In addition, a number of states use ARRT-administered exams for state licensing purposes. To be eligible for certification, technologists must graduate from an ARRT-approved accredited program and pass an examination. Many employers prefer to hire certified radiologic technologists. In order to maintain an ARRT certification, 24 hours of continuing education must be completed every 2 years.

Other Qualifications

Radiologic technologists should be sensitive to patients' physical and psychological needs. They must pay attention to detail, follow instructions, and work as part of a team. In addition, operating complicated equipment requires mechanical ability and manual dexterity.

Advancement

With experience and additional training, staff technologists may become specialists, performing CT scanning, MRI, mammography, or bone densitometry. Technologists also may advance, with additional education and certification, to become a radiologist assistant. The ARRT offers specialty certification in many radiologic specialties, as well as a credentialing for radiologist assistants.

Experienced technologists also may be promoted to supervisor, chief radiologic technologist, and, ultimately, department administrator or director. Depending on the institution, courses or a Master degree in business or health administration may be necessary for the director's position.

Some technologists progress by specializing in the occupation to become instructors or directors in radiologic technology educational programs; others take jobs as sales representatives or instructors with equipment manufacturers.

Employment Trends

Employment is projected to grow faster than average. Those with knowledge of more than one diagnostic imaging procedure—such as CT, MRI, and mammography—will have the best employment opportunities.

Employment Change

Employment of radiologic technologists is expected to increase by about 17% from 2008 to 2018, faster than the average for all occupations. As the population grows and ages, there will be an increasing demand for diagnostic imaging. With age comes an increased incidence of illness and injury, which often requires diagnostic imaging for diagnosis. In addition to diagnosis, diagnostic imaging is used to monitor the progress of disease treatment. With the increasing success of medical technologies in treating disease, diagnostic imaging will increasingly be needed to monitor the progress of treatment.

The extent to which diagnostic imaging procedures are performed largely depends on cost and reimbursement considerations. However, accurate early disease detection allows for lower cost of treatment in the long run, which many third-party payers find favorable.

Although hospitals will remain the principal employer of radiologic technologists, a number of new jobs will be found in offices of physicians and diagnostic imaging centers. As technology advances, many imaging modalities are becoming less expensive and more feasible to have in physicians' offices.

Job Prospects

In addition to job growth, job openings also will arise from the need to replace technologists who leave the occupation. Those with knowledge of more than one diagnostic imaging procedure—such as CT, MRI, and mammography—will have the best employment opportunities as employers seek to control costs by using multicredentialed employees.

Demand for radiologic technologists and technicians can tend to be regional with some areas having great demand, while other areas are saturated. Technologists and technicians willing to relocate may have better job prospects.

CT is continuing to become a frontline diagnosis tool. Instead of taking X-rays to decide whether a CT is needed, as was the practice before, it is often the first choice for imaging because of its accuracy. MRI also is increasingly used. Technologists with credentialing in either of these specialties will be very marketable to employers. **Table 16-1** shows some projection data provided by the Department of Labor.

TABLE 16-1 Projections Data from the National Employment Matrix for Radiologic Technologists and Technicians

Occupational Title	Employment, 2008	Projected Employment, 2018	Change, 2008–2018	
			Number	Percentage
Radiologic technologists and technicians	214,700	251,700	37,000	17

TABLE 16-2 Median Annual Earnings in the Industries Employing the Largest Number of Radiologic Technologists in May 2008

Medical and diagnostic laboratories	$55,210
Federal executive branch	53,650
General medical and surgical hospitals	52,890
Outpatient care centers	50,840
Offices of physicians	48,530

Earnings

The median annual wage of radiologic technologists was $52,210 in May 2008. The middle 50% earned between $42,710 and $63,010. The lowest 10% earned less than $35,100, and the highest 10% earned more than $74,970. Median annual wages in the industries employing the largest numbers of radiologic technologists in 2008 are shown in **Table 16-2**.

Related Occupations

Radiologic technologists operate sophisticated equipment to help physicians, dentists, and other health practitioners diagnose and treat patients. Workers in related healthcare occupations include cardiovascular technologists and technicians, diagnostic medical sonographers, nuclear medicine technologists, and radiation therapists.

Additional Information

For information on careers in radiologic technology, contact

- American Society of Radiologic Technologists, 15000 Central Ave. SE, Albuquerque, NM 87123. Internet: http://www.asrt.org

For the current list of accredited education programs in radiography, contact

- Joint Review Committee on Education in Radiologic Technology, 20 N. Wacker Dr., Suite 2850, Chicago, IL 60606-3182. Internet: http://www.jrcert.org

For certification information, contact

- American Registry of Radiologic Technologists, 1255 Northland Dr., St. Paul, MN 55120-1155. Internet: http://www.arrt.org

RADIATION THERAPISTS

SIGNIFICANT POINTS

- A Bachelor degree, Associate degree, or certificate in radiation therapy is generally required.

- Employment is projected to grow much faster than the average for all occupations.
- Good job opportunities are expected.
- Earnings are relatively high.

Work Description

Radiation therapy is used to treat cancer in the human body. As part of a medical radiation oncology team, radiation therapists use machines called linear accelerators to administer radiation treatment to patients. Linear accelerators are most commonly used in a procedure called external beam therapy, which projects high-energy X-rays at targeted cancer cells. As the X-rays collide with human tissue, they produce highly energized ions that can shrink and eliminate cancerous tumors. Radiation therapy is sometimes used as the sole treatment for cancer, but it is usually used in conjunction with chemotherapy or surgery.

Before treatment can begin, the oncology team has to develop a treatment plan. To create this plan, the radiation therapist must first use an X-ray imaging machine or computed tomography (CT) scan to pinpoint the location of the tumor. Then, a radiation oncologist (a physician who specializes in therapeutic radiology) and a radiation physicist (a worker who calibrates the linear accelerator) determine the best way to administer treatment. The therapist completes the plan by positioning the patient and adjusting the linear accelerator to the specifications developed by the team, and then recording the details so that those conditions can be replicated during treatment. The therapist later explains the treatment plan to the patient and answers any questions that the patient may have.

The next step in the process is treatment. To begin each treatment session, the radiation therapist uses the guidelines developed during the planning phase to position the patient and adjust the linear accelerator. Then, from a separate room that is protected from the X-ray radiation, the therapist operates the linear accelerator and monitors the patient's condition through a TV monitor and an intercom system. Treatment can take anywhere from 10 to 30 minutes.

During the treatment phase, the radiation therapist monitors the patient's physical condition to determine whether the patient is having any adverse reactions to the treatment. The therapist must also be aware of the patient's emotional well-being. Because many patients are under stress and are emotionally fragile, it is important for the therapist to maintain a positive attitude and provide emotional support.

Radiation therapists keep detailed records of their patients' treatments. These records include information such as the dose of radiation used for each treatment, the total amount of radiation used to date, the area treated, and the patient's reactions. Radiation oncologists and **dosimetrists** (technicians who calculate the dose of radiation that will be used for treatment) review these records to ensure that the treatment plan is working, to monitor the amount of radiation exposure that the patient has received, and to keep side effects to a minimum. Therapists also may assist dosimetrists with routine aspects of dosimetry, the process used to calculate radiation dosages.

Work Environment

Radiation therapists work in hospitals or in cancer treatment centers. These places are clean, well lighted, and well ventilated. Therapists do a considerable amount of lifting and must be able to help disabled patients get on and off treatment tables. They spend most of their time on their feet.

Radiation therapists generally work 40 hours a week, and unlike workers in some other healthcare occupations, they normally work only during the day. However, because radiation therapy emergencies do occur, some therapists are required to be on call and may have to work outside of their normal hours.

Working with cancer patients can be stressful, but many radiation therapists also find it rewarding. Because they work around radioactive materials, radiation therapists take great care to ensure that they are not exposed to dangerous levels of radiation. By following standard safety procedures, radiation therapists can prevent overexposure.

Employment Opportunities

Radiation therapists held about 15,200 jobs in 2008. About 70% worked in hospitals, and about 18% worked in the offices of physicians. A small proportion worked in outpatient care centers and medical and diagnostic laboratories.

Educational and Legal Requirements

A Bachelor degree, Associate degree, or certificate in radiation therapy generally is required. Many states require radiation therapists to be licensed, and most employers require certification. With experience, therapists can advance to managerial positions.

Education and Training

Employers usually require applicants to complete an Associate or a Bachelor degree program in radiation therapy. Individuals also may become qualified by completing an Associate or a Bachelor degree program in radiography, which is the study of radiological imaging, and then by completing a 12-month certificate program in radiation therapy. Radiation therapy programs include core courses on radiation therapy procedures and the scientific theories behind them. In addition, such programs often include courses on human anatomy and physiology, physics, algebra, precalculus, writing, public speaking, computer science, and research methodology. In 2009, there were 102 radiation therapy programs in the United States that were accredited by the American Registry of Radiologic Technologists (ARRT).

Licensure

In 2009, 33 states required radiation therapists to be licensed by a state accrediting board. Licensing requirements vary by state, but many states require applicants to pass the ARRT certification examination. Further information is available from individual state licensing offices.

Certification

Some states, as well as many employers, require radiation therapists to be certified by the ARRT. To become ARRT certified, an applicant must complete an accredited radiation therapy program, adhere to ARRT ethical standards, and pass the ARRT certification examination. The examination covers radiation protection and quality assurance, clinical concepts in radiation oncology, treatment planning, treatment delivery, and patient care and education. Candidates also must demonstrate competency in several clinical practices including patient care activities; simulation procedures; dosimetry calculations; fabrication of **beam modification devices**; low-volume, high-risk procedures; and the application of radiation.

ARRT certification is valid for 1 year, after which therapists must renew their certification. Requirements for renewal include abiding by the ARRT ethical standards, paying annual dues, and satisfying continuing education requirements. Continuing education requirements must be met every 2 years and include either the completion of 24 course credits related to radiation therapy or the attainment of ARRT certification in a discipline other than radiation therapy. However, states or employers that require initial certification may not require certification renewal.

Other Qualifications

All radiation therapists need good communication skills because their work involves a great deal of interaction with patients. Individuals interested in becoming radiation therapists should be psychologically capable of working with cancer patients. They should be caring and empathetic because they work with patients who are ill and under stress. They should be able to keep accurate, detailed records. They also should be physically fit because they work on their feet for long periods and lift and move disabled patients.

Advancement

Experienced radiation therapists may advance to manage radiation therapy programs in treatment centers or other healthcare facilities. Managers generally continue to treat patients while taking on management responsibilities. Other advancement opportunities include teaching, technical sales, and research. With additional training and certification, therapists also can become dosimetrists, who use complex mathematical formulas to calculate proper radiation doses.

Employment Trends

Employment is expected to increase much faster than average, and job prospects should be good.

Employment Change

Employment of radiation therapists is projected to grow by 27% between 2008 and 2018, which is much faster than the average for all occupations. The growing elderly population is expected to cause an increase in the number of people needing treatment. In addition, as radiation technology becomes safer and more effective, it will be prescribed more often, leading to an increased demand for radiation therapists. Growth is likely to be rapid across all practice settings, including hospitals, physicians' offices, and outpatient centers.

Job Prospects

Job prospects are expected to be good. Job openings will result from employment growth and from the need to replace workers who retire or leave the occupation for other reasons. Applicants with a Bachelor degree and related work experience may have the best opportunities. **Table 16-3** shows some projections data from the Department of Labor.

Earnings

Median annual wages of radiation therapists were $72,910 in May 2008. The middle 50% earned between $59,050 and $87,910. The lowest 10% earned less than $17,910, and the highest 10% earned more than $104,350. Some employers also reimburse their employees for the cost of continuing education.

Related Occupations

Other occupations that administer medical treatment to patients include cardiovascular technologists and technicians, dental hygienists, diagnostic medical sonographers, nuclear medicine technologists, nursing and psychiatric aides, physical therapist assistants and aides, radiologic technologists and technicians, and registered nurses.

Additional Information

Information on certification by the American Registry of Radiologic Technologists and on accredited radiation therapy programs may be obtained from

TABLE 16-3 Projections Data from the National Employment Matrix for Radiation Therapists

Occupational Title	Employment, 2008	Projected Employment, 2018	Change, 2008–2018	
			Number	Percentage
Radiation therapists	15,200	19,400	4200	27

- American Registry of Radiologic Technologists, 1255 Northland Dr., St. Paul, MN 55120. Internet: http://www.arrt.org

  Information on careers in radiation therapy may be obtained from

- American Society of Radiologic Technologists, 15000 Central Ave. SE, Albuquerque, NM 87123. Internet: http://www.asrt.org

DIAGNOSTIC MEDICAL SONOGRAPHERS
SIGNIFICANT POINTS

- Job opportunities should be favorable.
- Employment will grow as sonography becomes an increasingly attractive alternative to radiological procedures.
- Hospitals employed about 59% of all sonographers.
- Sonographers may receive education and training in hospitals, vocational-technical institutions, colleges or universities, or the armed forces.

Work Description

Diagnostic imaging embraces several procedures that aid in diagnosing ailments. The most familiar procedures are the X-ray and magnetic resonance imaging; however, not all imaging technologies use ionizing radiation or radio waves. Sonography, or ultrasonography, uses sound waves to generate an image for the assessment and diagnosis of various medical conditions. Sonography commonly is associated with obstetrics and the use of ultrasound imaging during pregnancy, but this technology has many other applications in the diagnosis and treatment of medical conditions throughout the body.

Diagnostic medical sonographers use special equipment to direct non-ionizing, high-frequency sound waves into areas of the patient's body. Sonographers operate the equipment, which collects reflected echoes and forms an image that may be videotaped, transmitted, or photographed for interpretation and diagnosis by a physician.

Sonographers begin by explaining the procedure to the patient and recording any medical history that may be relevant to the condition being viewed. They then select appropriate equipment settings and direct the patient to move into positions that will provide the best view. To perform the exam, sonographers use a transducer, which transmits sound waves in a cone or rectangle-shaped beam. Although techniques vary with the area being examined, sonographers usually spread a special gel on the skin to aid the transmission of sound waves.

Viewing the screen during the scan, sonographers look for subtle visual cues that contrast healthy areas with unhealthy ones. They decide whether the images are satisfactory for diagnostic purposes and select which ones to store and show to the physician. Sonographers take measurements, calculate values, and analyze the results in preliminary findings for the physicians.

In addition to working directly with patients, diagnostic medical sonographers keep patient records, and adjust and maintain equipment. They also may prepare work schedules, evaluate equipment purchases, or manage a sonography or diagnostic imaging department.

Diagnostic medical sonographers may specialize in obstetric and gynecologic sonography (the female reproductive system), abdominal sonography (the liver, kidneys, gallbladder, spleen, and pancreas), neurosonography (the brain), or breast sonography. In addition, sonographers may specialize in vascular sonography or cardiac sonography. (The work of vascular sonographers and cardiac sonographers is covered in Chapter 23 on cardiovascular technologists and technicians.)

Obstetric and gynecologic sonographers specialize in the imaging of the female reproductive system. Included in the discipline is one of the better-known uses of sonography: examining the fetus of a pregnant woman to track the baby's growth and health.

Abdominal sonographers inspect a patient's abdominal cavity to help diagnose and treat conditions primarily involving the gallbladder, bile ducts, kidneys, liver, pancreas, spleen, and male reproductive system. Abdominal sonographers also are able to scan parts of the chest, although echocardiographers usually perform studies of the heart using sonography.

Neurosonographers focus on the nervous system, including the brain. In neonatal care, neurosonographers study and diagnose neurological and nervous system disorders in premature infants. They also may scan blood vessels to check for abnormalities indicating a stroke in infants diagnosed with sickle-cell anemia. Like other sonographers, neurosonographers operate transducers to perform the sonogram, but use frequencies and beam shapes different from those used by obstetric and abdominal sonographers.

Breast sonographers use sonography to study diseases of the breasts. Sonography aids mammography in the detection of breast cancer. Breast sonography can also track tumors, blood supply conditions, and assist in the accurate biopsy of breast tissue. Breast sonographers use **high-frequency transducers**, made exclusively to study breast tissue.

Work Environment

Sonographers typically work in clean and well-maintained healthcare facilities. They usually work at diagnostic imaging machines in darkened rooms, but also may perform procedures at patients' bedsides. Sonographers may be on their feet for long periods of time and may have to lift or turn disabled patients. In addition, the nature of their work can put sonographers at an increased risk for musculoskeletal disorders such as carpal tunnel syndrome, or neck, back, and eye strain. The increasing use of ergonomically correct equipment, combined with an increasing awareness of potential problems, will help to minimize such risks.

Some sonographers work as contract employees and may travel to several different healthcare facilities within a given area. Similarly, some sonographers travel with mobile imaging service providers and bring mobile diagnostic imaging services to patients in areas who otherwise lack access to them.

Most full-time sonographers work about 40 hours a week. Hospital-based sonographers may have evening and weekend hours, including times when they are on call and must be ready to report to work on short notice.

Employment Opportunities

Diagnostic medical sonographers held about 50,300 jobs in 2008. About 59% of all sonographer jobs were in public and private hospitals. The remainder worked typically in physicians' offices, medical and diagnostic laboratories, and outpatient care centers.

Educational and Legal Requirements

Employers hiring in **diagnostic medical sonography** recognize and accept several levels of education and methods of acquiring it. Although no one level of education is preferred, employers do prefer registered sonographers who trained in accredited programs.

Education and Training

Several avenues exist for entry into the field of diagnostic medical sonography. Sonographers may train in hospitals, vocational-technical institutions, colleges and universities, or the armed forces. Some training programs prefer applicants with a background in science or experience in other healthcare professions. Some training programs also may consider high school graduates with courses in mathematics and science, as well as applicants with liberal arts backgrounds, but this practice is infrequent.

Colleges and universities offer formal training in both 2- and 4-year programs, culminating in an Associate or a Bachelor degree. Two-year programs are most prevalent. Course work includes classes in anatomy, physiology, instrumentation, basic physics, patient care, and medical ethics.

Employers also accept a few 1-year programs, some of which result in a certificate, as appropriate education. These programs typically are satisfactory education and training for workers already in health care who seek to increase their marketability by training in sonography. These programs are not accredited.

The Commission on Accreditation of Allied Health Education Programs (CAAHEP) accredited 150 diagnostic medical sonography training programs in 2008. These programs typically are the formal training programs offered by colleges and universities. Some hospital programs are accredited as well.

Certification and Other Qualifications

Although no state requires licensure in diagnostic medical sonography, organizations such as the **American Registry for Diagnostic Medical Sonographers**

(ARDMS) certify the skills and knowledge of sonographers through credentialing, including registration. Registration provides an independent, objective measure of an individual's professional standing, and many employers prefer to hire registered sonographers. Sonographers registered by the ARDMS are referred to as **Registered Diagnostic Medical Sonographers (RDMS)**. Registration with the ARDMS requires passing a general physical principles and instrumentation examination, in addition to passing an exam in a specialty such as obstetric and gynecologic sonography, abdominal sonography, or neurosonography. Sonographers must complete a required number of continuing education hours to maintain registration with the ARDMS and to stay abreast of technological advancements related to the occupation.

Sonographers need good communication and interpersonal skills because they must be able to explain technical procedures and results to their patients, some of whom may be nervous about the exam or the problems it may reveal. Good hand-eye coordination is particularly important to obtaining quality images. Sonographers should also enjoy learning because continuing education is the key to them staying abreast of the ever-changing field of diagnostic medicine. A background in mathematics and science is helpful for sonographers as well.

Advancement

Sonographers specializing in one particular discipline often seek competency in other specialties. For example, obstetric sonographers might seek training in abdominal sonography to broaden their opportunities and increase their marketability. Sonographers may also have advancement opportunities in education, administration, research, sales, or technical advising.

Employment Trends

Faster-than-average employment growth is expected. Job opportunities should be favorable.

Employment Change

As the U.S. population ages, demand for diagnostic imaging and therapeutic technology will increase. Employment of diagnostic medical sonographers is expected to increase by about 18% through 2018—faster than the average for all occupations.

Additional job growth also is expected as patients seek safer treatment methods and sonography becomes an increasingly attractive alternative to radiologic procedures. Unlike most diagnostic imaging methods, sonography does not involve radiation, so harmful side effects and complications from repeated use are less likely for both the patient and the sonographer. Sonographic technology is expected to evolve rapidly and to spawn many new sonography procedures, such as 3D- and 4D-sonography for use in obstetric and ophthalmologic diagnosis. However, high costs and necessary approval by the federal government may limit the rate at which some promising new technologies are adopted.

Hospitals will remain the principal employer of diagnostic medical sonographers. However, employment is expected to grow more rapidly in physicians' offices and in medical and diagnostic laboratories, including diagnostic imaging centers. Healthcare facilities such as these are expected to increase very rapidly because of the strong shift toward outpatient care, encouraged by third-party payers and made possible by technological advances that permit more procedures to be performed outside the hospital.

Job Prospects

Job opportunities should be favorable. In addition to job openings from growth, some openings will arise from the need to replace sonographers who retire or leave the occupation permanently for some other reason. Pain caused by musculoskeletal disorders has made it difficult for some sonographers to perform well. Some are forced to leave the occupation early because of such disorders. **Table 16-4** shows some projection data provided by the Department of Labor.

Earnings

Median annual earnings of diagnostic medical sonographers were $61,980 in May 2008. The middle 50% of sonographers earned wages between $52,570 and $73,680 a year. The lowest 10% earned less than $43,600, and the highest 10% earned more than $83,950. Median annual wages of diagnostic medical sonographers in May 2008 were $62,340 for those employed in offices of physicians and $61,870 for those working in general medical and surgical hospitals.

Related Occupations

Diagnostic medical sonographers operate sophisticated equipment to help physicians and other health practitioners diagnose and treat patients. Workers in related occupations include cardiovascular technologists and technicians, clinical laboratory technologists and technicians, nuclear medicine technologists, and respiratory therapists.

TABLE 16-4 Projections Data from the National Employment Matrix for Diagnostic Medical Sonographers

Occupational Title	Employment, 2008	Projected Employment, 2018	Change, 2008–2018	
			Number	Percentage
Diagnostic medical sonographers	50,300	59,500	9200	18

Additional Information

For information on a career as a diagnostic medical sonographer, contact

- Society of Diagnostic Medical Sonography, 2745 Dallas Pkwy., Suite 350, Plano, TX 75093-8730. Internet: http://www.sdms.org

For information on becoming a registered diagnostic medical sonographer, contact

- American Registry for Diagnostic Medical Sonography, 51 Monroe St., Plaza East 1, Rockville, MD 20850-2400. Internet: http://www.ardms.org

For certification information, contact

- American Registry of Radiologic Technologists, 1255 Northland Dr., St. Paul, MN 55120-1155. Internet: http://www.arrt.org/

For more information on ultrasound in medicine, contact

- American Institute of Ultrasound in Medicine, 14750 Sweitzer Ln., Suite 100, Laurel, MD 20707-5906. Internet: http://www.aium.org

For a current list of accredited education programs in diagnostic medical sonography, contact

- Joint Review Committee on Education in Diagnostic Medical Sonography, 2025 Woodlane Dr., St. Paul, MN 55125-2998. Internet: http://www.jrcdms.org
- Commission on Accreditation for Allied Health Education Programs, 1361 Park St., Clearwater, FL 33756. Internet: http://www.caahep.org

chapter seventeen

Social Workers*

*All information in this chapter, unless otherwise indicated, was obtained from Bureau of Labor Statistics. U.S. Department of Labor. *Occupational Outlook Handbook 2010–2011 Edition*. 2010.

INTRODUCTION

Health has been defined as not merely the absence of disease but as a condition of complete physical, mental, and social well-being. The effect of social, economic, and **environmental factors** on an individual's state of health is an accepted fact, and studies reveal a definite relationship between these factors and occurrence of disease. Recognizing this, health officials are placing increasing emphasis on the **psychological treatment** as well as the clinical treatment of patients in health facilities. Very often a patient's restoration to and maintenance of health is influenced by many factors that can be dealt with by other professionals, including competently trained social workers.

Social work in the health field involves programs and services that meet the special needs of the ill, disabled, elderly, or otherwise handicapped. Social workers deal with the total emotional, social, cultural, and physical needs of patients in whom the effects of illness go far beyond bodily discomfort. Such problems usually lie in three areas—problems within the patient, problems between the patient and family, or problems between the patient and the patient's environment. Illness invariably results in **emotional stress** and often causes significant changes in the lives of patients and their families. Medical care alone, even if it is of the highest quality, is often not sufficient. Social workers help patients and members of the health team to deal with these problems by providing a skilled appraisal of the source and significance of social, emotional, environmental, and economic factors affecting health. Their efforts with individual patients or groups of patients help to bring about constructive and meaningful changes in terms of total health.

SOCIAL WORKERS

SIGNIFICANT POINTS

- Employment is projected to grow faster than the average for all occupations.
- About 54% of jobs were in healthcare and social assistance industries, and 31% of social workers work for government.
- Although a Bachelor degree is necessary for entry-level positions, a Master degree in social work or a related field is necessary for some positions.
- Job prospects are expected to be favorable, particularly for social workers who specialize in the aging population or work in rural areas.

Work Description

Social work is a profession for those with a strong desire to help improve people's lives. Social workers assist people by helping them cope with and solve issues in their everyday lives, such as family and personal problems and dealing with relationships. Some social workers help clients who face a disability, life-threatening disease, or social problem, such as inadequate housing, unemployment, or substance abuse. Social workers also assist families that have serious domestic conflicts, sometimes involving child or spousal abuse. Additionally, they may conduct research, advocate for improved services, or become involved in planning or policy development. Many social workers specialize in serving a particular population or working in a specific setting. In all settings, these workers may also be called licensed **clinical social workers**, if they hold the appropriate state-mandated license.

Child, family, and **school social workers** provide social services and assistance to improve the social and psychological functioning of children and their families. Workers in this field assess their clients' needs and offer assistance to improve their situation. This often includes coordinating available services to assist a child or family. They may assist single parents in finding day care, arrange adoptions, or help find foster homes for neglected, abandoned, or abused children. These workers may specialize in working with a particular problem, population, or setting, such as child protective services, adoption, homelessness, domestic violence, or foster care.

In schools, social workers often serve as the link between students' families and the school, working with parents, guardians, teachers, and other school officials to ensure that students reach their academic and personal potential. They also assist students in dealing with stress or emotional problems. Many school social workers work directly with children with disabilities and their families. In addition, they address problems such as misbehavior, truancy, teenage pregnancy, and drug and alcohol problems, and advise teachers on how to cope with difficult students. School social workers may teach workshops to entire classes on topics like **conflict resolution**.

Child, family, and school social workers may be known as **child welfare social workers, family services social workers**, or **child protective services social workers**. These workers often work for individual and family services agencies, schools, or state or local governments.

Medical and public health social workers provide psychosocial support to individuals, families, or vulnerable populations so they can cope with chronic, acute, or terminal illnesses, such as Alzheimer's disease, cancer, or AIDS. They also advise family caregivers, counsel patients, and help plan for patients' needs after discharge from hospitals. They may arrange for at-home services, such as **Meals on Wheels** or home care. Some work on interdisciplinary teams that evaluate certain kinds of patients, such as geriatric or organ-transplant patients.

Some specialize in services for senior citizens and their families. These social workers may run support groups for the adult children of aging parents. Also, they may assess, coordinate, and monitor services such as housing, transportation, and long-term care. These workers may be known as gerontological social workers. Medical and public health social workers may work for hospitals, nursing and personal care facilities, individual and family services agencies, or local governments.

Mental health and substance abuse social workers assess and treat individuals with mental illness or substance abuse problems. Such services include

individual and group therapy, outreach, crisis intervention, social rehabilitation, and teaching skills needed for everyday living. They also may help plan
for supportive services to ease clients' return to the community when leaving inpatient facilities. They may provide services to assist family members of
those who suffer from addiction or other mental health issues. These workers may work in outpatient facilities, where clients come in for treatment and
then leave, or in inpatient programs, where patients reside at the facility. Some
mental health and substance social workers may work in employee-assistance
programs. In this setting, they may help people cope with job-related pressures
or with personal problems that affect the quality of their work. Other social
workers work in private practice, where they are employed directly by the client.
These social workers may be known as clinical social workers, **occupational
social workers**, or substance abuse social workers.

Other types of social workers include **social work administrators**, social
work researchers, and **social work planners and policy makers**, who develop
and implement programs to address issues such as child abuse, homelessness, substance abuse, poverty, and violence. These workers research and
analyze policies, programs, and regulations. They identify social problems
and suggest legislative and other solutions. They may help raise funds or
write grants to support these programs.

Work Environment

Social workers usually spend most of their time in an office or residential facility, but they also may travel locally to visit clients, meet with service providers,
or attend meetings. Some may meet with clients in one of several offices within
a local area. Social work, although satisfying, can be challenging. Understaffing
and large caseloads add to the pressure in some agencies. Full-time social workers usually work a standard 40-hour week, but some occasionally work evenings
and weekends to meet with clients, attend community meetings, and handle
emergencies. Some work part time, particularly in voluntary nonprofit agencies.

Employment Opportunities

Social workers held about 642,000 jobs, in 2008. About 54% jobs were
in healthcare and social assistance industries, and 31% or social workers
were employed by government agencies. Although most social workers are
employed in cities or suburbs, some work in rural areas. Employment by
type of social worker, in 2008, is shown in **Table 17-1**.

Educational and Legal Requirements

A Bachelor degree is the minimum requirement for entry into the occupation,
but some positions require an advanced degree. All states and the District of
Columbia have some licensure, certification, or registration requirement, but
these regulations vary.

TABLE 17-1 Employment by Type of Social Worker, in 2008

Child, family and school social workers	292,600
Medical and public health social workers	138,700
Mental health and substance abuse social workers	137,300
Social workers, all other	73,400

Education and Training

A Bachelor degree in social work (**BSW**) is the most common minimum requirement to qualify for a job as a social worker; however, majors in psychology, sociology, and related fields may qualify for some entry-level jobs, especially in small community agencies. Although a Bachelor degree is sufficient for entry into the field, an advanced degree is required for some positions. A Master degree in social work (MSW) is typically required for positions in health and school settings, and is required for clinical work as well. Some jobs in public and private agencies may require an advanced degree, such as an MSW with a concentration in social services policy or administration. Supervisory, administrative, and staff training positions usually require an advanced degree. College and university teaching positions and most research appointments normally require a doctorate in social work (DSW or PhD).

As of June 2009, the Council on Social Work Education accredited 468 Bachelor degree programs and 196 Master degree programs. The Group for the Advancement of Doctoral Education listed 74 doctoral programs in social work (DSW or PhD) in the United States. Bachelor degree programs prepare graduates for direct service positions, such as caseworker, mental health assistant, group home worker, and residential counselor. These programs include courses in social work values and ethics, dealing with a culturally diverse clientele and at-risk populations, the promotion of social and economic justice, human behavior and the social environment, social welfare policy and services, social work practice, social research methods, and field education. Accredited programs require a minimum of 400 hours of supervised field experience.

Master degree programs prepare graduates for work in their chosen field of concentration and continue to develop the skills required to perform clinical assessments, manage large caseloads, take on supervisory roles, and explore new ways of drawing upon social services to meet the needs of clients. Master degree programs usually last 2 years and include a minimum of 900 hours of supervised field instruction or internship. A part-time program may take 4 years. Entry into a Master degree program does not require a Bachelor degree in social work, but courses in psychology, biology, sociology, economics, political science, and social work are recommended. In addition, a second language can be very helpful. Most Master degree programs offer advanced standing for those with a Bachelor degree from an accredited social work program.

Licensure

All states and the District of Columbia have licensing, certification, or registration requirements regarding social work practice and the use of professional titles. Most states require 2 years or 3000 hours of supervised clinical experience for the licensure of clinical social workers. Because of some limitations on what settings unlicensed social workers may work and some variation in the requirements to obtain a license, those interested in becoming a social worker should research requirements in their state.

Other Qualifications

Social workers should be emotionally mature, objective, and sensitive to people and their problems. They must be able to handle responsibility, work independently, and maintain good working relationships with clients and coworkers. Volunteer or paid jobs as a social work aide can help people test their interest in this field.

Certification and Advancement

Advancement to supervisor, program manager, assistant director, or executive director of a social service agency or department usually requires an advanced degree and related work experience. Other career options for social workers include teaching, research, and consulting. Some of these workers help formulate government policies by analyzing and advocating policy positions in government agencies, in research institutions, and on legislators' staffs.

Some social workers go into private practice. Most private practitioners are clinical social workers who provide psychotherapy, usually paid for through health insurance or by the clients themselves. Private practitioners must have at least a Master degree and a period of supervised work experience. A network of contacts for referrals also is essential.

Employment Trends

Employment for social workers is expected to grow faster than the average for all occupations through 2018. Job prospects are expected to be favorable, particularly for social workers who specialize in the aging population or work in rural areas.

Employment Change

Employment of social workers is expected to increase by 16% during the 2008–2018 decade, which is faster than the average for all occupations. The growing elderly population and the aging baby-boom generation will create greater demand for health and social services, resulting in rapid job growth among gerontological social workers. Employment of social workers in private social service agencies also will increase.

Employment of child, family, and school social workers is expected to grow by about 12%, which is as fast as the average for all occupations. Demand for child and family social workers should continue, as these workers are needed to investigate child abuse cases and place children in foster care and with adoptive families. However, growth for these workers may be hampered by the budget constraints of state and local governments, who are among the largest employers of these workers. Furthermore, demand for school social workers will continue and lead to more jobs as efforts are expanded to respond to rising student enrollments, as well as the continued emphasis on integrating children with disabilities into the general school population. There could be competition for school social work jobs in some areas because of the limited number of openings. The availability of federal, state, and local funding will be a major factor in determining the actual job growth in schools.

Mental health and substance abuse social workers will grow by almost 20% over the 2008–2018 decade, which is much faster than the average. In particular, social workers specializing in substance abuse will experience strong demand. Substance abusers are increasingly being placed into treatment programs instead of being sentenced to prison. Also, growing numbers of the substance abusers sentenced to prison or probation are increasingly being required by correctional systems to have substance abuse treatment added as a condition to their sentence or probation. As this trend grows, demand will strengthen for treatment programs and social workers to assist abusers on the road to recovery. Opportunities for social workers in private practice will expand, as they are preferred over more costly psychologists. Furthermore, the passage of legislation that requires insurance plans offered by employers to cover mental health treatment in a manner that is equal to the treatment of physical health may increase the demand for mental health treatment.

Growth of medical and public health social workers is expected to be about 22%, which is much faster than the average for all occupations. One of the major contributing factors is the rise in the elderly population. These social workers will be needed to assist in finding the best care and assistance for the aging, as well as to support their families. Employment opportunities for social workers with backgrounds in gerontology should be excellent, particularly in the growing numbers of assisted-living and senior-living communities. The expanding senior population also will spur demand for social workers in nursing homes, long-term care facilities, home care agencies, and hospices.

Job Prospects

Job prospects are expected to be favorable. Many job openings will stem from growth and the need to replace social workers who leave the occupation. However, competition for social worker jobs is expected in cities where training programs for social workers are prevalent. Opportunities should be good in rural areas, which often find it difficult to attract and retain qualified staff. By specialty, job prospects may be best for those social workers with

TABLE 17-2 Projections Data from the National Employment Matrix for Different Categories of Social Workers

Occupational Title	Employment, 2008	Projected Employment, 2018	Change, 2008–2018	
			Number	Percentage
Social workers	642,000	745,400	103,400	16
Child, family, and school social workers	292,600	328,700	36,100	12
Medical and public health social workers	138,700	169,800	31,100	22
Mental health and substance abuse social workers	137,300	164,100	26,800	20
Social workers, all other	73,400	82,800	9400	13

a background in gerontology and substance abuse treatment. **Table 17-2** shows some job projections data from the Department of Labor.

Earnings

Median annual wages of child, family, and school social workers were $39,530 in May 2008. The middle 50% earned between $31,040 and $52,080. The lowest 10% earned less than $25,870, and the top 10% earned more than $66,430. Median annual wages in the industries employing the largest numbers of child, family, and school social workers in May 2008 are shown in **Table 17-3**.

Median annual wages of medical and public health social workers were $46,650 in May 2008. The middle 50% earned between $35,550 and $57,690. The lowest 10% earned less than $28,100, and the top 10% earned more than $69,090. Median annual wages in the industries employing the largest numbers of medical and public health social workers in May 2008 are shown in **Table 17-4**.

TABLE 17-3 Median Annual Wages in the Industries Employing the Largest Numbers of Child, Family, and School Social Workers in May 2008

Elementary and secondary schools	$53,860
Local government	46,650
State government	39,600
Individual and family services	34,450
Other residential care facilities	34,270

TABLE 17-4 Median Annual Wages in the Industries Employing the Largest Numbers of Medical and Public Health Social Workers in May 2008

General medical and surgical hospitals	$51,470
Home healthcare services	46,930
Local government	44,140
Nursing care facilities	41,080
Individual and family services	38,370

Median annual wages of mental health and substance abuse social workers were $37,210 in May 2008. The middle 50% earned between $28,910 and $48,560. The lowest 10% earned less than $21,770, and the top 10% earned more than $61,430. Median annual wages in the industries employing the largest numbers of mental health and substance abuse social workers in May 2008 are shown in **Table 17-5**.

Median annual wages of social workers, all others, were $46,220 in May 2008. The middle 50% earned between $34,420 and $60,850. The lowest 10% earned less than $27,400, and the top 10% earned more than $74,040. Median annual wages in the industries employing the largest numbers of social workers in May 2008 are shown in **Table 17-6**.

About 24% of social workers are members of a union or covered by a union contract.

Related Occupations

Through direct counseling or referral to other services, social workers help people solve a range of personal problems. Workers in occupations with similar duties include clergy, counselors, health educators, probation officers and correctional treatment specialists, psychologists, and social and **human service assistants**.

Additional Information

For information about career opportunities in social work and voluntary credentials for social workers, contact

- National Association of Social Workers, 750 First St. NE, Suite 700, Washington, DC 20002-4241. Internet: http://www.socialworkers.org/

TABLE 17-5 Median Annual Wages in the Industries Employing the Largest Numbers of Mental Health and Substance Abuse Social Workers in May 2008

Outpatient care centers	$36,660
Individual and family services	35,900
Residential mental retardation, mental health, and substance abuse facilities	33,950

TABLE 17-6 Median Annual Wages in the Industries Employing the Largest Numbers of Social Workers in May 2008

General medical and surgical hospitals	$55,940
Local government	51,700
Individual and family services	36,660
Residential mental retardation, mental health, and substance abuse facilities	36,460
Community food and housing, and emergency and other relief services	31,890

- Center for Clinical Social Work, 27 Congress St., Suite 501, Salem, MA 01970. Internet: http://www.centercsw.org

  For a listing of accredited social work programs, contact

- Council on Social Work Education, 1725 Duke St., Suite 500, Alexandria, VA 22314-3457. Internet: http://www.cswe.org

  Information on licensing requirements and testing procedures for each state may be obtained from state licensing authorities, or from

- Association of Social Work Boards, 400 South Ridge Pkwy., Suite B, Culpeper, VA 22701. Internet: http://www.aswb.org

SOCIAL AND HUMAN SERVICE ASSISTANTS

SIGNIFICANT POINTS

- A high school diploma is the minimum educational requirement, but employers often seek individuals with relevant work experience or education beyond high school.
- Employment is projected to grow much faster than the average for all occupations.
- Job opportunities should be excellent, particularly for applicants with appropriate postsecondary education, but wages remain low.

Work Description

Social and human service assistants help social workers, healthcare workers, and other professionals to provide services to people. Social and human service assistant is a generic term for workers with a wide array of job titles, including **human service worker, case management aide**, social work assistant, community support worker, mental health aide, community outreach worker, **life skills counselor**, social services aide, youth worker, psychological aide, client advocate, or gerontology aide. They usually work under the direction of workers from a variety of fields, such as nursing, psychiatry, psychology, or social work. The amount of responsibility and supervision they are given varies a great deal. Some have little direct supervision. For example, they may run a group home. Others work under close direction.

Social and human service assistants provide services to clients to help them improve their quality of life. They assess clients' needs; investigate their eligibility for benefits and services such as food stamps, Medicaid, and welfare; and help clients obtain them. They also arrange for transportation, if necessary, and provide emotional support. They monitor and keep case records on clients and report progress to supervisors and case managers.

Social and human service assistants play a variety of roles in the community. For example, they may organize and lead group activities, assist clients in need of counseling or crisis intervention, or administer food banks or emergency fuel programs. In halfway houses, group homes, and government-supported housing programs, they assist adults who need supervision with personal hygiene and daily living tasks. They review clients' records, ensure that clients take prescribed medication, talk with family members, and confer with medical personnel and other caregivers to provide insight into clients' needs. Assistants also give emotional support and help clients become involved in community recreation programs and other activities.

In psychiatric hospitals, rehabilitation programs, and outpatient clinics, social and human service assistants work with psychiatrists, psychologists, social workers, and others to help clients master everyday living skills, communicate more effectively, and live well with others. They support the client's participation in a treatment plan, such as individual or group counseling or occupational therapy. The work, while satisfying, can be emotionally draining. Understaffing and relatively low pay can add to the pressure.

Work Environment

Working conditions of social and human service assistants vary. Some work in offices, clinics, and hospitals, while others work in group homes, shelters, and day programs. Traveling to see clients is required for some jobs. Sometimes working with clients can be dangerous even though most agencies do everything they can to ensure their workers' safety. Some work in the evening and on weekends.

Educational and Legal Requirements

A high school diploma is the minimum education requirement, but employers often seek individuals with relevant work experience or education beyond high school.

Education and Training

Many employers prefer to hire people with some education beyond high school. Certificates or Associate degrees in subjects such as human services, gerontology, or one of the social or behavioral sciences meet many employers' requirements. Some jobs may require a Bachelor or Master degree in human services or a related field, such as counseling, rehabilitation, or social work.

Human services degree programs have a core curriculum that trains students to observe patients and record information, conduct patient interviews, implement treatment plans, employ problem-solving techniques, handle crisis intervention matters, and use proper case management and referral procedures. Many programs utilize fieldwork to give students hands-on experience. General education courses in liberal arts, sciences, and the humanities also are part of most curriculums. Most programs also offer specialized courses related to addictions, gerontology, child protection, and other areas. Many degree programs require the completion of a supervised internship.

Workers' level of education often determines the kind of work they are assigned and the degree of responsibility that is given to them. For example, workers with no more than a high school education are likely to work in direct-care services and help clients to fill out paperwork. They may receive extensive on-the-job training on how to perform these tasks. Workers with a college degree, however, might do supportive counseling, coordinate program activities, or manage a group home. Social and human service assistants with proven leadership ability, especially acquired from paid or volunteer experience in social services, often have greater autonomy in their work. Regardless of the academic or work background of employees, most employers provide some form of in-service training, such as seminars and workshops, to their employees.

Other Qualifications

These workers should have a strong desire to help others, effective communication skills, a sense of responsibility, and the ability to manage time effectively. Many human service jobs involve direct contact with people who are vulnerable to exploitation or mistreatment, so patience and understanding are also highly valued characteristics. It is becoming more common for employers to require a criminal background check, and in some settings, workers may be required to have a valid driver's license.

Advancement

Formal education is almost always necessary for advancement. In general, advancement to case management or social work jobs requires a Bachelor or Master degree in human services, counseling, rehabilitation, social work, or a related field.

Employment Opportunities

Social and human service assistants held about 352,000 jobs in 2008. More than 65% were employed in the healthcare and social assistance industries, and state and local governments employed almost 24%.

Employment Trends

Employment of social and human service assistants is expected to grow much faster than the average for all occupations. Job prospects are expected to be excellent, particularly for applicants with relevant postsecondary education.

Employment Change

The number of social and human service assistants is expected to grow by nearly 23% between 2008 and 2018, which is much faster than the average for all occupations. This is largely a result of the aging population and increased demand for mental health and substance abuse treatment.

As the elderly population continues to grow, the demand for social and human service assistants will expand. This is largely a result of the increased need for social services demanded by this population, such as adult day care, meal delivery programs, and support during medical crises. Social and human service assistants, who assist in locating and providing these services, will be needed to meet this increased demand.

Opportunities are expected to be good in private social service agencies. Employment in private agencies will grow as state and local governments continue to contract out services to the private sector in an effort to cut costs.

The number of jobs for social and human service assistants in state and local governments will grow, but not as fast as employment for social and human service assistants in other industries. Employment in the public sector may fluctuate with the level of funding provided by state and local governments and with the number of services contracted out to private organizations.

Job Prospects

Job prospects for social and human service assistants are expected to be excellent, particularly for individuals with appropriate education after high school. Job openings will come from job growth, but also from the need to replace workers, who advance into new positions, retire, or leave the workforce for other reasons. There will be more competition for jobs in urban areas than in rural ones, but qualified applicants should have little difficulty finding employment. **Table 17-7** shows some projections data from the Department of Labor.

Earnings

Median annual wages of social and human service assistants were $27,280 in May 2008. The middle 50% earned between $21,860 and $34,590. The top 10% earned more than $43,510, while the lowest 10% earned less than $17,900.

Median annual wages in the industries employing the largest numbers of social and human service assistants in May 2008 are shown in **Table 17-8**.

TABLE 17-7 Projections Data from the National Employment Matrix for Social and Human Service Assistants

Occupational Title	Employment, 2008	Projected Employment, 2018	Change, 2008–2018	
			Number	Percentage
Social and human service assistants	352,000	431,500	79,500	23

TABLE 17-8 Median Annual Wages in the Industries Employing the Largest Numbers of Social and Human Service Assistants in May 2008

State government	$35,510
Local government	32,560
Individual and family services	26,250
Vocational rehabilitation services	23,910
Residential mental retardation, mental health, and substance abuse facilities	23,580

Related Occupations

Workers in other occupations that require skills similar to those of social and human service assistants include child care workers, correctional officers, counselors, eligibility interviewers, government program workers, health educators, home health aides and personal and home care aides, occupational therapist assistants and aides, probation officers and correctional treatment specialists, psychologists, recreational therapists, and social workers.

Additional Information

For information on programs and careers in human services, contact

- Council for Standards in Human Services Education, 1935 S. Plum Grove Rd., PMB 297, Palatine, IL 60067. Internet: http://www.cshse.org
- National Organization for Human Services, 5341 Old Highway 5, Suite 206, #214, Woodstock, GA 30188. Internet: http://www.nationalhuman-services.org

Information on job openings may be available from state employment service offices or directly from city, county, or state departments of health, mental health and mental retardation, and human resources.

SOCIAL ASSISTANCE, EXCEPT CHILD DAY CARE
SIGNIFICANT POINTS

- Professional and service occupations each account for about 35% of jobs in this industry.
- Job opportunities in social assistance should be numerous through the year 2018 because of job turnover and rapid employment growth.
- Some of the fastest growing occupations in the nation, such as home health aides, personal and home care aides, and social and human service assistants, are concentrated in social assistance.
- Average earnings are low because of the large number of part-time and low-paying service jobs.

Work Description

At times, people need help to live a full and productive life. They may need assistance finding a job or appropriate child care, learning skills to find employment, locating safe and adequate housing, and getting nutritious food for their family. The **social assistance industry** provides help to individuals and families to aid them in becoming healthy and productive members of society.

Goods and Services

Social assistance establishments provide a wide array of services that include helping the homeless, counseling troubled individuals, training the unemployed or underemployed, and helping families to obtain financial assistance. In general, organizations in this industry work to improve the lives of the individuals and families they serve and to enrich their communities. The specific services provided vary greatly, depending on the population the establishment is trying to serve and its goals or mission.

Social assistance consists of four segments—individual and family services; community food and housing, and emergency and other relief services; **vocational rehabilitation services**; and child day care services.

Establishments in the individual and family services sector work to provide the skills and resources necessary for individuals to be more self-sufficient and for families to live in a stable and safe environment. Many of the services in this sector are often aimed at a particular population, such as children, the elderly, or those with mental or physical disabilities. Services targeted at children can vary greatly based on the goal of the establishment providing the assistance. Some programs provide youth services, such as after-school programs or youth centers. Generally, these programs are aimed at giving children a safe, supportive environment to spend their time after school or on weekends. Often provided are planned activities such as field trips, tutors to assist with homework, and games and sports equipment. Foster care and adoption agencies are responsible for locating safe families and environments for children who are in the foster care system. Other services aimed at children include drug prevention and mentoring programs.

Services provided to the elderly include senior centers, which hold activities geared toward senior citizens and are often used as a place for seniors to gather to talk or play games. Some services, like adult day care and support groups, are aimed at assisting both the elderly and disabled populations. Home care agencies provide services to the elderly and disabled to allow them to continue to live in their own homes. This may include assistance with errands, cleaning, and personal hygiene.

This sector of the industry also provides other support services to individuals and families. These often include programs for people addicted to drugs or alcohol, parenting support groups, and rape or abuse crisis centers.

Community food and housing, and emergency and other relief services establishments provide various types of assistance to members of the community.

This sector consists of three subsectors: community food services, community housing services, and emergency and other relief services.

Establishments in the community food services subsector collect, prepare, and deliver food for the needy. They may prepare and deliver meals to persons who by reason of age, disability, or illness are unable to prepare meals for themselves. They may also collect and distribute salvageable or donated food, or prepare and provide meals at fixed or mobile locations, and distribute clothing and blankets. Food banks, meal delivery programs, and soup kitchens are included in this industry.

Establishments in the community housing services sector provide short-term emergency shelter for victims of domestic violence, sexual assault, or child abuse. These establishments may operate their own shelter or may provide subsidized housing using existing homes. Also included in this sector are establishments that provide transitional housing for low-income individuals and families, as well as establishments that provide temporary residential shelter for the homeless, runaway youths, and patients and families caught in medical crises. Community housing establishments also perform volunteer construction or repair of homes of the elderly or disabled, or of low-cost housing—sometimes in partnership with a future homeowner, who may assist in construction or repair work.

Establishments in the emergency and other relief services sector provide assistance to those who have been directly affected by a disaster. These establishments may set up emergency shelters for those who have been evacuated from their homes. They may also provide medical assistance to those who have been injured by the disaster. In the aftermath, they may supply food and clothing, assist with resettlement, and provide counseling to victims of domestic or international disasters or conflicts.

Vocational rehabilitation services establishments provide vocational rehabilitation or life skills services. Workers in these establishments work with people who are disabled, either from birth or as a result of an illness or injury. They teach clients the skills necessary to live independently and to find employment. Often, services include assessing the abilities of their clients to determine what occupations they should pursue. These workers may also provide job counseling and assist in locating training and educational programs.

Thousands of other establishments, mainly in state and local government, provide additional social assistance.

Industry Organization

About 94,700 establishments in the private sector provided social assistance in 2008. Of that, 75,700 establishments were in individual and family services; about 9500 were in community food and housing, and emergency and other relief services; and 9500 were in vocational rehabilitation service organizations. Establishments within social assistance tend to be smaller than the average for all establishments. In 2008, 84,500 of social assistance establishments employed fewer than 50 workers; however, larger establishments accounted for most jobs.

Work Environment

Some social assistance establishments operate around the clock, and evening, weekend, and holiday work is common. Some establishments may be under-staffed, resulting in large caseloads for each worker. Jobs in voluntary, non-profit agencies often are part time.

Some workers spend a substantial amount of time traveling within the local area. For example, home health and personal care aides routinely visit clients in their homes; social workers and social and human service assistants also may make home visits.

Employment Opportunities

Social assistance provided 1.6 million nongovernment wage and salary jobs in 2008. About 67% were in individual and family services, as shown in **Table 17-9**.

Careers in social assistance appeal to people with a strong desire to make life better and easier for others. Workers in this industry are usually good communicators and enjoy interacting with people.

Professional and Related Occupations

More than 35% of all nongovernment social assistance jobs were in profes-sional and related occupations in 2008 (**Table 17-10**). Some of these workers may have direct interaction with clients, while others have limited interac-tion with the population they serve. These workers may spend their time on tasks like planning programs or events, organizing classes or workshops, grant writing, or creating educational material to be used by clients. Profes-sional and related occupations within this industry include social workers, counselors, health educators, teachers (adult literacy and remedial educa-tion), and social and human service assistants.

Social workers help clients function within the limitations of their envi-ronment, improve their relationships, and solve personal and family prob-lems. Often, this includes counseling and assessing the needs of clients, referring them to the appropriate sources of help, and monitoring their prog-ress. Many social workers specialize in a particular field. Child, family, and

TABLE 17-9 Percentage Distribution of Employment and Establishments in Social Assistance, Except Child Day Care, by Detailed Industry Sector, 2008

Industry Segment	Employment	Establishments
Total	100.0	100.0
Individual and family services	71.0	79.9
Vocational rehabilitation services	20.3	10.0
Emergency and other relief services	8.7	10.1

Source: Bureau of Labor Statistics: Quarterly Census of Employment and Wages, 2008.

TABLE 17-10 Employment of Wage and Salary Workers in Social Assistance, Except Child Day Care, by Occupation, 2008, and Projected Change, 2008–2018

Occupation	Employment (in Thousands), 2008		Percentage Change, 2008–2018
All occupations	*1649.5*	*100.0*	*40.1*
Management, business, and financial occupations	*144.7*	*8.8*	*23.4*
Professional and related occupations	578.7	35.1	30.2
Counselors	134.3	8.1	25.8
Social workers	131.8	8.0	25.9
Social and human service assistants	121.5	7.4	44.6
Service occupations	*615.1*	*37.3*	*62.5*
Home health aides	142.3	8.6	76.1
Nursing aides, orderlies, and attendants	18.1	1.1	31.2
Cooks and food preparation workers	18.6	1.1	25.3
Personal and home care aides	279.7	17.0	82.8
Recreation and fitness workers	26.1	1.6	25.3
Office and administrative support occupations	*188.5*	*11.4*	*19.8*
Financial clerks	28.7	1.7	21.3
Information and record clerks	34.3	2.1	19.6
Secretaries and administrative assistants	50.2	3.0	20.6
Office clerks, general	40.2	2.4	22.3

Columns may not add to the total due to the omission of occupations that have low employment.
Source: Bureau of Labor Statistics National Employment Matrix, 2008–2018.

school social workers aim to improve the social and psychological functioning of children and their families. This may involve work with single parents, parents seeking to adopt a child, or children in foster care. Medical and public health social workers provide support to individuals and families coping with illness or diseases; at times, this may include both terminal and chronic illnesses. These workers may help arrange for additional services to assist in caring for patients, including services such as Meals on Wheels or other home care services. Mental health and substance abuse social workers evaluate and treat individuals with mental health and substance abuse problems. They may provide treatment through group or individual therapy or work in community outreach and crisis intervention.

Counselors help people evaluate their interests and abilities, and advise and assist them with personal and social problems. Counselors often specialize, so their job duties vary greatly based on the population they serve.

Educational, vocational, and school counselors in this industry usually work in what is more commonly known as career counseling. They assist clients in determining what field of work they should enter and help them with job-seeking activities, like locating job openings for which they might apply or coaching them on proper interview conduct. Rehabilitation counselors assist people in living with the social, personal, and vocational effects of a disability. In some cases, they assist people who are adjusting to a disability caused by injury or illness, but they also counsel those who have had disabilities from birth. These counselors evaluate the abilities and limitations of the individual and arrange for vocational training, medical care, and job placement. Mental health counselors work with individuals and families to treat mental and emotional disorders. This is often done through individual or group therapy. Substance abuse and behavioral disorder counselors work with individuals who are addicted to substances, such as alcohol, tobacco, or other drugs, or a behavior, like gambling or an eating disorder. They often use techniques such as group and individual therapy, and in some settings they may be involved in crisis intervention and community outreach. Marriage and family therapists aim to improve an individual's or family's mental and emotional health through therapeutic techniques that focus on the family system. This is frequently done through individual, family, or group therapy.

Health educators encourage healthy lifestyles and wellness by educating individuals and communities about behaviors that promote health and prevent illness and diseases. They use many different mediums and methods to get their message to their target audience. They often teach classes and plan events or programs on health-related topics, create pamphlets and other written materials, and organize medical screenings for illnesses. In the social assistance industry, they may often be responsible for writing applications for grants.

Adult literacy and remedial education teachers instruct adults and out-of-school youths in reading, writing, speaking English, and basic math skills. These workers may work with adults who are in need of basic education or who are pursuing their General Educational Development (GED) certificate. They may also work with adults and children who are learning English as a second language.

Social and human service assistants work in a variety of social and human service delivery settings. However, in general, they provide services, both directly and indirectly, to ensure that individuals in their care can function to the best of their ability. Job titles and duties of these workers vary, but they include human service worker, case management aide, social work assistant, mental health aide, child abuse worker, community outreach worker, and gerontology aide.

Service Occupations

About 37% of the jobs in the social assistance industry were in service occupations in 2008. These workers generally provide direct services to their clients. Many do work that requires hands-on interaction with clients. These workers include personal and home care aides and home health aides who help elderly, disabled, and ill persons live in their own homes, instead of in an institution. Personal and home care aides provide routine personal care services. They perform nonmedical tasks, such as cooking meals, basic cleaning, assisting the client to bathe or dress, and, in some cases, accompanying the client to appointments. Home health aides provide health-related services, like administering oral medication or checking the client's pulse rate or temperature. They may assist the client in performing exercises and help them bathe, dress, and groom.

Other Occupations

Social and community service managers plan, organize, and coordinate the activities of a social service program or community outreach program. This includes overseeing the budget and the execution of programs, events, and services. They often may direct and supervise those who are providing both direct and indirect services to the population they serve. In some situations, they may be responsible for fundraising activities or speaking to donors.

As in most industries, office and administrative support workers—secretaries and bookkeepers, for example—help with record keeping and other administrative tasks. Table 17-10 shows the employment of wage and salary workers in social assistance, except child day care by occupation, 2008, and projected change, 2008–2018.

Educational and Legal Requirements

Training requirements within this industry vary greatly based on occupation, state licensure requirements, and the setting in which the work is done. Many workers begin in this industry by working as a volunteer. Volunteering with a student, religious, or charitable organization is a good way for job seekers to test their interest in social assistance, and may provide an advantage when applying for jobs in this industry. However, for many occupations, a Bachelor or Master degree is required for entrance into the industry.

Professional and Related Occupations

Entry requirements vary based on occupational specialty and state licensure and certification requirements. A Bachelor degree is the minimum educational requirement for entry-level positions as social workers, health educators, and counselors. However, some specialties and employers may require additional education, like a Master degree, or some previous experience. In some settings and specialties, social workers, marriage and family therapists, and counselors may be required to obtain a state-issued license. Licensure requirements vary from state to state, but most states require a Master degree and 2 years or 3000 hours of supervised clinical experience.

Educational requirements are less stringent for social and human service assistants. Some employers do not require any education beyond high school, but they may prefer some related work experience. Other employers favor workers who have completed some coursework in human services, social work, or another social or behavioral science. Employers may also prefer an Associate degree or a Bachelor degree in human services or social work. A number of employers also provide in-service training, such as seminars and workshops.

Professional workers in this industry often advance to a supervisory position, such as supervisor, program manager, assistant director, or executive director. Often, advancing to this level requires a Master degree and the appropriate licenses. Some workers opt to move away from positions that provide services directly to clients and become involved in policy making, grant writing, or research. Others enter private practice and provide psychotherapeutic counseling and other services on a contract basis.

Service Occupations

Service occupations within this industry require little to no education beyond a high school diploma. Personal and home care aides receive some basic on-the-job training. The federal government has guidelines for home health aides whose employers receive reimbursement from Medicare. These workers must complete both a training program consisting of a minimum of 75 hours and a competency or state licensure program. Training includes information regarding personal hygiene, **safe transfer techniques**, reading and recording vital signs, infection control, and basic nutrition. However, aides may take a competency exam to become certified without taking this training. At a minimum, 16 hours of supervised practical training are required before an aide has direct contact with a resident. These licensure requirements represent the minimum, as outlined by the federal government. Some states require additional hours of training to become certified.

Workers in service occupations may opt to get some additional training and may advance to, for example, licensed practical nurse. Some personal and home care aides may opt to open their own businesses.

Employment Trends

Job opportunities in social assistance should be plentiful, because employment is expected to grow rapidly, and many workers leave the industry and need to be replaced.

Employment Change

Employment within this industry is expected to grow rapidly relative to all other industries through 2018. The number of nongovernment wage and salary jobs is expected to increase 40%, compared with 11% for all industries combined. However, growth will not be evenly distributed among the industry's subsectors (**Table 17-11**). The individual and family services industry is expected to grow by 48%, making it one of the fastest-growing industries in the economy. The community food and housing, and emergency and other relief services industry is expected to grow by 22%, and vocational rehabilitation

TABLE 17-11 Employment in Social Assistance, Except Child Day Care, by Industry Segment, 2008, and Projected Change, 2008–2018

Industry Segment	Employment (in Thousands), 2008	Percentage Change, 2008–2018
Social assistance, except child day care, total	1649.5	40.1
Individual and family services	1108.6	47.8
Vocational and rehabilitation services	402.8	25.1
Community food and housing, and emergency and other relief services	138.1	21.7

Source: Bureau of Labor Statistics National Employment Matrix, 2008–2018.

services is expected to grow 25% over the 2008–2018 projection period. Table 17-11 shows employment in social assistance, except child day care by industry segment, 2008, and projected change, 2008–2018.

Growth of employment in the social assistance industry may depend, in large part, on the amount of funding made available by government and managed-care organizations. Employment in private social service agencies may grow if state and local governments contract out some of their social services functions in an effort to cut costs.

Projected job growth in individual and family services will result mostly from an increase in the population that will demand additional services from this sector. As baby boomers age, there is expected to be a substantial increase in the elderly population, one of the primary segments of the population that requires services from this industry. As a result, there should be an expansion in programs that serve the elderly, such as adult day care or services that provide home care, allowing the elderly to remain in their homes for as long as possible. Furthermore, the demand will increase for drug and alcohol abuse treatment programs, as those with drug and alcohol addictions are increasingly required to attend treatment programs—rather than being sent to jail.

Growth in the community food and housing, and emergency and other services industry will result from an increase in urbanization. As urban areas become more densely populated, and if natural disasters hit these populous areas, more people will be affected, thus increasing the demand for disaster relief. Furthermore, demand for housing and food assistance will remain steady.

Employment growth in vocational rehabilitation services is expected because of a steady demand for services for individuals with some form of physical or mental disability. Workers in this sector will continue to serve people who are injured on the job and need assistance moving back into the work environment. But the main source of growing demand for this sector is the expected increase in the elderly population, which frequently uses services provided by this industry to recover from illnesses or injuries.

Some of the fastest-growing occupations in the nation are concentrated in social assistance, like home health aides and personal and home care aides. Employment growth for these two occupations is driven predominantly by the need to provide services to the elderly and ill in their homes and to avoid expensive hospital or nursing home care.

Job Prospects

Besides job openings arising from employment growth, many additional openings will stem from the need to replace workers who transfer to other occupations or stop working. Workers leave jobs in this industry at a higher rate than the rest of the economy, making job prospects excellent.

Earnings
Industry Earnings

Average earnings in the social assistance industry are lower than the average for all industries, as shown in **Table 17-12**.

Wages in selected occupations in the social assistance industry, except the child day care industry, appear in **Table 17-13**. As in most industries, professionals and managers commonly earn more than other workers, reflecting higher education levels, broader experience, and greater responsibility.

Benefits and Union Membership

Professional workers in this industry typically receive benefits, such as medical insurance and paid time off. However, those working in service occupations may receive no benefits. About 8% of workers in the social assistance industry were union members or were covered by union contracts in 2008, as opposed to 14% throughout all industries.

Related Occupations

Workers in other occupations that require skills similar to those of social and human service assistants include counselors, health educators, home

TABLE 17-12 Average Earnings of Nonsupervisory Workers in Social Assistance, 2008

Industry Segment	Hourly	Weekly
Total, private industry	$18.08	$608
Social assistance	12.47	375
Community food and housing, and emergency and other relief services	14.72	466
Individual and family services	13.13	394
Vocational rehabilitation services	12.45	360

Source: Bureau Labor Statistics Current Employment Statistics, 2008.

TABLE 17-13 Median Hourly Wages of the Largest Occupations in Social Assistance, Except Child Day Care, May 2008

Occupation	Individual and Family Services	Community Food and Housing, and Emergency and Other Relief Services	Vocational Rehabilitation Services	All Industries
Social and community service managers	$25.01	$24.23	$24.40	$26.92
Mental health and substance abuse social workers	17.26	16.02	15.64	17.89
Child, family, and school social workers	16.56	15.80	16.22	19.01
Community and social service specialists, all other	15.67	15.09	14.58	18.11
Rehabilitation counselors	13.60	14.85	13.97	14.87
Social and human service assistants	12.62	11.94	11.50	13.12
Office clerks, general	11.31	10.72	11.08	12.17
Personal and home care aides	9.77	10.50	9.58	9.22
Home health aides	9.48	9.43	9.71	9.84
Janitors and cleaners, except maids and housekeeping cleaners	9.41	10.34	9.45	10.31

Source: Bureau of Labor Statistics Occupational Employment Statistics, May 2008.

health aides and personal and home care aides, social and human service assistants, social workers, teachers (adult literacy and remedial education, and self-enrichment education).

Additional Information

For information about careers in social work and voluntary credentials for social workers, contact

- National Association of Social Workers, 750 First St. NE, Suite 700, Washington, DC 20002-4241. Internet: http://www.socialworkers.org

For information on programs and careers in human services, contact

- Council for Standards in Human Services Education, 1935 S. Plum Grove Rd., PMB 297, Palatine, IL 60067. Internet: http://www.cshse.org
- National Human Services Assembly, 1319 F St. NW, Suite 402, Washington, DC 20004. Internet: http://www.nassembly.org
- National Association for Home Care and Hospice, 228 Seventh St. SE, Washington, DC 20003. Internet: http://www.nahc.org

For information regarding jobs in nonprofit organizations and voluntary credential information, contact

- **American Humanics**, 1100 Walnut St., Suite 1900, Kansas City, MO 64106. Internet: http://www.humanics.org

State employment service offices also may be able to provide information on job opportunities in social assistance.

chapter eighteen

Psychology*

---

*All information in this chapter, unless otherwise indicated, was obtained from Bureau of Labor Statistics. U.S. Department of Labor. *Occupational Outlook Handbook 2010–2011 Edition*. 2010.

PSYCHOLOGISTS

SIGNIFICANT POINTS

- About 34% of psychologists are self-employed, mainly as private practitioners and independent consultants.
- Employment growth will vary by specialty, for example, clinical, counseling, and school psychologists will have 11% growth; industrial-organizational psychologists, 26% growth; and 14% growth is expected for all other psychologists.
- Acceptance to graduate psychology programs is highly competitive.
- Job opportunities should be the best for those with a doctoral degree in a subfield, such as health; those with a Master degree will have good prospects in industrial-organization; Bachelor degree holders will have limited prospects.

Psychologists study the human mind and human behavior. Psychology examines both normal and abnormal aspects of human behavior. It involves a scientific approach to gathering, quantifying, analyzing, and interpreting data on why people act as they do, and it provides insight into varied forms of human behavior and related mental and physical processes. Through the application of highly developed skills and knowledge, psychologists seek to identify, prevent, and solve various problems of human behavior.

As a health career, psychology is one of the allied professions devoted to mental health. Along with psychiatry, psychiatric nursing, and psychiatric social work, psychology contributes both to the prevention of mental illness and to its diagnosis and treatment. As distinguished from psychiatry, which is a branch of medicine, psychology is a nonmedical science. As distinguished from psychiatric social work, psychology looks first at the individual's reaction to his or her circumstances—family, job, and social relationships. The psychiatric social worker looks first at the individual's surrounding circumstances and relationships.

Work Description

Psychologists study the behavior of individuals or groups to ascertain and understand the fundamental processes of human behavior. Some psychologists interview people and develop, administer, and score a variety of psychological tests. Others work in mental health and rehabilitation centers, hospitals, and private practice providing counseling and therapy to persons suffering emotional or adjustment problems. Because psychology is basically a science, the psychologist is often the most knowledgeable member among mental health team members regarding research. The science of psychology is one of the main sources of our increasing understanding of mental capacity and intelligence, and of the effect of emotions on health. Psychological research contributes continuously to the improvement of diagnostic methods, and to the treatment and prevention of mental and emotional disorders. Psychologists also work with disabled persons, either individually or in groups, to diagnose behavioral problems and to help correct or compensate for these impairments.

A psychologist may also design, develop, and evaluate materials and procedures in order to resolve problems in educational and training programs. In addition, psychologists employ scientific techniques to deal with problems of motivation and morale in the work setting. Psychologists design and conduct experiments and analyze the results in an effort to improve understanding of human and animal behavior.

Some psychologists engage in private practice; others work in colleges and universities, where they train graduate and undergraduate students and engage in basic research. Increasingly, they work as administrators of psychology programs in hospitals, clinics, and community health agencies. Many psychologists practice in federal, state, and local agencies; a variety of business and industrial organizations; and various branches of the armed forces.

The field of psychology offers a number of specializations that an individual can consider when planning a career. These include clinical psychology, counseling psychology, developmental psychology, educational psychology, engineering psychology, personnel psychology, experimental psychology, industrial psychology, psychometric psychology, rehabilitation psychology, and school and social psychology.

Clinical psychologists specialize in the assessment and treatment of persons with mental and emotional problems and illnesses. They apply experience and scientific knowledge of human behavior to diagnose and treat psychological problems ranging from the developmental crises of adolescence to extreme psychotic conditions. Working in hospitals, clinics, or similar medical institutions, clinical psychologists design and conduct research either alone or in conjunction with physicians or other social scientists. Although the emphasis may differ considerably from one position to another, all clinical psychologists apply scientific knowledge of human behavior to the care and treatment of the handicapped and the disturbed. Their purpose is to help the individual who is maladjusted learn new and better habits of behavior so as to find a more satisfactory way of living.

Clinical psychologists work directly with the patient, or client, to uncover everything that will help in understanding his or her difficulties. They also talk with the patient's family, friends, physicians, and teachers to round out this background. At times they consult with the psychiatrist, social worker, and others concerned with diagnosis and treatment.

Areas of specialization within clinical psychology include health psychology, neuropsychology, and geropsychology. **Health psychologists** promote good health through health maintenance counseling programs designed to help people achieve health-oriented goals, such as to stop smoking or lose weight. **Neuropsychologists** study the relationship between the brain and behavior. They often work in stroke and head injury programs. **Geropsychologists** deal with the special problems faced by the elderly. The emergence and subsequent growth of these specialties reflect the increasing participation of psychologists in providing direct services to special patient populations.

Counseling psychologists help normal or moderately maladjusted persons, either individually or in groups, to gain self-understanding, recognize problems, and develop methods of coping with their difficulties. Counseling psychologists pay particular attention to the role of education and work in a person's behavior and to the interaction between individuals and the environments in which they live. This type of counseling primarily emphasizes preventing or forestalling the onset of mental illness. Growing public awareness of mental health problems has highlighted the importance of and need for the services that counseling psychologists provide.

Developmental psychologists specialize in investigating the development of individuals from prenatal origins through old age. In studying the changes involved in mental, physical, emotional, and social growth, psychologists seek to determine the origins of human behavior and the reasons for human growth and decline. For example, psychologists study how an infant's behavior and feelings are related to the biological growth of the body. Another example is the study of the influence of social learning and socialization on an infant's development into a socialized person.

Educational psychologists design, develop, and evaluate materials and procedures to resolve problems in educational and training programs. These psychologists analyze educational problems, develop instructional materials, determine the best conditions for instruction, and evaluate the effectiveness of educational programs. Educational psychologists are employed by school systems, the military, private research and development firms, and industrial concerns.

Engineering psychologists deal with the design and use of the systems and environments in which people live and work. Their main purpose is the development of efficient and acceptable interactions between individuals and the environments in which they function. These psychologists help to design equipment, work areas, and systems involving the direct interaction of humans with machines. In addition, they develop the aids, training devices, and requirements necessary to train personnel to operate such systems successfully.

Personnel psychologists apply their professional knowledge and skills to the hiring, assignment, and promotion of employees in order to increase productivity and job satisfaction. These psychologists place great emphasis on data gathered from tests and interviews, and apply the techniques of other psychological specialties, such as experimental, developmental, and psychometric, to normal work activities.

The **experimental psychologist** designs, conducts, and analyzes experiments to develop knowledge regarding human and animal behavior. Experimental psychology is a general term referring to the methods employed in studying behavioral processes. There are different types of experimental psychologists who are identified by their areas of specialization, such as comparative psychologists, learning psychologists, and physiological psychologists.

Industrial psychologists use scientific techniques to deal with problems of motivation and morale in the work setting. These psychologists study how work is organized and suggest improvements designed to increase quality, productivity, and worker satisfaction. They consult with all levels of management and present recommendations for developing better training programs and preretirement counseling services.

Psychometric psychologists directly measure human behavior, primarily through the use of tests. Typically well-trained in mathematics, statistics, and the use of computers, they design, develop, and validate intelligence, aptitude, and personality tests; analyze complex statistical data; and design various types of research investigations. In addition, they conduct pilot studies of newly developed materials and devise and apply procedures for measuring the **psychological variables** affecting human behavior.

Rehabilitation psychologists work with disabled persons, either individually or in groups, to assess the degree of disability and develop ways to correct or compensate for these impairments. The primary concern of these psychologists is the restoration of the patient's emotional, physical, social, and **economic effectiveness**.

School psychologists are concerned with developing effective programs for improving the intellectual, social, and emotional development of children in an educational system or school. They diagnose the needs of gifted, handicapped, and disturbed children, and plan and carry out corrective programs to enable them to do schoolwork at their highest potential and to adjust to everyday pressures. To determine a child's needs, limitations, and potential, school psychologists often observe the child in the classroom and at play, study school records, consult with teachers and parents, and administer and interpret various tests. They advise school administrators and parent–teacher groups in matters involving psychological services within the school system and serve as consultants in education for children who are handicapped, mentally disturbed, or mentally retarded. School psychologists also engage in planning and developing special programs in the area of adult education.

Social psychologists study the effects of groups and individuals on the thoughts, feelings, attitudes, and behavior of the individual. They study, for example, the ways in which social attitudes develop and how members of families, neighborhoods, and communities influence each other.

Experimental or research psychologists work in university and private research centers and in business, nonprofit, and governmental organizations. They study the behavior of both human beings and animals such as rats, monkeys, and pigeons. Prominent areas of study in experimental and research psychology include motivation, thought, attention, learning and memory, sensory and perceptual processes, and the effects of substance abuse. Research and experimental psychologists also study genetic and neurological factors affecting behavior.

Work Environment

A psychologist's specialty and place of employment determine his or her working conditions. Clinical, school, and counseling psychologists in private practice have their own offices and set their own hours. They often offer evening and weekend hours to accommodate their clients. Psychologists employed in hospitals, nursing homes, and other health facilities may work shifts including evenings and weekends, whereas those who work in schools and clinics generally work regular hours.

Psychologists employed as faculty by colleges and universities divide their time between teaching and research and may also have administrative responsibilities. Many have part-time consulting practices. Most psychologists in government and industry have well-structured schedules.

Increasingly, many psychologists work as part of a team and consult with other psychologists and various healthcare professionals. Many experience pressures due to deadlines, tight schedules, and overtime work. Their routines may be interrupted frequently. Travel is required to attend conferences or conduct research.

Employment Opportunities

Psychologists held about 170,200 jobs in 2008. Educational institutions employed about 29% of psychologists in positions other than teaching, such as counseling, testing, research, and administration. About 21% were employed in health care, primarily in offices of mental health practitioners, hospitals, physicians' offices, and outpatient mental health and substance abuse centers. Government agencies at the state and local levels employed psychologists in correctional facilities, law enforcement, and other settings.

After several years of experience, some psychologists—usually those with doctoral degrees—enter private practice or set up private research or consulting firms. About 34% of psychologists were self-employed in 2008, compared with only 8% of all professional workers.

In addition to the previously mentioned jobs, many psychologists held faculty positions at colleges and universities and as high school psychology teachers.

Educational and Legal Requirements

A Master or doctoral degree and a license are required for most psychologists.

Education and Training

A doctoral degree usually is required for independent practice as a psychologist. Psychologists with a PhD or Doctor of Psychology (PsyD) qualify for a wide range of teaching, research, clinical, and counseling positions in universities, healthcare services, elementary and secondary schools, private industry, and government. Psychologists with a doctoral degree often work in clinical positions or in private practice, but they also sometimes teach, conduct research, or carry out administrative responsibilities.

A doctoral degree generally requires about 5 years of graduate study, culminating in a dissertation based on original research. Courses in quantitative research methods, which include the use of computer-based analysis, are an integral part of graduate study and are necessary to complete the dissertation. The PsyD degree may be based on practical work and examinations rather than a dissertation. In clinical, counseling, and school psychology, the requirements for the doctoral degree include an internship of at least 1 year.

A specialist degree or its equivalent is required in most states for an individual to work as a school psychologist, although a few states still credential school psychologists with Master degrees. A specialist (EdS) degree in school psychology requires a minimum of 2 years of full-time graduate study (at least 60 graduate semester hours) and a 1-year full-time internship during the third year. In professional practice school psychologists address both the educational and the mental health components of students' development; as a consequence, their training includes coursework in both education and psychology.

People with a Master degree in psychology may work as industrial-organizational psychologists. They also may work as psychological assistants under the supervision of doctoral-level psychologists and may conduct research or psychological evaluations. A Master degree in psychology requires at least 2 years of full-time graduate study. Degree requirements usually include practical experience in an applied setting and a master's thesis based on an original research project.

Competition for admission to graduate psychology programs is keen. Some universities require applicants to have an undergraduate major in psychology. Others prefer only coursework in basic psychology with additional courses in statistics, mathematics, and the biological, physical, and social sciences.

A Bachelor degree in psychology qualifies a person to assist psychologists and other professionals in community mental health centers, vocational rehabilitation offices, and correctional programs. Bachelor degree holders may also work as research or administrative assistants for psychologists. Some work as technicians in related fields, such as marketing research. Many find employment in other areas, such as sales, service, or business management.

In the federal government, candidates having at least 24 semester hours in psychology and one course in statistics qualify for entry-level positions. However, competition for these jobs is keen because this is one of the few ways in which one can work as a psychologist without an advanced degree.

The American Psychological Association (**APA**) presently accredits doctoral training programs in clinical, counseling, and school psychology, as well as institutions that provide internships for doctoral students in school, clinical, and counseling psychology. The National Association of School Psychologists, with the assistance of the National Council for Accreditation of Teacher Education, helps to approve advanced degree programs in school psychology.

Licensure

Psychologists in independent practice or those who offer any type of patient care—including clinical, counseling, and school psychologists—must meet certification or licensing requirements in all states and the District of Columbia.

Licensing laws vary by state and by type of position, but require licensed or certified psychologists to limit their practice to areas in which they have developed professional competence through training and experience. Clinical and counseling psychologists usually need a doctorate in psychology, an approved internship, and 1 to 2 years of professional experience. In addition, all states require that applicants pass an examination. Most state licensing boards administer a standardized test, and many supplement that with additional oral or essay questions. Some states require continuing education for renewal of the license.

The National Association of School Psychologists (**NASP**) awards the Nationally Certified School Psychologist (NCSP) designation, which recognizes professional competency in school psychology at a national level. Currently, 31 states recognize the NCSP and allow those with the certification to transfer credentials from one state to another without taking a new certification exam. In states that recognize the NCSP, the requirements for certification or licensure and those for the NCSP often are the same or similar. Requirements for the NCSP include the completion of 60 graduate semester hours in school psychology; a 1200-hour internship, 600 hours of which must be completed in a school setting; and a passing score on the National School Psychology Examination.

Other Qualifications

Aspiring psychologists who are interested in direct patient care must be emotionally stable, mature, and able to deal effectively with people. Sensitivity, compassion, good communication skills, and the ability to lead and inspire others are particularly important qualities for people wishing to do clinical work and counseling. Research psychologists should be able to do detailed work both independently and as part of a team. Patience and perseverance are vital qualities, because achieving results in the psychological treatment of patients or in research may take a long time.

Certification and Advancement

The American Board of Professional Psychology (ABPP) recognizes professional achievement by awarding specialty certification in 13 different areas, such as psychoanalysis, rehabilitation, forensic, group, school, clinical health, and couple and family. Candidates for ABPP certification must meet general criteria that consist of a doctorate in psychology, as well as state licensure. Each candidate must then meet additional criteria of the specialty field, which is usually a combination of postdoctoral training in their specialty, several years of experience, and professional endorsements, as determined by the ABPP. Applicants are then required to pass the specialty board examination. Psychologists can improve their advancement opportunities by earning an advanced degree and by participation in continuing education. Many psychologists opt to start their own practice after gaining experience working in the field.

Employment Trends

Fast-as-average employment growth is expected for psychologists. Job prospects should be best for people who have a doctoral degree from a leading university in an applied specialty, such as counseling or health, and people with a specialist or doctoral degree in school psychology. Master degree holders in fields other than industrial-organizational psychology will face keen competition. Opportunities will be limited for Bachelor degree holders.

Employment Change

Employment of psychologists is expected to grow 12% from 2008 to 2018, faster than the average for all occupations. Employment will grow because of increased demand for psychological services in schools, hospitals, social service agencies, mental health centers, substance abuse treatment clinics, consulting firms, and private companies.

Employment growth will vary by specialty. Growing awareness of how students' mental health and behavioral problems, such as bullying, affect learning will increase demand for school psychologists to offer student counseling and mental health services.

The rise in healthcare costs associated with unhealthy lifestyles, such as smoking, alcoholism, and obesity, has made prevention and treatment more critical. An increase in the number of employee assistance programs, which help workers deal with personal problems, also should lead to employment growth for clinical and counseling specialties. Clinical and counseling psychologists also will be needed to help people deal with depression and other mental disorders, marriage and family problems, job stress, and addiction. The growing number of elderly will increase the demand for psychologists trained in geropsychology to help people deal with the mental and physical changes that occur as individuals grow older. There also will be an increased need for psychologists to work with military veterans returning from armed conflicts.

Industrial-organizational psychologists also will be in demand to help to boost worker productivity and retention rates in a wide range of businesses. Industrial-organizational psychologists will help companies deal with issues such as workplace diversity and antidiscrimination policies. Companies also will use psychologists' expertise in survey design, analysis, and research to develop tools for marketing evaluation and statistical analysis.

Job Prospects

Job prospects should be the best for people who have a doctoral degree from a leading university in an applied specialty, such as counseling or health, and people with a specialty or doctoral degree in school psychology. Psychologists with extensive training in quantitative research methods and computer science may have a competitive edge over applicants without such a background.

TABLE 18-1 Projections Data from the National Employment Matrix for Psychologists

Occupational Title	Employment, 2008	Projected Employment, 2018	Change, 2008–2018	
			Number	Percentage
Psychologists	170,200	190,000	19,800	12
Clinical, counseling, and school psychologists	152,000	168,800	16,800	11
Industrial-organizational psychologists	2300	2900	600	26
Psychologists, all other	15,900	18,300	2300	14

Master degree holders in fields other than industrial-organizational psychology will face keen competition for jobs because of the limited number of positions that require only a Master degree. Master degree holders may find jobs as psychological assistants or counselors, providing mental health services under the direct supervision of a licensed psychologist. Still others may find jobs involving research and data collection and analysis in universities, government, or private companies.

Opportunities directly related to psychology will be limited for Bachelor degree holders. Some may find jobs as assistants in rehabilitation centers or other jobs involving data collection and analysis. Those who meet state certification requirements may become high school psychology teachers. **Table 18-1** shows some projection data provided by the Department of Labor.

Earnings

Median annual earnings of wage and salary clinical, counseling, and school psychologists in May 2008 were $64,140. The middle 50% earned between $48,700 and $82,800. The lowest 10% earned less than $37,900, and the highest 10% earned more than $106,840. Median annual earnings in the industries employing the largest numbers of clinical, counseling, and school psychologists are shown in **Table 18-2**.

TABLE 18-2 Median Annual Earnings in the Industries Employing the Largest Numbers of Clinical, Counseling, and School Psychologists in May 2008

Offices of other health practitioners	$68,400
Elementary and secondary schools	65,710
State government	63,710
Outpatient care centers	59,130
Individual and family services	57,440

Median annual earnings of wage and salary industrial-organizational psychologists in May 2008 were $77,010. The middle 50% earned between $54,100 and $115,720. The lowest 10% earned less than $38,690, and the highest 10% earned more than $149,120. In 2008, about 31% of all psychologists were members of a union.

Related Occupations

Psychologists work with people, developing relationships and comforting them. Other occupations with similar duties include counselors, social workers, clergy, sociologists, special education teachers, funeral directors, market and survey researchers, recreation workers, and managers and specialists in human resources, training, and labor relations. Psychologists also sometimes diagnose and treat problems, and assist patients in recovery. These duties are similar to those for physicians and surgeons, radiation therapists, audiologists, dentists, optometrists, and speech-language pathologists.

Additional Information

For information on careers, educational requirements, financial assistance, and licensing in all fields of psychology, contact

- American Psychological Association, Center for Psychology Workforce Analysis and Research and Education Directorate, 750 1st St. NE, Washington, DC 20002. Internet: http://www.apa.org/students

For information on careers, educational requirements, certification, and licensing of school psychologists, contact

- National Association of School Psychologists, 4340 East West Hwy., Suite 402, Bethesda, MD 20814. Internet: http://www.nasponline.org

Information about state licensing requirements is available from

- Association of State and Provincial Psychology Boards, P.O. Box 241245, Montgomery, AL 36124. Internet: http://www.asppb.org

Information about psychology specialty certifications is available from

- American Board of Professional Psychology, 600 Market St., Suite 300, Chapel Hill, NC 27516. Internet: http://www.abpp.org

chapter nineteen

Respiratory Care Practitioners*

*All information in this chapter, unless otherwise indicated, was obtained from Bureau of Labor Statistics, U.S. Department of Labor. *Occupational Outlook Handbook 2010–2011 Edition*. 2010.

MAINTAINING THE BREATH OF LIFE

A person can live without water for a few days and without food for a few weeks, but if someone stops breathing for more than a few minutes, serious brain damage occurs. If oxygen is cut off for more than 9 minutes, death usually results. Respiratory therapists, also known as respiratory care personnel, specialize in the evaluation, treatment, and care of patients with breathing disorders. Whenever the breath of life is at risk, the respiratory therapist is called upon to intervene. Respiratory therapists perform procedures that are crucial in maintaining the lives of seriously ill patients with breathing problems and assist in the treatment of patients with cardiopulmonary (heart and lung) diseases and disorders.

RESPIRATORY THERAPISTS

SIGNIFICANT POINTS

- Job opportunities should be very good.
- Hospitals will account for the vast majority of job openings, but a growing number of openings will arise in other settings.
- An Associate degree is the minimum educational requirement, but a Bachelor or Master degree may be important for advancement.
- All states except Alaska and Hawaii require respiratory therapists to be licensed.

Work Description

Respiratory therapists—also known as respiratory care practitioners—evaluate, treat, and care for patients with breathing or other cardiopulmonary disorders. Practicing under the direction of a physician, respiratory therapists assume primary responsibility for all respiratory care therapeutic treatments and diagnostic procedures, including the supervision of respiratory therapy technicians. They consult with physicians and other healthcare staff to help develop and modify patient care plans. Therapists also provide complex therapy requiring considerable independent judgment, such as caring for patients on life support in intensive-care units of hospitals.

Respiratory therapists evaluate and treat all types of patients, ranging from premature infants whose lungs are not fully developed to elderly people whose lungs are diseased. They provide temporary relief to patients with chronic asthma or emphysema and give emergency care to patients who are victims of a heart attack, stroke, drowning, or shock.

Respiratory therapists interview patients, perform limited physical examinations, and conduct diagnostic tests. For example, respiratory therapists test patients' breathing capacity and determine the concentration of oxygen and other gases in their blood. They also measure a patients' pH, which indicates the acidity or alkalinity of the blood. To evaluate a patient's **lung capacity**, respiratory therapists have the patient breathe into an instrument that measures the volume and flow of oxygen during inhalation and exhalation. By comparing the reading with the norm for the patient's age, height, weight, and sex, respiratory therapists can provide information that helps determine whether the patient has any lung deficiencies. To analyze oxygen, carbon dioxide, and **blood pH** levels, therapists draw an **arterial blood sample**, place it in a blood gas analyzer, and relay the results to a physician, who then makes treatment decisions.

To treat patients, respiratory therapists use **oxygen or oxygen mixtures**, **chest physiotherapy**, and **aerosol** medications—liquid medications suspended in a gas that forms a mist that is inhaled. They teach patients how to inhale the aerosol properly to ensure its effectiveness. When a patient has difficulty getting enough oxygen into his or her blood, therapists increase the patient's concentration of oxygen by placing an oxygen mask or nasal cannula on the patient and setting the oxygen flow at the level prescribed by a physician. Therapists also connect patients who cannot breathe on their own to **ventilators** that deliver pressurized oxygen into the lungs. The therapists insert a tube into the patient's trachea, or windpipe; connect the tube to the ventilator; and set the rate, volume, and oxygen concentration of the oxygen mixture entering the patient's lungs.

Therapists perform regular assessments of patients and equipment. If a patient appears to be having difficulty breathing or if the oxygen, carbon dioxide, or pH level of the blood is abnormal, therapists change the ventilator setting according to the doctor's orders or check the equipment for mechanical problems.

Respiratory therapists perform chest physiotherapy on patients to remove mucus from their lungs and make it easier for them to breathe. Therapists place patients in positions that help drain mucus, and then vibrate the patients' rib cages, often by tapping on the chest, and tell the patients to cough. Chest physiotherapy may be needed after surgery, for example, because anesthesia depresses respiration. As a result, physiotherapy may be prescribed to help get the patient's lungs back to normal and to prevent congestion. Chest physiotherapy also helps patients suffering from lung diseases, such as cystic fibrosis, that cause mucus to collect in the lungs.

Therapists who work in home care teach patients and their families to use ventilators and other life-support systems. In addition, these therapists visit patients in their homes to inspect and clean equipment, evaluate the home environment, and ensure that patients have sufficient knowledge of their diseases and the proper use of their medications and equipment. Therapists also make emergency visits if equipment problems arise.

In some hospitals, therapists perform tasks that fall outside their traditional role. Therapists are becoming involved in areas such as pulmonary rehabilitation, smoking-cessation counseling, disease prevention, case management, and polysomnography—the diagnosis of breathing disorders during sleep, such as apnea. Respiratory therapists also increasingly treat critical-care patients, either as part of surface and air transport teams or as part of rapid-response teams in hospitals.

Work Environment

Respiratory therapists generally work between 35 and 40 hours a week. Because hospitals operate around the clock, therapists can work evenings, nights, or weekends. They spend long periods standing and walking between patients' rooms. In an emergency, therapists work under the stress of the situation. Respiratory therapists employed in home health care must travel frequently to patients' homes.

Respiratory therapists are trained to work with gases stored under pressure. Adherence to safety precautions and the regular maintenance and testing of equipment minimize the risk of injury. As in many other health occupations, respiratory therapists are exposed to infectious diseases, but by carefully following proper procedures, they can minimize these risks.

Employment Opportunities

Respiratory therapists held about 105,900 jobs in 2008. About 81% of jobs were in hospitals, mainly in departments of respiratory care, anesthesiology, or pulmonary medicine. Most of the remaining jobs were in offices of physicians or other health practitioners, consumer-goods rental firms that supply respiratory equipment for home use, nursing care facilities, employment services, and home healthcare services.

Educational and Legal Requirements

An Associate degree is the minimum educational requirement, but a Bachelor or Master degree may be important for advancement. All states except Alaska and Hawaii require respiratory therapists to be licensed.

Education and Training

An Associate degree is required to become a respiratory therapist. Training is offered at the postsecondary level by colleges and universities, medical schools, vocational-technical institutes, and the armed forces. Most programs award Associate or Bachelor degrees and prepare graduates for jobs as advanced respiratory therapists. A limited number of Associate degree programs lead to jobs as entry-level respiratory therapists. According to the Commission on Accreditation of Allied Health Education Programs (CAA-HEP), 31 entry-level and 346 advanced respiratory therapy programs were accredited in the United States in 2008.

Among the areas of study in respiratory therapy programs are human anatomy and physiology, pathophysiology, chemistry, physics, microbiology, pharmacology, and mathematics. Other courses deal with therapeutic and diagnostic procedures and tests, equipment, patient assessment, cardiopulmonary resuscitation, the application of clinical practice guidelines, patient care outside of hospitals, cardiac and pulmonary rehabilitation, respiratory health promotion and disease prevention, and medical record keeping and reimbursement.

High school students interested in applying to respiratory therapy programs should take courses in health, biology, mathematics, chemistry, and physics. Respiratory care involves basic mathematical problem solving and an understanding of chemical and physical principles. For example, respiratory care workers must be able to compute dosages of medication and calculate gas concentrations.

Licensure and Certification

A license is required to practice as a respiratory therapist, except in Alaska and Hawaii. Also, most employers require respiratory therapists to maintain a cardiopulmonary resuscitation (CPR) certification.

Licensure is usually based, in large part, on meeting the requirements for certification from the National Board for Respiratory Care (NBRC). The board offers the **Certified Respiratory Therapist (CRT)** credential to those who graduate from entry-level or advanced programs accredited by the CAAHEP or the **Committee on Accreditation for Respiratory Care (CoARC)** and who also pass an exam.

The board also awards the **Registered Respiratory Therapist (RRT)** to CRTs who have graduated from advanced programs and pass two separate examinations. Supervisory positions and intensive-care specialties usually require the RRT.

Other Qualifications

Therapists should be sensitive to patients' physical and psychological needs. Respiratory care practitioners must pay attention to detail, follow instructions, and work as part of a team. In addition, operating advanced equipment requires proficiency with computers.

Advancement

Respiratory therapists advance in clinical practice by moving from general care to the care of critically ill patients who have significant problems in other organ systems, such as the heart or kidneys. Respiratory therapists, especially those with a Bachelor or Master degree, also may advance to supervisory or managerial positions in a respiratory therapy department. Respiratory therapists in home health care and equipment rental firms may become branch managers. Some respiratory therapists advance by moving into teaching positions. Others use the knowledge gained as a respiratory therapist to work in another industry, such as developing, marketing, or selling pharmaceuticals and medical devices.

Employment Trends

Much faster than average growth is projected for respiratory therapists. Job opportunities should be very good.

Employment Change

Employment of respiratory therapists is expected to grow by 21% from 2008 to 2018, much faster than the average for all occupations. The increasing demand will come from substantial growth in the middle-aged and elderly population—a development that will heighten the incidence of **cardiopulmonary disease**. Growth in demand also will result from the expanding role of respiratory therapists in case management, disease prevention, emergency care, and the early detection of pulmonary disorders.

Older Americans suffer most from respiratory ailments and cardiopulmonary diseases, such as pneumonia, chronic bronchitis, emphysema, and heart disease. As the number of older persons increases, the need for respiratory therapists is expected to increase as well. In addition, advances in inhalable medications and in the treatment of lung transplant patients, heart attack and accident victims, and premature infants—many of whom depend on a ventilator during part of their treatment—will increase the demand for the services of respiratory care practitioners.

Job Prospects

Job opportunities are expected to be very good, especially for those with a Bachelor degree and certification, and those with cardiopulmonary care skills or experience working with infants. The vast majority of job openings will continue to be in hospitals. However, a growing number of openings are expected to be outside of hospitals, especially in home healthcare services, offices of physicians or other health practitioners, consumer-goods rental firms, or in the employment services industry as temporary workers in various settings. **Table 19-1** provides projections data from the National Employment Matrix.

Earnings

Median annual wages of wage and salary respiratory therapists were $52,200 in May 2008. The middle 50% earned between $44,490 and $61,720. The lowest 10% earned less than $37,920, and the highest 10% earned more than $69,800.

Additional Information

Information concerning a career in respiratory care is available from

- American Association for Respiratory Care, 9425 N. MacArthur Blvd., Suite 100, Irving, TX 75063. Internet: http://www.aarc.org

TABLE 19-1   Projections Data from the National Employment Matrix for Respiratory Therapists

Occupational Title	Employment, 2008	Projected Employment, 2018	Change, 2008–2018	
			Number	Percentage
Respiratory therapists	105,900	128,100	22,200	21

For a list of accredited educational programs for respiratory care practitioners, contact either of the following organizations:

- Commission on Accreditation for Allied Health Education Programs, 1361 Park St., Clearwater, FL 33756. Internet: http://www.caahep.org
- Committee on Accreditation for Respiratory Care, 1248 Harwood Rd., Bedford, TX 76021.

Information on gaining credentials in respiratory care and a list of state licensing agencies can be obtained from

- National Board for Respiratory Care, Inc., 18000 W. 105th St., Olathe, KS 66061. Internet: http://www.nbrc.org

RESPIRATORY THERAPY TECHNICIANS

Work Description

Respiratory therapy technicians follow specific, well-defined respiratory care procedures under the direction of respiratory therapists and physicians. They help to evaluate, treat, and care for patients with breathing or other cardiopulmonary disorders.

Educational and Legal Requirements

An Associate degree generally is required to work as a respiratory therapy technician. However, the entry-level requirement is a postsecondary certificate from an accredited school.

Employment Trends

Employment Change

Little or no change in employment growth is projected for respiratory therapy technicians. Most work in respiratory care is being done by respiratory therapists, resulting in limited demand for respiratory therapy technicians. **Table 19-2** shows some projection data provided by the Department of Labor.

Job Prospects

Respiratory therapy technicians can expect keen competition. Very few openings for respiratory therapy technicians are expected, as the work is increasingly performed by respiratory therapists.

TABLE 19-2   Projections Data from the National Employment Matrix for Respiratory Therapy Technicians

Occupational Title	Employment, 2008	Projected Employment, 2018	Change, 2008–2018	
			Number	Percentage
Respiratory Therapy Technicians	16,500	16,400	–100	–1

Earnings

Median annual wages for respiratory therapy technicians were $42,430 in May 2008.

Related Occupations

They include physicians and surgeons, and respiratory therapists.

Additional Information

- American Association for Respiratory Care, 9425 N. MacArthur Blvd., Suite 100, Irving, TX 75063. Internet: http://www.aarc.org

chapter twenty

Physical Therapy*

*All information in this chapter, unless otherwise indicated, was obtained from Bureau of Labor Statistics. U.S. Department of Labor. *Occupational Outlook Handbook 2010–2011 Edition*. 2010.

PHYSICAL THERAPY AND OUR HEALTH

Physical therapy is a health profession whose primary purpose is the promotion of optimal human health and functioning through the application of scientific principles to prevent, identify, assess, correct, or alleviate acute or prolonged movement dysfunction. Physical therapy encompasses areas of specialized competence and includes the development of new principles and applications to effectively meet existing and emerging health needs. **Physical therapists** restore, maintain, and promote overall fitness and health. Their patients include accident victims and individuals with disabling conditions such as lower-back pain, arthritis, heart disease, fractures, head injuries, and cerebral palsy. Other professional activities in which physical therapists engage are **research**, education, consultation, and administration.

Possible therapeutic interventions include, but are not limited to, the use of **therapeutic exercise** with or without **assistive devices**, physical agents, electricity, manual procedures such as joint and **soft tissue mobilization**, neuromuscular reeducation, bronchopulmonary hygiene, and ambulation or gait training.

Physical therapists use **tests and measurements** to evaluate muscle strength, force, endurance, and tone; joint motion, mobility, and stability; reflexes and automatic reactions; movement skill and accuracy; sensations and perception; peripheral nerve integrity; locomotor skill, stability, and endurance; activities of daily living; cardiac, pulmonary, and vascular functions; fit, function, and comfort of prosthetic, orthotic, and other assistive devices; posture and body mechanics; limb length, circumference, and volume; thoracic excursion and breathing patterns; vital signs; **photosensitivity**; and home and work physical environments.

PHYSICAL THERAPISTS

SIGNIFICANT POINTS

- Employment is projected to grow much faster than average.
- Physical therapist assistants should have very good job prospects; on the other hand, aides may face keen competition from the large pool of qualified applicants.
- Aides usually learn skills on the job, while physical therapist assistants have an Associate degree; most states require licensing for assistants.
- Most jobs are in offices of other health practitioners and in hospitals.

Work Description

Physical therapists provide services that help restore function, improve mobility, relieve pain, and prevent or limit permanent physical disabilities. They restore, maintain, and promote overall fitness and health. Their patients include accident victims and individuals with disabling conditions such as lower-back pain, arthritis, heart disease, fractures, head injuries, and cerebral palsy.

Therapists examine patients' medical histories and then test and measure the patients' strength, range of motion, balance and coordination, posture, muscle performance, respiration, and motor function. Next, physical therapists develop plans describing a treatment strategy and its anticipated outcome.

Treatment often includes exercise, especially for patients who have been immobilized or who lack flexibility, strength, or endurance. Physical therapists encourage patients to use their muscles to increase their flexibility and range of motion. More advanced exercises focus on improving strength, balance, coordination, and endurance. The goal is to improve how an individual functions at work and at home.

Physical therapists also use **electrical stimulation**, hot packs or cold compresses, and ultrasound to relieve pain and reduce swelling. They may use traction or **deep-tissue massage** to relieve pain and improve circulation and flexibility. Therapists also teach patients to use assistive and adaptive devices, such as crutches, prostheses, and wheelchairs. They also may show patients how to do exercises at home to expedite their recovery. As treatment continues, physical therapists document the patient's progress, conduct periodic examinations, and modify treatments when necessary.

Physical therapists often consult and practice with a variety of other professionals, such as physicians, dentists, nurses, educators, social workers, occupational therapists, speech-language pathologists, and audiologists.

Some physical therapists treat a wide range of ailments; others specialize in areas such as pediatrics, geriatrics, orthopedics, **sports medicine**, neurology, and **cardiopulmonary physical therapy**.

Work Environment

Physical therapists practice in hospitals, clinics, and private offices that have specially equipped facilities. They also treat patients in hospital rooms, homes, or schools. These jobs can be physically demanding because therapists often have to stoop, kneel, crouch, lift, and stand for long periods. In addition, physical therapists move heavy equipment and lift patients or help them turn, stand, or walk.

In 2008, most full-time physical therapists worked a 40-hour week; some worked evenings and weekends to fit their patients' schedules. About 27% of physical therapists worked part time.

Employment Opportunities

Physical therapists held about 185,500 jobs in 2008. The number of jobs is greater than the number of practicing physical therapists because some physical therapists hold two or more jobs. For example, some may work in a private practice, but also work part time in another healthcare facility.

About 60% of physical therapists worked in hospitals or in offices of other physical therapists. Additional jobs were in the home healthcare services industry, nursing care facilities, outpatient care centers, and offices of physicians. Some self-employed physical therapists in private practice saw individual patients and contracted to provide services in hospitals, rehabilitation centers, nursing care facilities, home healthcare agencies, adult day care programs, and schools. Physical therapists also teach in academic institutions and conduct research.

Educational and Legal Requirements

Today's entrants to this profession need a post-baccalaureate degree from an accredited physical therapy program. All states regulate the practice of physical therapy, which usually requires passing scores on national and state examinations.

Education and Training

The **American Physical Therapy Association**'s **(APTA)** accrediting body, called the Commission on Accreditation of Physical Therapy Education **(CAPTE)**, accredits entry-level academic programs in physical therapy. In 2009, there were 212 physical therapist education programs. Of these accredited programs, 12 awarded Master degrees and 200 awarded doctoral degrees. Currently, only graduate-degree physical therapist programs are accredited. Master degree programs typically are 2 to 2.5 years in length, while doctoral degree programs last 3 years.

Physical therapist education programs include foundational science courses, such as biology, anatomy, physiology, cellular histology, exercise physiology, neuroscience, biomechanics, pharmacology, pathology, and radiology/imaging, as well as behavioral science courses, such as **evidence-based practice** and clinical reasoning. Some of the clinically based courses include medical screening, examination tests and measures, diagnostic process, therapeutic interventions, **outcomes assessment**, and practice management. In addition to classroom and laboratory instruction, students receive supervised clinical experience.

Among the undergraduate courses that are useful when one applies to a physical therapist education program are anatomy, biology, chemistry, physics, social science, mathematics, and statistics. Before granting admission, many programs require volunteer experience in the physical therapy department of a hospital or clinic.

Licensure

All states regulate the practice of physical therapy. Eligibility requirements vary by state. Typical requirements for physical therapists include graduation from an accredited physical therapy education program, passing the National Physical Therapy Examination, and fulfilling state requirements such as **jurisprudence exams**. A number of states require continuing education as a condition of maintaining licensure.

Other Qualifications

Physical therapists should have strong interpersonal and communication skills, so they can educate patients about their condition and physical therapy treatments and communicate with patients' families. Physical therapists also should be compassionate and possess a desire to help patients.

Advancement

Physical therapists are expected to continue their professional development by participating in continuing education courses and workshops. Some physical therapists become board certified in a clinical specialty. Opportunities for physical therapists exist in academia and research. Some become self-employed, providing contract services or opening a private practice.

Employment Trends

Employment of physical therapists is expected to grow much faster than average. Job opportunities will be good, especially in acute hospital, **rehabilitation**, and orthopedic settings.

Employment Change

Employment of physical therapists is expected to grow 30% from 2008 to 2018, much faster than the average for all occupations. The impact of proposed federal legislation imposing limits on reimbursement for therapy services may adversely affect the short-term job outlook for physical therapists. However, the long term demand for physical therapists should continue to rise as new treatments and techniques expand the scope of physical therapy practices. Moreover, the increasing numbers of individuals with disabilities or limited function will spur demand.

The increasing elderly population will drive growth in the demand for physical therapy services. The elderly population is particularly vulnerable to chronic and debilitating conditions that require therapeutic services. Also, the baby-boom generation is entering the prime age for heart attacks and strokes, increasing the demand for cardiac and physical rehabilitation. And increasing numbers of children will need physical therapy as technological advances save the lives of a larger proportion of newborns with severe birth defects.

Future medical developments also should permit a higher percentage of trauma victims to survive, creating additional demand for rehabilitative care. In addition, growth may result from advances in medical technology that could permit the treatment of an increasing number of disabling conditions that were untreatable in the past.

Widespread interest in health promotion also should increase demand for physical therapy services. A growing number of employers are using physical therapists to evaluate work sites, develop exercise programs, and teach safe work habits to employees.

TABLE 20-1 Projections Data from the National Employment Matrix for Physical Therapists

Occupational Title	Employment, 2008	Projected Employment, 2018	Change, 2008–2018	
			Number	Percentage
Physical therapists	185,500	241,700	56,200	30

Job Prospects

Job opportunities will be good for licensed physical therapists in all settings. Job opportunities should be particularly good in acute hospital, rehabilitation, and orthopedic settings, where the elderly are most often treated. Physical therapists with specialized knowledge of particular types of treatment also will have excellent job prospects. **Table 20-1** shows some projection data provided by the Department of Labor.

Earnings

Median annual wages of physical therapists were $72,790 in May 2008. The middle 50% earned between $60,300 and $85,540. The lowest 10% earned less than $50,350, and the highest 10% earned more than $104,350. Median annual wages in the industries employing the largest numbers of physical therapists in May 2008 are shown in **Table 20-2**.

Related Occupations

Physical therapists rehabilitate people with physical disabilities. Others who work in the rehabilitation field include audiologists, chiropractors, occupational therapists, recreational therapists, rehabilitation counselors, respiratory therapists, and speech-language pathologists.

Additional Information

Career information on physical therapy and a list of schools offering accredited programs can be obtained from

- The American Physical Therapy Association, 1111 North Fairfax St., Alexandria, VA 22314-1488. Internet: http://www.apta.org

TABLE 20-2 Median Annual Wages in the Industries Employing the Largest Numbers of Physical Therapists in May 2008

Home healthcare services	$77,630
Nursing care facilities	76,680
General medical and surgical hospitals	73,270
Offices of physicians	72,790
Offices of other health practitioners	71,400

PHYSICAL THERAPIST ASSISTANTS AND AIDES
SIGNIFICANT POINTS

- Employment is projected to grow much faster than average.
- Physical therapist assistants should have very good job prospects; on the other hand, aides may face keen competition from the large pool of qualified applicants.
- Aides usually learn skills on the job, while physical therapist assistants have an Associate degree; most states require licensing for assistants.
- Most jobs are in offices of other health practitioners and in hospitals.

Work Description

Physical therapist assistants and aides help physical therapists to provide treatment that improves patient mobility, relieves pain, and prevents or lessens physical disabilities of patients. A physical therapist might ask an assistant to help patients exercise or learn to use crutches, for example, or an aide to gather and prepare therapy equipment. Patients include accident victims and individuals with disabling conditions such as lower-back pain, arthritis, heart disease, fractures, head injuries, and cerebral palsy.

Physical therapist assistants perform a variety of tasks. Under the direction and supervision of physical therapists, they provide part of a patient's treatment. This might involve exercises, massages, electrical stimulation, **paraffin baths**, hot and cold packs, traction, and ultrasound. Physical therapist assistants record the patient's responses to treatment and report the outcome of each treatment to the physical therapist.

Physical therapist aides help make therapy sessions productive, under the direct supervision of a physical therapist or physical therapist assistant. They usually are responsible for keeping the treatment area clean and organized and for preparing for each patient's therapy. When patients need assistance moving to or from a treatment area, aides push them in a wheelchair or provide them with a shoulder to lean on. Physical therapist aides are not licensed and do not perform the clinical tasks of a physical therapist assistant in states where licensure is required.

The duties of aides include some clerical tasks, such as ordering depleted supplies, answering the phone, and filling out insurance forms and other paperwork. The extent to which an aide or an assistant performs clerical tasks depends on the size and location of the facility.

Work Environment

Physical therapist assistants and aides need a moderate degree of strength because of the physical exertion required in assisting patients with their treatment. In some cases, assistants and aides need to lift patients. Frequent kneeling, stooping, and standing for long periods also are part of the job.

The hours and days that physical therapist assistants and aides work vary with the facility. About 28% of all physical therapist assistants and aides work part time. Many outpatient physical therapy offices and clinics keep evening and weekend hours to accommodate patients' personal schedules.

Employment Opportunities

Physical therapist assistants and aides held about 109,900 jobs in 2008. Physical therapist assistants held about 63,800 jobs; physical therapist aides approximately 46,100. Both work with physical therapists in a variety of settings. About 72% of jobs were in offices of physical therapists or in hospitals. Others worked primarily in nursing care facilities, offices of physicians, home healthcare services, and outpatient care centers.

Educational and Legal Requirements

Most physical therapist aides are trained on the job, but most physical therapist assistants earn an Associate degree from an accredited physical therapist assistant program. Some states require licensing for physical therapist assistants.

Education and Training

Employers typically require physical therapist aides to have a high school diploma. They are trained on the job, and most employers provide clinical on-the-job training.

In most states, physical therapist assistants are required by law to hold an Associate degree. The American Physical Therapy Association's Commission on Accreditation in Physical Therapy Education accredits postsecondary physical therapy assistant programs. In 2009, there were 223 accredited programs, which usually last 2 years and culminate in an Associate degree.

Programs are divided into academic study and hands-on clinical experience. Academic course work includes algebra, anatomy and physiology, biology, chemistry, and psychology. Clinical work includes certifications in cardiopulmonary resuscitation (CPR) and other first aid, and field experience in treatment centers. Both educators and prospective employers view clinical experience as essential to ensuring that students understand the responsibilities of a physical therapist assistant.

Licensure

Licensing is not required to practice as a physical therapist aide. However, some states require licensure or registration in order to work as a physical therapist assistant. States that require licensure stipulate specific educational and examination criteria. Additional requirements may include certification in CPR and other first aid, and a minimum number of hours of clinical experience. Complete information on regulations can be obtained from state licensing boards.

Other Qualifications

Physical therapist assistants and aides should be well organized, detail oriented, and caring. They usually have strong interpersonal skills and a desire to help people in need.

Advancement

Some physical therapist aides advance to become therapist assistants after gaining experience and, often, additional education. Sometimes, this education is required by law. Some physical therapist assistants advance by specializing in a clinical area. They gain expertise in treating a certain type of patient, such as geriatric or pediatric, or a type of ailment, such as sports injuries. Many physical therapist assistants advance to administrative positions. These positions might include organizing all the assistants in a large physical therapy organization or acting as the director for a specific department such as sports medicine. Other assistants go on to teach in accredited physical therapist assistant academic programs, lead health risk reduction classes for the elderly, or organize community activities related to fitness and risk reduction.

Employment Trends

Employment is expected to grow much faster than average because of increasing consumer demand for physical therapy services. Job prospects for physical therapist assistants are expected to be very good. Aides should experience keen competition for jobs.

Employment Change

Employment of physical therapist assistants and aides is expected to grow by 35% over the 2008 to 2018 decade, much faster than the average for all occupations. The impact of federal limits on Medicare and Medicaid reimbursement for therapy services may adversely affect the short-term job outlook for physical therapist assistants and aides. However, long-term demand for physical therapist assistants and aides will continue to rise, as the number of individuals with disabilities or limited function grows.

The increasing number of people who need therapy reflects, in part, the increasing elderly population. The elderly population is particularly vulnerable to chronic and debilitating conditions that require therapeutic services. These patients often need additional assistance in their treatment, making the roles of assistants and aides vital. In addition, the large baby-boom generation is entering the prime age for heart attacks and strokes, further increasing the demand for cardiac and physical rehabilitation. Moreover, future medical developments should permit an increased percentage of trauma victims to survive, creating added demand for therapy services.

Physical therapists are expected to increasingly use assistants to reduce the cost of physical therapy services. Once a patient is evaluated and a treatment plan is designed by the physical therapist, the physical therapist assistant can provide many parts of the treatment, as approved by the therapist.

Job Prospects

Opportunities for individuals interested in becoming physical therapist assistants are expected to be very good. Physical therapist aides may face keen competition from the large pool of qualified individuals. In addition

TABLE 20-3 Projections Data from the National Employment Matrix for Physical Therapist Assistants and Aides

Occupational Title	Employment, 2008	Project Employment, 2018	Change, 2008–2018	
			Number	Percentage
Physical therapist assistants and aides	109,900	147,800	37,900	35
Physical therapist assistants	63,800	85,000	21,200	33
Physical therapist aides	46,100	62,800	16,700	36

to employment growth, job openings will result from the need to replace workers who leave the occupation permanently. Physical therapist assistants and aides with prior experience working in a physical therapy office or other healthcare setting will have the best job opportunities. **Table 20-3** shows some projection data provided by the Department of Labor.

Earnings

Median annual wages of physical therapist assistants were $46,140 in May 2008. The middle 50% earned between $37,170 and $54,900. The lowest 10% earned less than $28,580, and the highest 10% earned more than $63,830. Median annual wages in the industries employing the largest numbers of physical therapist assistants in May 2008 are included in **Table 20-4**.

Median annual wages of physical therapist aides were $23,760 in May 2008. The middle 50% earned between $19,910 and $28,670. The lowest 10% earned less than $17,270, and the highest 10% earned more than $33,540. Median annual wages in the industries employing the largest numbers of physical therapist aides in May 2008 are shown in **Table 20-5**.

Related Occupations

Physical therapist assistants and aides work under the supervision of physical therapists. Other workers in the healthcare field who work under similar supervision include dental assistants; medical assistants; occupational therapist assistants and aides; pharmacy aides; pharmacy technicians; nursing,

TABLE 20-4 Median Annual Earnings in the Industries Employing the Largest Numbers of Physical Therapist Assistants in May 2008

Home healthcare services	$51,950
Nursing care facilities	51,090
General medical and surgical hospitals	45,510
Offices of other health practitioners	44,580
Offices of physicians	43,390

TABLE 20-5 **Median Annual Earnings in the Industries Employing the Largest Numbers of Physical Therapist Aides in May 2008**

Nursing care facilities	$26,530
General medical and surgical hospitals	24,780
Specialty (except psychiatric and substance abuse) hospitals	24,590
Offices of physicians	23,730
Offices of other health practitioners	22,550

psychiatric, and home health aides; personal and home care aides; and social and human service assistants.

Additional Information

Career information on physical therapy and a list of schools offering accredited programs can be obtained from

- The American Physical Therapy Association, 1111 North Fairfax St., Alexandria, VA 22314-1488. Internet: http://www.apta.org

chapter twenty-one

Occupational Therapy*

KEY TERMS		
Adaptive equipment	Mental health	Outpatient care
Cognitive skills	Multidisciplinary team	Pediatrics
COTA	Nursing care	Perceptual skills
Emotional disorders	Occupational therapist registered (OTR)	Physical disabilities
Family services	Occupational therapy aide	Rehabilitation center
Gerontology	Occupational therapy assistant	Wellness and health promotion
Home health care		
Home healthcare services		

---

*All information in this chapter, unless otherwise indicated, was obtained from Bureau of Labor Statistics. U.S. Department of Labor. *Occupational Outlook Handbook 2010–2011 Edition*. 2010.

OCCUPATIONAL THERAPISTS
SIGNIFICANT POINTS

- Employment is expected to grow much faster than average, and job opportunities should be good, especially for therapists treating the elderly.
- Occupational therapists are regulated in all 50 states; requirements vary by state.
- Occupational therapists are increasingly taking on supervisory roles, allowing assistants and aides to work more closely with clients under the guidance of a therapist.

Work Description

Occupational therapists treat people with mental, physical, developmental, or emotional disabilities. They employ a variety of techniques designed to help individuals develop or maintain daily living skills, and cope with the physical and emotional effects of disability. With support and direction from the therapist, patients learn (or relearn) many of the "ordinary" tasks that are performed every day at home, at work, at school, and in the community. The therapist's goal is to help clients establish a lifestyle that is as independent, productive, and satisfying as possible.

Like other health professionals, occupational therapists often work as members of a **multidisciplinary team** whose members may include a physician, nurse, physical therapist, psychologist, rehabilitation counselor, and social worker. Team members evaluate the patient in terms of their individual specialties and work together to develop goals that meet the patient's needs. During the course of treatment, team meetings are held to evaluate progress and to modify the treatment plan, if necessary.

Activities of various kinds can be used for treatment purposes. When working with children, for example, occupational therapists often use toys. For adults, therapy may include anything from activities that strengthen muscles to using a computer. Although some treatments may give the appearance of recreation, all have a serious purpose. Working in the kitchen may produce a cake, but the skills practiced include memory, sequencing, coordination, and safety precautions, which are important for independent living at home. "Word find" games can help improve visual acuity and the ability to discern patterns. Specially designed computer programs help patients improve **cognitive skills**, including decision making, abstract reasoning, and problem solving, along with **perceptual skills**, such as peripheral vision and discrimination of letters, colors, and shapes. All of these treatments are designed to foster independence at home and at work.

During each therapy session, the therapist assesses the patient to determine treatment effectiveness and progress made toward meeting the treatment's goals. These assessments are then a basis for modifying goals and therapeutic procedures. A person with short-term memory loss, for instance, might be encouraged to make lists to aid recall. One with coordination problems might be given tasks to improve eye–hand coordination.

In addition to helping individuals strengthen basic motor functions and reasoning abilities, occupational therapists help them master daily living skills. Helping individuals with severe disabilities learn to cope with seemingly ordinary tasks such as getting dressed, using a bathroom, or driving a car requires sensitivity as well as skill. Disability may be recently acquired, such as a spinal cord injury resulting from a traffic accident, or a chronic condition present at birth, such as cerebral palsy. Therapists provide individuals with **adaptive equipment** such as wheelchairs, splints, and aids for eating and dressing. They may design and make special equipment and recommend changes in the home or work environment to facilitate functioning.

Computer-aided adaptive equipment offers the prospect of independence to some people with severe disabilities. Occupational therapists often work with rehabilitation engineers to develop such special equipment. Examples include microprocessing devices that permit individuals with paraplegia and quadriplegia to operate wheelchairs and household switches for appliances such as telephones, television sets, and radios. As such devices move out of the research and development stage, occupational therapists become involved in helping patients learn to use them.

An occupational therapist tends to work with a particular disability or age group. Approximately three out of five therapists work principally with persons who have **physical disabilities**; the rest work with those who have psychological, emotional, or developmental problems. A growing number of therapists are working in the **wellness and health promotion** areas. Often, the practice setting determines the age level and treatment needs of a therapist's patients. In **home health care**, for instance, a growing number of referrals involve older individuals with conditions such as arthritis, cardiac problems, and hip and other fractures.

The goals of occupational therapy in public schools focus not on treatment or rehabilitation, but on the resources that an individual child needs to participate effectively in the educational program. This may involve making an initial evaluation of a child's abilities and the implications for learning, recommending special therapeutic activities, consulting with parents and teachers, modifying classroom equipment or school facilities, and developing the functional, motor, and perceptual skills necessary for learning. Like teachers, these occupational therapists work regular school hours and participate in teachers' meetings and other activities.

Occupational therapists in **mental health** settings treat individuals with mental illness or emotional problems. Among the disorders and diseases often treated mainly as **emotional disorders**, occupational therapists encounter alcoholism, drug abuse, depression, eating disorders, and stress-related disorders. Therapists provide individual and group activities that simulate real-life experiences to help people learn to cope with the daily stresses of life and to manage their work and leisure more effectively. These activities include tasks that require planning and time-management skills, budgeting, shopping, meal preparation and homemaking, self-care, and using community resources such as public transportation and service agencies.

Keeping notes is an important part of an occupational therapist's job. Some of the records for which an occupational therapist may be responsible include an initial evaluation, progress notes, written reports to the physician, special internal staff notes, Medicare records, and discharge notes. Careful and complete documentation is required for reimbursement by insurance companies and Medicare.

Besides working with patients, occupational therapists may supervise student therapists, **occupational therapy assistants**, volunteers, and auxiliary nursing workers. Chief occupational therapists in a hospital may teach medical and nursing students the principles of occupational therapy. Many therapists supervise occupational therapy departments, coordinate patients' activities, or act as consultants to public health departments and mental health agencies. Some teach or conduct research in colleges and universities.

Work Environment

Although occupational therapists generally work a standard 40-hour week, they may occasionally have to work evenings or weekends. Their work environment varies according to the setting and available facilities. In a large **rehabilitation center**, for example, the therapist may work in a spacious room with a variety of equipment. In a nursing home, the therapist may work in a kitchen when using food preparation as therapy. Wherever they work and whatever equipment they use, they generally have adequate lighting and ventilation. The job can be physically tiring because therapists are on their feet much of the time. Those providing home health care may spend several hours a day driving from appointment to appointment. Therapists also face hazards such as back strain from lifting and moving patients and equipment.

Therapists are increasingly taking on supervisory roles. In an effort to curtail rising healthcare costs, third-party payers are beginning to encourage occupational therapy assistants and aides to take more hands-on responsibility. Having assistants and aides work more closely with clients under the guidance of a therapist should reduce the cost of therapy. Around 31% of occupational therapists worked part time.

Employment Opportunities

Occupational therapists held about 104,500 jobs in 2008. The largest number of jobs was in ambulatory healthcare services, which employed about 29% of occupational therapists. Other major employers included hospitals, offices of other health practitioners (including offices of other occupational therapists), public and private educational services, and **nursing care** facilities. Some occupational therapists were employed by **home healthcare services**, **outpatient care** centers, offices of physicians, individual and **family services**, community care facilities for the elderly, and government agencies.

A small number of occupational therapists were self-employed in private practice. These practitioners treated clients referred by other health professionals. They also provided contract or consulting services to nursing care facilities, schools, adult day care programs, and home healthcare agencies.

Educational and Legal Requirements

Occupational therapists must be licensed, requiring a Master degree in occupational therapy, 6 months of supervised fieldwork, and passing scores on national and state examinations.

Education and Training

A Master degree or higher in occupational therapy is the minimum requirement for entry into the field. In addition, occupational therapists must attend an academic program accredited by the Accreditation Council for Occupational Therapy Education (ACOTE) in order to sit for the national certifying exam. In 2009, 150 Master degree programs or combined Bachelor and Master degree programs were accredited, and four doctoral degree programs were accredited.

Most schools have full-time programs, although a growing number are offering weekend or part-time programs as well. Coursework in occupational therapy programs includes the physical, biological, and behavioral sciences, as well as applied occupational therapy theory and skills. Programs also require the completion of at least 24 weeks of supervised fieldwork as part of the academic curriculum.

People considering the profession of occupational therapy should take high school courses in biology, chemistry, physics, health, art, and the social sciences. College admissions offices also look favorably on paid or volunteer experience in the healthcare field. Relevant undergraduate majors include biology, psychology, sociology, anthropology, liberal arts, and anatomy.

Licensure

All 50 states, Puerto Rico, Guam, and the District of Columbia regulate the practice of occupational therapy. To obtain a license, applicants must graduate from an accredited educational program and pass a national certification examination. Those who pass the exam are awarded the title "**Occupational Therapist Registered (OTR)**." Some states have additional requirements for therapists who work in schools or early intervention programs. These requirements may include education-related classes, an education practice certificate, or early intervention certification.

Certification and Other Qualifications

Certification is voluntary. The National Board for Certifying Occupational Therapy certifies occupational therapists through a national certifying exam. Those who pass the test are awarded the title "Occupational Therapist Registered (OTR)." In some states, the national certifying exam meets requirements for regulation, while other states have their own licensing exam.

Occupational therapists need patience and strong interpersonal skills to inspire trust and respect in their clients. Patience is necessary because many clients may not show rapid improvement. Ingenuity and imagination in adapting activities to individual needs are assets. Occupational therapists working in home healthcare services also must be able to adapt to a variety of settings.

Advancement

Occupational therapists are expected to continue their professional development by participating in continuing education courses and workshops. In fact, a number of states require continuing education as a condition of maintaining licensure.

Therapists are increasingly taking on supervisory roles. Because of rising healthcare costs, third-party payers are beginning to encourage occupational therapy assistants and aides to take more hands-on responsibility for clients. Occupational therapists can choose to advance their careers by taking on administrative duties and supervising assistants and aides.

Occupational therapists also can advance by specializing in a clinical area and gaining expertise in treating a particular type of patient or ailment. Therapists have specialized in **gerontology**, mental health, **pediatrics**, and physical rehabilitation. In addition, some occupational therapists choose to teach classes in accredited occupational therapy educational programs.

Employment Trends

Employment of occupational therapists is expected to grow much faster than the average for all occupations. Job opportunities should be good, especially for occupational therapists treating the elderly.

Employment Change

Employment of occupational therapists is expected to increase 26% between 2008 and 2018, much faster than the average for all occupations. The increasing elderly population will drive growth in the demand for occupational therapy services. In the short term, the impact of proposed federal legislation imposing limits on reimbursement for therapy services may adversely affect the job market for occupational therapists. However, over the long term, the demand for occupational therapists should continue to rise as a result of the increasing number of individuals with disabilities or limited function who require therapy services. The baby-boom generation's movement into middle age, a period when the incidence of heart attack and stroke increases, will spur demand for therapeutic services. Growth in the population of those 75 years and older—an age group that suffers from high incidences of disabling conditions—also will increase demand for therapeutic services. In addition, medical advances now enable more patients with critical problems to survive—patients who ultimately may need extensive therapy.

TABLE 21-1   Projections Data from the National Employment Matrix for Occupational Therapists

Occupational Title	Employment, 2008	Projected Employment, 2018	Change, 2008–2018	
			Number	Percentage
Occupational therapists	104,500	131,300	26,800	26

Hospitals will continue to employ a large number of occupational therapists to provide therapy services to acutely ill inpatients. Hospitals also will need occupational therapists to staff their outpatient rehabilitation programs.

Employment growth in schools will result from the expansion of the school-age population, the extension of services for disabled students, and an increasing prevalence of sensory disorders in children. Therapists will be needed to help children with disabilities prepare to enter special education programs.

Job Prospects

Job opportunities should be good for licensed occupational therapists in all settings, particularly in acute hospital, rehabilitation, and orthopedic settings because the elderly receive most of their treatment in these settings. Occupational therapists with specialized knowledge in a treatment area also will have increased job prospects. Driver rehabilitation and fall-prevention training for the elderly are emerging practice areas for occupational therapy. **Table 21-1** shows some projection data provided by the Department of Labor.

Earnings

Median annual earnings of occupational therapist were $66,780 in May 2008. The middle 50% earned between $55,090 and $81,290. The lowest 10% earned less than $42,820, and the highest 10% earned more than $98,310. Median annual earnings in the industries employing the largest numbers of occupational therapist in May 2008 are shown in **Table 21-2**.

Related Occupations

Occupational therapists use specialized knowledge to help individuals perform daily living skills and achieve maximum independence. Other workers

TABLE 21-2   Median Annual Earnings in the Industries Employing the Largest Numbers of Occupational Therapists, May 2008

Home healthcare services	$74,510
Nursing care facilities	72,790
Offices of other health practitioners	69,360
General medical and surgical hospitals	68,100
Elementary and secondary schools	60,020

performing similar duties include athletic trainers, audiologists, chiropractors, physical therapists, recreational therapists, rehabilitation counselors, respiratory therapists, and speech-language pathologists.

Additional Information

For information on a career in occupational therapy and a list of accredited programs, contact

- American Occupational Therapy Association, 4720 Montgomery Ln., P.O. Box 31220, Bethesda, MD 20824-1220. Internet: http://www.aota.org

OCCUPATIONAL THERAPY ASSISTANTS AND AIDES
SIGNIFICANT POINTS

- Typical entry-level education for occupational therapy assistants is an Associate degree; in contrast, occupational therapy aides usually receive their training on the job.

- Many states regulate the practice of occupational therapy assistants either by licensing, registration, or certification; requirements vary by state.

- Employment is projected to grow much faster than average as demand for occupational therapist services rises and as occupational therapists increasingly use assistants and aides.

- Job prospects should be very good for occupational therapy assistants; job seekers holding only a high school diploma might face keen competition for occupational therapy aide jobs.

Work Description

Occupational therapy assistants and aides work under the direction of occupational therapists to provide rehabilitative services to patients suffering from mental, physical, emotional, or developmental impairments. The ultimate goal is to improve clients' quality of life by helping them compensate for limitations. For example, occupational therapy assistants help injured workers reenter the labor force by helping them improve their motor skills; alternatively, they may help persons with learning disabilities increase their independence by teaching them to prepare meals or use public transportation.

Occupational therapy assistants help clients with the rehabilitative activities and exercises that are outlined in the treatment plan devised by the occupational therapist. The activities range from teaching the patient the proper method of moving from a bed into a wheelchair to the best way to stretch and limber the muscles of the hand. Assistants monitor the individual to ensure that the client is performing the activities correctly and to provide encouragement. They also record their observations with regard to the patient's progress for use by the occupational therapist. If the treatment is not having the intended effect or if the client is not improving as expected, the treatment program may be altered to obtain better results. Assistants also document billing submitted to the patient's health insurance provider.

Occupational therapy aides typically prepare materials and assemble equipment used during treatment and are responsible for performing a range of clerical tasks. Their duties may include scheduling appointments, answering the telephone, restocking or ordering depleted supplies, and filling out insurance forms or other paperwork. Aides are not licensed, so by law they are not allowed to perform as wide a range of tasks as occupational therapy assistants do.

Work Environment

Occupational therapy assistants and aides need to have a moderate degree of strength because of the physical exertion required to assist patients. For example, assistants and aides may need to lift patients. Constant kneeling, stooping, and standing for long periods also are part of the job.

The work schedules of occupational therapy assistants and aides vary by facility and whether they are full or part time. For example, many outpatient therapy offices and clinics have evening and weekend hours to accommodate patients' schedules.

Employment Opportunities

Occupational therapy assistants and aides held about 34,400 jobs in 2008. Occupational therapy assistants held about 26,600 jobs, and occupational therapy aides held approximately 7800. About 28% of jobs for assistants and aides were in offices of other health practitioners, 27% were in hospitals, and 20% were in nursing care facilities. The rest were primarily in community care facilities for the elderly, home healthcare services, individual and family services, and state government agencies.

Educational and Legal Requirements

An Associate degree or a certificate from an accredited community college or technical school is generally required to qualify for occupational therapy assistant jobs. In contrast, occupational therapy aides usually receive most of their training on the job.

Education and Training

There were 135 accredited occupational therapy assistant programs in 2009. The first year of study typically involves an introduction to health care, basic medical terminology, anatomy, and physiology. In the second year, courses are more rigorous and usually include occupational therapy courses in areas such as mental health, adult physical disabilities, gerontology, and pediatrics.

Students also must complete 16 weeks of supervised fieldwork in a clinic or community setting.

Applicants to occupational therapy assistant programs can improve their chances of admission by taking high school courses in biology and health and by performing volunteer work in nursing care facilities, occupational or physical therapists' offices, or other healthcare settings.

Occupational therapy aides usually receive most of their training on the job. Qualified applicants must have a high school diploma, strong interpersonal skills, and a desire to help people in need. Applicants may increase their chances of getting a job by volunteering their services, thus displaying initiative and aptitude to the employer.

Licensure

In most states, occupational therapy assistants are regulated and must pass a national certification examination after they graduate. Those who pass the test are awarded the title "Certified Occupational Therapy Assistant."

Certification and Other Qualifications

Certification is voluntary. The National Board for Certifying Occupational Therapy certifies occupational therapy assistants through a national certifying exam. Those who pass the test are awarded the title Certified Occupational Therapy Assistant (**COTA**). In some states, the national certifying exam meets requirements for regulation, but other states have their own licensing exam.

Occupational therapist assistants are expected to continue their professional development by participating in continuing education courses and workshops in order to maintain certification. A number of states require continuing education as a condition of maintaining licensure.

Assistants and aides must be responsible, patient, and willing to take directions and work as part of a team. Furthermore, they should be caring and want to help people who are not able to help themselves.

Advancement

Occupational therapy assistants may advance into administration positions. They might organize all the assistants in a large occupational therapy department or act as the director for a specific department such as sports medicine. Some assistants go on to teach classes in accredited occupational therapy assistant academic programs or lead health risk reduction classes for the elderly.

Employment Trends

Employment is expected to grow much faster than average as demand for occupational therapy services rises and as occupational therapists increasingly use assistants and aides. Job prospects should be very good for occupational therapy assistants. Job seekers holding only a high school diploma might face keen competition for occupational therapy aide jobs.

Employment Change

Employment of occupational therapy assistants and aides is expected to grow 30% from 2008 to 2018, much faster than the average for all occupations. In the short term, the impact of proposed federal legislation imposing limits on reimbursement for therapy services may adversely affect the job market for occupational therapy assistants and aides. Over the long term, however, demand for both will continue to rise because of the increasing number of individuals with disabilities or limited function.

The growing elderly population is particularly vulnerable to chronic and debilitating conditions that require therapeutic services. These patients often need additional assistance in their treatment, making the role of assistants and aides vital. As the large baby-boom generation ages, it enters the prime age bracket for heart attacks and strokes, further increasing the demand for cardiac and physical rehabilitation. In addition, future medical developments should permit an increasing percentage of trauma victims to survive, creating added demand for therapy services. An increase of sensory disorders in children will also spur demand for occupational therapy services.

Occupational therapists are expected to increase their utilization of assistants and aides to reduce the cost of occupational therapy services. Once a patient is evaluated and the therapist designs a treatment plan, the occupational therapy assistant can provide many aspects of treatment, as prescribed by the therapist.

Job Prospects

Opportunities for individuals interested in becoming occupational therapy assistants are expected to be very good. In addition to employment growth, job openings will result from the need to replace occupational therapy assistants and aides who leave the occupation permanently between 2008 and 2018. Occupational therapy assistants and aides with prior experience working in an occupational therapy office or other healthcare setting will have the best job opportunities. However, individuals with only a high school diploma may face keen competition for occupational therapy aide jobs. **Table 21-3** shows some projection data provided by the Department of Labor.

TABLE 21-3 Projections Data from the National Employment Matrix for Occupational Therapy Assistants and Aides, Occupational Therapy Assistants, and Occupational Therapy Aides

Occupational Title	Employment, 2008	Projected Employment, 2018	Change, 2008–2018	
			Number	Percentage
Occupational therapy assistants and aides	34,400	44,800	10,400	30
Occupational therapy assistants	26,600	34,600	8000	30
Occupational therapy aides	7800	10,200	2400	31

TABLE 21-4 Median Annual Earnings in the Industries Employing the Largest Numbers of Occupational Therapy Assistants, May 2008

Home healthcare services	$53,090
Offices of other health practitioners	50,810
Nursing care facilities	50,790
General medical and surgical hospitals	45,760
Elementary and secondary schools	41,850

Earnings

Median annual earnings of occupational therapy assistants were $48,230 in May 2008. The middle 50% earned between $39,240 and $57,810. The lowest 10% earned less than $31,150, and the highest 10% earned more than $65,160. Median annual earnings in the industries employing the largest numbers of occupational therapy assistants in May 2008 are included in **Table 21-4**.

Median annual earnings of occupational therapy aides were $26,960 in May 2008. The middle 50% earned between $21,930 and $33,340. The lowest 10% earned less than $17,850, and the highest 10% earned more than $46,910. Median annual earnings in the industries employing the largest numbers of occupational therapy aides in May 2008 are shown in **Table 21-5**.

Related Occupations

Occupational therapy assistants and aides work under the supervision and direction of occupational therapists. Other workers in the healthcare field who work under similar supervision include dental assistants; medical assistants; nursing, psychiatric, and home health aides; personal and home care aides; pharmacy aides; pharmacy technicians; and physical therapist assistants and aides.

Additional Information

For information on a career in occupational therapy and a list of accredited programs, contact

- American Occupational Therapy Association, 4720 Montgomery Ln., P.O. Box 31220, Bethesda, MD 20824-1220. Internet: http://www.aota.org

TABLE 21-5 Median Annual Earnings in the Industries Employing the Largest Numbers of Occupational Therapy Assistants, May 2008

Specialty (except psychiatric and substance abuse) hospitals	$30,400
General medical and surgical hospitals	27,750
Offices of other health practitioners	26,850
Elementary and secondary schools	26,820
Nursing care facilities	25,790

chapter twenty-two

Athletic Trainers*

KEY TERMS

BOC
Bone injuries
Communication skills
Fitness trainers
Injury preventive devices
Medical equipment
or machinery
Muscle injuries

National Athletic
Trainers' Association
National Collegiate
Athletic Association
Division I
Physician practice
manager
Preventing work-related
injuries

Recreational sports
Repetitive stress injuries
Spectator sports
Sports centers
Teaching certificate
or license
Third-party
reimbursement

---

*All information in this chapter, unless otherwise indicated, was obtained from Bureau of Labor Statistics. U.S. Department of Labor. *Occupational Outlook Handbook 2010–2011 Edition*. 2010.

ATHLETIC TRAINERS

SIGNIFICANT POINTS

- A Bachelor degree is usually the minimum requirement, but many athletic trainers hold a Master or doctoral degree.
- Long hours, sometimes including nights and weekends, are common.
- Job prospects should be good in the healthcare industry and in high schools, but competition is expected for positions with professional and college sports teams.

Work Description

Athletic trainers help prevent and treat injuries for people of all ages. Their patients and clients include everyone from professional athletes to industrial workers. Recognized by the American Medical Association as allied health professionals, athletic trainers specialize in the prevention, diagnosis, assessment, treatment, and rehabilitation of **muscle injuries**, **bone injuries**, and illnesses. Athletic trainers, as one of the first healthcare providers on the scene when injuries occur, must be able to recognize, evaluate, and assess injuries and provide immediate care when needed. Athletic trainers should not be confused with **fitness trainers** or personal trainers, who are not healthcare workers, but rather train people to become physically fit.

Athletic trainers try to prevent injuries by educating people on how to reduce their risk for injuries and by advising them on the proper use of equipment, exercises to improve balance and strength, and home exercises and therapy programs. They also help apply protective or **injury-preventive devices** such as tape, bandages, and braces.

Athletic trainers may work under the direction of a licensed physician and in cooperation with other healthcare providers. The extent of the direction ranges from discussing specific injuries and treatment options with a physician to performing evaluations and treatments as directed by a physician. Some athletic trainers meet with the team physician or consulting physician once or twice a week; others interact with a physician every day. Athletic trainers often have administrative responsibilities. These may include regular meetings with an athletic director, **physician practice manager**, or other administrative officer to deal with budgets, purchasing, policy implementation, and other business-related issues.

Work Environment

The industry and individual employer are significant in determining the work environment of athletic trainers. Many athletic trainers work indoors most of the time; others, especially those in some sports-related jobs, spend much of their time working outdoors. The job also might require standing for long periods, working with **medical equipment or machinery**, and being able to walk, run, kneel, stoop, or crawl. Travel may be required.

Schedules vary by work setting. Athletic trainers in nonsports settings generally have an established schedule—usually about 40 to 50 hours per week—with nights and weekends off. Athletic trainers working in hospitals and clinics may spend part of their time working at other locations doing outreach services. The most common outreach programs include conducting athletic training services and speaking at high schools, colleges, and commercial businesses.

Athletic trainers in sports settings have schedules that are longer and more variable. These athletic trainers must be present for team practices and competitions, which often are on evenings and weekends, and their schedules can change on short notice when games and practices have to be rescheduled. In high schools, athletic trainers who also teach may work 60 to 70 hours a week, or more. In **National Collegiate Athletic Association Division I** colleges and universities, athletic trainers generally work with one team; when that team's sport is in season, working at least 50 to 60 hours a week is common. Athletic trainers in smaller colleges and universities often work with several teams and have teaching responsibilities. During the off-season, a 40- to 50-hour workweek may be normal in most settings. Athletic trainers for professional sports teams generally work the most hours per week. During training camps, practices, and competitions, they may be required to work up to 12 hours a day.

There is some stress involved with being an athletic trainer. The work of athletic trainers requires frequent interaction with others. They consult with physicians as well as have frequent contact with athletes and patients to discuss and administer treatments, rehabilitation programs, injury-preventive practices, and other health related issues. Athletic trainers are responsible for their clients' health and sometimes have to make quick decisions that could affect the health or career of their clients. Athletics trainers also can be affected by the pressure to win, which is typical of competitive sports teams.

Employment Opportunities

Athletic trainers held about 16,300 jobs in 2008 and are found in every part of the country. Most athletic trainer jobs are related to sports, although an increasing number also work in nonsports settings. About 39% were found in public and private educational services, primarily in colleges, universities, and high schools. Another 38% of athletic trainers worked in health care, including jobs in hospitals, offices of physicians, and offices of other health practitioners. About 13% worked in fitness and **recreational sports** centers. Around 5% work in **spectator sports**.

Education and Legal Requirements

A Bachelor degree is usually the minimum requirement, but many athletic trainers hold a Master or doctoral degree. In 2009, 47 states required athletic trainers to be licensed or hold some form of registration.

Education and Training

A Bachelor degree from an accredited college or university is required for almost all jobs as an athletic trainer. In 2009, there were about 350 accredited undergraduate programs nationwide. Students in these programs are educated both in the classroom and in clinical settings. Formal education includes many science and health-related courses, such as human anatomy, physiology, nutrition, and biomechanics.

According to the **National Athletic Trainers' Association**, almost 70% of athletic trainers have a Master degree or higher. Athletic trainers may need a Master or higher degree to be eligible for some positions, especially those in colleges and universities, and to increase their advancement opportunities. Because some positions in high schools involve teaching along with athletic trainer responsibilities, a **teaching certificate or license** could be required.

Licensure and Certification

In 2009, 47 states required athletic trainers to be licensed or registered; this requires certification from the Board of Certification, Inc. (**BOC**). For BOC certification, athletic trainers need a Bachelor or Master degree from an accredited athletic training program and must pass a rigorous examination. To retain certification, credential holders must continue taking medical-related courses and adhere to the BOC standards of practice. In Alaska, California, West Virginia, and the District of Columbia where licensure is not required, certification is voluntary but may be helpful for those seeking jobs and advancement.

Other Qualifications

Because all athletic trainers deal directly with a variety of people, they need good social and **communication skills**. They should be able to manage difficult situations and the stress associated with them, such as when disagreements arise with coaches, patients, clients, or parents regarding suggested treatment. Athletic trainers also should be organized, be able to manage time wisely, be inquisitive, and have a strong desire to help people.

Advancement

There are a few ways for athletic trainers to advance. Some athletic trainers advance by switching teams or sports to gain additional responsibility or pay. Assistant athletic trainers may become head athletic trainers and, eventually, athletic directors or physician, hospital, or clinic practice administrators where they assume a management role. Some athletic trainers move into sales and marketing positions, using their expertise to sell medical and athletic equipment.

Employment Trends

Employment is projected to grow much faster than average. Job prospects should be good in the healthcare industry and in high schools, but competition is expected for positions with professional and college sports teams.

Employment Change

Employment of athletic trainers is projected to grow 37% from 2008 to 2018, much faster than the average for all occupations, because of their role in preventing injuries and reducing healthcare costs. Job growth will be concentrated in the healthcare industry, including hospitals and offices of health practitioners. Fitness and recreation **sports centers** also will provide new jobs, as these establishments grow and continue to need additional athletic trainers to provide support for their clients. Growth in positions with sports teams will be somewhat slower, however, as most professional sports clubs and colleges and universities already have complete athletic training staffs.

The demand for health care, with an emphasis on preventive care, should grow as the population ages and as a way to reduce healthcare costs. Increased licensure requirements and regulation has led to a greater acceptance of athletic trainers as qualified healthcare providers. As a result, **third-party reimbursement** is expected to continue to grow for athletic training services. Athletic trainers will benefit from this expansion because they provide a cost-effective way to increase the number of health professionals in an office or other setting.

In some states, efforts are under way to have an athletic trainer in every high school to work with student-athletes, which may lead to growth in the number of athletic trainers employed in high schools. In addition, as more young athletes specialize in certain sports, there is increasing demand for athletic trainers to deal with **repetitive stress injuries**.

As athletic trainers continue to expand their services, more employers are expected to use these workers to reduce healthcare costs by **preventing work-related injuries**. Athletic trainers can help prevent injuries and provide immediate treatment for many injuries that do occur. For example, some athletic trainers may be hired to increase the fitness and performance of police and firefighters.

Job Prospects

Job prospects should be good for athletic trainers in the healthcare industry and in high schools. Those looking for a position with a professional or college sports team may face competition. Because of relatively low turnover, the settings with the best job prospects will be the ones that are expected to have the most job growth, primarily positions in the healthcare and fitness and recreational sports centers industries. Additional job opportunities may arise in elementary and secondary schools as more positions are created. Some of these positions also will require teaching responsibilities.

There are relatively few positions for professional and collegiate sports teams in comparison to the number of applicants. Turnover among professional sports team athletic trainers is also limited. Many athletic trainers prefer to continue to work with the same coaches, administrators, and players when a good working relationship already exists.

There also are opportunities for athletic trainers to join the military, although they would not be classified as athletic trainers. Enlisted soldiers and officers who are athletic trainers are usually placed in another program, such as health educator or training specialist, in which their skills are useful.

This occupation is expected to continue to change over the next decade, including more administrative responsibilities, adapting to new technology, and working with larger populations, and job seekers must be prepared to adapt to these changes. **Table 22-1** shows some projection data from the National Employment Matrix.

Earnings

Most athletic trainers work in full-time positions and typically receive benefits. The salary of an athletic trainer depends on experience and job responsibilities, and varies by job setting. Median annual wages for athletic trainers were $39,640 in May 2008. The middle 50% earned between $32,070 and $49,250. The lowest 10% earned less than $23,450, and the top 10% earned more than $60,960.

Many employers pay for some of the continuing education required for athletic trainers to remain certified, although the amount covered varies from employer to employer.

Related Occupations

Other American Medical Association allied health professionals include chiropractors, emergency medical technicians and paramedics, licensed practical and licensed vocational nurses, massage therapists, occupational therapists, physical therapists, physician assistants, physicians and surgeons, podiatrists, recreational therapists, registered nurses, and respiratory therapists.

TABLE 22-1 Projections Data from the National Employment Matrix for Athletic Trainers

Occupational Title	Employment, 2008	Projected Employment, 2018	Change, 2008–2018	
			Number	Percentage
Athletic trainers	16,300	22,400	6100	37

Additional Information

For further information on careers in athletic training, contact

- National Athletic Trainers' Association, 2952 Stemmons Freeway, Suite 200, Dallas, TX 75247. Internet: http://www.nata.org

  For further information on certification, contact

- Board of Certification, Inc., 1415 Harney St., Suite 200, Omaha, NE 68102. Internet: http://www.bocatc.org

chapter twenty-three

Additional Technologists and Technicians*

*All information in this chapter, unless otherwise indicated, was obtained from Bureau of Labor Statistics. U.S. Department of Labor. *Occupational Outlook Handbook 2010–2011 Edition*. 2010.

CARDIOVASCULAR TECHNOLOGISTS AND TECHNICIANS
SIGNIFICANT POINTS

- Employment is expected to grow much faster than average.
- Technologists and technicians with multiple professional credentials, trained to perform a wide range of procedures, will have the best prospects.
- About 77% of jobs are in hospitals.
- Workers typically need a 2-year Associate degree at a junior or community college; most employers also require a professional credential.

Work Descriptions

Cardiovascular technologists and technicians assist physicians in diagnosing and treating cardiac (heart) and peripheral vascular (blood vessel) ailments. Cardiovascular technologists and technicians schedule appointments, perform ultrasound or cardiovascular procedures, review doctors' interpretations and patient files, and monitor patients' heart rates. They also operate and maintain testing equipment, explain test procedures, and compare test results to a standard to identify problems. Other day-to-day activities vary significantly between specialties. Cardiovascular technologists may specialize in any of three areas of practice: **invasive cardiology**, echocardiography, or vascular technology.

Invasive Cardiology

Cardiovascular technologists specializing in invasive procedures are called **cardiology technologists**. They assist physicians with cardiac catheterization procedures in which a small tube, or catheter, is threaded through a patient's artery from a spot on the patient's groin to the heart. The procedure can determine whether a blockage exists in the blood vessels that supply the heart muscle. The procedure also can help to diagnose other problems. Part of the procedure may involve balloon angioplasty, which can be used to treat blockages of blood vessels or heart valves without the need for heart surgery. Cardiology technologists assist physicians as they insert a catheter with a balloon on the end to the point of the obstruction. Another procedure using the catheter is the electrophysiology test, which helps locate the specific areas of heart tissue that give rise to the abnormal electrical impulses that cause arrhythmias.

Technologists prepare patients for cardiac catheterization by first positioning them on an examining table and then shaving, cleaning, and administering anesthesia to the top of their leg near the groin. During the catheterization procedures, they monitor patients' blood pressure and heart rate with electrocardiogram (EKG) equipment and notify the physician if something appears to be wrong. Technologists also may prepare and monitor patients during open-heart surgery and during the insertion of pacemakers and stents that open up blockages in arteries to the heart and major blood vessels.

Noninvasive Technology

Technologists who specialize in vascular technology or echocardiography perform noninvasive tests. Tests are called "noninvasive" if they do not require the insertion of probes or other instruments into the patient's body. For example, procedures such as Doppler ultrasound transmit high-frequency sound waves into areas of the patient's body and then process reflected echoes of the sound waves to form an image. Technologists view the ultrasound image on a screen and may record the image on videotape or photograph it for interpretation and diagnosis by a physician. As the technologist uses the instrument to perform scans and record images, technologists check the image on the screen for subtle differences between healthy and diseased areas, decide which images to include in the report to the physician, and judge whether the images are satisfactory for diagnostic purposes. They also explain the procedure to patients, record any additional medical history the patient relates, select appropriate equipment settings, and change the patient's position as necessary.

Vascular Technology

Technicians who assist physicians in the diagnosis of disorders affecting the circulation are known as **vascular technologists** or vascular sonographers. Vascular technologists complete patients' medical history, evaluate pulses and assess blood flow in arteries and veins by listening to vascular flow sounds for abnormalities, and confirm that the appropriate vascular test has been ordered. Once confirmed, they perform a noninvasive procedure using ultrasound instruments to record vascular information such as vascular blood flow, blood pressure, oxygen saturation, cerebral circulation, peripheral circulation, and abdominal circulation. Many of these tests are performed during or immediately after surgery. Vascular technologists then provide a summary of findings to the physician to aid in patient diagnosis and management.

Echocardiography

This area of practice includes taking electrocardiographs (EKGs) and sonograms of the heart. Cardiovascular technicians who specialize in EKGs and **stress testing**, and perform Holter monitor procedures are known as cardiographic or **electrocardiograph (EKG) technicians**.

A basic EKG, which traces electrical impulses transmitted by the heart, requires technicians to attach electrodes to the patient's chest, arms, and legs, and then manipulate switches on an EKG machine to obtain a reading. An EKG is printed out for interpretation by the physician. This test is done before most kinds of surgery, or as part of a routine physical examination, especially on persons who have reached middle age or who have a history of cardiovascular problems.

Electrocardiograph technicians with advanced training perform Holter monitor and stress testing. For **Holter monitoring**, technicians place electrodes on the patient's chest and attach a portable EKG monitor to the patient's belt. Following 24 or more hours of normal activity by the patient, the technician removes a tape from the monitor and places it in a scanner. After checking the quality of the recorded impulses on an electronic screen, the technician usually prints the information from the tape for analysis by a physician. Physicians use the output from the scanner to diagnose heart ailments, such as heart rhythm abnormalities or problems with pacemakers.

For a treadmill stress test, EKG technicians document the patient's medical history, explain the procedure, connect the patient to an EKG monitor, and obtain a baseline reading and resting blood pressure. Next, they monitor the heart's performance while the patient is walking on a treadmill, gradually increasing the treadmill's speed to observe the effect of increased exertion. Like vascular technologists and cardiac sonographers, cardiographic technicians who perform EKG, Holter monitor, and stress tests are known as "noninvasive" technicians.

Technologists who use ultrasound to examine the heart chambers, valves, and vessels are referred to as cardiac sonographers, or **echocardiographers**. They use ultrasound instrumentation to create images called echocardiograms. An echocardiogram may be performed while the patient is either resting or physically active. Technologists may administer medication to physically active patients to assess their heart function. Cardiac sonographers also may assist physicians who perform **transesophageal** echocardiography, which involves placing a tube in the patient's esophagus to obtain ultrasound images.

Work Environment

Cardiovascular technologists and technicians spend a lot of time walking and standing. Heavy lifting may be involved to move equipment or transfer patients. These workers wear heavy protective aprons while conducting some procedures. Those who work in catheterization laboratories may face stressful working conditions because they are in close contact with patients with serious heart ailments. For example, some patients may encounter complications that have life-or-death implications.

Some cardiovascular technologists and technicians may have the potential for radiation exposure, which is kept to a minimum by strict adherence to radiation safety guidelines. In addition, those who use sonography can be at an increased risk for musculoskeletal disorders such as carpel tunnel syndrome, neck and back strain, and eyestrain. However, the greater use of ergonomically correct equipment and an increasing awareness of hazards will continue to minimize such risks.

Technologists and technicians generally work a 5-day, 40-hour week that may include weekends. Those in catheterization laboratories tend to work longer hours and may work evenings. They also may be on call during the night and on weekends. About 18% worked part time in 2008.

Employment Opportunities

Cardiovascular technologists and technicians held about 49,500 jobs in 2008. About 77% of jobs were in public and private hospitals, primarily in cardiology departments. The remaining jobs were mostly in offices of physicians, including cardiologists, or in medical and diagnostic laboratories, including diagnostic imaging centers.

Educational and Legal Requirements

An Associate degree is the most common level of education completed by cardiovascular technologists and technicians. Certification, although not required in all cases, is available.

Education and Training

Although a few cardiovascular technologists, vascular technologists, and cardiac sonographers are currently trained on the job, most receive training in 2- to 4-year programs. The majority of technologists complete a 2-year junior or community college program, but 4-year programs are increasingly available. The first year is dedicated to core courses and is followed by a year of specialized instruction in either invasive or noninvasive cardiovascular, or noninvasive vascular technology. Those who are already qualified in an allied health profession need to complete only the year of specialized instruction.

The Joint Review Committee on Education in Cardiovascular Technology reviews education programs seeking accreditation. The Commission on Accreditation of Allied Health Education Programs (CAAHEP) accredits these education programs; as of January 2009, there were 34 programs accredited in cardiovascular technology in the United States. Similarly, students who want to study echocardiography or vascular sonography may also attend CAAHEP-accredited programs in diagnostic medical sonography. In 2009, there were 168 diagnostic medical sonography programs accredited by CAAHEP. Those who attend these accredited programs are eligible to obtain professional certification.

Unlike most other cardiovascular technologists and technicians, most EKG technicians are trained on the job by an EKG supervisor or a cardiologist. On-the-job training usually lasts about 4 to 6 weeks. Most employers prefer to train people already in the healthcare field—nursing aides, for example. Some EKG technicians are students enrolled in 2-year programs to become technologists, working part time to gain experience and make contact with employers. For technicians who perform Holter monitoring, on-the-job training may last around 18 to 24 months.

Licensure and Certification

Some states require workers in this occupation to be licensed. For information on a particular state, contact that state's medical board. Certification is available from two organizations: Cardiovascular Credentialing International (CCI) and the American Registry for Diagnostic Medical Sonographers (ARDMS). The CCI offers four certifications—Certified Cardiographic Technician (CCT), Registered Cardiac Sonographer (RCS), Registered Vascular Specialist (RVS), and Registered Cardiovascular Invasive Specialist (RCIS). The ARDMS offers Registered Diagnostic Cardiac Sonographer (RDCS) and Registered Vascular Technologist (RVT) credentials. Some states require certification as part of licensure. In other states, certification is not required, but many employers prefer it.

Other Qualifications

Cardiovascular technologists and technicians must be reliable, have mechanical aptitude, and be able to follow detailed instructions. A pleasant, relaxed manner for putting patients at ease is an asset. They must be articulate and well spoken as they must communicate in technical detail with physicians and also explain procedures in a simple manner to patients.

Advancement

Technologists and technicians can advance to higher levels of the profession as many institutions structure the occupation in multiple levels, each having an increasing amount of responsibility. Technologists and technicians also can advance into supervisory or management positions. Other common possibilities include working in an educational setting or conducting laboratory work.

Employment Trends

Employment is expected to grow much faster than average; technologists and technicians with multiple professional credentials, trained to perform a wide range of procedures, will have the best prospects.

Employment Change

Employment of cardiovascular technologists and technicians is expected to increase by 24% through the year 2018, much faster than the average for all occupations. Growth will occur as the population ages, because older people have a higher incidence of heart disease and other complications of the heart and vascular system. Noninvasive procedures, such as ultrasound, are being performed more often as an alternative to more expensive and invasive procedures. Due to advances in medicine and greater public awareness, signs of vascular disease can be detected earlier, creating demand for cardiovascular technologists and technicians to perform various procedures.

Employment of vascular technologists and echocardiographers will grow as advances in vascular technology and sonography reduce the need for more costly and invasive procedures. Electrophysiology is also becoming a rapidly growing specialty. However, fewer EKG technicians will be needed, as hospitals train nursing aides and others to perform basic EKG procedures. Individuals trained in Holter monitoring and stress testing are expected to have more favorable job prospects than those who can perform only a basic EKG.

Medicaid has relaxed some of the rules governing reimbursement for vascular exams, which is resulting in vascular studies becoming a more routine practice. As a result of the increased use of these procedures, individuals with training in vascular studies should have more favorable employment opportunities.

Job Prospects

Some additional job openings for cardiovascular technologists and technicians will arise from replacement needs as individuals transfer to other jobs or leave the labor force. Job prospects will be best for those with multiple professional credentials, trained to perform a wide range of procedures. Those willing to relocate or work irregular hours also will have better job opportunities.

It is not uncommon for cardiovascular technologists and technicians to move between the specialties within the occupation by obtaining certification in more than one specialty. **Table 23-1** shows some projection data provided by the Department of Labor.

Median annual earnings of cardiovascular technologists and technicians were $47,010 in May 2008. The middle 50% earned between $32,800 and $61,580. The lowest 10% earned less than $25,510, and the highest 10% earned more than $74,760. Median annual earnings of cardiovascular technologists and technicians in 2008 were $48,590 in offices of physicians and $46,670 in general medical and surgical hospitals.

Related Occupations

Cardiovascular technologists and technicians operate sophisticated equipment that helps physicians and other health practitioners to diagnose and treat patients. So do diagnostic medical sonographers, nuclear medicine technologists, radiation therapists, radiologic technologists and technicians, and respiratory therapists.

TABLE 23-1 Projections Data from the National Employment Matrix for Cardiovascular Technologists and Technicians

Occupational Title	Employment, 2008	Projected Employment, 2018	Change, 2008–2018	
			Number	Percentage
Cardiovascular technologists and technicians	49,500	61,400	11,900	24

Additional Information

For general information about a career in cardiovascular technology, contact

- Alliance of Cardiovascular Professionals, P.O. Box 2007, Midlothian, VA 23113. Internet: http://www.acp-online.org

For a list of accredited programs in cardiovascular technology, contact

- Committee on Accreditation for Allied Health Education Programs, 1361 Park St., Clearwater, FL 33756. Internet: http://www.caahep.org
- Society for Vascular Ultrasound, 4601 Presidents Dr., Suite 260, Lanham, MD 20706-4381. Internet: http://www.svunet.org

For information regarding registration and certification, contact

- Cardiovascular Credentialing International, 1500 Sunday Dr., Suite 102, Raleigh, NC 27607. Internet: http://www.cci-online.org
- American Registry of Diagnostic Medical Sonographers, 51 Monroe St., Plaza East One, Rockville, MD 20850-2400. Internet: http://www.ardms.org

NUCLEAR MEDICINE TECHNOLOGISTS
SIGNIFICANT POINTS

- Keen competition is expected for most positions.

- Technologists with training in multiple diagnostic methods, or in nuclear cardiology, should have the best prospects.

- Nuclear medicine technology programs range in length from 1 to 4 years and lead to a certificate, an Associate degree, or a Bachelor degree.

- About 66% of nuclear medicine technologists work in hospitals.

Work Descriptions

Diagnostic imaging embraces several procedures that aid in diagnosing ailments, the most familiar being the X-ray. In **nuclear medicine**, **radio-nuclides**—unstable atoms that emit radiation spontaneously—are used to diagnose and treat disease. Radionuclides are purified and compounded to form **radiopharmaceuticals**. Nuclear medicine technologists administer radiopharmaceuticals to patients and then monitor the characteristics and functions of tissues or organs in which the drugs localize. Abnormal areas show higher-than-expected or lower-than-expected concentrations of radio-activity. Nuclear medicine differs from other diagnostic imaging technologies because it determines the presence of disease on the basis of metabolic changes rather than changes in organ structure.

Nuclear medicine technologists operate cameras that detect and map the radioactive drug in a patient's body to create diagnostic images. After explaining test procedures to patients, technologists prepare a dose of the radiopharmaceutical and administer it by mouth, injection, inhalation, or other means. They position patients and start a **gamma scintillation camera**, or "scanner," which creates images of the distribution of a radiopharmaceutical as it localizes in, and emits signals from, the patient's body. The images are produced on a computer screen or on film for a physician to interpret.

When preparing radiopharmaceuticals, technologists adhere to safety standards that keep the radiation exposure as low as possible to workers and patients. Technologists maintain patient records and document the amount and type of radionuclides that they receive, use, and discard.

Work Environment

Physical stamina is important because nuclear medicine technologists are on their feet much of the day and may have to lift or turn disabled patients. In addition, technologists must operate complicated equipment that requires mechanical ability and manual dexterity.

Although the potential for radiation exposure exists in this field, it is minimized by the use of shielded syringes, gloves, and other protective devices, and by adherence to strict radiation safety guidelines. The amount of radiation in a nuclear medicine procedure is comparable to that received during a diagnostic X-ray procedure. Technologists also wear badges that measure radiation levels. Because of safety programs, badge measurements rarely exceed established safety levels.

Nuclear medicine technologists generally work a 40 hour week, perhaps including evening or weekend hours, in departments that operate on an extended schedule. Opportunities for part-time and shift work also are available. In addition, technologists in hospitals may have on-call duty on a rotational basis, and those employed by mobile imaging services may be required to travel to several locations.

There are two areas of specialty for nuclear medicine technologists—nuclear cardiology and positron emission tomography (**PET**). Nuclear cardiology typically involves myocardial perfusion imaging, which, like most nuclear medicine, uses radiopharmaceuticals and cameras to image the body. Myocardial perfusion imaging, however, requires that patients perform exercise so the technologist can image the heart and blood flow. Technologists specializing in PET operate a special medical imaging device that produces a 3-D image of the body.

Employment Opportunities

Nuclear medicine technologists held about 21,800 jobs in 2008. About 66% of all nuclear medicine technologist jobs were in hospitals—private and public. Most of the rest were in offices of physicians or in medical and diagnostic laboratories, including diagnostic imaging centers.

Educational and Legal Requirements

Nuclear medicine technology programs range in length from 1 to 4 years and lead to a certificate, an Associate degree, or a Bachelor degree. Many employers and an increasing number of states require certification or licensure. Aspiring nuclear medicine technologists should check the requirements of the state in which they plan to work.

Education and Training

Completion of a nuclear medicine technology program takes 1 to 4 years and leads to a certificate, an Associate degree, or a Bachelor degree. Generally, certificate programs are offered in hospitals, Associate degree programs in community colleges, and Bachelor degree programs in 4-year colleges and universities. Courses cover the physical sciences, the biological effects of radiation exposure, radiation protection and procedures, the use of radiopharmaceuticals, imaging techniques, and computer applications.

One-year certificate programs are for health professionals who already possess an Associate degree—especially radiologic technologists and diagnostic medical sonographers—but who wish to specialize in nuclear medicine. The programs also attract medical technologists, registered nurses, and others who wish to change fields or specialize.

The Joint Review Committee on Education Programs in Nuclear Medicine Technology accredits most formal training programs in nuclear medicine technology. In 2008, there were more than 100 accredited programs available.

Licensure and Certification

Educational requirements for nuclear medicine technologists vary from state to state, so it is important that aspiring technologists check the requirements of the state in which they plan to work. In 2008, 25 states licensed nuclear medicine technologists. In addition, many third-party payers require nuclear medicine technologists to be certified in order for the healthcare facility to receive reimbursement for imaging procedures. Certification is available from the American Registry of Radiologic Technologists (**ARRT**) and from the Nuclear Medicine Technology Certification Board (NMTCB). Although not required, some workers receive certification from both agencies. Nuclear medicine technologists must meet the minimum federal standards on the administration of radioactive drugs and the operation of radiation detection equipment.

The most common way to become eligible for certification by ARRT or NMTCB is to complete a training program recognized by those organizations. Other ways to become eligible are completing a Bachelor or Associate degree in biological science or a related health field, such as registered nursing, or acquiring, under supervision, a certain number of hours of experience in nuclear medicine technology. ARRT and NMTCB have different requirements, but in all cases, one must pass a comprehensive exam to become certified.

In addition to the general certification requirements, certified technicians also must complete a certain number of continuing education hours. Continuing education is required primarily because of the frequent technological and innovative changes in the field of nuclear medicine. Typically, technologists must register annually with both the ARRT and the NMTCB.

Other Qualifications

Nuclear medicine technologists should have excellent communication skills, be detail oriented, and have a desire to continue learning. Technologists must effectively interact with patients and their families and should be sensitive to patients' physical and psychological needs. Nuclear medicine technologists must be able to work independently as they usually have little direct supervision. Technologists also must be detailed oriented and meticulous when performing procedures to ensure that all regulations are being followed.

Advancement

Technologists may advance to supervisor, then to chief technologist, and to department administrator or director. Some technologists specialize in a clinical area, such as nuclear cardiology or computer analysis, or leave patient care to take positions in research laboratories. Some become instructors in, or directors of, nuclear medicine technology programs, a step that usually requires a Bachelor or Master degree in the subject. Others leave the occupation to work as sales or training representatives for medical equipment and radiopharmaceutical manufacturing firms or as radiation safety officers in regulatory agencies or hospitals.

Employment Trends

Faster-than-average job growth will arise from an increase in the number of middle-aged and elderly persons, who are the primary users of diagnostic and treatment procedures. However, the number of job openings each year will be relatively low because the occupation is small.

Employment Change

Employment of nuclear medicine technologists is expected to increase by 16% from 2008 to 2018, faster than the average for all occupations. Growth will arise from technological advancement, the development of new nuclear medicine treatments, and an increase in the number of middle-aged and older persons, who are the primary users of diagnostic procedures, including nuclear medicine tests.

Technological innovations may increase the diagnostic uses of nuclear medicine. New nuclear medical imaging technologies, including positron emission tomography (PET) and single photon emission computed tomography (SPECT), are expected to be used increasingly and to contribute further to employment growth. The wider use of nuclear medical imaging to observe metabolic and biochemical changes during **neurology**, cardiology, and oncology procedures also will spur demand for nuclear medicine technologists.

Nonetheless, cost considerations will affect the speed with which new applications of nuclear medicine grow. Some promising nuclear medicine procedures, such as positron emission tomography, are extremely costly, and hospitals contemplating these procedures will have to consider equipment costs, reimbursement policies, and the number of potential users.

Job Prospects

In spite of fast growth in nuclear medicine, the number of openings in the occupation each year will be relatively low because of the small size of the occupation. Technologists who have additional training in other diagnostic methods, such as radiologic technology or diagnostic medical sonography, will enjoy the best prospects. **Table 23-2** shows some projection data provided by the Department of Labor.

Earnings

Median annual earnings of nuclear medicine technologists were $66,660 in May 2008. The middle 50% earned between $57,270 and $78,240. The lowest 10% earned less than $48,450, and the highest 10% earned more than $87,770. Median annual earnings of nuclear medicine technologists in 2008 were $66,320 in general medical and surgical hospitals.

Related Occupations

Nuclear medicine technologists operate sophisticated equipment to help physicians and other health practitioners diagnose and treat patients. Cardiovascular technologists and technicians, clinical laboratory technologists and technicians, diagnostic medical sonographers, radiation therapists, radiologic technologists and technicians, and respiratory therapists perform similar functions.

Additional Information

Additional information on a career as a nuclear medicine technologist is available from

TABLE 23-2 Projections Data from the National Employment Matrix for Nuclear Medicine Technologists

Occupational Title	Employment, 2008	Projected Employment, 2018	Change, 2008–2018	
			Number	Percentage
Nuclear medicine technologists	21,800	25,400	3600	16

- Society of Nuclear Medicine Technologists, 1850 Samuel Morse Dr., Reston, VA 20190. Internet: http://www.snm.org

    For a list of accredited programs in nuclear medicine technology, contact

- Joint Review Committee on Educational Programs in Nuclear Medicine Technology, 2000 W. Danforth Rd., Suite 130 #203, Edmond, OK 73003. Internet: http://www.jrcnmt.org

    Information on certification is available from

- Nuclear Medicine Technology Certification Board, 3558 Habersham at Northlake, Building 1, Tucker, GA 30084. Internet: http://www.nmtcb.org
- American Registry of Radiologic Technologists, 1255 Northland Dr., St. Paul, MN 55120-1155. Internet: http://www.arrt.org

SURGICAL TECHNOLOGISTS
SIGNIFICANT POINTS

- Employment is expected to grow much faster than average.
- Job opportunities will be best for technologists who are certified and for those who are willing to relocate.
- Training programs last 9 to 24 months and lead to a certificate, diploma, or Associate degree.
- Hospitals will continue to be the primary employers, although much faster employment growth is expected in other healthcare industries.

Work Descriptions

Surgical technologists, also called scrubs and surgical or operating room technicians, assist in surgical operations under the supervision of surgeons, registered nurses, or other surgical personnel. Surgical technologists are members of operating room teams, which most commonly include surgeons, anesthesiologists, and circulating nurses.

Before an operation, surgical technologists help prepare the **operating room** by setting up surgical instruments and equipment, sterile drapes, and sterile solutions. They assemble both sterile and nonsterile equipment, as well as check and adjust it to ensure that it is working properly. Technologists also get patients ready for surgery by washing, shaving, and disinfecting incision sites. They transport patients to the operating room, help position them on the operating table, and cover them with sterile surgical drapes. Technologists also observe patients' vital signs, check charts, and help the surgical team put on sterile gowns and gloves.

During surgery, technologists pass instruments and other sterile supplies to surgeons and surgeon assistants. They may hold retractors, cut sutures, and help count sponges, needles, supplies, and instruments. Surgical technologists help prepare, care for, and dispose of specimens taken for laboratory analysis, and help apply dressings. Some operate sterilizers, lights, or suction machines, and help operate diagnostic equipment.

After an operation, surgical technologists may help transfer patients to the recovery room and clean and restock the operating room. Certified surgical technologists with additional specialized education or training also may act as the surgical first assistant or circulator. The surgical first assistant, as defined by the American College of Surgeons (ACS), provides aid in exposure, hemostasis (controlling blood flow and stopping or preventing hemorrhage), and other technical functions under the surgeon's direction, to assist the surgeon in carrying out a safe operation. A circulating technologist is the "unsterile" member of the surgical team. The circulator interviews and prepares the patient prior to surgery, assists with anesthesia, obtains and opens packages from which the "sterile" team members remove sterile contents during the procedure, keeps a written account of the surgical procedure, and answers the surgeon's questions about the patient during the surgery.

Work Environment

Surgical technologists work in clean, well-lighted, cool environments. They must stand for long periods and remain alert during operations. At times, they may be exposed to communicable diseases and unpleasant sights, odors, and materials. Most surgical technologists work a regular 40-hour week, although they may be on call or work nights, weekends, and holidays on a rotating basis.

Employment Opportunities

Surgical technologists held about 91,500 jobs in 2008. About 71% of jobs for surgical technologists were in hospitals, mainly in operating and delivery rooms. Other jobs were in offices of physicians or dentists who perform outpatient surgery and in outpatient care centers, including ambulatory surgical centers. A few technologists, known as private scrubs, are employed directly by surgeons who maintain specialized surgical teams, such as those for liver transplants.

Educational and Legal Requirements

Training programs last 9 to 24 months and lead to a certificate, diploma, or Associate degree. Professional certification can help in getting jobs and promotions.

Education and Training

Surgical technologists receive their training in formal programs offered by community and junior colleges, vocational schools, universities, hospitals, and the military. In 2008, the Commission on Accreditation of Allied Health Education Programs (CAAHEP) recognized more than 450 accredited training programs. Programs last from 9 to 24 months and lead to a certificate, diploma, or Associate degree. High school graduation normally is required for admission. Recommended high school courses include health, biology, chemistry, and mathematics.

Surgical technologist training programs provide classroom education and supervised clinical experience. Students take courses in anatomy, physiology, microbiology, pharmacology, professional ethics, and medical terminology. Other topics covered include the care and safety of patients during surgery, sterile techniques, and surgical procedures. Students also learn to sterilize instruments, prevent and control infection, and handle special drugs, solutions, supplies, and equipment.

Certification and Other Qualifications

Most employers prefer to hire certified surgical technologists. Technologists may obtain voluntary professional certification from the Liaison Council on Certification for the Surgical Technologist by graduating from a CAAHEP-accredited program and passing a national certification examination. They may then use the Certified Surgical Technologist (CST) designation. Continuing education or reexamination is required to maintain certification, which must be renewed every 4 years.

Certification also may be obtained from the National Center for Competency Testing (NCCT). Candidates qualify for the exam by following one of three paths: they complete an accredited training program; undergo a 2-year hospital on-the-job training program; or acquire 7 years of experience working in the field. After passing the exam, individuals may use the designation Tech in Surgery-Certified, (TS-C). This certification must be renewed every 5 years through either continuing education or reexamination.

Surgical technologists need manual dexterity sufficient to handle instruments quickly. They also must be conscientious, orderly, and emotionally stable to handle the demands of the operating room environment. Technologists must respond quickly and be familiar enough with operating room procedures to have instruments on hand for surgeons as needed. They are expected to keep abreast of new developments in the field.

Advancement

Technologists advance by specializing in a particular area of surgery, such as neurosurgery or open-heart surgery. They also may work as circulating technologists. With additional training, some technologists advance to surgical first assistant. Some surgical technologists manage central supply departments in hospitals or take positions with insurance companies, sterile supply services, and operating equipment firms.

Employment Trends

Employment of surgical technologists is expected to grow much faster than the average for all occupations. Job opportunities will be best for technologists who are certified and for those who are willing to relocate.

Employment Change

Employment of surgical technologists is expected to grow 25% between 2008 and 2018, much faster than the average for all occupations, as the volume of surgeries increases. The number of surgical procedures is expected to rise as the population grows and ages. Older people, including the baby-boom generation, who generally require more surgical procedures, will account for a larger portion of the general population. In addition, technological advances, such as fiber optics and laser technology, will permit an increasing number of new surgical procedures to be performed and also will allow surgical technologists to assist with a greater number of procedures.

Hospitals will continue to be the primary employer of surgical technologists, although much faster employment growth is expected in offices of physicians and in outpatient care centers, including ambulatory surgical centers.

Job Prospects

Job opportunities will be best for technologists who are certified. **Table 23-3** shows some projection data provided by the Department of Labor.

Earnings

Median annual earnings of wage and salary surgical technologists were $38,740 in May 2008. The middle 50% earned between $32,490 and $46,910. The lowest 10% earned less than $27,510, and the highest 10% earned more than $54,300. Median annual earnings in the industries employing the largest numbers of surgical technologists are shown in **Table 23-4**.

Wages of surgical technologists vary with their experience and education, the responsibilities of the position, the working hours, and the economy of a given region of the country. Benefits provided by most employers include paid vacation and sick leave; health, medical, vision, dental, and life insurance; and retirement programs. A few employers also provide tuition reimbursement and child-care benefits.

TABLE 23-3 Projections Data from the National Employment Matrix for Surgical Technologists

Occupational Title	Employment, 2008	Projected Employment, 2018	Change, 2008–2018 Number	Percentage
Surgical technologists	91,500	114,700	23,200	25

TABLE 23-4   Median Annual Earnings in Industries, May 2008

Specialty (psychiatric and substance) hospitals	$40,880
Outpatient care centers	39,660
General medical and surgical hospitals	38,640
Offices of physicians	38,520
Offices of dentists	36,380

Related Occupations

Other health occupations requiring approximately 1 year of training after high school include dental assistants, licensed practical and licensed vocational nurses, clinical laboratory technologists and technicians, and medical assistants.

Additional Information

For additional information on a career as a surgical technologist and a list of CAAHEP-accredited programs, contact

- Association of Surgical Technologists, 6 West Dry Creek Cir., Suite 200, Littleton, CO 80120. Internet: http://www.ast.org

  For information on becoming a Certified Surgical Technologist, contact

- Liaison Council on Certification for the Surgical Technologist, 6 West Dry Creek Cir., Suite 100, Littleton, CO 80120. Internet: http://www.lcc-st.org

  For information on becoming a Tech in Surgery-Certified, contact

- National Center for Competency Testing, 7007 College Blvd., Suite 705, Overland Park, KS 66211.

MEDICAL, DENTAL, AND OPHTHALMIC LABORATORY TECHNICIANS
SIGNIFICANT POINTS

- Around 58% of jobs were in medical equipment and supplies manufacturing, usually in small, privately owned businesses.
- Most technicians learn their craft on the job, but many employers prefer to hire those with formal training.
- Faster-than-average employment growth is expected for dental and ophthalmic laboratory technicians, while average employment growth is expected for medical appliance technicians.
- Job opportunities should be favorable because few people seek these positions.

Work Descriptions

When patients require a medical device to help them see clearly, chew and speak well, or walk better, their healthcare providers send requests for such devices to medical, dental, and **ophthalmic laboratory technicians**. These technicians produce a variety of implements to help patients.

Medical appliance technicians construct, fit, maintain, and repair braces, artificial limbs, joints, arch supports, and other surgical and medical appliances. They follow prescriptions or detailed instructions from podiatrists or orthotists, who request braces, supports, corrective shoes, or other devices. They also follow the instructions of prosthetists in constructing replacement limbs—arms, legs, hands, or feet—for patients who need them due to a birth defect, accident, or amputation. Other health professionals may also order medical appliances to be produced by medical appliance technicians. Medical appliance technicians who work with orthotic and prosthetic devices are called orthotic and prosthetic technicians. Other medical appliance technicians work with medical appliances that help correct other medical problems, such as aids to correct hearing loss.

Creating medical devices takes several steps. To make arch supports, for example, technicians first make a wax or plastic impression of the patient's foot. Then they bend and form a material so that it conforms to prescribed contours required to fabricate structural components. If a support is mainly required to correct the balance of a patient with legs of different lengths, a rigid material is used. If the support is primarily intended to protect those with arthritic or diabetic feet, a soft material is used. Supports and braces are polished with grinding and buffing wheels. Technicians may cover arch supports with felt to make them more comfortable.

For prostheses, technicians construct or receive a plaster cast of the patient's limb to use as a pattern. Then, they lay out parts and use precision measuring instruments to measure them. Technicians may use wood, plastic, metal, or other material for the parts of the artificial limb. Next, they carve, cut, or grind the material using hand or power tools. Then, they drill holes for rivets and glue, rivet, or weld the parts together. They are able to do very precise work using common tools. Next, technicians use grinding and buffing wheels to smooth and polish artificial limbs. Last, they may cover or pad the limbs with rubber, leather, felt, plastic, or another material. Also, technicians may mix pigments according to formulas to match the patient's skin color and apply the mixture to the artificial limb.

After fabrication, medical appliance technicians test devices for proper alignment, movement, and biomechanical stability using meters and alignment fixtures. They also may fit the appliance on the patient and adjust it as necessary. Over time the appliance will wear down, so technicians must repair and maintain the device. They also may service and repair the machinery used for the fabrication of orthotic and prosthetic devices.

Dental laboratory technicians fill prescriptions from dentists for crowns, bridges, dentures, and other dental prosthetics. First, dentists send a specification of the item to be manufactured, along with an impression or mold of the patient's mouth or teeth. With new technology, a technician may receive a digital impression rather than a physical mold. Then dental laboratory technicians, also called dental technicians, create a model of the patient's mouth by pouring plaster into the impression and allowing it to set. They place the model on an apparatus that mimics the bite and movement of the patient's jaw. The model serves as the basis of the prosthetic device. Technicians examine the model, noting the size and shape of the adjacent teeth, as well as gaps within the gum line. Based on these observations and the dentist's specifications, technicians build and shape a wax tooth or teeth model, using small hand instruments called wax spatulas and wax carvers. The wax model is used to cast the metal framework for the prosthetic device.

After the wax tooth has been formed, dental technicians pour the cast and form the metal and, using small handheld tools, prepare the surface to allow the metal and porcelain to bond. They then apply porcelain in layers, to arrive at the precise shape and color of a tooth. Technicians place the tooth in a porcelain furnace to bake the porcelain onto the metal framework, and then adjust the shape and color, with subsequent grinding and addition of porcelain to achieve a sealed finish. The final product is a nearly exact replica of the lost tooth or teeth.

In some dental laboratories, technicians perform all stages of the work, whereas in other labs, each technician works on only a few. Dental laboratory technicians can specialize in one of five areas: orthodontic appliances, crowns and bridges, complete dentures, partial dentures, or ceramics. Job titles can reflect specialization in these areas. For example, technicians who make porcelain and acrylic restorations are called **dental ceramists**.

Ophthalmic laboratory technicians —also known as manufacturing opticians, optical mechanics, or optical goods workers—make prescription eyeglass or contact lenses. Prescription lenses are curved in such a way that light is correctly focused onto the retina of the patient's eye, improving his or her vision. Some ophthalmic laboratory technicians manufacture lenses for other optical instruments, such as telescopes and binoculars. Ophthalmic laboratory technicians cut, grind, edge, and finish lenses according to specifications provided by dispensing opticians, optometrists, or ophthalmologists, and may insert lenses into frames to produce finished glasses. Although some lenses still are produced by hand, technicians are increasingly using automated equipment to make lenses.

Ophthalmic laboratory technicians should not be confused with workers in other vision care occupations. Ophthalmologists and optometrists are "eye doctors" who examine eyes, diagnose and treat vision problems, and prescribe corrective lenses. Ophthalmologists are physicians who also perform eye surgery. Dispensing opticians, who also may do the work of ophthalmic laboratory technicians, help patients select frames and lenses, and adjust finished eyeglasses. (See Chapter 7.)

Ophthalmic laboratory technicians read prescription specifications, select standard glass or plastic lens blanks, and then mark them to indicate where the curves specified on the prescription should be ground. They place the lens in the lens grinder, set the dials for the prescribed curvature, and start the machine. After a minute or so, the lens is ready to be "finished" by a machine that rotates it against a fine abrasive to grind it and smooth out rough edges. The lens is then placed in a polishing machine with an even finer abrasive, to polish it to a smooth, bright finish.

Next, the technician examines the lens through a **lensometer**, an instrument similar in shape to a microscope, to make sure that the degree and placement of the curve are correct. The technician then cuts the lenses and bevels the edges to fit the frame, dips each lens into dye if the prescription calls for tinted or coated lenses, polishes the edges, and assembles the lenses and frame parts into a finished pair of glasses.

In small laboratories, technicians usually handle every phase of the operation. In large ones, in which virtually every phase of the operation is automated, technicians may be responsible for operating computerized equipment. Technicians also inspect the final product for quality and accuracy.

Work Environment

Medical, dental, and ophthalmic laboratory technicians generally work in clean, well-lighted, and well-ventilated laboratories. They have limited contact with the public. Salaried laboratory technicians usually work 40 hours a week, but some work part time. At times, technicians wear goggles to protect their eyes, gloves to handle hot objects, or masks to avoid inhaling dust. They may spend a great deal of time standing. Medical appliance technicians should be particularly careful when working with tools because there is a risk of injury.

Dental technicians usually have their own workbenches, which can be equipped with Bunsen burners, grinding and polishing equipment, and hand instruments, such as wax spatulas and wax carvers. Some dental technicians have **computer-aided milling equipment** to assist them with creating artificial teeth.

Employment Opportunities

Medical, dental, and ophthalmic laboratory technicians held about 95,200 jobs in 2008. About 58% of salaried jobs were in medical equipment and supply manufacturing laboratories, which usually are small, privately owned businesses with fewer than five employees. However, some laboratories are large; a few employ more than 1000 workers. **Table 23-5** shows employment by detailed occupation.

TABLE 23-5   Employment by Detailed Occupation

Dental laboratory technicians	46,000
Ophthalmic laboratory technicians	35,200
Medical appliance technicians	13,900

In addition to manufacturing laboratories, many medical appliance technicians worked in health and personal care stores, while others worked in public and private hospitals, professional and commercial equipment and supplies merchant wholesalers, or consumer goods rental centers. Some were self-employed. In addition to manufacturing laboratories, many dental laboratory technicians worked in offices of dentists. Some dental laboratory technicians open their own offices.

Most ophthalmic laboratory technician jobs were in medical equipment and supplies manufacturing laboratories. Others worked in health and personal care stores, offices of optometrists, and professional and commercial equipment and supplies merchant wholesalers.

Educational and Legal Requirements

Most medical, dental, and ophthalmic laboratory technicians learn their craft on the job; many employers, however, prefer to hire those with formal training or at least a high school diploma.

Education and Training

High school students interested in becoming medical appliance technicians should take mathematics, metal and wood shop, and drafting. Medical appliance technicians usually begin as helpers and gradually learn new skills as they gain experience.

Formal training is also available. In 2008, there were five orthotic and prosthetic technician programs accredited by the National Commission on Orthotic and Prosthetic Education (NCOPE). These programs offer either an Associate degree or a 1-year certificate for orthotic or prosthetic technicians. The programs instruct students on human anatomy and physiology, orthotic and prosthetic equipment and materials, and applied biomechanical principles to customize orthotics or prostheses. The programs also include clinical rotations to provide hands-on experience.

Dental laboratory technicians begin by learning simple tasks, such as pouring plaster into an impression, and progress to more complex procedures, such as making porcelain crowns and bridges. Becoming a fully trained technician requires an average of 3 to 4 years, depending on the individual's aptitude and ambition, but it may take a few years more to become an accomplished technician. High school students interested in becoming dental laboratory technicians should take courses in art, metal and wood shop, drafting, and sciences. Courses in management and business may help those wishing to operate their own laboratories. Training in dental laboratory technology also is available through universities, community and junior colleges, vocational-technical institutes, and the armed forces. Formal training programs vary greatly both in length and in the level of skill they impart. In 2008, the Commission on Dental Accreditation, in conjunction with the American Dental Association, accredited 20 programs in dental laboratory technology.

These programs provide classroom instruction in materials science, oral anatomy, fabrication procedures, ethics, and related subjects. In addition, each student is given supervised practical experience in a school or an associated dental laboratory. Accredited programs normally take 2 years to complete and lead to an Associate degree. A few programs take about 4 years to complete and offer a Bachelor degree in dental technology. Graduates of 2-year training programs need additional hands-on experience to become fully qualified.

Each dental laboratory owner operates in a different way, and classroom instruction does not necessarily expose students to techniques and procedures favored by individual laboratory owners. Students who have taken enough courses to learn the basics of the craft usually are considered good candidates for training, regardless of whether they have completed a formal program. Many employers will train someone without any classroom experience.

Ophthalmic laboratory technicians start on simple tasks if they are training to produce lenses by hand. They may begin with marking or blocking lenses for grinding then progress to grinding, cutting, edging, and beveling lenses, and finally to assembling the eyeglasses. Depending on individual aptitude, it may take up to 6 months to become proficient in all phases of the work.

Employers filling trainee jobs prefer applicants who are high school graduates. Courses in science, mathematics, and computers are valuable; manual dexterity and the ability to do precision work are essential. Technicians using automated systems will find computer skills valuable.

A few ophthalmic laboratory technicians learn their trade in the armed forces or in the few programs in optical technology offered by vocational-technical institutes or trade schools. In 2008, there were two programs in ophthalmic technology accredited by the Commission on Opticianry Accreditation (COA).

Other Qualifications

Dental technicians need a high degree of manual dexterity, good vision, and the ability to recognize very fine color shadings and variations in shape. An artistic aptitude for detailed and precise work also is important.

Certification and Advancement

Voluntary certification for orthotic and prosthetic technicians is available through The American Board for Certification in Orthotics, Prosthetics & Pedorthics (**ABC**). Applicants are eligible for an exam after completing a program accredited by NCOPE, or obtaining 2 years of experience as a technician under the direct supervision of an ABC-certified practitioner. After successfully passing the appropriate exam, technicians receive the Registered Orthotic Technician, Registered Prosthetic Technician, or Registered Prosthetic-Orthotic Technician credential. Certification may help those orthotic and prosthetic technicians seeking to advance.

With additional formal education, medical appliance technicians who make orthotics and prostheses can advance to become orthotists or prosthetists, technicians who work with patients who need braces, artificial limbs, or related devices and help to determine the specifications for those devices.

In large dental laboratories, dental technicians may become supervisors or managers. Experienced technicians may teach or take jobs with dental suppliers in such areas as product development, marketing, and sales. Opening one's own laboratory is another, and more common, way to advance and earn more.

The National Board for Certification, an independent board established by the National Association of Dental Laboratories, offers certification in dental laboratory technology. Certification, which is voluntary except in three states, can be obtained in five specialty areas: crowns and bridges, ceramics, partial dentures, complete dentures, and orthodontic appliances. Certification may increase chances of advancement. Ophthalmic laboratory technicians can become supervisors and managers. Some become dispensing opticians, although further education or training generally is required in that occupation.

Employment Trends

Overall, faster-than-average growth is expected for employment of medical, dental, and ophthalmic laboratory technicians, but varies by detailed occupation. Job opportunities should be favorable because few people seek these positions.

Employment Change

Overall employment for these occupations is expected to grow 14% from 2008 to 2018, faster than the average for all occupations.

Employment of medical appliance technicians will grow 11%, about as fast as the average for all occupations, because of the increasing prevalence of the two leading causes of limb loss—diabetes and cardiovascular disease. In addition, advances in technology may spur demand for prostheses that allow for greater movement.

Employment of dental laboratory technicians is expected to grow 14%, which is faster than the average for all occupations. During the last few years, demand has arisen from an aging public that is growing increasingly interested in cosmetic prostheses. For example, many dental laboratories are filling orders for composite fillings that are the same shade of white as natural teeth to replace older, less attractive fillings. However, job growth for dental laboratory technicians will be limited. The overall dental health of the population has improved because of the fluoridation of drinking water and greater emphasis on preventive dental care, which has reduced the incidence of dental cavities. As a result, full dentures will be less common, as most people will need only a bridge or crown.

Ophthalmic laboratory technicians are expected to experience employment growth of 15%, faster than the average for all occupations. Demographic trends make it likely that many more Americans will need vision care in the years ahead. Not only will the population grow, but also the proportion of middle-aged and older adults is projected to increase rapidly. Middle age is a time when many people use corrective lenses for the first time, and elderly persons usually require more vision care than others. However, the increasing use of automated machinery will temper job growth for ophthalmic laboratory technicians.

Job Prospects

Job opportunities for medical, dental, and ophthalmic laboratory technicians should be favorable, due to expected faster-than-average growth. Those with formal training in a medical, dental, or ophthalmic laboratory technology program will have the best job prospects. In addition to openings from job growth, many job openings also will arise from the need to replace technicians who transfer to other occupations or who leave the labor force. **Table 23-6** shows some projection data provided by the Department of Labor.

Earnings

Median annual wages of wage and salary medical appliance technicians were $34,460 in May 2008. The middle 50% earned between $26,600 and $47,210. The lowest 10% earned less than $21,720, and the highest 10% earned more than $63,750.

Median annual earnings of wage and salary dental laboratory technicians were $34,170 in May 2008. The middle 50% earned between $26,260 and $44,790. The lowest 10% earned less than $20,740, and the highest 10% earned more than $58,140. In the two industries that employed the most dental laboratory technicians—medical equipment and supplies manufacturing and offices of dentists—median annual earnings were $33,700 and $35,000, respectively.

TABLE 23-6 Projections Data from the National Employment Matrix for Medical, Dental, and Ophthalmic Laboratory Technicians, Dental Laboratory Technicians, Medical Laboratory Technicians, and Ophthalmic Laboratory Technicians

Occupational Title	Employment, 2008	Project Employment, 2018	Change, 2008–2018	
			Number	Percentage
Medical, dental, and ophthalmic laboratory technicians	95,200	108,300	13,100	14
Dental laboratory technicians	46,000	52,400	6400	14
Medical laboratory technicians	13,900	15,400	1500	11
Ophthalmic laboratory technicians	35,200	40,400	5200	15

Median annual earnings of wage and salary ophthalmic laboratory technicians were $27,210 in May 2008. The middle 50% earned between $21,580 and $34,810. The lowest 10% earned less than $18,080, and the highest 10% earned more than $42,890. Median annual earnings were $25,250 in medical equipment and supplies manufacturing and $25,580 in health and personal care stores, the two industries that employ the most ophthalmic laboratory technicians.

Related Occupations

Medical, dental, and ophthalmic laboratory technicians manufacture and work with the same devices that are used by dispensing opticians, orthotists, and prosthetists. Other occupations that work with or manufacture goods using similar tools and skills are precision instrument and equipment repair, and textile, apparel, and furnishings occupations.

Additional Information

For information on careers in orthotics and prosthetics, contact

- American Academy of Orthotists and Prosthetists, 1331 H St. NW, Suite 501, Washington, DC 20005. Internet: http://www.opcareers.org

For a list of accredited programs for orthotic and prosthetic technicians, contact

- National Commission on Orthotic and Prosthetic Education, 330 John Carlyle St., Suite 200, Alexandria, VA 22314. Internet: http://www.ncope.org

For information on requirements for the certification of orthotic and prosthetic technicians, contact

- American Board for Certification in Orthotics and Prosthetics, 330 John Carlyle St., Suite 210, Alexandria, VA 22314. Internet: http://www.abcop.org

For a list of accredited programs in dental laboratory technology, contact

- Commission on Dental Accreditation, American Dental Association, 211 E. Chicago Ave., Chicago, IL 60611. Internet: http://www.ada.org

For information on requirements for the certification of dental laboratory technicians, contact

- National Board for Certification in Dental Technology, 325 John Knox Rd., L103, Tallahassee, FL 32303. Internet: http://www.nbccert.org

For information on career opportunities in commercial dental laboratories, contact

• National Association of Dental Laboratories, 325 John Knox Rd., L103, Tallahassee, FL 32303. Internet: http://www.nadl.org

For information on an accredited program in ophthalmic laboratory technology, contact

• Commission on Opticianry Accreditation, P.O. Box 142, Florence, IN 47020. Internet: http://www.coaccreditation.com/

General information on grants and scholarships is available from individual schools. State employment service offices can provide information about job openings for medical, dental, and ophthalmic laboratory technicians.

chapter twenty-four

Additional Health Therapists, Assistants, and Aides*

KEY TERMS

Art therapy	Medical assistants	Personal and home
Behavioral therapist	Mental health	care aides
CNAs	assistants	Physical therapy
Corrective therapy	Music therapy	Psychiatric aides
Dance therapy	Nursing aides	Recreational therapy
Home health aides	Occupational therapists	Rehabilitation counselors
Horticultural therapy	Orderlies	Speech pathologists
Manual arts therapy	Orthopedists	and audiologists

---

*Information for the following professions was obtained from Bureau of Labor Statistics, U.S. Department of Labor, *Occupational Outlook Handbook 2010–2011 Edition*, 2010:

- Recreational therapists
- Medical assistants
- Nursing and psychiatric aides
- Home health aides and personal and home care aides

HEALTH AND THERAPISTS

The objective of therapy is to help individuals with physical, mental, or social handicaps to regain their capacity for self-help and independence. To meet this goal, different kinds of therapists are employed, each with special knowledge and skills that can be used in rehabilitation. For example, art, dance, and music therapists bring both artistic and therapeutic skills to their work and try to improve the mental and physical well-being of their patients. Dance and art techniques are used as nonverbal means of communication, and, along with music, are often useful in helping patients resolve physical, emotional, and social problems. Horticultural therapists use gardening, an enjoyable and relaxing activity, for such purposes as training disabled or handicapped patients, evaluating the abilities of patients, or as a social activity for patients. Corrective therapists treat their patients by using medically prescribed exercises and activities. Physical therapists work with persons who are physically disabled by illness, accident, or birth defects. They use exercise and such treatments as heat, cold, and electricity to improve the patient's condition.

Occupational therapists help individuals with physical or emotional disabilities by teaching daily living skills or job skills. Manual arts therapists use industrial arts such as graphics or wood- or metalworking to rehabilitate their patients. Recreation therapists use sports, games, crafts, camping, and hobbies as part of the rehabilitation of ill, disabled, or handicapped persons. Athletic trainers care for and try to prevent injuries of individuals engaged in professional, amateur, and school athletics.

Persons whose limbs are lost or disabled through injury, disease, or birth defects require highly skilled and specialized services, provided by **orthopedists** and prosthetists. Orthopedists make and fit orthopedic braces, while prosthetists make and fit artificial limbs.

Speech pathologists and audiologists work with children and adults who have speech, language, or hearing impairments. **Rehabilitation counselors** help persons with physical, mental, or social problems return to or begin a normal life by obtaining satisfactory work.

Therapy and its related activities offer a broad spectrum of opportunities for career exploration by interested individuals; the following pages will explore in greater detail some of the specializations not described in previous chapters.

RECREATIONAL THERAPISTS

SIGNIFICANT POINTS

- Applicants for recreational therapist jobs will experience competition.
- A Bachelor degree in therapeutic recreation is the usual educational requirement.
- Some states regulate recreational therapists through licensure, registration, or regulation of titles, but requirements vary.
- Recreational therapists should be comfortable working with persons who are ill or who have disabilities.

Work Descriptions

Recreational therapists, also referred to as therapeutic recreation specialists, provide treatment services and recreation activities for individuals with disabilities or illnesses. Using a variety of techniques, including arts and crafts, animals, sports, games, dance and movement, drama, music, and community outings, therapists improve and maintain the physical, mental, and emotional well-being of their clients. Therapists help individuals reduce depression, stress, and anxiety; recover basic motor functioning and reasoning abilities; build confidence; and socialize effectively so that they can enjoy greater independence and reduce or eliminate the effects of their illness or disability. In addition, therapists help people with disabilities integrate into the community by teaching them how to use community resources and recreational activities. Recreational therapists are different from recreation workers, who organize recreational activities primarily for enjoyment.

In acute healthcare settings, such as hospitals and rehabilitation centers, recreational therapists treat and rehabilitate individuals with specific health conditions, usually in conjunction or collaboration with physicians, nurses, psychologists, social workers, and physical and occupational therapists. In long-term and residential care facilities, recreational therapists use leisure activities, especially structured group programs, to improve and maintain their clients' general health and well-being. They also may provide interventions to prevent the client from suffering further medical problems and complications.

Recreational therapists assess clients by gathering information from observations, medical records, standardized assessments, medical staff, clients' families, and clients themselves. Based on this information they develop and carry out therapeutic interventions consistent with the clients' needs and interests. For example, they may encourage clients who are isolated from others or who have limited social skills to play games with others, and they may teach right-handed people with right-side paralysis how to use their unaffected left side to throw a ball or swing a racket. Recreational therapists may instruct patients in relaxation techniques to reduce stress and tension, stretching and limbering exercises, proper body mechanics for participation in recreational activities, pacing and energy conservation techniques, and team activities. As they work, therapists observe and document a patient's participation, reactions, and progress.

Community-based recreational therapists may work in parks and recreation departments, special-education programs for school districts, or assisted-living, adult day care, and substance abuse rehabilitation centers. In these programs, therapists use interventions to develop specific skills, while providing opportunities for exercise, mental stimulation, creativity, and fun. Those few who work in schools help counselors, teachers, and parents address the special needs of students, including easing disabled students' transition into adult life.

Work Environment

Recreational therapists provide services in special activity rooms, but also use offices to plan their activities and prepare documentation. When working with clients during community integration programs, they may travel locally to teach clients how to use public transportation and other public amenities, such as parks, playgrounds, swimming pools, restaurants, and theaters. Therapists often lift and carry equipment. Recreational therapists generally work a 40-hour week that may include some evenings, weekends, and holidays.

Employment Opportunities

Recreational therapists held about 23,300 jobs in 2008. About 24% of these were in nursing and residential care facilities and hospitals. Other recreational therapists worked in state and local government agencies and in community care facilities for the elderly, including assisted-living facilities. The rest worked primarily in residential mental retardation, mental health, and substance abuse facilities; individual and family services; federal government agencies; educational services; and outpatient care centers. Only a small number of therapists were self-employed, generally contracting with long-term care facilities or community agencies to develop and oversee programs.

Educational and Legal Requirements

A Bachelor degree with a major or concentration in therapeutic recreation is the usual requirement for entry-level positions. Some states regulate recreational therapists, but requirements vary.

Education and Training

Most entry-level recreational therapists need a Bachelor degree in therapeutic recreation, or in recreation with a concentration in therapeutic recreation. People may qualify for paraprofessional positions with an Associate degree in therapeutic recreation or another subject related to health care. An Associate degree in **recreational therapy**; training in art, drama, or **music therapy**; or qualifying work experience may be sufficient for activity director positions in nursing homes.

There are more than 100 academic programs that prepare students to become recreational therapists. Most offer Bachelor degrees, although some also offer Associate, Master, or doctoral degrees. Therapeutic recreation programs include courses in assessment, treatment and program planning, intervention design, and evaluation. Students also study human anatomy, physiology, abnormal psychology, medical and psychiatric terminology, characteristics of illnesses and disabilities, professional ethics, and the use of assistive devices and technology.

Licensure

Some states regulate recreational therapists through licensure, registration, or the regulation of titles. Requirements vary by state. In 2009, Oklahoma, North Carolina, Utah, and New Hampshire required licensure to practice as a recreational therapist.

Certification and Other Qualifications

Although certification is usually voluntary, most employers prefer to hire candidates who are certified therapeutic recreation specialists. Work in a clinical setting often requires certification by the National Council for Therapeutic Recreation Certification. The council offers the Certified Therapeutic Recreation Specialist credential to candidates who have a Bachelor or graduate degree from an accredited educational institution, pass a written certification examination, and complete a supervised internship of at least 480 hours. Therapists must meet additional requirements to maintain certification. Therapists can also earn certifications in specific areas, such as **art therapy** and aquatic therapy.

Recreational therapists must be comfortable working with people who are ill or disabled. Therapists must be patient, tactful, and persuasive when working with people who have a variety of special needs. Ingenuity, a sense of humor, and imagination are needed to adapt activities to individual needs, and good physical coordination is necessary to demonstrate or participate in recreational activities.

Advancement

Therapists may advance to supervisory or administrative positions. Some teach, conduct research, or consult for health or social service agencies.

Employment Trends

Overall employment of recreational therapists is expected to grow faster than the average for all occupations. Competition for jobs is expected.

Employment Change

Employment of recreational therapists is expected to increase 15% from 2008 to 2018, faster than the average for all occupations. Employment of recreational therapists will grow to meet the therapy needs of the increasing number of older adults. In nursing care facilities—the largest industry employing recreational therapists—employment will grow faster than the occupation as a whole as the number of older adults continues to grow. Fast employment growth is expected in the residential and outpatient settings that serve people who are physically disabled, cognitively disabled, elderly, or have mental illness or substance abuse problems. Employment is expected to decline in hospitals, however, as services shift to outpatient settings and employers emphasize cost containment.

TABLE 24-1 Projections Data from the National Employment Matrix for Recreational Therapists

Occupational Title	Employment, 2008	Projected Employment, 2018	Change, 2008–2018	
			Number	Percentage
Recreational therapists	23,300	26,700	3400	15

Healthcare facilities will support a growing number of jobs in adult day care and outpatient settings offering short-term mental health and alcohol or drug abuse treatment services. Rehabilitation, home health care, and transitional programs will provide additional jobs.

Job Prospects

Recreational therapists will experience competition for jobs. Lower paid recreational therapy aides may be increasingly used in an effort to contain costs. Job opportunities should be best for people with a Bachelor degree in therapeutic recreation or in recreation with courses in therapeutic recreation. Opportunities also should be good for therapists who hold specialized certifications such as aquatic therapy, meditation, or crisis intervention. Recreational therapists might experience more competition for jobs in certain regions of the country. **Table 24-1** shows some projection data provided by the Department of Labor.

Earnings

Median annual earnings of recreational therapists were $38,370 in May 2008. The middle 50% earned between $29,660 and $49,140. The lowest 10% earned less than $23,150, and the highest 10% earned more than $60,280. Median annual earnings in the industries employing the largest numbers of recreational therapists in May 2008 are included in **Table 24-2**.

Related Occupations

Recreational therapists primarily design activities to help people with disabilities lead more fulfilling and independent lives. Other workers who have similar jobs are occupational therapists, physical therapists, recreation workers, rehabilitation counselors, and special education teachers.

TABLE 24-2 Median Annual Earnings in the Industries

General medical and surgical hospitals	$42,120
State government	40,310
Psychiatric and substance abuse hospitals	40,150
Nursing care facilities	33,920
Community care facilities for the elderly	33,490

Additional Information

For information and materials on careers and academic programs in recreational therapy, contact

- American Therapeutic Recreation Association, 629 N. Main St., Hattiesburg, MS 39401. Internet: http://atra-online.com/
- National Therapeutic Recreation Society, 22377 Belmont Ridge Rd., Ashburn, VA 20148-4501. Internet: http://www.nrpa.org/

Information on certification may be obtained from

- National Council for Therapeutic Recreation Certification, 7 Elmwood Dr., New City, NY 10956. Internet: http://www.nctrc.org

For information on licensure requirements, contact the appropriate recreational therapy regulatory agency for your state.

BEHAVIORAL THERAPISTS

An Overview

A **behavioral therapist** is a trained professional who uses common human behavioral modifications to improve the quality of life for a patient with a health problem. For example, a person may be depressed after surgery. Recovery may be better and faster if an art therapist assists the patient. That is, the patient is assisted or encouraged to develop the enjoyment of painting, going to museums, visiting homes of famous artists, and so on. Obviously the process of behavioral modification is much more complicated than, for example, going to a museum. Thus, there are therapists specializing in modifying a patient's behavior or attitude toward art, dance, horticulture, music and so on.

This chapter discusses some of the most common or popular aspects of working as a behavioral therapist, but with the following premise in mind:

1. Educational and legal requirements are highly variable because practically every state has its own. It is not possible to provide standard information.
2. The pay scale is also highly variable in both private and public sectors, varying from state to state, county to county, and city to city.
3. The same applies to employment trends. As a result, there is not a single source in the federal government for an interested party to obtain reliable information. In view of this, there are two ways to obtain information and assistance:

   Employment bureaus, human resource departments, and similar units exist in the central government of each state. The easiest way to obtain relevant information is to use the state website to find specific data for each job category of behavioral therapy, for example, art therapists.

Practically every job category of behavior therapy is represented and promoted by its own nonprofit trade association. Most offer up-to-date employment information. The list is as follows:

American Art Therapy Association
225 North Fairfax Street
Alexandria, VA 22314
http://www.arttherapy.org

American Dance Therapy Association
10632 Little Patuxent Parkway, Suite 108
Columbia, MD 21044-3263
http://www.adta.org

The American Horticultural Therapy Association
150 South Warner Road, Suite 156
King of Prussia, PA 19406
http://www.ahta.org

American Kinesiology (Corrective) Therapy Association
118 College Drive, #5142
Hattiesburg, MS 39406
http://www.akta.org

American Music Therapy Association, Inc.
8455 Colesville Road, Suite 1000
Silver Spring, MD 20910
http://www.musictherapy.org

National Coalition of Creative Arts Therapy Associations
c/o AMTA
8455 Colesville Road, Suite 1000
Silver Spring, MD 20910
http://www.nccata.org

Art Therapists

Expressing ideas and feelings through art and achieving some sense of well-being as a result is a very old concept. Pictures scratched or painted by primitive man have been found on cave walls, and many ancient tools and objects were designed to be not only useful but also artistically pleasing. Exactly what made the cave dwellers and their ancestors draw the pictures or design the objects is not known, but we can assume that they must have received some sort of emotional satisfaction from creating them. Art therapy is based on the use of art as a device for nonverbal expression and communication. Art therapy attempts to resolve the individual's emotional conflicts and encourages personal growth and self-understanding.

The most practical application of art therapy has been with those suffering from mental disorders, mental retardation, or other problems of social and psychological development, but innovative work has also been done on a variety of other problems. Art therapists confer with members of the medical health team to diagnose patients' problems. Combining art, education, and insight, art therapists assess their patients' problems, strengths, and weaknesses, and determine a course of treatment best suited to accomplish specific treatment goals. Art therapists plan art activities, maintain and distribute supplies and materials, provide art instruction, and observe and record the various interactions that occur during therapy sessions. Emphasis is not placed on the quality of the product, but rather on the well-being of the patient. Art therapists often work as members of teams of other professionals and coordinate their activities with those of other therapists.

Art therapists work with people of all ages who have various degrees of impairment. They may practice with individuals, groups, or families in clinical, educational, or rehabilitative settings, which include private psychiatric hospitals and clinics, community health centers, geriatric centers, drug and alcohol clinics, nursing homes, halfway houses, prisons, public and private schools, and institutions for the emotionally disturbed, learning disabled, brain damaged, deaf, blind, physically handicapped, and multiple disabled. Many art therapists who work in clinics also teach art therapy in colleges or universities, and may do research on some aspect of therapy. However, the primary involvement of most art therapists is with clients in some type of clinical setting.

Art therapists normally work a 40-hour week, although the hours and degree of responsibility vary with the setting. The facilities in which they work are usually fully equipped with art materials, tables, chairs, art desks, and storage areas; general working conditions are good.

Corrective Therapists

Corrective therapy treats patients by applying medically prescribed physical exercises and activities to strengthen and coordinate body functions and prevent muscular deterioration caused by inactivity due to illness. Corrective therapists apply the principles, tools, techniques, and psychology of medically oriented physical education to help persons with physical and mental problems meet their treatment goals. Corrective therapists design or adjust equipment and devise exercises to meet the needs of patients. They instruct patients in proper exercise techniques and equipment usage to meet specified objectives such as walking, joint flexibility, endurance, strength, and emotional self-confidence and security. For the physically handicapped, the exercise routines are aimed at developing strength, dexterity, and muscle coordination. Therapists teach exercise routines to patients who use wheelchairs, instruct amputees or partially paralyzed patients how to walk and move around, and sometimes give driving lessons to handicapped persons using specially equipped automobiles. They also advise patients on the use of braces, artificial limbs, and other devices. For the emotionally ill or mentally retarded, therapists use exercises to relieve frustration or tension, or to bring about social involvement.

Corrective therapists also judge strength, endurance, and self-care ability to gauge the patient's recovery at successive stages. They participate in staff planning sessions and make hospital ward rounds as members of healthcare teams. They prepare progress reports on patients' responses to therapeutic treatment exercises and present findings orally or in writing at staff meetings and conferences. Therapists also counsel patients' family members on therapeutic matters.

Corrective therapy should not be confused with **physical therapy**. Physical therapists employ physical agents such as heat, water, and light in treatment routines, and perform tests to determine nerve, muscle, and skin condition and reaction. Corrective therapy is used mainly in the more advanced stages of rehabilitation where functional training is required.

Some corrective therapists choose areas of specialization. Corrective therapists who specialize in driver training are concerned with teaching handicapped persons safe driving methods, developing their remaining skills, and teaching them to use special driving devices. Seminars and workshops in driver training are required for this specialization, and the Veterans Administration primarily employs therapists working in this area. Corrective therapists who specialize in cardiac rehabilitation check patients' pulmonary function, establish work performance limits, and establish levels of progression to attain optimal fitness capabilities. Therapists receive specialized training in cardiopulmonary theory, methodology, and techniques, and the use of specialized equipment. Some corrective therapists are beginning to specialize in therapeutic pool work in numerous hospital and health education sites. This specialization requires water safety certifications, such as those given by the Red Cross or YMCA/YWCA, and knowledge of the effects of water activities and of water on exercise performance.

Corrective therapists work in a variety of government, public, and private facilities, including hospitals, rehabilitation clinics, schools, colleges, nursing homes, special schools, recreation facilities, and camps for the handicapped. They work a 40-hour week, usually in an indoor setting, although outdoor recreation areas and pools are also used. A variety of physical demands are involved in being a corrective therapist, including demonstrating exercises and equipment use, lifting and balancing patients, and handling and adjusting therapeutic exercise equipment.

Dance Therapists

For centuries, dancing and related types of body movement have been recognized and used as a form of entertainment and as a way to ease tension and obtain other physical and emotional benefits. For many, this type of physical activity renews emotional well-being, encourages self-expression, and recharges energy drained by the frustrations of everyday living. For these reasons, dancing and body movement can be therapeutic activities. **Dance therapy**, used with individuals who have emotional and often physical impairments caused by injury, illness, or birth defects, has been developed by dance therapists and uses dance and body movement as a tool to further emotional and physical integration and well-being. Dance therapists take advantage of the expressive and communicative aspects of dance to help people resolve social, emotional, and physical disorders.

Dance therapists assess their clients' emotional and social behavior, movement capabilities, and general posture. They determine what types of movement experiences will best help clients develop an increased awareness of feelings and nonverbal behavior, a broader scope of interaction of mind and body, an improved body image, improved social relations, and relief from physical and emotional blocks. Working with individuals and groups, dance therapists plan and conduct movement sessions designed to achieve those goals and objectives. Dance therapists also participate in case conferences, staff meetings, community meetings, verbal therapy sessions, and other activities, depending on the setting in which they work. Some engage in research on movement behavior, teach or train others in educational or employment settings, or act as consultants to various agencies or organizations.

Dance therapy takes place in a wide variety of settings, but movement research is its only real area of specialization. The movement researcher observes, records, and analyzes nonverbal behavior in live settings, on videotape, or on film. In addition to the general knowledge and experience required of dance therapists, movement researchers must have completed advanced courses in movement observation and research methods.

Dance therapists work in a variety of mental health settings, including psychiatric hospitals, clinics, developmental centers, correctional facilities, special schools, substance abuse programs, and facilities for the aged. Registered dance therapists may also work in private practice or teach in educational facilities.

Hours and other working conditions vary, as do facilities. Some are modern and well equipped; others are older and sometimes quite sparse in terms of equipment and other elements that contribute to a pleasant work/ therapy setting. Most aspects of dance therapy involve close physical contact with different types of patient groups, as well as a good deal of physical activity. In all instances, strength, flexibility, stamina, and a strong desire to relate to and help others are necessary.

Horticulture Therapists

Horticultural therapy uses horticultural activities as the primary treatment method to bring about a beneficial change in an individual with a physical, mental, or social handicap. Horticulture therapists use gardening for a variety of purposes, such as to rehabilitate patients after illness or injury; train impaired, disabled, and handicapped persons; evaluate patients' disabilities and capabilities; and provide a social activity for physically and mentally impaired persons.

Horticulture therapists organize indoor or outdoor activities, usually in a group setting, for patients with different types of problems. They use plants and related materials to help handicapped individuals improve their emotional attitudes through a change in self-concept; their social skills through nonthreatening interactions with others; their physical skills through activities requiring both gross and fine-motor coordination; and their mental skills through planning, preparing, and caring for their plants. Horticulture therapists work closely with other staff members to design and conduct a program suited to the needs of the particular client. In some programs, particularly those related to vocational rehabilitation, the plants may be sold, and in this situation the therapist may also have some business responsibilities. In addition to working directly with patients, horticulture therapists often teach at local colleges or universities and conduct workshops and other training programs.

Most horticulture therapists work in public or private facilities for the handicapped, including convalescent homes, juvenile centers, schools and training centers for the mentally retarded, psychiatric hospitals, and general care hospitals. Horticulture therapists work closely with both people and plants, and the work setting is often a greenhouse or outside garden. Care of plants can be demanding, and the ability to move the hands easily and skillfully is very important. However, there are no physical requirements for the job, and handicapped individuals may, in fact, have the advantage of serving as role models for patients.

Manual Arts Therapists

Manual arts therapy uses mechanical, technical, and industrial activities that are vocationally significant to assist patients in their recovery and in maintaining, improving, or developing work skills. Under the direction of a physician, manual arts therapists develop a program of actual or simulated work situations, which help patients to prepare for an early return to their communities, as well as to the world of work.

In rehabilitation, manual arts therapists apply clinical techniques for treating the physical or mental conditions of their patients, observe patient behavior, assist in patient adjustment to work situations, and evaluate manual abilities and work skills. The primary purpose is to engage patients in therapeutic activities that prove absorbing to them and help in their recovery, giving them a sense of confidence and achievement. These work activities also have a practical value because they serve to retrain patients in their own skills or trades or, where disability makes this reentry impossible, to help them explore and learn new work skills or avocational activities. Manual arts therapists cooperate with other members of the patient's rehabilitation team to plan and organize work activities, while considering the patient's disabilities and capabilities. Manual arts therapy may be the only therapy prescribed for a patient, or it may be used in conjunction with other therapies in a combined treatment program. It may be prescribed at any stage during hospitalization, depending on the patient's condition and rehabilitation goals.

Patients may explore various work activities offered in manual arts therapy, including woodworking, metalworking, electronics, printing and graphic arts, and sometimes agriculture. For example, a construction worker who has lost a leg in a fall may discover an interest in drawing and be taught technical drafting. A bedridden patient may learn basic electricity by using batteries and simple hookups and later advance to electronics. A patient in a wheelchair may explore jewelry or watch repair. A group of mental patients may help maintain hospital grounds. It is the job of the manual arts therapist to observe, evaluate, and guide patients in their work activities toward their rehabilitation goals.

Manual arts therapists prepare reports describing patients' emotional and social adjustment, physical performance, and work tolerance. The rehabilitation team uses these reports to judge the progress of patients and their ability to meet the physical and mental demands of their place in the community and in the world of work.

Most manual arts therapists are employed in hospitals and centers operated by the Veterans Administration, but they also work in sheltered workshops, mental health clinics, workers' compensation rehabilitation centers, and rehabilitation centers for the blind. The federal law that requires schooling for all handicapped children has opened a new field to manual arts therapy. Therapists normally work indoors from 8:00 a.m. to 4:30 p.m. 5 days a week, do little traveling, and generally have good working conditions. Because of the workshop setting, some noise and dust fumes are normally present, but these factors are usually controlled.

Music Therapists

Music therapy is an allied health profession in which music is used within a therapeutic relationship to address the physical, psychological, cognitive, and social needs of individuals. Music has been a part of almost every culture and is recognized everywhere as having healing value. Much has been written about its effects, and it is often described as soothing, relaxing, exciting, moving, or in terms of some other emotional feeling it creates in the listener or performer. For each individual it serves a different purpose and, for some, many purposes. For those who are disabled, music may become part of medical treatment.

Music therapists understand music psychology and specialize in using music to accomplish treatment goals involving the restoration, maintenance, and improvement of mental and physical health. In its use with the mentally ill, music therapy may achieve changes in patients' behavior that will give them a new understanding of themselves and of the world around them. This new understanding can serve as a basis for improved mental health and more effective adjustment to normal living.

Often working as one member of a team that may include other therapists, psychiatrists, psychologists, social workers, and special educators, music therapists evaluate how a client might be helped through a music program. They determine what goals and objectives can probably be met and plan musical activities and experiences that are likely to meet them, on both an individual and a group basis. Music therapists treat patients of all ages, ranging from disturbed small children and adolescents to adults who suffer from mental illnesses of many types and various degrees of seriousness. The mentally retarded, those with cerebral palsy, individuals with physical impairments, and the blind make up a group that is second only to the mentally ill in the number receiving music therapy.

As members of the mental health team, music therapists devise programs to achieve aims prescribed by attending psychiatrists, and the treatment results are evaluated periodically. Music therapists may create programs of many kinds in an effort to gain and to hold the patient's interest. Much depends on the patient's potential for training; what would be possible for one would be inappropriate for another. Group singing is commonly used. Music appreciation and music education are appealing to others. Every effort is made to improve skills acquired in past years and to develop an interest that will give a new dimension to normal living.

Unlike most music programs, music therapy programs focus on the well-being of the client rather than a perfected musical product. Voice, as well as traditional and nontraditional instruments and music are used, and individual lessons are provided. In addition, instrumental and vocal music are often combined with body movements as a part of therapy.

Music therapists find employment in a variety of facilities throughout the country. They are usually employed in psychiatric hospitals, mental retardation centers, physical disability treatment and training institutions, day care centers, nursing homes, special education programs, community mental health centers, special service agencies, and other related facilities.

As in many therapy situations, music therapists work very closely with their clients and must be able to relate to them and their problems in a warm, professional manner. The work is not always a relaxing, pleasurable experience. The process of strengthening discipline and changing behavior can arouse temporary anxiety and negative attitudes. Music therapists must be able to deal with these problems when they arise and use tact and resourcefulness in solving them. They often must work in close cooperation with therapists in other disciplines when physical facilities are shared to plan and schedule activities. Standard work hours are usual, but music therapists may be called on from time to time to work evening hours and weekends.

Music therapists usually enter this career field for the stimulation of working with people in a therapy situation that involves music. There are rewards within the field itself, and there is always the possibility of being recognized for outstanding accomplishments or for having developed new and innovative methods.

MEDICAL ASSISTANTS
SIGNIFICANT POINTS

- Employment is projected to grow much faster than average, ranking medical assistants among the fastest-growing occupations over the 2008 to 2018 decade.
- Job prospects should be excellent.
- About 62% of medical assistants work in offices of physicians.
- Some medical assistants are trained on the job, but many complete 1-year or 2-year programs.

Work Descriptions

Medical assistants perform administrative and clinical tasks to keep the offices of physicians, podiatrists, chiropractors, and other health practitioners running smoothly. They should not be confused with physician assistants, who examine, diagnose, and treat patients under the direct supervision of a physician. Physician assistants are discussed in a separate chapter.

The duties of medical assistants vary from office to office, depending on the location and size of the practice and the practitioner's specialty. In small practices, medical assistants usually do many different kinds of tasks, handling both administrative and clinical duties and reporting directly to an office manager, physician, or other health practitioner. Those in large practices tend to specialize in a particular area, under the supervision of department administrators.

Medical assistants who perform administrative tasks have many duties. They update and file patients' medical records, fill out insurance forms, and arrange for hospital admissions and laboratory services. They also perform tasks less specific to medical settings, such as answering telephones, greeting patients, scheduling appointments, and handling correspondence, billing, and bookkeeping.

For clinical medical assistants, duties vary according to what is allowed by state law. Some common tasks include taking medical histories and recording vital signs, explaining treatment procedures to patients, preparing patients for examinations, and assisting physicians during examinations. Medical assistants collect and prepare laboratory specimens and sometimes perform basic laboratory tests on the premises, dispose of contaminated supplies, and sterilize medical instruments. They might instruct patients about medications and special diets, prepare and administer medications as directed by a physician, authorize drug refills as directed, telephone prescriptions to a pharmacy, draw blood, prepare patients for X-rays, take electrocardiograms, remove sutures, and change dressings. Medical assistants also may arrange examining room instruments and equipment, purchase and maintain supplies and equipment, and keep waiting and examining rooms neat and clean.

Ophthalmic medical assistants, optometric assistants, and podiatric medical assistants are examples of specialized medical assistants who have additional duties. Ophthalmic medical assistants help ophthalmologists provide eye care. They conduct diagnostic tests, measure and record vision, and test eye muscle function. They also show patients how to insert, remove, and care for contact lenses, and they apply eye dressings. Under the direction of the physician, ophthalmic medical assistants may administer eye medications. They also maintain optical and surgical instruments and may assist the ophthalmologist in surgery. Optometric assistants also help provide eye care, working with optometrists. They provide chair-side assistance, instruct patients about contact lens use and care, conduct preliminary tests on patients, and otherwise provide assistance while working directly with an optometrist. Podiatric medical assistants make castings of feet, expose and develop X-rays, and assist podiatrists in surgery.

Work Environment

Medical assistants work in well-lighted, clean environments. They constantly interact with other people and may have to handle several responsibilities at once. Most full-time medical assistants work a regular 40-hour week. However, many medical assistants work part time, evenings, or weekends.

Employment Opportunities

Medical assistants held about 483,600 jobs in 2009. About 62% worked in offices of physicians; 13% worked in public and private hospitals, including inpatient and outpatient facilities; and 11% worked in offices of other health practitioners, such as chiropractors, optometrists, and podiatrists. Most of the remainder worked in other healthcare industries such as outpatient care centers and nursing and residential care facilities.

Educational and Legal Requirements

Some medical assistants are trained on the job, but many complete 1-year or 2-year programs.

Education and Training

Postsecondary medical assisting programs are offered in vocational-technical high schools, postsecondary vocational schools, and community and junior colleges. Programs usually last either 1 year and result in a certificate or diploma, or 2 years and result in an Associate degree. Courses cover anatomy, physiology, and medical terminology, as well as typing, transcription, record keeping, accounting, and insurance processing. Students learn laboratory techniques, clinical and diagnostic procedures, pharmaceutical principles, the administration of medications, and first aid. They study office practices, patient relations, medical law, and ethics. There are various organizations that accredit medical assisting programs. Accredited programs often include an internship that provides practical experience in physicians' offices, hospitals, or other healthcare facilities.

Formal training in medical assisting, while generally preferred, is not always required. Some medical assistants are trained on the job, although this practice is less common than in the past. Applicants usually need a high school diploma or the equivalent. Recommended high school courses include mathematics, health, biology, typing, bookkeeping, computers, and office skills. Volunteer experience in the healthcare field also is helpful. Medical assistants who are trained on the job usually spend their first few months attending training sessions and working closely with more experienced workers. Some states allow medical assistants to perform more advanced procedures, such as giving injections, after passing a test or taking a course.

Certification and Other Qualifications

Employers prefer to hire experienced or certified workers. Although not required, certification indicates that a medical assistant meets certain standards of competence. The certification process varies. There are various associations—some listed among the sources of information that follow—that award certification credentials to medical assistants. A medical assistant may choose to become certified in a specialty, such as podiatry, optometry, or ophthalmology.

Medical assistants deal with the public; therefore, they must be neat, well groomed, and have a courteous, pleasant manner, and they must be able to put patients at ease and explain physicians' instructions. They must respect the confidential nature of medical information. Clinical duties require a reasonable level of manual dexterity and visual acuity.

Advancement

Medical assistants may advance to other occupations through experience or additional training. For example, some may go on to teach medical assisting, and others pursue additional education to become nurses or other healthcare workers. Administrative medical assistants may advance to office manager, or qualify for a variety of administrative support occupations.

Employment Trends

Employment is projected to grow much faster than average, ranking medical assistants among the fastest-growing occupations over the 2008 to 2018 decade. Job opportunities should be excellent, particularly for those with formal training or experience, and certification.

Employment Change

Employment of medical assistants is expected to grow 34% from 2008 to 2018, much faster than the average for all occupations. As the healthcare industry expands because of technological advances in medicine and the growth and aging of the population, an increased need for all healthcare workers will be felt. The increasing use of medical assistants in the rapidly growing healthcare industry will further stimulate job growth.

Helping to drive job growth is the increasing number of group practices, clinics, and other healthcare facilities that need a high proportion of support personnel, particularly medical assistants who can handle both administrative and clinical duties. In addition, medical assistants work primarily in outpatient settings, a rapidly growing sector of the healthcare industry.

Job Prospects

Job seekers who want to work as medical assistants should encounter excellent job prospects. Medical assistants are projected to account for a very large number of new jobs, and many other opportunities will come from the need to replace workers leaving the occupation. Those with formal training or experience—particularly those with certification—should have the best job opportunities. **Table 24-3** shows some projection data provided by the Department of Labor.

Earnings

The earnings of medical assistants vary, depending on experience, skill level, and location. Median annual earnings of wage and salary medical assistants were $28,300 in May 2008. The middle 50% earned between $23,700 and $33,050. The lowest 10% earned less than $20,600, and the highest 10% earned more than $39,570. Median annual earnings in the industries employing the largest numbers of medical assistants in May 2008 are shown in **Table 24-4**.

Related Occupations

Medical assistants perform work similar to the tasks completed by other workers in medical support occupations. Administrative medical assistants do work similar to that of medical secretaries, medical transcriptionists, and medical records and health information technicians. Clinical medical assistants perform duties similar to those of dental assistants; dental hygienists; occupational therapist assistants and aides; pharmacy aides; licensed practical and licensed vocational nurses; surgical technologists; physical therapist assistants and aides; and nursing, psychiatric, and **home health aides**.

TABLE 24-3 Projections Data from the National Employment Matrix for Medical Assistants

Occupational Title	Employment, 2008	Projected Employment, 2018	Change, 2008–2018	
			Number	Percentage
Medical assistants	483,600	647,500	163,900	34

TABLE 24-4 Median Annual Earnings in the Industries Employing the Largest Numbers of Medical Assistants in May 2008

General medical and surgical hospitals	$29,720
Colleges, universities, and professional schools	28,820
Offices of physicians	28,710
Outpatient care centers	28,570
Offices of other health practitioners	25,240

Additional Information

Information about career opportunities and certification for medical assistants is available from

- American Association of Medical Assistants, 20 North Wacker Dr., Suite 1575, Chicago, IL 60606. Internet: http://www.aama-ntl.org/
- American Medical Technologists, 10700 West Higgins Rd., Suite 150, Rosemont, IL 60018. Internet: http://www.amt1.com/
- National Healthcareer Association, 7 Ridgedale Ave., Suite 203, Cedar Knolls, NJ 07927. Internet: http://www.nhanow.com/

For lists of accredited educational programs in medical assisting, contact

- Accrediting Bureau of Health Education Schools, 7777 Leesburg Pike, Suite 314 N, Falls Church, VA 22043. Internet: http://www.abhes.org/
- Commission on Accreditation of Allied Health Education Programs, 1361 Park St., Clearwater, FL 33756. Internet: http://www.caahep.org/

Information about career opportunities, training programs, and certification for ophthalmic medical personnel is available from

- Joint Commission on Allied Health Personnel in Ophthalmology, 2025 Woodlane Dr., St. Paul, MN 55125. Internet: http://www.jcahpo.org/

Information about career opportunities, training programs, and certification for optometric assistants is available from

- American Optometric Association, 243 N. Lindbergh Blvd., St. Louis, MO 63141. Internet: http://www.aoa.org/

Information about certification for podiatric assistants is available from

- American Society of Podiatric Medical Assistants, 2124 South Austin Blvd., Cicero, IL 60804. Internet: http://www.aspma.org/

NURSING AND PSYCHIATRIC AIDES
SIGNIFICANT POINTS

- Numerous job openings and excellent job opportunities are expected.
- Most jobs are in nursing and residential care facilities and in hospitals.
- A high school diploma is required for many jobs; specific qualifications vary by occupation, state laws, and work setting.
- This occupation is characterized by modest entry requirements, low pay, high physical and emotional demands, and limited advancement opportunities.

Work Description

Nursing and **psychiatric aides** help care for physically or mentally ill, injured, disabled, or infirm individuals in hospitals, nursing care facilities, and mental health settings. **Nursing aides** and home health aides are among the occupations commonly referred to as direct care workers, due to their role in working with patients who need long-term care. The specific care they give depends on their specialty.

Nursing aides, also known as nurse aides, nursing assistants, certified nursing assistants, geriatric aides, unlicensed assistive personnel, **orderlies**, or hospital attendants, provide hands-on care and perform routine tasks under the supervision of nursing and medical staff. Specific tasks vary, with aides handling many aspects of a patient's care. They often help patients to eat, dress, and bathe. They also answer calls for help, deliver messages, serve meals, make beds, and tidy up rooms. Aides sometimes are responsible for taking a patient's temperature, pulse rate, respiration rate, or blood pressure. They also may help provide care to patients by helping them get out of bed and walk, escorting them to operating and examining rooms, or providing skin care. Some aides help other medical staff by setting up equipment, storing and moving supplies, and assisting with some procedures. Aides also observe patients' physical, mental, and emotional conditions and report any change to the nursing or medical staff.

Nursing aides employed in nursing care facilities often are the principal caregivers and have more contact with residents than do other members of the staff. Because some residents may stay in a nursing care facility for months or even years, aides develop positive, caring relationships with their patients.

Psychiatric aides, also known as **mental health assistants** or psychiatric nursing assistants, care for mentally impaired or emotionally disturbed individuals. They work under a team that may include psychiatrists, psychologists, psychiatric nurses, social workers, and therapists. In addition to helping patients to dress, bathe, groom themselves, and eat, psychiatric aides socialize with patients and lead them in educational and recreational activities. Psychiatric aides may play card games or other games with patients, watch television with them, or participate in group activities, such as playing sports or going on field trips. They observe patients and report any physical or behavioral signs that might be important for the professional staff to know. They accompany patients to and from therapy and treatment. Because they have such close contact with patients, psychiatric aides can have a great deal of influence on patients' outlook and treatment.

Work Environment

Work as an aide can be physically demanding. Aides spend many hours standing and walking, and they often face heavy workloads. Aides must guard against back injury, because they may have to move patients into and out of bed or help them stand or walk. It is important for aides to be trained in and to follow the proper procedures for lifting and moving patients. Aides also may face hazards from minor infections and major diseases, such as hepatitis, but can avoid infections by following proper procedures. Nursing aides, orderlies, and attendants and psychiatric aides have some of the highest nonfatal injuries and illness rates for all occupations, in the ninety-eighth and ninety-ninth percentiles in 2007.

Aides also perform tasks that some may consider unpleasant, such as emptying bedpans and changing soiled bed linens. The patients they care for may be disoriented, irritable, or uncooperative. Psychiatric aides must be prepared to care for patients whose illnesses may cause violent behavior. Although their work can be emotionally demanding, many aides gain satisfaction from assisting those in need.

Most full-time aides work about 40 hours per week, but because patients need care 24 hours a day, some aides work evenings, nights, weekends, and holidays. In 2008 about 24% of nursing aides, orderlies, and attendants and psychiatric aides worked part time.

Employment Opportunities

Nursing and psychiatric aides held about 1.5 million jobs in 2008. Nursing aides, orderlies, and attendants held the most jobs—approximately 1.5 million, and psychiatric aides held about 62,500 jobs. About 41% of nursing aides, orderlies, and attendants worked in nursing care facilities and another 29% worked in hospitals. About 50% of all psychiatric aides worked in hospitals. Others were employed in residential care facilities, government agencies, outpatient care centers, and individual and family services.

Educational and Legal Requirements

In many cases, a high school diploma or equivalent is necessary for a job as a nursing or psychiatric aide. Specific qualifications vary by occupation, state laws, and work setting. Advancement opportunities are limited.

Education and Training

Nursing and psychiatric aide training is offered in high schools, vocational-technical centers, some nursing care facilities, and some community colleges. Courses cover body mechanics, nutrition, anatomy and physiology, infection control, communication skills, and resident rights. Personal care skills, such as how to help patients bathe, eat, and groom themselves, also are taught. Hospitals may require previous experience as a nursing aide or home health aide. Some states also require psychiatric aides to complete a formal training program. However, most psychiatric aides learn their skills on the job from experienced workers.

Some employers provide classroom instruction for newly hired aides, while others rely exclusively on informal on-the-job instruction by a licensed nurse or an experienced aide. Such training may last from several days to a few months. Aides also may attend lectures, workshops, and in-service training.

Licensure and Certification

Federal government requirements exist for nursing aides who work in nursing care facilities. These aides must complete a minimum of 75 hours of state-approved training and pass a competency evaluation. Aides who complete the program are known as certified nurse assistants (**CNAs**) and are placed on the state registry of nurse aides. Additional requirements may exist, but vary by state. Therefore, individuals should contact their state board directly for applicable information.

Other Qualifications

Aides must be in good health. A physical examination, including state-regulated disease tests, may be required. A criminal background check also is usually required for employment. Applicants should be tactful, patient, understanding, emotionally stable, and dependable, and should have a desire to help people. They also should be able to work as part of a team, have good communication skills, and be willing to perform repetitive, routine tasks.

Advancement

Opportunities for advancement within these occupations are limited. Aides generally need additional formal training or education to enter other health occupations. The most common healthcare occupations for former aides are licensed practical nurse, registered nurse, and medical assistant.

For some individuals, these occupations serve as entry-level jobs. For example, some high school and college students gain experience working in these occupations while attending school. And experience as an aide can help individuals decide whether to pursue a career in health care.

Employment Trends

Employment is projected to grow faster than the average. Excellent job opportunities are expected.

Employment Change

Overall employment of nursing and psychiatric aides is projected to grow 18% between 2008 and 2018, faster than the average for all occupations. However, growth will vary for individual occupations. Employment for nursing aides, orderlies, and attendants will grow 19%, faster than the average for all occupations, predominantly in response to the long-term care needs of an increasing elderly population. Financial pressures on hospitals to discharge patients as soon as possible should boost admissions to nursing care facilities. As a result, new jobs will be more numerous in nursing and residential care facilities than in hospitals, and growth will be especially strong in community care facilities for the elderly. Modern medical technology will also drive demand for nursing aides, because as the technology saves and extends more lives, it increases the need for long-term care provided by aides. However, employment growth is not expected to be as fast as for other healthcare support occupations, largely because nursing aides are concentrated in the relatively slower-growing nursing and residential care facilities industry sector. In addition, growth will be hindered by nursing facilities' reliance on government funding, which does not increase as fast as the cost of patient care. Government funding limits the number of nursing aides nursing facilities can afford to have on staff.

The employment of psychiatric aides is expected to grow 6%, more slowly than average. Psychiatric aides are a small occupation compared to nursing aides, orderlies, and attendants. Most psychiatric aides currently work in hospitals, but the industries most likely to see growth will be residential facilities for people with developmental disabilities, mental illness, and substance abuse problems. There is a long-term trend toward treating psychiatric patients outside of hospitals, because it is more cost-effective and allows patients greater independence. Demand for psychiatric aides in residential facilities will rise in response to increases in the number of older persons, many of whom will require mental health services. Demand for these workers will also grow as an increasing number of mentally disabled adults, formerly cared for by their elderly parents, will need care. Job growth also could be affected by changes in government funding of programs for the mentally ill.

Job Prospects

High replacement needs for nursing and psychiatric aides reflect modest entry requirements, low pay, high physical and emotional demands, and limited opportunities for advancement within the occupation. For these same reasons, the number of people looking to enter the occupation will be limited. Many aides leave the occupation to attend training programs for other healthcare occupations. Therefore, people who are interested in, and suited for, this work should have excellent job opportunities. **Table 24-5** shows some projection data provided by the Department of Labor.

TABLE 24-5   Projections Data for Employment Trends

Occupational Title	Employment, 2008	Projected Employment, 2018	Change, 2008–2018	
			Number	Percentage
Nursing and psychiatric aides	1,532,300	1,811,800	279,500	18
Nursing aides, orderlies, and attendants	1,469,800	1,745,800	276,000	19
Psychiatric aides	62,500	66,100	3600	6

Earnings

Median hourly wages of nursing aides, orderlies, and attendants were $11.46 in May 2008. The middle 50% earned between $9.71 and $13.76 an hour. The lowest 10% earned less than $8.34, and the highest 10% earned more than $15.97 an hour. Median hourly wages in the industries employing the largest numbers of nursing aides, orderlies, and attendants in May 2008 is shown in **Table 24-6**.

Median hourly wages of psychiatric aides were $12.77 in May 2008. The middle 50% earned between $10.00 and $15.63 an hour. The lowest 10% earned less than $8.35, and the highest 10% earned more than $18.77 an hour. Median hourly wages in the industries employing the largest numbers of psychiatric aides in May 2008 is shown in **Table 24-7**.

Related Occupations

Other occupations that help people who need routine care or treatment include child care workers, home health aides and **personal and home care aides**, licensed practical and licensed vocational nurses, medical assistants, occupational therapist assistants and aides, registered nurses, and social and human service assistants

Additional Information

Information about employment opportunities may be obtained from local hospitals, nursing care facilities, home healthcare agencies, psychiatric facilities, state boards of nursing, and local offices of the state employment service.

TABLE 24-6   **Median Hourly Wages in the Industries Employing the Largest Numbers of Nursing Aides, Orderlies, and Attendants**

Employment services	$12.10
General medical and surgical hospitals	12.05
Nursing care facilities	11.13
Community care facilities for the elderly	10.91
Home healthcare services	10.58

TABLE 24-7   Median Hourly Wages in the Industries Employing the Largest Numbers of Psychiatric Aides, May 2008

Psychiatric and substance abuse hospitals	$13.43
General medical and surgical hospitals	13.29
Nursing care facilities	11.66
Individual and family services	10.78
Residential mental retardation, mental health, and substance abuse facilities	9.89

Information on licensing requirements for nursing aides, and lists of state-approved nursing aide programs are available from state departments of public health, departments of occupational licensing, and boards of nursing.

For more information on nursing aides, orderlies, and attendants, contact

- National Association of Health Care Assistants, 1201 L St. NW, Washington, DC 20005. Internet: http://www.nahcacares.org
- National Network of Career Nursing Assistants, 3577 Easton Rd., Norton, OH 44203. Internet: http://www.cna-network.org

For more information on the assisted living, nursing facility, developmentally disabled, and subacute care provider industry, contact

- American Health Care Association, 1201 L St. NW, Washington, DC 20005. Internet: http://www.ahca.org/

HOME HEALTH AIDES AND PERSONAL AND HOME CARE AIDES
SIGNIFICANT POINTS

- Job opportunities are expected to be excellent because of rapid growth in home health care and high replacement needs.
- Training requirements vary from state to state, the type of home services agency, and the funding source covering the costs of services.
- Many of these workers work part time and weekends or evenings to suit the needs of their clients.

Work Description

Home health aides and personal and home care aides help people who are disabled, chronically ill, or cognitively impaired, and older adults, who may need assistance, live in their own homes or in residential facilities instead of in health facilities or institutions. They also assist people in hospices and day programs, and help individuals with disabilities go to work and remain engaged in their communities. Most aides work with elderly or physically or mentally disabled clients who need more care than family or friends can provide. Others help discharge hospital patients who have relatively short-term needs.

Aides provide light housekeeping and homemaking tasks such as laundry, changing bed linens, shopping for food, and planning and preparing meals. Aides also may help clients get out of bed, bathe, dress, and groom. Some accompany clients to doctors' appointments or on other errands.

Home health aides and personal and home care aides provide instruction and psychological support to their clients. They may advise families and patients on nutrition, cleanliness, and household tasks.

Aides' daily routine may vary. They may go to the same home every day or week for months or even years and often visit four or five clients on the same day. However, some aides may work solely with one client who is in need of more care and attention. In some situations, this may involve working with other aides in shifts so that the client has an aide throughout the day and night. Aides also work with clients, particularly younger adults, at schools or at the client's work site. In general, home health aides and personal and home care aides have similar job duties. However, there are some small differences.

Home health aides typically work for certified home health or hospice agencies that receive government funding and therefore must comply with regulations to receive funding. This means that they must work under the direct supervision of a medical professional, usually a nurse. These aides keep records of services performed and of clients' condition and progress. They report changes in the client's condition to the supervisor or case manager. Aides also work with therapists and other medical staff.

Home health aides may provide some basic health-related services, such as checking patients' pulse rate, temperature, and respiration rate. They also may help with simple prescribed exercises and assist with medications administration. Occasionally, they change simple dressings, give massages, provide skin care, or assist with braces and artificial limbs. With special training, experienced home health aides also may assist with medical equipment such as ventilators, which help patients breathe.

Personal and home care aides—also called homemakers, caregivers, companions, and personal attendants—work for various public and private agencies that provide home care services. In these agencies, caregivers are likely supervised by a licensed nurse, social worker, or other nonmedical managers. Aides receive detailed instructions explaining when to visit clients and what services to perform for them. However, personal and home care aides work independently, with only periodic visits by their supervisors. These caregivers may work with only one client each day or five or six clients once a day every week or every 2 weeks.

Some aides are hired directly by the patient or the patient's family. In these situations, personal and home care aides are supervised and assigned tasks directly by the patient or the patient's family.

Aides may also work with individuals who are developmentally or intellectually disabled. These workers are often called direct support professionals, and they may assist in implementing a behavior plan, teaching self-care skills, and providing employment support, as well as providing a range of other personal assistance services.

Work Environment

Work as an aide can be physically demanding. Aides must guard against back injury because they may have to move patients into and out of bed or help them to stand or walk. Aides also may face hazards from minor infections and exposure to communicable diseases, such as hepatitis, but can avoid infections by following proper procedures. Because mechanical lifting devices available in institutional settings are not as frequently available in patients' homes, home health aides must take extra care to avoid injuries resulting from overexertion when they assist patients. These workers experience a larger-than-average number of work-related injuries or illnesses.

Aides also perform tasks that some may consider unpleasant, such as emptying bedpans and changing soiled bed linens. The patients they care for may be disoriented, irritable, or uncooperative. Although their work can be emotionally demanding, many aides gain satisfaction from assisting those in need.

Most aides work with a number of different patients, each job lasting a few hours, days, or weeks. They often visit multiple patients on the same day. Surroundings differ by case. Some homes are neat and pleasant, whereas others are untidy and depressing. Some clients are pleasant and cooperative; others are angry, abusive, depressed, or otherwise difficult.

Home health aides and personal and home care aides generally work alone, with periodic visits from their supervisor. They receive detailed instructions explaining when to visit patients and what services to perform. Aides are responsible for getting to patients' homes, and they may spend a good portion of the workday traveling from one patient to another. Many of these workers work part time and weekends or evenings to suit the needs of their clients.

Employment Opportunities

Home health aides and personal and home care aides held about 1.7 million jobs in 2008. The majority of jobs were in home healthcare services, individual and family services, residential care facilities, and private households.

Educational and Legal Requirements

Home health aides must receive formal training and pass a competency test to work for certified home health or hospice agencies that receive reimbursement from Medicare or Medicaid. Personal and home care aides, however, face a wide range of requirements, which vary from state to state.

Education and Training

Home health aides and personal and home care aides are generally not required to have a high school diploma. They usually are trained on the job by registered nurses, licensed practical nurses, experienced aides, or their supervisor. Aides are instructed on how to cook for clients, including those on special diets. Furthermore, they may be trained in basic housekeeping tasks, such as making a bed and keeping the home sanitary and safe for the client. Generally, they are taught how to respond to an emergency, learning basic safety techniques. Employers also may train aides to conduct themselves in a professional and courteous manner while in a client's home. Some clients prefer that tasks are done a certain way and will teach the aide. A competency evaluation may be required to ensure that the aide can perform the required tasks.

Licensure

Home health aides who work for agencies that receive reimbursement from Medicare or Medicaid must receive a minimum level of training. They must complete both a training program consisting of a minimum of 75 hours and a competency evaluation or state certification program. Training includes information regarding personal hygiene, safe transfer techniques, reading and recording vital signs, infection control, and basic nutrition. Aides may take a competency exam to become certified without taking any of the training. At a minimum, 16 hours of supervised practical training are required before an aide has direct contact with a resident. These certification requirements represent the minimum, as outlined by the federal government. Some states may require additional hours of training to become certified. Personal and home care aides are not required to be certified.

Other Qualifications

Aides should have a desire to help people. They should be responsible, compassionate, patient, emotionally stable, and cheerful. In addition, aides should be tactful, honest, and discreet, because they work in private homes. Aides also must be in good health. A physical examination, including state-mandated tests for tuberculosis and other diseases, may be required. A criminal background check and a good driving record also may be required for employment.

Certification and Advancement

The National Association for Home Care and Hospice (NAHC) offers national certification for aides. Certification is a voluntary demonstration that the individual has met industry standards. Certification requires the completion of 75 hours of training; observation and documentation of 17 skills for competency, assessed by a registered nurse; and the passing of a written exam developed by the NAHC.

Advancement for home health aides and personal and home care aides is limited. In some agencies, workers start out performing homemaker duties, such as cleaning. With experience and training, they may take on more personal care duties. Some aides choose to receive additional training to become nursing aides, licensed practical nurses, or registered nurses. Some may start their own home care agency or work as a self-employed aide. Self-employed aides have no agency affiliation or supervision and accept clients, set fees, and arrange work schedules on their own.

Employment Trends

Excellent job opportunities are expected for this occupation because rapid employment growth and high replacement needs are projected to produce a large number of job openings.

Employment Change

Employment of home health aides is projected to grow by 50% between 2008 and 2018, which is much faster than the average for all occupations. Employment of personal and home care aides is expected to grow by 46% from 2008 to 2018, which is much faster than the average for all occupations. For both occupations, the expected growth is due, in large part, to the projected rise in the number of elderly people, an age group that often has mounting health problems and that needs some assistance with daily activities. The elderly and other clients, such as the mentally disabled, increasingly rely on home care.

This trend reflects several developments. Inpatient care in hospitals and nursing homes can be extremely expensive, so more patients return to their homes from these facilities as quickly as possible in order to contain costs. Patients, who need assistance with everyday tasks and household chores rather than medical care, can reduce medical expenses by returning to their homes. Furthermore, most patients—particularly the elderly—prefer care in their homes rather than in nursing homes or other inpatient facilities. This development is aided by the realization that treatment can be more effective in familiar surroundings.

Job Prospects

In addition to job openings created by the increased demand for these workers, replacement needs are expected to lead to many openings. The relatively low skill requirements, low pay, and high emotional demands of the work result in high replacement needs. For these same reasons, many people are reluctant to seek jobs in the occupation. Therefore, persons who are interested in and suited for this work—particularly those with experience or training as personal care, home health, or nursing aides—should have excellent job prospects.

Earnings

Median hourly wages of wage and salary personal and home care aides were $9.22 in May 2008. The middle 50% earned between $7.81 and $10.98 an hour. The lowest 10% earned less than $6.84, and the highest 10% earned more than $12.33 an hour. Median hourly wages in the industries employing the largest numbers of personal and home care aides are shown in **Table 24-8**.

Median hourly wages of home health aides were $9.84 in May 2008. The middle 50% earned between $8.52 and $11.69 an hour. The lowest 10% earned less than $7.65, and the highest 10% earned more than $13.93 an hour. Median hourly wages in the industries employing the largest numbers of home health aides in May 2008 are shown in **Table 24-9**.

TABLE 24-8 Median Hourly Wages in the Industries Employing the Largest Numbers of Personal and Home Care Aides

Individual and family services	$9.77
Employment services	9.76
Residential mental retardation, mental health, and substance abuse facilities	9.70
Vocational rehabilitation services	9.58
Home healthcare services	7.94

Aides receive slight pay increases with experience and added responsibility. Usually, they are paid only for the time worked in the home, not for travel time between jobs, and must pay for their travel costs from their earnings. Most employers hire only on-call hourly workers.

Related Occupations

Home health aides and personal and home care aides combine the duties of caregivers and social service workers. Workers in related occupations that involve personal contact to help others include child care workers, licensed practical and licensed vocational nurses, medical assistants, nursing and psychiatric aides, occupational therapist assistants and aides, physical therapist assistants and aides, radiation therapists, registered nurses, and social and human service assistants.

Additional Information

Information on licensing requirements for nursing and home health aides, as well as lists of state-approved nursing aide programs, are available from state departments of public health, departments of occupational licensing, boards of nursing, and home care associations.

For information about voluntary credentials for personal and home care aides, contact

- National Association for Home Care and Hospice, 228 Seventh St. SE, Washington, DC 20003. Internet: http://www.nahc.org

TABLE 24-9 Median Hourly Wages in the Industries Employing the Largest Numbers of Home Health Aides, May 2008

Nursing care facilities	$10.20
Residential mental retardation, mental health, and substance abuse facilities	10.02
Home healthcare services	9.70
Individual and family services	9.48
Community care facilities for the elderly	9.44

chapter twenty-five

Veterinary Medicine*

KEY TERMS

AALAS
A bridge
Animal and human
 health
Animal technician
Biosecurity
CKOs
Food safety inspection

Germicides
Groom
Groomers
Jurisprudence
Keepers
LATG
Livestock health
NVT

Public health
Research
Standards for pure food
 from animal sources
Transmissible diseases
Veterinarians
Veterinary assistants

*All information in this chapter, unless otherwise indicated, was obtained from Bureau of Labor Statistics, U.S. Department of Labor. *Occupational Outlook Handbook 2010–2011 Edition*. 2010.

VETERINARY MEDICINE

Veterinary medicine is one of the oldest healing arts and involves both **animal and human health**. One of its main functions is the control of diseases transmissible from animals to humans, and the discovery of new knowledge in comparative medicine.

Veterinary medicine has come to the rescue of a disappearing food supply. Doctors of Veterinary Medicine (DVMs) monitor the food supply. They guard the health of all domestic protein-producing animals, and set and enforce **standards for pure food from animal sources**. Safeguarding our food supply by ensuring **livestock health** and wholesomeness is one of veterinary medicine's most important functions. Through this work the whole population is served directly.

VETERINARIANS

SIGNIFICANT POINTS

- Veterinarians should love animals and be able to get along with their owners.
- Graduation from an accredited college of veterinary medicine and a state license are required; admission to veterinary school is competitive.
- Job opportunities should be excellent.
- About 80% of veterinarians work in private practice.

Work Description

Veterinarians diagnose and treat diseases and dysfunctions of animals. Specifically, they care for the health of pets, livestock, and animals in zoos, racetracks, and laboratories. Some veterinarians use their skills to protect humans against diseases carried by animals and conduct clinical **research** on human and animal health problems. Others work in basic research, broadening our knowledge of animals and medical science, and in applied research, developing new ways to use knowledge.

Most veterinarians diagnose animal health problems, vaccinate against diseases, medicate animals suffering from infections or illnesses, treat and dress wounds, set fractures, perform surgery, and advise owners about animal feeding, behavior, and breeding.

According to the American Medical Veterinary Association, 77% of veterinarians who work in private medical practices treat pets. These practitioners usually care for dogs and cats, but also treat birds, reptiles, rabbits, ferrets, and other animals that can be kept as pets. About 16% of veterinarians work in private mixed and food animal practices, where they see pigs, goats, cattle, sheep, and some wild animals in addition to farm animals. A small proportion of private-practice veterinarians, about 6%, work exclusively with horses.

Veterinarians who work with food animals or horses usually drive to farms or ranches to provide veterinary services for herds or individual animals.

These veterinarians test for and vaccinate against diseases and consult with farm or ranch owners and managers regarding animal production, feeding, and housing issues. They also treat and dress wounds, set fractures, and perform surgery, including cesarean sections on birthing animals. Other veterinarians care for zoo, aquarium, or laboratory animals. Veterinarians of all types euthanize animals when necessary.

Veterinarians who treat animals use medical equipment such as stethoscopes, surgical instruments, and diagnostic equipment, including radiographic and ultrasound equipment. Veterinarians working in research use a full range of sophisticated laboratory equipment.

Some veterinarians contribute to human as well as animal health. A number of veterinarians work with physicians and scientists as they research ways to prevent and treat various human health problems. For example, veterinarians contributed greatly to conquering malaria and yellow fever, solved the mystery of botulism, produced an anticoagulant used to treat some people with heart disease, and defined and developed surgical techniques for humans, such as hip and knee joint replacements and limb and organ transplants. Today, some determine the effects of drug therapies, antibiotics, or new surgical techniques by testing them on animals.

Some veterinarians are involved in food safety and inspection. Veterinarians who are livestock inspectors, for example, check animals for **transmissible diseases** such as *E. coli*, advise owners on the treatment of their animals, and may quarantine animals. Veterinarians who are meat, poultry, or egg product inspectors examine slaughtering and processing plants, check live animals and carcasses for disease, and enforce government regulations regarding food purity and sanitation. More veterinarians are finding opportunities in food security as they ensure that the nation has abundant and safe food supplies. Veterinarians involved in food security often work along the country's borders as animal and plant health inspectors, where they examine imports and exports of animal products to prevent disease here and in foreign countries. The Department of Agriculture's Animal and Plant Health Inspection Service division or the U.S. Food and Drug Administration's Center for Veterinary Medicine employs many of these workers.

Work Environment

Veterinarians in private or clinical practice often work long hours in a noisy indoor environment. Sometimes they have to deal with emotional or demanding pet owners. When working with animals that are frightened or in pain, veterinarians risk being bitten, kicked, or scratched.

Veterinarians who work with food animals or horses spend time driving between their offices and farms or ranches. They work outdoors in all kinds of weather and may have to treat animals or perform surgery, often under unsanitary conditions.

Veterinarians working in nonclinical areas, such as **public health** and research, work in clean, well-lighted offices or laboratories and have working conditions similar to those of other professionals who work in these environments. Veterinarians in nonclinical areas spend much of their time dealing with people rather than animals.

Veterinarians often work long hours. Those in group practices may take turns being on call for evening, night, or weekend work; solo practitioners may work extended hours (including weekend hours), responding to emergencies or squeezing in unexpected appointments.

Employment Opportunities

Veterinarians held about 59,700 jobs in 2008. According to the American Veterinary Medical Association, 80% of veterinarians were employed in a solo or group practice. Most others were salaried employees of colleges or universities; medical schools; private industry, such as research laboratories and pharmaceutical companies; and federal, state, or local government.

The federal government employed about 1300 civilian veterinarians, chiefly in the U.S. Department of Agriculture and the U.S. Food and Drug Administration's Center for Veterinary Medicine. A few veterinarians work for zoos, but most veterinarians caring for zoo animals are private practitioners who contract with the zoos to provide services, usually on a part-time basis. In addition, many veterinarians hold veterinary faculty positions in colleges and universities and are classified as teachers.

Educational and Legal Requirements

Veterinarians must obtain a Doctor of Veterinary Medicine degree and a state license. Admission to veterinary school is competitive.

Education and Training

Prospective veterinarians must graduate with a Doctor of Veterinary Medicine (DVM or VMD) degree from a 4-year program at an accredited college of veterinary medicine. There are 28 colleges in 26 states that meet accreditation standards set by the Council on Education of the American Veterinary Medical Association (AVMA).

The prerequisites for admission to veterinary programs vary. Many programs do not require a Bachelor degree for entrance, but all require a significant number of credit hours—ranging from 45 to 90 semester hours—at the undergraduate level. However, most of the students admitted have completed an undergraduate program and earned a Bachelor degree. Applicants without a degree face a difficult task in gaining admittance.

Preveterinary courses should emphasize the sciences. Veterinary medical colleges typically require applicants to have taken classes in organic and inorganic chemistry, physics, biochemistry, general biology, animal biology, animal nutrition, genetics, vertebrate embryology, cellular biology, microbiology, zoology, and systemic physiology. Some programs require calculus; some require only statistics, college algebra and trigonometry, or precalculus. Most veterinary medical colleges also require some courses in English or literature, other humanities, and the social sciences. Increasingly, courses in general business management and career development have become a standard part of the curriculum to teach new graduates how to effectively run a practice.

In addition to satisfying preveterinary course requirements, applicants must submit test scores from the Graduate Record Examination (GRE), the Veterinary College Admission Test (VCAT), or the Medical College Admission Test (MCAT), depending on the preference of the college to which they are applying. Currently, 22 schools require the GRE, 4 require the VCAT, and 2 accept the MCAT.

Admission to veterinary school is competitive. The number of accredited veterinary colleges has remained largely the same since 1983, but the number of applicants has risen significantly. Only about 1 in 3 applicants was accepted in 2007.

New graduates with a Doctor of Veterinary Medicine degree may begin to practice veterinary medicine once they receive their license, but many new graduates choose to enter a 1-year internship. Interns receive a small salary but often find that their internship experience leads to better paying opportunities later, relative to those of other veterinarians. Veterinarians who then seek board certification also must complete a 3- to 4-year residency program that provides intensive training in one of the 39 AVMA-recognized veterinary specialties including internal medicine, oncology, pathology, dentistry, nutrition, radiology, surgery, dermatology, anesthesiology, neurology, cardiology, ophthalmology, preventive medicine, and exotic-small-animal medicine.

Licensure

All states and the District of Columbia require that veterinarians be licensed before they can practice. The only exemptions are for veterinarians working for some federal agencies and some state governments. Licensing is controlled by the states and is not uniform, although all states require the successful completion of the DVM degree—or equivalent education—and a passing grade on a national board examination, the North American Veterinary Licensing Exam. This 8-hour examination consists of 360 multiple-choice questions covering all aspects of veterinary medicine as well as visual materials designed to test diagnostic skills.

The Educational Commission for Foreign Veterinary Graduates grants certification to individuals trained outside the United States who demonstrate that they meet specified requirements for English language and clinical proficiency. This certification fulfills the educational requirement for licensure in all states.

Most states also require candidates to pass a state **jurisprudence** examination covering state laws and regulations. Some states do additional testing on clinical competency as well. There are few reciprocal agreements between states, so veterinarians who wish to practice in a different state usually must first pass that state's examinations.

Other Qualifications

When deciding whom to admit, some veterinary medical colleges place heavy consideration on candidates' veterinary and animal experience. Formal experience, such as work with veterinarians or scientists in clinics, agribusiness, research, or some area of health science, is particularly advantageous. Less formal experience, such as working with animals on a farm, or at a stable or animal shelter, also can be helpful. Students must demonstrate ambition and an eagerness to work with animals.

Prospective veterinarians should love animals and have the ability to get along with their owners, especially pet owners, who usually have strong bonds with their pets. They need good manual dexterity. Veterinarians who intend to go into private practice should possess excellent communication and business skills, because they will need to successfully manage their practice and employees and promote, market, and sell their services.

Advancement

Most veterinarians begin as employees in established group practices. Despite the substantial financial investment in equipment, office space, and staff, many veterinarians with experience eventually set up their own practice or purchase an established one.

Newly trained veterinarians can become U.S. government meat and poultry inspectors, disease-control workers, animal welfare and safety workers, epidemiologists, research assistants, or commissioned officers in the U.S. Public Health Service or various branches of the U.S. armed forces. A state license may be required.

Nearly all states have continuing education requirements for licensed veterinarians. Requirements differ by state and may involve attending a class or otherwise demonstrating knowledge of recent medical and veterinary advances.

Employment Trends

Employment is expected to increase much faster than average. Excellent job opportunities are expected.

Employment Change

Employment of veterinarians is expected to increase 33% over the 2008 to 2018 decade, much faster than the average for all occupations. Veterinarians usually practice in animal hospitals or clinics and care primarily for small pets. Recent trends indicate particularly strong interest in cats as pets. Faster growth of the cat population is expected to increase the demand for feline medicine and veterinary services, while demand for veterinary care for dogs should continue to grow at a more modest pace.

Many pet owners consider their pets as members of the family, which serves as evidence that people are placing a higher value on their pets and is an example of the human-animal bond. These pet owners are becoming more aware of the availability of advanced care and are more willing to pay for intensive veterinary care than owners in the past. Furthermore, the number of pet owners purchasing pet insurance is rising, increasing the likelihood that considerable money will be spent on veterinary care.

More pet owners also will take advantage of nontraditional veterinary services, such as cancer treatment and preventive dental care. Modern veterinary services have caught up to human medicine; certain procedures, such as hip replacement, kidney transplants, and blood transfusions, which were once only available for humans, are now available for animals.

Continued support for public health and food and animal safety, national disease control programs, and biomedical research on human health problems will contribute to the demand for veterinarians, although the number of positions in these areas is smaller than the number in private practice. Homeland security also may provide opportunities for veterinarians involved in efforts to maintain abundant food supplies and minimize animal diseases in the United States and in foreign countries.

Job Prospects

Excellent job opportunities are expected because there are only 28 accredited schools of veterinary medicine in the United States, resulting in a limited number of graduates—about 2500—each year. However, admission to veterinary school is competitive.

New graduates continue to be attracted to companion-animal medicine because they usually prefer to deal with pets and to live and work near heavily populated areas, where most pet owners live. Employment opportunities are very good in cities and suburbs, but are even better in rural areas because fewer veterinarians compete to work there.

Beginning veterinarians may take positions requiring evening or weekend work to accommodate the extended hours of operation that many practices are offering. Some veterinarians take salaried positions in retail stores offering veterinary services. Self-employed veterinarians usually have to work hard and long to build a sufficient client base.

The number of jobs for farm-animal veterinarians is likely to grow more slowly than the number of jobs for companion-animal veterinarians. Nevertheless, job prospects should be excellent for farm-animal veterinarians because of their lower earnings and because many veterinarians do not want to work outside or in rural or isolated areas.

Veterinarians with training in food safety and security, animal health and welfare, and public health and epidemiology should have the best opportunities for a career in the federal government. **Table 25-1** shows some projections data from the National Employment Matrix.

TABLE 25-1 Projections Data from the National Employment Matrix for Veterinarians

Occupational Title	Employment, 2008	Projected Employment, 2018	Change, 2008–2018	
			Number	Percentage
Veterinarians	59,700	79,400	19,700	33

TABLE 25-2 Average Starting Salaries of Veterinary Medical College Graduates, 2008

Small animals, exclusively	$66,000
Large animals, exclusively	63,220
Small animals, predominantly	62,510
Mixed animals	59,660
Large animals, predominantly	58,420
Equine (horses)	42,750

Note: All figures are rounded.

Earnings

Median annual wages of veterinarians were $79,050 in May 2008. The middle 50% earned between $61,370 and $104,110. The lowest 10% earned less than $46,610, and the highest 10% earned more than $143,660. The average annual salary for veterinarians in the federal government was $93,398 in March 2009.

According to employment data from state Department of Labor, average starting salaries of veterinary medical college graduates in 2008 varied by type of practice, as indicated in **Table 25-2**.

Related Occupations

Related occupations include animal care and service workers, biological scientists, chiropractors, dentists, medical scientists, optometrists, physicians and surgeons, podiatrists, and veterinary technologists and technicians.

Additional Information

For additional information on careers in veterinary medicine, a list of U.S. schools and colleges of veterinary medicine, and accreditation policies, send a letter-sized, self-addressed, stamped envelope to

• American Veterinary Medical Association, 1931 N. Meacham Rd., Suite 100, Schaumburg, IL 60173. Internet: http://www.avma.org

  For information on veterinary education, contact

• Association of American Veterinary Medical Colleges, 1101 Vermont Ave. NW, Suite 301, Washington, DC 20005. Internet: http://www.aavmc.org

  For information on scholarships, grants, and loans, contact the financial aid officer at the veterinary schools to which you wish to apply.

For information on veterinarians working in zoos, see the *Occupational Outlook Quarterly* article, "Wild Jobs with Wildlife," online at http://www. bls.gov/opub/ooq/2001/spring/art01.pdf.

Information on obtaining a veterinary position with the federal government is available from the Office of Personnel Management through USA-JOBS, the federal government's official employment information system. This resource for locating and applying for job opportunities can be accessed through the Internet at http://www.usajobs.opm.gov.

VETERINARY TECHNOLOGISTS AND TECHNICIANS
SIGNIFICANT POINTS

- Animal lovers get satisfaction from this occupation, but aspects of the work can be unpleasant, physically and emotionally demanding, and sometimes dangerous.

- There are primarily two levels of education and training for entry to this occupation: a 2-year program for veterinary technicians and a 4-year program for veterinary technologists.

- Employment is expected to grow much faster than average.

- Overall job opportunities should be excellent; however, keen competition is expected for jobs in zoos and aquariums.

Work Description

Owners of pets and other animals today expect superior veterinary care. To provide this service, veterinarians use the skills of veterinary technologists and technicians, who perform many of the same duties for a veterinarian that a nurse would for a physician. Although specific job duties vary by employer, there is often little difference between the tasks carried out by technicians and technologists, despite differences in formal education and training. However, most technicians work in private clinical practice, while many technologists have the option to work in more advanced research-related jobs.

Veterinary technologists and technicians typically conduct clinical work in a private practice under the supervision of a licensed veterinarian. Veterinary technologists and technicians often perform various medical tests and treat and diagnose medical conditions and diseases in animals. For example, they may perform laboratory tests such as urinalysis and blood counts, assist with dental care, prepare tissue samples, take blood samples, and assist veterinarians in a variety of other diagnostic tests. Although most of these duties are performed in a laboratory setting, many are not. For example, some veterinary technicians record patients' case histories, expose and develop X-rays and radiographs, and provide specialized nursing care. In addition, experienced veterinary technicians may discuss a pet's condition with its owners and train new clinic personnel. Veterinary technologists and technicians assisting small-animal practitioners usually care for small pets, such as cats and dogs, but can perform a variety of duties with mice, rats, sheep, pigs, cattle, monkeys, birds, fish, and frogs. Very few veterinary technologists work in mixed-animal practices where they care for both small pets and large, nondomestic animals.

Besides working in private clinics and animal hospitals, some veterinary technologists and technicians work in research facilities under the guidance of veterinarians or physicians. In this role, they may administer medications, prepare samples for laboratory examinations, or record information on an animal's genealogy, diet, weight, medications, food intake, and clinical signs of pain and distress. Some may sterilize laboratory and surgical equipment and provide routine postoperative care. Occasionally, veterinary technologists vaccinate newly admitted animals and may have to euthanize seriously ill, severely injured, or unwanted animals.

Although the goal of most veterinary technologists and technicians is to promote animal health, some contribute to human health as well. Veterinary technologists occasionally assist veterinarians in implementing research projects as they work with other scientists in medical-related fields such as gene therapy and cloning. Some find opportunities in biomedical research, wildlife medicine, livestock management, pharmaceutical sales, and increasingly in **biosecurity** and disaster preparedness.

Work Environment

Although people who love animals get satisfaction from helping them, some of the work may be unpleasant, physically and emotionally demanding, and sometimes dangerous. Data from the U.S. Bureau of Labor Statistics show that full-time veterinary technologists and technicians experienced a work-related injury and illness rate that was much higher than the national average. At times, veterinary technicians must clean cages and lift, hold, or restrain animals, risking exposure to bites or scratches. These workers must take precautions when treating animals with **germicides** or insecticides. The work setting can be noisy.

Veterinary technologists and technicians who witness abused animals or who euthanize unwanted, aged, or hopelessly injured animals may experience emotional stress. Those working for humane societies and animal shelters often deal with the public, some of whom might react with hostility to any implication that the owners are neglecting or abusing their pets. Such workers must maintain a calm and professional demeanor while they enforce the laws regarding animal care.

In some animal hospitals, research facilities, and animal shelters, a veterinary technician is on duty 24 hours a day, which means that some work night shifts. Most full-time veterinary technologists and technicians work about 40 hours a week, although some work 50 or more hours a week.

Employment Opportunities

Veterinary technologists and technicians held about 79,600 jobs in 2008. About 91% worked in veterinary services. The remainder worked in boarding kennels, animal shelters, rescue leagues, and zoos.

Educational and Legal Requirements

There are primarily two levels of education and training for entry to this occupation: a 2-year program for veterinary technicians and a 4-year program for veterinary technologists.

Education and Training

Most entry-level veterinary technicians have a 2-year Associate degree from an American Veterinary Medical Association (AVMA)-accredited community college program in veterinary technology in which courses are taught in clinical and laboratory settings using live animals. Currently, about 20 colleges offer veterinary technology programs that are longer and that culminate in a 4-year Bachelor degree in veterinary technology. These 4-year colleges, in addition to some vocational schools, also offer 2-year programs in laboratory animal science. About 10 schools offer distance learning.

In 2009, about 160 veterinary technology programs in 45 states were accredited by the AVMA. Graduation from an AVMA-accredited veterinary technology program allows students to take the credentialing exam in any state in the country.

Those interested in careers as veterinary technologists and technicians should take as many high school science, biology, and math courses as possible. Science courses taken beyond high school, in an Associate or Bachelor degree program, should emphasize practical skills in a clinical or laboratory setting.

Technologists and technicians usually begin work as trainees under the direct supervision of a veterinarian. Entry-level workers whose training or educational background encompasses extensive hands-on experience with diagnostic and medical equipment usually require a shorter period of on-the-job training.

Licensure and Certification

Each state regulates veterinary technicians and technologists differently; however, all states require them to pass a credentialing exam following coursework. Passing the state exam assures the public that the technician or technologist has sufficient knowledge to work in a veterinary clinic or hospital. Candidates are tested for competency through an examination that includes oral, written, and practical portions, and that is regulated by the State Board of Veterinary Examiners or the appropriate state agency. Depending on the state, candidates may become registered, licensed, or certified. Most states, however, use the National Veterinary Technician (**NVT**) exam.

Prospects usually can have their passing scores transferred from one state to another, so long as both states use the same exam.

Employers recommend American Association for Laboratory Animal Science (**AALAS**) certification for those seeking employment in a research facility. AALAS offers certification for three levels of technician competence, with a focus on three principal areas—animal husbandry, facility management, and animal health and welfare. Those who wish to become certified must satisfy a combination of education and experience requirements prior to taking the AALAS examination. Work experience must be directly related to the maintenance, health, and well-being of laboratory animals and must be gained in a laboratory animal facility as defined by AALAS. Candidates who meet the necessary criteria can begin pursuing the desired certification on the basis of their qualifications. The lowest level of certification is Assistant Laboratory Animal Technician (ALAT), the second level is Laboratory Animal Technician (LAT), and the highest level of certification is Laboratory Animal Technologist (**LATG**). The AALAS examination consists of multiple-choice questions and is longer and more difficult for higher levels of certification, ranging from 2 hours and 120 multiple choice questions for the ALAT, to 3 hours and 180 multiple choice questions for the LATG.

Other Qualifications

As veterinary technologists and technicians often deal with pet owners, communication skills are very important. In addition, technologists and technicians should be able to work well with others, because teamwork with veterinarians and other veterinary technicians is common. Organizational ability and the ability to pay attention to detail also are important.

Advancement

As they gain experience, technologists and technicians take on more responsibility and carry out more assignments with little veterinary supervision. Some eventually may become supervisors.

Employment Trends

Excellent job opportunities will stem from the need to replace veterinary technologists and technicians who leave the occupation and from the limited output of qualified veterinary technicians from 2-year programs, which are not expected to meet the demand over the 2008 to 2018 period. Employment is expected to grow much faster than average.

Employment Change

Employment of veterinary technologists and technicians is expected to grow 36% over the 2008 to 2018 projection period, which is much faster than the average for all occupations. Pet owners are becoming more affluent and more willing to pay for advanced veterinary care because many of them consider their pet to be part of the family. This growing affluence and view of pets will continue to increase the demand for veterinary care. The vast majority of veterinary technicians work at private clinical practices under veterinarians. As the number of veterinarians grows to meet the demand for veterinary care, so will the number of veterinary technicians needed to assist them.

The number of pet owners who take advantage of veterinary services for their pets is expected to grow over the projection period, increasing employment opportunities. The availability of advanced veterinary services, such as preventive dental care and surgical procedures, also will provide opportunities for workers specializing in those areas as they will be needed to assist licensed veterinarians. The growing number of cats kept as companion pets is expected to boost the demand for feline medicine and services. Further demand for these workers will stem from the desire to replace **veterinary assistants** with more highly skilled technicians in animal clinics and hospitals, shelters, boarding kennels, animal control facilities, and humane societies.

Continued support for public health, food and animal safety, and national disease control programs, as well as biomedical research on human health problems, also will contribute to the demand for veterinary technologists, although the number of positions in these areas is lower than in private practice.

Job Prospects

Excellent job opportunities are expected because of the relatively few veterinary technology graduates each year. The number of 2-year programs has recently grown to about 160, but due to small class sizes, fewer than 3800 graduates are anticipated each year, a number that is not expected to meet demand. Additionally, many veterinary technicians remain in the field less than 10 years, so the need to replace workers who leave the occupation each year also will produce many job opportunities.

Veterinary technologists also will enjoy excellent job opportunities due to the relatively few graduates from 4-year programs—about 500 annually. However, unlike veterinary technicians who usually work in private clinical practice, veterinary technologists will have better opportunities for research jobs in a variety of settings, including biomedical facilities, diagnostic laboratories, wildlife facilities, drug and food manufacturing companies, and **food safety inspection** facilities.

Despite the relatively small number of graduates each year, keen competition is expected for veterinary technician jobs in zoos and aquariums, due to expected slow growth in facility capacity, low turnover among workers, the limited number of positions, and the fact that the work in zoos and aquariums attracts many candidates.

Employment of veterinary technicians and technologists is relatively stable during periods of economic recession. Layoffs are less likely to occur among veterinary technologists and technicians than in some other occupations because animals will continue to require medical care. **Table 25-3** shows some projections data from the National Employment Matrix.

TABLE 25-3 Projections Data from the National Employment Matrix for Veterinary Technologists and Technicians

Occupational Title	Employment, 2008	Projected Employment, 2018	Change, 2008–2018	
			Number	Percentage
Veterinary technologists and technicians	79,600	108,100	28,500	36

Earnings

Median annual wages of veterinary technologists and technicians were $28,900 in May 2008. The middle 50% earned between $23,580 and $34,960. The lowest 10% earned less than $19,770, and the highest 10% earned more than $41,490. Veterinary technologists in research jobs may earn more than veterinary technicians in other types of jobs.

Related Occupations

Others who work extensively with animals include animal care and service workers, veterinarians, and veterinary assistants and laboratory animal caretakers.

Additional Information

For information on certification as a laboratory **animal technician** or technologist, contact

- American Association for Laboratory Animal Science, 9190 Crestwyn Hills Dr., Memphis, TN 38125. Internet: http://www.aalas.org/

For information on careers in veterinary medicine and a listing of AVMA-accredited veterinary technology programs, contact

- American Veterinary Medical Association, 1931 N. Meacham Rd., Suite 100, Schaumburg, IL 60173-4360. Internet: http://www.avma.org/

ANIMAL CARE AND SERVICE WORKERS
SIGNIFICANT POINTS

- Animal lovers get satisfaction in this occupation, but the work can be unpleasant, physically and emotionally demanding, and sometimes dangerous.
- Most workers are trained on the job, but employers generally prefer to hire people who have experience with animals; some jobs require formal education.
- Most positions will present excellent employment opportunities; however, keen competition is expected for jobs as zookeepers and marine mammal trainers.
- Earnings are relatively low.

Work Description

Many people like animals. But, as pet owners will admit, taking care of them is hard work. Animal care and service workers—who include animal caretakers and animal trainers—train, feed, water, **groom**, bathe, and exercise animals and clean, disinfect, and repair their cages. They also play with the animals, provide companionship, and observe behavioral changes that could indicate illness or injury. Boarding kennels, pet stores, animal shelters, rescue leagues, veterinary hospitals and clinics, stables, laboratories, aquariums and natural aquatic habitats, and zoological parks all house animals and employ animal care and service workers. Job titles and duties vary by employment setting.

Kennel attendants care for pets while their owners are working or traveling out of town. Beginning attendants perform basic tasks, such as cleaning both the cages and the dog runs, filling food and water dishes, and exercising animals. Experienced attendants may provide basic animal health care, as well as bathe animals, trim nails, and attend to other grooming needs. Attendants who work in kennels also may sell pet food and supplies, assist in obedience training, or prepare animals for shipping.

Groomers are animal caretakers who specialize in maintaining a pet's appearance. Most groom dogs and a few groom cats. Some groomers work in kennels, veterinary clinics, animal shelters, or pet supply stores. Others operate their own grooming business, typically at a salon or, increasingly, by making house calls. Such mobile services are growing rapidly because they offer convenience for pet owners, flexibility of schedules for groomers, and minimal trauma for pets resulting from their being in unfamiliar surroundings. Groomers clean and sanitize equipment to prevent the spread of disease, as well as maintaining a clean and safe environment for the animals. Groomers also schedule appointments, discuss pets' grooming needs with clients, and collect general information on the pets' health and behavior. Groomers sometimes are the first to notice a medical problem, such as an ear or skin infection, that requires veterinary care.

Grooming the pet involves several steps: an initial brush-out is followed by a clipping of hair with combs and grooming shears; the groomer then cuts the animal's nails, cleans the ears, bathes and blow-dries the animal, and ends with a final trim and styling.

Animal caretakers in animal shelters work mainly with cats and dogs and perform a variety of duties typically determined by the worker's experience. In addition to attending to the basic needs of the animals, caretakers at shelters keep records of the animals, including information about any tests or treatments performed on them. Experienced caretakers may vaccinate newly admitted animals under the direction of a veterinarian or veterinary technician and euthanize (painlessly put to death) seriously ill, severely injured, or unwanted animals. Animal caretakers in animal shelters also interact with the public, answering telephone inquiries, screening applicants who wish to adopt an animal, or educating visitors on neutering and other animal health issues.

Pet sitters look after one or more animals when their owner is away. They do this by traveling to the pet owner's home to carry out the daily routine. Most pet sitters feed, walk, and play with the animal, but some more experienced sitters also may be required to bathe, train, or groom them. Most watch over dogs and a few take care of cats. By not removing the pet from its normal surroundings, trauma is reduced and the animal can maintain its normal diet and exercise regimen.

Grooms, or caretakers, care for horses in stables. They saddle and unsaddle horses, give them rubdowns, and walk them to cool them off after a ride. They also feed, groom, and exercise the horses; clean out stalls and replenish bedding; polish saddles; clean and organize the tack (harness, saddle, and bridle) room; and store supplies and feed. Experienced grooms may help train horses.

In zoos, animal care and service workers, called **keepers**, prepare the diets and clean the enclosures of animals and sometimes assist in raising them when they are very young. They watch for any signs of illness or injury, monitor eating patterns or any changes in behavior, and record their observations. Keepers also may answer questions and ensure that the visiting public behaves responsibly toward the exhibited animals. Depending on the zoo, keepers may be assigned to work with a broad group of animals, such as mammals, birds, or reptiles, or they may work with a limited collection of animals such as primates, large cats, or small mammals.

Animal trainers train animals for riding, security, performance, obedience, or assisting people with disabilities. Animal trainers do this by accustoming the animal to the human voice and human contact and teaching the animal to respond to commands. The three most commonly trained animals are dogs, horses, and marine mammals, including dolphins and sea lions. Trainers use several techniques to help them train animals. One technique, known as **a bridge**, is a stimulus that a trainer uses to communicate the precise moment an animal does something correctly. When the animal responds correctly, the trainer gives positive reinforcement in a variety of ways: offering food, toys, play, and rubdowns or speaking the word "good." Animal training takes place in small steps and often takes months and even years of repetition. During the teaching process, trainers provide animals with mental stimulation, physical exercise, and husbandry. A relatively new form of training teaches animals to cooperate with workers giving medical care: animals learn "veterinary" behaviors, such as allowing for the collection of blood samples; physical, X-ray, ultrasonic, and dental exams; physical therapy; and the administration of medicines and replacement fluids.

Training also can be a good tool for facilitating the relocation of animals from one habitat to another, easing, for example, the process of loading horses onto trailers. Trainers often work in competitions or shows, such as circuses, marine parks, and aquariums; many others work in animal shelters, dog kennels and salons, or horse farms. Trainers in shows work to display the talent and ability of an animal, such as a dolphin, through interactive programs to educate and entertain the public.

In addition to their hands-on work with the animals, trainers often oversee other aspects of animals' care, such as preparing their diet and providing a safe and clean environment and habitat.

Work Environment

People who love animals get satisfaction from working with and helping them. However, some of the work may be unpleasant, physically or emotionally demanding, and sometimes dangerous. Data from the U.S. Bureau of Labor Statistics show that full-time animal care and service workers experienced a work-related injury and illness rate that was higher than the national average. Most animal care and service workers have to clean animal cages and lift, hold, or restrain animals, risking exposure to bites or scratches. Their work often involves kneeling, crawling, repeated bending, and, occasionally, lifting heavy supplies such as bales of hay or bags of feed. Animal caretakers must take precautions when treating animals with germicides or insecticides. They may work outdoors in all kinds of weather, and the work setting can be noisy. Caretakers of show and sports animals travel to competitions.

Animal care and service workers who witness abused animals or who assist in euthanizing unwanted, aged, or hopelessly injured animals may experience emotional distress. Those working for private humane societies and municipal animal shelters often deal with the public, some of whom may be hostile. Such workers must maintain a calm and professional demeanor while helping to enforce the laws regarding animal care.

Animal care and service workers often work irregular hours. Most animals are fed every day, so caretakers often work weekend and holiday shifts. In some animal hospitals, research facilities, and animal shelters, an attendant is on duty 24 hours a day, which means night shifts.

Employment Opportunities

Animal care and service workers held 220,400 jobs in 2008. Nearly 4 out of 5 worked as nonfarm animal caretakers; the remainder worked as animal trainers. Nonfarm animal caretakers often worked in boarding kennels, animal shelters, rescue leagues, stables, grooming shops, pet stores, animal hospitals, and veterinary offices. A significant number of caretakers worked for animal humane societies, racing stables, dog and horse racetrack operators, zoos, theme parks, circuses, and other amusement and recreation services.

Employment of animal trainers is concentrated in animal services that specialize in training and in commercial sports, where racehorses and dogs are trained. About 54% of animal trainers were self-employed.

Educational and Legal Requirements

On-the-job training is the most common way animal care and service workers learn their work; however, employers generally prefer to hire people who have experience with animals. Some jobs require formal education.

Education and Training

Animal trainers often need a high school diploma or GED equivalent. Some animal training jobs may require a Bachelor degree and additional skills. For example, marine mammal trainers usually need a Bachelor degree in biology, marine biology, animal science, psychology, or a related field. An animal health technician degree also may qualify trainers for some jobs.

Most equine trainers learn their trade by working as a groom at a stable. Some study at an accredited private training school.

Many dog trainers attend workshops and courses at community colleges and vocational schools. Topics include the basic study of canines, learning theory of animals, teaching obedience cues, problem-solving methods, and safety. Many such schools also offer business training. Pet sitters are not required to have any specific training, but knowledge of and some form of previous experience with animals often are recommended.

Many zoos require their caretakers to have a Bachelor degree in biology, animal science, or a related field. Most require experience with animals, preferably as a volunteer or paid keeper in a zoo.

Pet groomers typically learn their trade by completing an informal apprenticeship, usually lasting 6 to 10 weeks, under the guidance of an experienced groomer. Prospective groomers also may attend one of the 50 state-licensed grooming schools throughout the country, with programs varying in length from 2 to 18 weeks. Beginning groomers often start by taking on one duty, such as bathing and drying the pet. They eventually assume responsibility for the entire grooming process, from the initial brush-out to the final clipping.

Animal caretakers in animal shelters are not required to have any specialized training, but training programs and workshops are available through the Humane Society of the United States, the American Humane Association, and the National Animal Control Association. Workshop topics include investigations of cruelty, appropriate methods of euthanasia for shelter animals, proper guidelines for capturing animals, techniques for preventing problems with wildlife, and dealing with the public. Beginning animal caretakers in kennels learn on the job and usually start by cleaning cages and feeding animals.

Certification and Other Qualifications

Certifications are available in many animal service occupations. For dog trainers, certification by a professional association or one of the hundreds of private vocational or state-approved trade schools can be advantageous. The National Dog Groomers Association of America offers certification for master status as a groomer. To earn certification, applicants must demonstrate their practical skills and pass two exams. The National Association of Professional Pet Sitters offers a two-stage, home-study certification program for those who wish to become pet care professionals. Topics include business management, animal care, and animal health issues, and applicants must pass a written exam to earn certification. The Pet Care Services Association offers a three-stage, home-study program for individuals interested in pet care. Levels I and II focus on basic principles of animal care and customer service, while Level III spotlights management and professional aspects of the pet care business. Those who complete the third stage and pass oral and written examinations become Certified Kennel Operators (**CKOs**).

All animal care and service workers need patience, sensitivity, and problem-solving ability. Those who work in shelters also need tact and communication skills, because they often deal with individuals who abandon their pets. The ability to handle emotional people is vital for workers at shelters.

Animal trainers especially need problem-solving skills and experience in animal obedience. Successful marine mammal trainers also should have good public-speaking skills, because presentations are a large part of the job. Usually four to five trainers work with a group of animals at one time; therefore, trainers should be able to work as part of a team. Marine mammal trainers must also be good swimmers; certification in SCUBA is a plus. Most horse-training jobs have minimum weight requirements for candidates.

Advancement

With experience and additional training, caretakers in animal shelters may become adoption coordinators, animal control officers, emergency rescue drivers, assistant shelter managers, or shelter directors. Pet groomers who work in large retail establishments or kennels may, with experience, move into supervisory or managerial positions. Experienced groomers often choose to open their own salons or mobile grooming business. Advancement for kennel caretakers takes the form of promotion to kennel supervisor, assistant manager, and manager; those with enough capital and experience may open up their own kennels. Zookeepers may advance to senior keeper, assistant head keeper, head keeper, and assistant curator, but very few openings occur, especially for the higher-level positions.

Employment Trends

Because many workers leave this occupation each year, there will be excellent job opportunities for most positions. Because employment growth is much faster than average, this also will add to job openings. However, keen competition is expected for jobs as zookeepers and marine mammal trainers.

Employment Change

Employment of animal care and service workers is expected to grow 21% over the 2008 to 2018 decade, much faster than the average for all occupations. The companion pet population, which drives employment of animal caretakers in kennels, grooming shops, animal shelters, and veterinary clinics and hospitals, is anticipated to increase. Pet owners—including a large number of baby boomers, whose disposable income is expected to increase as they age—are expected to increasingly purchase grooming services, daily and overnight boarding services, training services, and veterinary services, resulting in more jobs for animal care and service workers. As more pet owners consider their pets part of the family, demand for luxury animal services and the willingness to spend greater amounts of money on pets should continue to grow. Demand for marine mammal trainers, on the other hand, should grow slowly.

Demand for animal care and service workers in animal shelters is expected to grow as communities increasingly recognize the connection between animal abuse and abuse toward humans and continue to commit private funds to animal shelters, many of which are working hand in hand with social service agencies and law enforcement teams.

Job Prospects

Due to employment growth and the need to replace workers who leave the occupation, job opportunities for most positions should be excellent. The need to replace pet sitters, dog walkers, kennel attendants, and animal control and shelter workers leaving the field will create the overwhelming majority of job openings. Many animal caretaker jobs require little or no training and have flexible work schedules, making them suitable for people seeking a first job or for temporary or part-time work. Prospective groomers also will face excellent opportunities as the companion dog population is expected to grow and services such as mobile grooming continue to grow in popularity. The outlook for caretakers in zoos and aquariums, however, is not favorable, due to slow job growth and keen competition for the few positions.

Prospective mammal trainers also will face keen competition as the number of applicants greatly exceeds the number of available positions. Prospective horse trainers should anticipate an equally challenging labor market because the number of entry-level positions is limited. Dog trainers, however, should experience conditions that are more favorable, driven by their owners' desire to instill obedience in their pet. Opportunities for dog trainers should be best in large metropolitan areas.

Job opportunities for animal care and service workers may vary from year to year because the strength of the economy affects demand for these workers. Pet owners tend to spend more on animal services when the economy is strong. **Table 25-4** shows some projections data from the National Employment Matrix.

TABLE 25-4 Projections Data from the National Employment Matrix for Animal Care and Service Workers, Animal Trainers, and Nonfarm Animal Caretakers

Occupational Title	Employment, 2008	Projected Employment, 2018	Change, 2008–2018	
			Number	Percentage
Animal care and service workers	220,400	265,900	45,500	21
Animal trainers	47,100	56,700	9600	20
Nonfarm animal caretakers	173,300	209,100	35,800	21

TABLE 25-5   Median Annual Wages in the Industries Employing
the Largest Numbers of Nonfarm Animal Caretakers, May 2008

Spectator sports	$20,520
Other personal services	19,530
Social advocacy organizations	18,640
Veterinary services	18,380
Other miscellaneous store retailers	18,320

Earnings

Wages are relatively low. Median annual wages of nonfarm animal caretakers were $19,360 in May 2008. The middle 50% earned between $16,720 and $24,300. The lowest 10% earned less than $15,140, and the highest 10% earned more than $31,590. Median annual wages in the industries employing the largest numbers of nonfarm animal caretakers in May 2008 are shown in **Table 25-5**.

Median annual wages of animal trainers were $27,270 in May 2008. The middle 50% earned between $19,880 and $38,280. The lowest 10% earned less than $16,700, and the highest 10% earned more than $51,400.

Related Occupations

Others who work extensively with animals include agricultural workers, animal control workers, biological scientists, farmers, ranchers, agricultural managers, veterinarians, veterinary assistants and laboratory animal caretakers, and veterinary technologists and technicians.

Additional Information

For career information and information on training, certification, and earnings of a related occupation—animal control officers—contact

- National Animal Control Association, P.O. Box 480851, Kansas City, MO 64148-0851. Internet: http://www.nacanet.org

For information on becoming an advanced pet care technician at a kennel, contact

- Pet Care Services Association, 2760 N. Academy Blvd., Suite 120, Colorado Springs, CO 80917. Internet: http://www.petcareservices.org

For general information on pet grooming careers, including workshops and certification information, contact

- National Dog Groomers Association of America, P.O. Box 101, Clark, PA 16113. Internet: http://www.nationaldoggroomers.com

For information on pet sitting, including certification information, contact

- National Association of Professional Pet Sitters, 15000 Commerce Parkway, Suite C, Mount Laurel, NJ 08054. Internet: http://www.petsitters.org

part three

Health-Related Professions

chapter twenty-six

Clinical Laboratory Technology*

KEY TERMS

Automated analyzers

Blood bank technologists

Cell counters

Clinical chemistry

Clinical laboratory technicians

Clinical laboratory technologists

Cytotechnologists

Hematological

Histotechnicians

Immunology

Materials scientists

Medical technologists

Microbiology

NAACLS

Phlebotomists

Prescribed drug regimen

The Clinical Laboratory Improvement Act

*All information in this chapter, unless otherwise indicated, was obtained from Bureau of Labor Statistics. U.S. Department of Labor. *Occupational Outlook Handbook 2010–2011 Edition*. 2010.

OBJECTIVES

The following objectives are for all chapters in Part III. After studying these chapters the student should be able to:

- Describe the responsibilities and work of each profession.
- Classify the specialties in each profession.
- Discuss the environment in which the work takes place.
- Identify any adjunct personnel who assist the professionals with their work.
- Compare and contrast the following factors among the professions: educational requirements, employment trends, opportunities for advancement, salary potential, and career ladders.
- Identify other professionals who do similar tasks or have similar responsibilities.
- Discuss the advantages of the national organizations to which professionals belong.
- Explain the concept and functions of interdisciplinary teams.

THE LABORATORY TEAM

The practice of modern medicine would be impossible without the tests performed in the clinical laboratory. A medical team of pathologists, specialists, technologists, and technicians work together to determine the presence, extent, or absence of disease, and to provide data to evaluate the effectiveness of treatment.

Physicians order laboratory work for a wide variety of reasons: Test results may be used to establish values against which future measurements can be compared; to monitor treatment, as with tests for drug levels in the blood that can indicate whether a patient is adhering to a **prescribed drug regimen**; to reassure patients that a disease is absent or under control; or to assess the status of a patient's health, as with cholesterol measurements.

Although physicians depend heavily on laboratory results, they do not ordinarily perform the tests themselves. This job falls to clinical laboratory personnel. Clinical laboratory testing plays a crucial role in the detection, diagnosis, and treatment of disease. **Clinical laboratory technologists** and technicians, also known as **medical technologists** and technicians, perform most of these tests.

CLINICAL LABORATORY TECHNOLOGISTS AND TECHNICIANS
SIGNIFICANT POINTS

- Excellent job opportunities are expected.
- Clinical laboratory technologists usually have a Bachelor degree with a major in medical technology or in one of the life sciences; **clinical laboratory technicians** generally need either an Associate degree or a certificate.
- Most jobs will continue to be in hospitals, but employment will grow rapidly in other settings as well.

Work Description

Clinical laboratory testing plays a crucial role in the detection, diagnosis, and treatment of disease. Clinical laboratory technologists, also referred to as clinical laboratory scientists or medical technologists, and clinical laboratory technicians, also known as medical technicians or medical laboratory technicians, perform most of these tests.

Clinical laboratory personnel examine and analyze body fluids and cells. They look for bacteria, parasites, and other microorganisms; analyze the chemical content of fluids; match blood for transfusions; and test for drug levels in the blood that show how a patient is responding to treatment. Technologists also prepare specimens for examination, count cells, and look for abnormal cells in blood and body fluids. They use microscopes, **cell counters**, and other sophisticated laboratory equipment. They also use automated equipment and computerized instruments capable of performing a number of tests simultaneously. After testing and examining a specimen, they analyze the results and relay them to physicians.

With increasing automation and the use of computer technology, the work of technologists and technicians has become less hands on and more analytical. The complexity of tests performed, the level of judgment needed, and the amount of responsibility workers assume depend largely on the amount of education and experience they have. Clinical laboratory technologists usually do more complex tasks than clinical laboratory technicians do.

Clinical laboratory technologists perform complex chemical, biological, **hematological**, immunologic, microscopic, and bacteriological tests. Technologists microscopically examine blood and other body fluids. They make cultures of body fluid and tissue samples to determine the presence of bacteria, fungi, parasites, or other microorganisms. Technologists analyze samples for chemical content or a chemical reaction and determine concentrations of compounds such as blood glucose and cholesterol levels. They also type and cross-match blood samples for transfusions.

Clinical laboratory technologists evaluate test results, develop and modify procedures, and establish and monitor programs to ensure the accuracy of tests. Some technologists supervise clinical laboratory technicians.

Technologists in small laboratories perform many types of tests, whereas those in large laboratories generally specialize. **Clinical chemistry** technologists, for example, prepare specimens and analyze the chemical and hormonal contents of body fluids. **Microbiology** technologists examine and identify bacteria and other microorganisms. **Blood bank technologists**, or immunohematology technologists, collect, type, and prepare blood and its components for transfusions. **Immunology** technologists examine elements of the human immune system and its response to foreign bodies. **Cytotechnologists** prepare slides of body cells and examine these cells microscopically for abnormalities that may signal the beginning of a cancerous growth. Molecular biology technologists perform complex protein and nucleic acid testing on cell samples.

Clinical laboratory technicians perform less complex tests and laboratory procedures than technologists do. Technicians may prepare specimens and operate **automated analyzers**, for example, or they may perform manual tests in accordance with detailed instructions. They usually work under the supervision of medical and clinical laboratory technologists or laboratory managers. Like technologists, clinical laboratory technicians may work in several areas of the clinical laboratory or specialize in just one. **Phlebotomists** collect blood samples, for example, and **histotechnicians** cut and stain tissue specimens for microscopic examination by pathologists.

Work Environment

Clinical laboratory personnel are trained to work with infectious specimens. When proper methods of infection control and sterilization are followed, few hazards exist. Protective masks, gloves, and goggles often are necessary to ensure the safety of laboratory personnel.

Working conditions vary with the size and type of employment setting. Laboratories usually are well lighted and clean; however, specimens, solutions, and reagents used in the laboratory sometimes produce fumes. Laboratory workers may spend a great deal of time on their feet.

The hours that clinical laboratory technologists and technicians work vary with the size and type of employment setting. In large hospitals or in independent laboratories that operate continuously, personnel usually work the day, evening, or night shift, and may work weekends and holidays. Laboratory personnel in small facilities may work on rotating shifts, rather than on a regular shift. In some facilities, laboratory personnel are on call several nights a week or on weekends, in case of an emergency.

Employment Opportunities

Clinical laboratory technologists and technicians held about 328,100 jobs in 2008. More than half of the jobs were in hospitals. Most of the remaining jobs were in offices of physicians and in medical and diagnostic laboratories. A small proportion was in educational services and in all other ambulatory healthcare services.

Educational and Legal Requirements

Clinical laboratory technologists generally require a Bachelor degree in medical technology or in one of the life sciences; clinical laboratory technicians usually need an Associate degree or a certificate.

Education and Training

The usual requirement for an entry-level position as a clinical laboratory technologist is a Bachelor degree with a major in medical technology or one of the life sciences; however, it is possible to qualify for some jobs with a combination of education and on-the-job and specialized training. Universities and hospitals offer medical technology programs.

Bachelor degree programs in medical technology include courses in chemistry, biological sciences, microbiology, mathematics, and statistics, as well as specialized courses devoted to knowledge and skills used in the clinical laboratory. Many programs also offer or require courses in management, business, and computer applications. **The Clinical Laboratory Improvement Act** requires technologists who perform highly complex tests to have at least an Associate degree.

Medical and clinical laboratory technicians generally have either an Associate degree from a community or junior college or a certificate from a hospital, a vocational or technical school, or the armed forces. A few technicians learn their skills on the job.

The National Accrediting Agency for Clinical Laboratory Sciences (**NAACLS**) fully accredits about 479 programs for medical and clinical laboratory technologists, medical and clinical laboratory technicians, histotechnologists and histotechnicians, cytogenetic technologists, and diagnostic molecular scientists. NAACLS also approves about 60 programs in phlebotomy and clinical assisting. Other nationally recognized agencies that accredit specific areas for clinical laboratory workers include the Commission on Accreditation of Allied Health Education Programs and the Accrediting Bureau of Health Education Schools.

Licensure

Some states require laboratory personnel to be licensed or registered. Licensure of technologists often requires a Bachelor degree and the passing of an exam, but requirements vary by state and specialty. Information on licensure is available from state departments of health or boards of occupational licensing.

Certification and Other Qualifications

Many employers prefer applicants who are certified by a recognized professional association. Associations offering certification include the Board of Registry of the American Society for Clinical Pathology, the American Medical Technologists, the National Credentialing Agency for Laboratory Personnel, and the Board of Registry of the American Association of Bioanalysts.

These agencies have different requirements for certification and different organizational sponsors.

In addition to certification, employers seek clinical laboratory personnel with good analytical judgment and the ability to work under pressure. Technologists in particular are expected to be good at problem solving. Close attention to detail is also essential for laboratory personnel because small differences or changes in test substances or numerical readouts can be crucial to a diagnosis. Manual dexterity and normal color vision are highly desirable, and with the widespread use of automated laboratory equipment, computer skills are important.

Advancement

Technicians can advance and become technologists through additional education and experience. Technologists may advance to supervisory positions in laboratory work or may become chief medical or clinical laboratory technologists or laboratory managers in hospitals. Manufacturers of home diagnostic testing kits and laboratory equipment and supplies also seek experienced technologists to work in product development, marketing, and sales.

Professional certification and a graduate degree in medical technology, one of the biological sciences, chemistry, management, or education usually speeds advancement. A doctorate usually is needed to become a laboratory director. Federal regulation requires directors of moderately complex laboratories to have either a Master degree or a Bachelor degree, combined with the appropriate amount of training and experience.

Employment Trends

Rapid job growth and excellent job opportunities are expected. Most jobs will continue to be in hospitals, but employment will grow rapidly in other settings as well.

Employment Change

Employment of clinical laboratory workers is expected to grow by 14% between 2008 and 2018, faster than the average for all occupations. The volume of laboratory tests continues to increase with both population growth and the development of new types of tests.

Technological advances will continue to have opposing effects on employment. On the one hand, new, increasingly powerful diagnostic tests and advances in genomics—the study of the genetic information of a cell or organism—will encourage additional testing and spur employment. On the other hand, research and development efforts targeted at simplifying and automating routine testing procedures may enhance the ability of nonlaboratory personnel—physicians and patients in particular—to perform tests now conducted in laboratories.

TABLE 26-1   Projections Data from the National Employment Matrix for Clinical and Medical Laboratory Technologists and Technicians

Occupational Title	Employment, 2008	Projected Employment, 2018	Change, 2008–2018	
			Number	Percentage
Clinical laboratory technologists and technicians	328,100	373,600	45,500	14
Medical and clinical laboratory technologists	172,400	193,000	20,500	12
Medical and clinical laboratory technicians	155,600	180,700	25,100	16

Although hospitals are expected to continue to be the major employer of clinical laboratory workers, employment is expected also to grow rapidly in medical and diagnostic laboratories, offices of physicians, and all other ambulatory healthcare services.

Job Prospects

Job opportunities are expected to be excellent because the number of job openings is expected to continue to exceed the number of job seekers. Although significant, job growth will not be the only source of opportunities. As in most occupations, many additional openings will result from the need to replace workers who transfer to other occupations, retire, or stop working for some other reason. Willingness to relocate will further enhance one's job prospects. **Table 26-1** provides some projections data from the National Employment Matrix.

Earnings

Median annual wages of medical and clinical laboratory technologists were $53,500 in May 2008. The middle 50% earned between $44,560 and $63,420. The lowest 10% earned less than $36,180, and the highest 10% earned more than $74,680. Median annual wages in the industries employing the largest numbers of medical and clinical laboratory technologists are shown in **Table 26-2**.

TABLE 26-2   Median Annual Wages in the Industries Employing the Largest Numbers of Medical and Clinical Laboratory Technologists

Federal executive branch	$59,800
General medical and surgical hospitals	54,220
Medical and diagnostic laboratories	53,360
Offices of physicians	49,080
Colleges, universities, and professional schools	47,890

TABLE 26-3 Median Annual Wages in the Industries Employing the Largest Numbers of Medical and Clinical Laboratory Technicians

General medical and surgical hospitals	$36,840
Colleges, universities, and professional schools	36,290
Offices of physicians	33,980
Medical and diagnostic laboratories	32,630
Other ambulatory healthcare services	31,320

Median annual wages of medical and clinical laboratory technicians were $35,380 in May 2008. The middle 50% earned between $28,420 and $44,310. The lowest 10% earned less than $23,480, and the highest 10% earned more than $53,520. Median annual wages in the industries employing the largest numbers of medical and clinical laboratory technicians are shown in **Table 26-3**.

According to data compiled from the published job statistics of various states in the country, median hourly wages of staff clinical laboratory technologists and technicians, in various specialties and laboratory types, in 2008 are shown in **Table 26-4**.

Related Occupations

Clinical laboratory technologists and technicians analyze body fluids, tissue, and other substances using a variety of tests. Chemists and **materials scientists**, science technicians, and veterinary technologists and technicians perform similar or related procedures.

TABLE 26-4 Median Hourly Wages of Staff Clinical Laboratory Technologists and Technicians in Various Specialties and Laboratory Types

Specialty	Hospital	Private Clinic	Physician Office Laboratory
Cytotechnologist	$28.00	$29.00	$27.00
Histotechnologist	23.00	24.00	26.00
Medical technologist	24.00	24.00	21.00
Histotechnician	21.00	21.00	22.00
Medical laboratory technician	19.00	18.00	17.00
Phlebotomist	13.00	13.00	14.00

Note: All figures are rounded.

Additional Information

For a list of accredited and approved educational programs for clinical laboratory personnel, contact

- National Accrediting Agency for Clinical Laboratory Sciences, 5600 N. River Rd., Suite 720, Rosemont, IL 60018. Internet: http://www.naacls.org

Information on certification is available from

- American Association of Bioanalysts, Board of Registry, 906 Olive St., Suite 1200, St. Louis, MO 63101. Internet: http://www.aab.org
- American Medical Technologists, 10700 W. Higgins Rd., Suite 150, Rosemont, IL 60018. Internet: http://www.amt1.com
- American Society for Clinical Pathology, 33 West Monroe St., Suite 1600, Chicago, IL 60603. Internet: http://www.ascp.org
- National Credentialing Agency for Laboratory Personnel, P.O. Box 15945-289, Lenexa, KS 66285. Internet: http://www.nca-info.org

Additional career information is available from

- American Association of Blood Banks, 8101 Glenbrook Rd., Bethesda, MD 20814. Internet: http://www.aabb.org
- American Society for Clinical Laboratory Science, 6701 Democracy Blvd., Suite 300, Bethesda, MD 20817. Internet: http://www.ascls.org
- American Society for Cytopathology, 100 West 10th St., Suite 605, Wilmington, DE 19801. Internet: http://www.cytopathology.org
- Clinical Laboratory Management Association, 993 Old Eagle School Rd., Suite 405, Wayne, PA 19087.

chapter twenty-seven

Health Information Personnel*

*All information in this chapter was obtained from Bureau of Labor Statistics. U.S. Department of Labor. *Occupational Outlook Handbook 2010–2011 Edition*. 2010.

PERSONNEL

SIGNIFICANT POINTS

- Employment is expected to grow much faster than average.
- Job prospects should be very good, particularly for technicians with strong computer software skills.
- Entrants usually have an Associate degree.
- This is one of the few health-related occupations in which there is no direct hands-on patient care.

PROVIDING AND PRESERVING ESSENTIAL INFORMATION

Providing and preserving information of ethical, scientific, and legal value to the appropriate professional personnel is one of the most valuable aspects of health care. Managing an information system that meets medical, administrative, ethical, and legal requirements involves the teamwork of administrators, technicians, transcriptionists, and medical librarians, collectively known as **health information personnel**.

Just as schools and colleges keep transcripts of grades and employers maintain personnel records, doctors and hospitals set up a permanent file for every patient they treat. This file is known as the patient's medical record or chart. It includes the patient's medical history, results of physical examinations, results of X-ray and laboratory tests, diagnoses, treatment plans, doctors' orders and notes, and nurses' notes. The medical record is the centerpiece of the health information system because it contains the entire history of each patient who receives health care. This medical record—a permanent document of the history and progress of one person's illness or injury—preserves information of medical, scientific, legal, and planning value. It is compiled from observations and findings recorded by the patient's physician and other professional members of the medical team. The entries and reports noted in it originate from various points in the hospital, clinic, nursing home, health center, or other healthcare facility. Through a network of communications systems, they are entered in the individual patient's record. This vital medical profile constitutes each patient's unique medical history.

The medical record shows the **diagnosis and treatment plan** and the patient's **symptoms and response** to treatment. Although accurate and orderly records are essential for clinical purposes, medical records have other important uses as well. They provide background and **documentation** for **insurance claims** and **Medicare reimbursement**, legal actions, professional review of treatment and medications prescribed, and training of health professions personnel. Medical records are used for research and planning purposes. They provide data for clinical studies, evaluations of the benefits and costs of various medical and surgical procedures, and **assessments** of community health needs.

The increasing use of **electronic health records (EHRs)** will continue to broaden and alter the job responsibilities of **health information technicians**.

For example, with the use of EHRs, technicians must be familiar with EHR computer software, maintaining EHR security, and analyzing electronic data to improve healthcare information. Health information technicians use EHR software to maintain data on patient safety, patterns of disease, and disease treatment and outcomes, and to conduct clinical research. Technicians also may assist with improving EHR software usability and may contribute to the development and maintenance of health information networks.

HEALTH INFORMATION ADMINISTRATORS

Work Description

Health information administrators direct and control the activities of the medical record department. They train and supervise the medical record staff and develop systems for documenting, storing, and retrieving medical information. Information administrators compile **statistics** required by federal and state agencies, assist the medical staff in evaluations of patient care or research studies, and sometimes testify in court about medical records and procedures of record keeping.

Health information managers are responsible for the maintenance and security of all patient records. Recent regulations enacted by the federal government require that all healthcare providers maintain secure electronic patient records. As a result, health information managers must keep up with current computer and software technology and with legislative requirements. In addition, as patient data become more frequently used for quality management and in medical research, health information managers ensure that databases are complete, accurate, and available only to authorized personnel.

Increasingly, medical record administrators are viewed as key members of the management team, and they work closely with the finance department to monitor hospital spending patterns. As part of the management team, health administrators establish and implement policies, objectives, and procedures for their department; evaluate personnel and work performance; develop reports and budgets; coordinate activities with other managers, and work closely with physicians.

Work Environment

Most health information administrators work in pleasant and comfortable offices, but they may work long hours if they are called in to help solve unexpected problems. Those who work at computers for prolonged periods may experience muscle pain and eyestrain.

Employment Opportunities

Employment of medical and health services managers is expected to grow 16% from 2008 to 2018, faster than the average for all occupations. Managers will be needed to oversee the computerization of patient records and to ensure their security as required by law. Additional demand for managers will stem from the need to recruit workers and increase employee retention, to comply with changing regulations, and to implement new technology. Hospitals will continue to employ the majority of medical and health services managers; however, the number of new jobs created in hospitals is expected to increase at a slower rate than in many other industries because of the growing use of clinics and other outpatient care sites. Employment will grow fastest in practitioners' offices, home healthcare agencies, and consulting firms.

Educational and Legal Requirements

The minimum educational program for a registered record administrator is a Bachelor degree in health information or medical record administration. In 2008, there were 48 accredited Bachelor degree programs and 5 Master degree programs in health information management, according to the Commission on Accreditation for Health Informatics and Information Management Education (CAHIIM).

Health information managers who hold a Bachelor degree or postbaccalaureate degree from an approved program and who pass an exam can earn certification as a Registered Health Information Administrator from the American Health Information Management Association. The preprofessional curriculum includes studies in the humanities and behavioral, biological, and physical sciences. The professional curriculum covers medical terminology, medical care organizations, disease classifications, organization, supervision, healthcare statistics, and principles of law, as well as advanced data processing.

Earnings

Earnings of health information administrators vary by type and size of the facility as well as by the level of education and responsibility. Salaries also vary according to geographic region. According to the latest statistics available in 2008, mean annual earnings for health information administrators for those with a Bachelor's degree were $68,213, and for those with a Master degree they were $81,879.

Related Occupations

Health information administrators receive training and experience in both health sciences and management. Other occupations and services requiring knowledge of both fields include hospital and nursing home administrators, public health directors, health agency directors, clinical laboratory workers, nursing services, physical therapists, rehabilitation services, radiology, respiratory therapists, and outpatient services administrators.

Additional Information

Information on careers in health information management may be obtained from

- American Health Information Management Association, 233 N. Michigan Ave., 21st Floor, Chicago, IL 60601-5800. Internet: http://www.ahima.org

HEALTH INFORMATION TECHNICIANS

Work Description

Every time a patient receives health care, a record is maintained of the observations, medical or surgical interventions, and treatment outcomes. This record includes information that the patient provides concerning his or her symptoms and medical history, the results of examinations, results of X-rays and laboratory tests, diagnoses, and treatment plans. Medical record and health information technicians organize and evaluate these records for completeness and accuracy.

Technicians assemble patients' health information, making sure that patients' initial medical charts are complete. They also ensure that all forms are completed, properly identified, and authenticated, and that all necessary information is placed on file in the computer. They regularly communicate with physicians and other healthcare professionals to clarify diagnoses or to obtain additional information.

Technicians regularly use computer programs to tabulate and analyze data in order to improve patient care, contain costs, and provide documentation for use in legal actions or research studies.

Some medical record and health information technicians specialize in coding patients' medical information for insurance purposes. These technicians assign a **code** to each diagnosis and procedure, relying on their knowledge of disease processes. Technicians then use classification systems software to assign the patient to one of several hundred **diagnosis-related groups (DRGs)**. The DRG determines the amount for which Medicare or other insurance programs using the DRG system will reimburse the hospital if the patient is covered. In addition to the DRG system, coders use other coding systems, such as those required for ambulatory settings, physician offices, or long-term care.

Health information technicians' duties vary according to the size of the facility. In large to medium facilities, technicians may specialize in one aspect of health information or supervise health information clerks and transcribers while a health information administrator manages the department. In small facilities, an accredited health information technician sometimes manages the department.

Work Environment

Medical records personnel generally work a standard 40-hour week. Some overtime may be required. In hospitals where medical record departments are open 18 to 24 hours a day, 7 days a week, medical record personnel work on day, evening, and night shifts. Part-time work is generally available.

This is one of the few health occupations in which there is little or no physical contact with patients. The work environment is usually pleasant and comfortable, but some aspects of the job can be stressful. The utmost accuracy is essential, which demands concentration and close attention to detail. The emphasis on accuracy can cause fatigue and mental strain. Medical record technicians who work at video display terminals for prolonged periods may experience eyestrain and musculoskeletal pain.

Employment Opportunities

Medical records and health information technicians held about 172,500 jobs in 2008. About 2 out of 5 jobs were in hospitals. The rest were mostly in offices of physicians, nursing care facilities, outpatient care centers, and home healthcare services.

Insurance firms that deal in health matters employ a small number of health information technicians to tabulate and analyze health information. Public health departments also employ technicians to supervise data collection from healthcare institutions and to assist in research.

Employment of medical records and health information technicians is expected to increase by 20%, much faster than the average for all occupations through 2018. Employment growth will result from the increase in the number of medical tests, treatments, and procedures that will be performed. As the population continues to age, the occurrence of health-related problems will increase. Tumor registrars should experience job growth as the incidence of cancer increases from an aging population.

In addition, with the increasing use of electronic health records, more technicians will be needed to complete the new responsibilities associated with electronic data management.

Educational and Legal Requirements

Medical record and health information technicians entering the field usually have a 2-year Associate degree from a community or junior college. Associate degree coursework includes classes in medical terminology and diseases, anatomy and physiology, legal aspects of medical records, coding and abstraction of data, statistics, databases, quality assurance methods, and computer training, as well as general education. High school students can improve their chances of acceptance into a health information education program by taking courses in biology, chemistry, health, and especially computer training.

Many employers favor technicians who have become **Registered Health Information Technicians (RHITs)**. Registered Health Information Technicians must pass a written examination offered by the American Health Information Management Association (AHIMA). To take the examination, a person must graduate from a 2-year Associate degree program accredited by the Commission on Accreditation for Health Informatics and Information

Management Education (CAHIIM). Technicians trained in non-CAHIIM-accredited programs or trained on the job are not eligible to take the examination. In 2007, there were about 245 CAHIIM-accredited programs in Health Informatics and Information Management Education.

Experienced health information technicians usually advance in one of two ways—by specializing or by managing. Many senior health information technicians specialize in coding—particularly Medicare coding—or as a **Certified Tumor Registrar (CTR)**. Technicians who specialize in coding may also obtain voluntary certification.

In large health information departments, experienced technicians may advance to section supervisor, overseeing the work of coding, correspondence, or discharge sections. Senior technicians with RHIT credentials may become director or assistant director of a health information department in a small facility. In large institutions, however, the director is typically a health information administrator with a Bachelor degree in health information administration.

Employment Trends

New jobs are expected in offices of physicians because of increasing demand for detailed records, especially in large group practices. New jobs also are expected in home healthcare services, outpatient care centers, and nursing and residential care facilities. Although employment growth in hospitals will not keep pace with growth in other healthcare industries, many new jobs will, nevertheless, be created. Cancer registrars should experience job growth. As the population continues to age, the incidence of cancer may increase.

Earnings

According to the latest information, median annual earnings of health information technicians were $30,610. The middle 50% earned between $24,290 and $39,490 per year. The lowest 10% earned less than $20,440, and the highest 10% earned more than $50,060 per year. Median annual earnings in the industries employing the largest number of health information technicians are shown in **Table 27-1**.

TABLE 27-1 Median Annual Earnings in the Industries Employing the Largest Number of Health Information Technicians

General medical and surgical hospitals	$29,400
Nursing care facilities	28,410
Outpatient care centers	26,680
Offices of physicians	24,170

Related Occupations

Health information technicians need strong clinical background knowledge to analyze the contents of medical records. Other occupations that require knowledge of medical terminology, anatomy, and physiology, but do not interact directly with patients, are medical secretaries, transcriptionists, writers, and illustrators.

Additional Information

Information on careers in medical record and health information technology, including a list of accredited programs, is available from

- American Health Information Management Association, 233 N. Michigan Ave., 21st Floor, Chicago, IL 60601-5800. Internet: http://www.ahima.org

MEDICAL TRANSCRIPTIONISTS

Work Description

Medical transcriptionists translate and edit recorded dictation by physicians and other healthcare providers regarding patient assessment and treatment. They use headsets and transcribing machines to listen to recordings made by physicians and other healthcare professionals. These workers transcribe a variety of medical reports about emergency room visits, diagnostic imaging studies, operations, chart reviews, and final summaries.

To understand and accurately transcribe dictated reports into a format that is clear and comprehensible for the reader, the medical transcriptionist must understand the language of medicine, anatomy and physiology, diagnostic procedures, and treatment. They also must be able to translate medical jargon and abbreviations into their expanded forms. After reviewing and editing for grammar and clarity, the medical transcriptionist transcribes the dictated reports and returns them in either printed or electronic form to the dictating physician or care provider for review and signature, or correction. These reports eventually become a part of the patient's permanent file.

Work Environment

The majority of medical transcriptionists are employed in comfortable settings. They usually work in hospitals, doctors' offices, or medical transcription services. An increasing number of court reporters and medical transcriptionists work from home-based offices as subcontractors for law firms, hospitals, and transcription services.

The work presents few hazards. Sitting in the same position for long periods can be tiring, however, and workers can suffer wrist, back, neck, or eye problems due to strain, and risk incurring repetitive motion injuries such as carpal tunnel syndrome. The pressure to be both accurate and fast also can prove stressful.

Most medical transcriptionists work a standard 40-hour week, although about 1 out of 4 works part time. A substantial number of medical transcriptionists are self-employed, which may allow for irregular working hours.

Employment Opportunities

Employment of medical transcriptionists is projected to grow by 11% from 2008 to 2018, about as fast as the average for all occupations. A growing and aging population will spur demand for medical transcription services because older age groups receive proportionately greater numbers of medical tests, treatments, and procedures requiring documentation. The continuing need for electronic documentation that can be shared easily among providers, third-party payers, regulators, consumers, and health information systems will sustain a high level of demand for transcription services. Growing numbers of medical transcriptionists will be needed to amend patients' records, edit documents produced by speech recognition systems, and identify discrepancies in medical reports.

Outsourcing of transcription work overseas and advancements in speech recognition technology are not expected to reduce the need for well-trained medical transcriptionists within the United States. Outsourcing transcription work abroad—to countries such as India, Pakistan, Philippines, and the Caribbean—has grown more popular as transmitting confidential health information over the Internet has become more secure; however, the demand for overseas transcription services is expected only to supplement the demand for well-trained domestic medical transcriptionists. In addition, reports transcribed by overseas medical transcription services usually require editing for accuracy by domestic medical transcriptionists before they meet U.S. quality standards.

Speech recognition technology allows physicians and other health professionals to dictate medical reports into a computerized program that converts speech to text. In spite of advancements in this technology, speech recognition software has been slow to grasp and analyze the human voice and the English language, and the medical vernacular with all its diversity. As a result, there will continue to be a need for skilled medical transcriptionists to identify and appropriately edit the inevitable errors created by speech recognition systems, and to create a final document.

Job opportunities should be best for those who earn an Associate degree or certification from the American Association for Medical Transcription.

Education and Legal Requirements

Employers prefer to hire transcriptionists who have completed postsecondary training in medical transcription offered by many vocational schools, community colleges, and distance-learning programs.

Completion of a 2-year Associate degree or 1-year certificate program—including coursework in anatomy, medical terminology, legal issues relating to healthcare documentation, and English grammar and punctuation—is highly recommended, but not always required. Many of these programs include supervised on-the-job experience. Some transcriptionists, especially those already familiar with medical terminology from previous experience as a nurse or medical secretary, become proficient through refresher courses and training.

Formal accreditation is not required for medical transcription programs. However, the Approval Committee for Certificate Programs (ACCP)—established by the Association for Healthcare Documentation Integrity (AHDI) and the American Health Information Management Association—offers voluntary accreditation for medical transcription programs. Although voluntary, completion of an ACCP-approved program may be required for transcriptionists seeking certification.

The AHDI awards two voluntary designations, the Registered Medical Transcriptionist (RMT) and the Certified Medical Transcriptionist (CMT). Medical transcriptionists who are recent graduates of medical transcription educational programs or have fewer than 2 years' experience in acute care may become a registered RMT. The RMT credential is awarded upon successfully passing the AHDI level 1 registered medical transcription exam. The CMT designation requires at least 2 years of acute care experience working in multiple specialty surgery areas using different format, report, and dictation types. Candidates also must earn a passing score on a certification examination. Because medicine is constantly evolving, medical transcriptionists are encouraged to update their skills regularly. RMTs and CMTs must earn continuing education credits every 3 years to be recertified. As in many other fields, certification is recognized as a sign of competence.

For those seeking work as medical transcriptionists, understanding medical terminology is essential. Good English grammar and punctuation skills are required, as well as familiarity with personal computers and word processing software. Good listening skills are also necessary, because some doctors and health care professionals speak English as a second language.

Earnings

Medical transcriptionists had median hourly wages of $15.41 in May 2008. The middle 50% earned between $13.02 and $18.55. The lowest 10% earned less than $10.76, and the highest 10% earned more than $21. Median hourly earnings in the industries employing the largest numbers of medical transcriptionists are detailed in **Table 27-2**.

TABLE 27-2   Median Hourly Earnings in the Industries Employing the Largest Numbers of Medical Transcriptionists

Medical and diagnostic laboratories	$15.68
General medical and surgical hospitals	14.62
Business support services	14.34
Outpatient care centers	14.31
Offices of physicians	14.00

Compensation methods for medical transcriptionists vary. Some are paid based on the number of hours worked or on the number of lines transcribed. Others receive a base pay per hour with incentives for extra production. Large hospitals and healthcare organizations usually prefer to pay for the time an employee works. Independent contractors and employees of transcription services usually receive production-based pay.

Related Occupations

A number of other workers type, record information, and process paperwork. Among these are administrative assistants, bookkeepers, receptionists, secretaries, and human resource clerks. Medical secretaries may also transcribe as part of their job. Other workers who provide medical support include medical assistants and medical record technicians.

Additional Information

For information on a career as a medical transcriptionist, contact

- Association for Healthcare Documentation Integrity, 4230 Kierman Ave., Suite 130, Modesto, CA 95356. Internet: http://www.ahdionline.org

MEDICAL LIBRARIANS

Work Description

Medical or health science librarians provide essential services to professional staff and personnel in medicine, dentistry, nursing, pharmacy, the allied health professions, and other related technologies. Because health and related fields are growing rapidly, professional staff need quick and efficient access to large volumes of information and materials to keep abreast of developments, new procedures and techniques, and other relevant data. Relevant information and materials are used in education and training programs, in exchange-of-information activities among different health professions, and in biomedical research. Health science librarians make this information available to those who need it, utilizing knowledge of both library science and health science in their work.

Depending on the size of the facility where they work, health science librarians may take charge of an entire library or be assigned to specific functions. They select and order books, journals, and other materials, and classify and catalog acquisitions to allow their easy retrieval. Other duties include preparing guides to reference materials, compiling bibliographies, and selecting and acquiring films and other audiovisual materials.

Readers and researchers frequently call on the specialized skills of the librarian to track down information on a particular subject. The material may be bound in obscure documents or scattered in many places, requiring detective work to locate it. If the document is in another language, the librarian may be called on to obtain a translation. Frequently, the librarian is asked to compile a bibliography or to provide a comprehensive review or summary on a particular subject.

Aside from assisting patrons in person, the medical librarian also responds to mail, e-mail, and phone inquiries. Success in handling these inquiries depends largely on the librarian's skill. Librarians may have only very general knowledge of medicine, but they must know how and where to locate all types of information on short notice.

In hospitals, services offered by the medical library may depend on whether the hospital conducts research and training, or on the categories of illness treated there. Some hospitals have separate medical, nursing, and patient libraries. Increasingly, however, these collections are grouped together under the direction of one chief librarian, with assistants in charge of the separate services.

The medical librarian also plays an important role in the hospital's rehabilitation services. In addition, librarians serving patients provide book cart services, develop programs of interest for ambulatory patients, and visit new patients to learn about their reading interests.

Work Environment

In addition to hospitals, medical librarians work in schools of medicine, nursing, dentistry, and pharmacy; research institutes; pharmaceutical and related industries; health departments; professional societies; and voluntary health agencies. Medical libraries are found in numerous locations throughout the country but tend to be concentrated in or near population centers. Individual size and working conditions vary greatly from library to library. For instance, hospital libraries may range from a staff size of 1 to slightly fewer than 100. In ill-equipped offices, librarians may risk eyestrain, backache, and carpal tunnel syndrome. Nevertheless, surroundings are usually pleasant and free of hazards or unusual environmental working conditions.

Employment Opportunities

Employment of librarians is expected to grow by 8% between 2008 and 2018, which is as fast as the average for all occupations. Growth in the number of librarians will be limited by government budget constraints and the increasing use of electronic resources. Both will result in the hiring of fewer librarians and the replacement of librarians with less costly library technicians and assistants. As electronic resources become more common and patrons and support staff become more familiar with their use, fewer librarians are needed to maintain and assist users with these resources. In addition, many libraries are equipped for users to access library resources directly from their homes or offices through library websites. Some users bypass librarians altogether and conduct research on their own. Librarians will still be needed, however, to manage staff, help users define their research needs and develop database search techniques, address complicated reference requests, and choose appropriate materials.

Over the next decade, jobs for medical librarians outside traditional settings will grow fastest. These settings include private industry, nonprofit organizations, and consulting firms. Examples of jobs in industry for medical librarians include the biotechnology, insurance, pharmaceutical, publishing, and medical equipment industries.

Many companies are turning to librarians because of their research and organizational skills, and their knowledge of computer databases and library automation systems. Librarians also are hired by organizations to organize information on the Internet. Librarians working in these settings may be classified as systems analysts, database specialists and trainers, webmasters or web developers, or local area network (LAN) coordinators.

Most recently, medical and other librarians held about 159,900 jobs. Most were in school and academic libraries; others were in public and special libraries. A small number of librarians worked for hospitals and religious organizations. Others worked for governments. Entrepreneurial librarians sometimes start their own consulting practices, acting as freelance librarians or information brokers and providing services to other libraries, business, or government agencies. Replacement needs will account for more job openings over the next decade, as more than 2 out of 3 librarians are aged 45 or older, which will result in many job openings as these librarians retire. Slower than average employment growth, coupled with an increasing number of graduates with Master degrees in library science (MLSs), will result in more applicants competing for fewer jobs. Applicants for librarian jobs in large cities or suburban areas will face competition, while those willing to work in rural areas should have better job prospects.

Educational and Legal Requirements

An MLS degree is necessary for librarian positions in most public, academic, and special libraries, and in some school libraries. The federal government requires an MLS or the equivalent in education and experience. Many colleges and universities offer MLS programs, but employers often prefer graduates of the approximately 50 schools accredited by the American Library Association. Most MLS programs require a Bachelor degree; a major in liberal arts is appropriate preparation for such graduate work.

Most MLS programs take 1 year to complete, but some take 2 years. A typical graduate program includes courses in the foundations of library and information science, including the history of books and printing, intellectual freedom and censorship, and the role of libraries and information in society. Other basic courses cover material selection and processing, the organization of information, reference tools and strategies, and user services. Courses are adapted to educate librarians in using such new resources as online reference systems, Internet search methods, and automated circulation systems.

Computer-related coursework is an increasingly important component of an MLS degree.

An MLS degree provides general preparation for library work, but some individuals specialize in one particular area. The minimum qualifications for librarians specializing in medicine are as follows:

- A Master degree in library and information science from an American Library Association–accredited school
- Strong oral and written communication skills
- Strong interpersonal skills
- Strong computer skills

Librarians participate in continuing training once they are on the job to keep abreast of new information systems brought about by changing technology. Most MLS schools offer courses in Health Sciences Information, which is recommended for those interested in becoming a medical librarian.

Earnings

Salaries of librarians vary according to the individual's qualifications and the type, size, and location of the library. Librarians with primarily administrative duties often have greater earnings. Median annual wages of librarians in May 2008 were $52,530. The middle 50% earned between $42,240 and $65,300. The lowest 10% earned less than $33,190, and the highest 10% earned more than $81,130. The Medical Library Association reports that the average starting salary was $42,000 in 2008. The lowest 10% earned $42,000, and the highest 10% earned $96,879 in 2008. The overall average salary for medical librarians in 2008 was $65,796. Library directors can earn up to $158,000.

Related Occupations

Librarians play an important role in the transfer of knowledge and ideas by providing people with access to the information they need and want. Jobs requiring similar analytical, organizational, and communication skills include physicians, nurses, health educators, allied healthcare professionals, administrators, and information technology programmers and specialists.

Additional Information

Information on librarianship, including information on scholarships or loans, is available from the American Library Association. Consult its website for a listing of accredited library education programs.

- American Library Association, Office for Human Resource Development and Recruitment, 50 East Huron St., Chicago, IL 60611. Internet: http://www.ala.org

For information on employment opportunities as a health science librarian, scholarship information, credentialing information, and a list of MLA-accredited schools offering programs in health sciences librarianship, contact

• Medical Library Association, 65 East Wacker Pl., Suite 1900, Chicago, IL 60601-7246. Internet: http://www.mlanet.org

For information about medical librarians in academic settings, contact

• Association of Academic Health Sciences Libraries (AAHSL), 2150 North 107th St., Suite 205, Seattle, WA 98133-9009. Internet: http://aahsl.org

chapter twenty-eight

Health Services Administration*

KEY TERMS

Assistant administrators
Associate administrator
Budgets
Chief executive officer
  (CEO)
Coordinate

Executive health services
  (generalist, clinical)
Financial viability
Marketing
Negotiation
Organization

Philosophy
Policies
Programs
Strategic planning

*All information in this chapter was obtained from Bureau of Labor Statistics. U.S. Department of Labor. *Occupational Outlook Handbook 2010–2011 Edition*. 2010.

ADMINISTRATION

SIGNIFICANT POINTS

- Job opportunities will be good, especially for applicants with work experience in health care and strong business and management skills.
- A Master degree is the standard credential, although a Bachelor degree is adequate for some entry-level positions.
- Medical and health services managers typically work long hours and may be called at all hours to deal with problems.

THE NEED FOR PROFESSIONAL MANAGEMENT

Health care is a business and, like every business, it needs good management to keep the business running smoothly. Medical and health services managers, also referred to as healthcare executives or healthcare administrators, plan, direct, coordinate, and supervise the delivery of health care. These workers are either specialists in charge of a specific clinical department or generalists who manage an entire facility or system.

The structure and financing of health care are changing rapidly. Future medical and health services managers must be prepared to deal with the integration of healthcare delivery systems, technological innovations, an increasingly complex regulatory environment, restructuring of work, and an increased focus on preventive care. They will be called on to improve efficiency in healthcare facilities and the quality of the care provided.

Large facilities usually have several **assistant administrators** who aid the top administrator and handle daily decisions. Assistant administrators direct activities in clinical areas, such as nursing, surgery, therapy, medical records, and health information.

In smaller facilities, top administrators handle more of the details of daily operations. For example, many nursing home administrators manage personnel, finances, facility operations, and admissions, while also providing resident care.

Clinical managers have training or experience in a specific clinical area and, accordingly, have more specific responsibilities than do generalists. For example, directors of physical therapy are experienced physical therapists, and most health information and medical record administrators have a Bachelor degree in health information or medical record administration. Clinical managers establish and implement **policies**, objectives, and procedures for their departments; evaluate personnel and work quality; develop reports and **budgets**; and **coordinate** activities with other managers.

In group medical practices, managers work closely with physicians. Whereas an office manager might handle business affairs in small medical groups, leaving policy decisions to the physicians themselves, larger groups usually employ a full-time administrator to help formulate business strategies and coordinate day-to-day business.

A small group of 10 to 15 physicians might employ 1 administrator to oversee personnel matters, billing and collection, budgeting, planning, equipment outlays, and patient flow. A large practice of 40 to 50 physicians might have a chief administrator and several assistants, each responsible for a different area of expertise.

Medical and health services managers in managed care settings perform functions similar to those of their counterparts in large group practices, except that they could have larger staffs to manage. In addition, they might do more community outreach and preventive care than do managers of a group practice.

Some medical and health services managers oversee the activities of a number of hospitals in health systems. Such systems might contain both inpatient and outpatient facilities and offer a wide range of patient services.

Managers in all settings will be needed to improve the quality and efficiency of health care, while controlling costs, as insurance companies and Medicare demand higher levels of accountability. Managers also will be needed to oversee the computerization of patient records and ensure their security as required by law. Additional demand for managers will stem from the need to recruit workers and increase employee retention, to comply with changing regulations, to implement new technology, and to help improve the health of their communities by emphasizing preventive care.

In line with their training and/or experience in a specific clinical area, clinical managers have more specific responsibilities than generalist managers. For example, directors of physical therapy are experienced physical therapists, and most health information and medical record administrators have a Bachelor degree in health information or medical record administration. These managers establish and implement policies, objectives, and procedures for their departments; evaluate personnel and work performance; develop reports and budgets; and coordinate activities with other managers.

Another aspect of professional management is the need to address the extensive oversight and scrutiny to which health facilities are subject. Both past performance and future plans are subject to review by a variety of groups and organizations, including consumer groups, government agencies, professional oversight bodies, insurance companies and other third-party payers, business coalitions, and even the courts. Preparing for inspection visits by observers from regulatory bodies and submitting appropriate records and documentation can be time-consuming as well as technically demanding.

HEALTH SERVICES MANAGERS

Work Description

Health services manager is an inclusive term for individuals in many different positions who plan, organize, and coordinate the delivery of health care. Hospitals provide more than half of all jobs in this field. Other employers of health services managers include medical group practices; outpatient clinics;

HMOs; nursing homes; hospices; home health agencies; rehabilitation, community mental health, emergency care, and diagnostic imaging centers; and offices of doctors, dentists, and other health practitioners.

Three functional levels of administration are found in hospitals and other large facilities—executive, internal management, and specialized staff. The **chief executive officer (CEO)** provides overall management direction, but also is concerned with community outreach, planning, policy making, response to government agencies and regulations, and **negotiation**. The CEO often speaks before civic groups, promotes public participation in health **programs**, and coordinates the activities of the hospital or facility with those of government or community agencies. Institutional planning is an increasingly important responsibility of chief administrators, who continually must assess the need for services, personnel, facilities, and equipment, and periodically recommend changes such as shutting down a maternity ward or opening an outpatient clinic.

Chief administrators need leadership ability as well as technical skills to respond effectively to community requirements for health care, while at the same time satisfying demand for **financial viability**, cost containment, and public and professional accountability. Within a single institution, such as a community hospital, the healthcare administrator is directly accountable to a board of trustees made up of community leaders who are voted onto the board to determine broad policies and objectives for the hospital. Day-to-day management, particularly in large facilities, may be the responsibility of one or more associate or assistant administrators, who work with service unit managers and staff specialists.

Depending on the size of the facility, associate or assistant administrators may be responsible for budget and finance; human resources, including personnel administration, education, and in-service training; information management; and direction of the medical, nursing, ancillary services, housekeeping, physical plant, and other operating departments. As the healthcare system becomes more specialized, skills in financial management, **marketing**, **strategic planning**, systems analysis, and labor relations will be needed as well.

Hospital and nursing home administration differ in important respects. Hospitals are complex organizations, housing as many as 30 highly specialized departments, including admissions, surgery, clinical laboratory, therapy, emergency medicine, nursing, physical plant, medical records, accounting, and so on. The hospital administrator works with the governing board in establishing general policies and operating **philosophy** and provides direction to the department heads and the assistant administrators (or vice presidents), who implement those policies. The hospital administrator coordinates the activities of the assistant administrators and department heads to ensure that the hospital runs efficiently, provides high-quality medical care, and recovers adequate revenue to remain solvent or profitable. Administrators represent the hospital to the community and the state. Nationally, they participate in professional associations such as the American Hospital

Association, the American Public Health Association, and the Association of Mental Health Administrators.

Nursing home administrators need many of the same management skills as hospital administrators. Administrative staffs in nursing homes, however, are typically much smaller than those in hospitals. Nursing home administrators often have only one or two assistant administrators, and sometimes none. As a result, nursing home administrators are involved in day-to-day management decisions much more often than hospital administrators in all but the smallest hospitals. Nursing home administrators wear various hats— personnel director, director of finance, director of facilities, and admissions director, for example. They analyze data and then make daily management decisions in all of these areas. In addition, because many nursing home residents stay for months or even years, administrators must try to create an environment that nourishes residents' psychological, social, and spiritual well-being, as well as tends to their healthcare needs.

In the growing field of group practice management, administrators and managers need to be able to work effectively with the physicians who own the practice. Specific job duties vary according to the size of the practice. While an office manager handles the business side in very small medical groups, leaving policy decisions to the physicians themselves, larger groups generally employ a full-time administrator to provide advice on business strategies and coordinate the day-to-day management of the practice.

A group of 10 or 15 physicians might employ a single administrator to oversee personnel matters, billing and collection, budgeting, planning, equipment outlays, advertising, and patient flow, whereas a practice of 40 or 50 physicians would require a chief administrator and several assistants, each responsible for a different area of management. In addition to providing overall management direction, the chief administrator of a group practice is responsible for ensuring that the practice maintains or strengthens its competitive position. This is no small task, given the rapidly changing nature of the healthcare environment. Ensuring competitiveness might entail market research to analyze the services the practice currently offers and those it might offer, negotiating contracts with hospitals or other healthcare providers to gain access to specialized facilities and equipment, or entering into joint ventures for the purchase of an expensive piece of medical equipment, such as a magnetic resonance imager.

Managers in HMOs perform all the functions of administrators and managers in large medical group practices, plus one additional function— administering what amounts to an insurance company. HMO subscribers pay an annual fee that covers almost all of their care. HMO managers must establish a comprehensive medical benefits package with enrollment fees low enough to attract adequate enrollments but high enough to operate successfully. In addition, they may work more in the areas of community outreach and preventive care than do managers of a group practice. The size of the administrative staff in HMOs varies according to the size and type of HMO.

Some health services managers oversee the activities of health systems that may encompass a number of inpatient and outpatient facilities and offer a wide range of patient services.

Work Environment

Health services managers often work long hours. Facilities such as nursing homes and hospitals operate around the clock, and administrators and managers may be called at all hours to deal with emergencies. The job also may include travel to attend meetings or to inspect healthcare facilities.

Employment Opportunities

Medical and health services managers held about 283,500 jobs in 2008. About 38% worked in hospitals, and another 19% worked in offices of physicians or in nursing and residential care facilities. Most of the remainder worked in home healthcare services, federal government healthcare facilities, outpatient care centers, insurance companies, and community care facilities for the elderly.

Educational and Legal Requirements

Health services managers must be familiar with management principles and practices. A Master degree in health services administration, long-term care administration, health sciences, public health, public administration, or business administration is the standard credential for most generalist positions in this field. However, a Bachelor degree is adequate for some entry-level positions in smaller facilities and for some entry-level positions at the departmental level within healthcare organizations. In addition, physicians' offices and some other facilities may accept on-the-job experience as a substitute for formal education.

For clinical department heads, a degree and work experience in the appropriate field may be sufficient for entry, but a Master degree in health services administration or a related field may be required to advance. For example, nursing services administrators are usually chosen from among supervisory registered nurses who have administrative abilities and a graduate degree in nursing or health services administration.

Bachelor, Master, and doctoral degree programs in health administration are offered by colleges, universities, and schools of public health, medicine, allied health, public administration, and business administration. In 2008, 72 schools had accredited programs leading to a Master degree in health services administration, according to the Accrediting Commission on Education for Health Services Administration.

Some graduate programs seek out students with undergraduate degrees in business or health administration; others prefer students with a liberal arts or health profession background. Candidates with previous work experience in health care may also have an advantage. Competition for entry into these graduate programs is keen, and applicants need above-average grades to gain admission.

Graduate degree programs usually last between 2 and 3 years. They may include as much as 1 year of supervised administrative experience and coursework in hospital **organization** and management, marketing, accounting and budgeting, human resource administration, strategic planning, law and ethics, biostatistics or epidemiology, health economics, and health information systems. Some programs allow students to specialize in one type of facility—hospitals, nursing homes, mental health facilities, or medical groups. Other programs encourage a generalist approach to health administration education.

Recent graduates with Master degrees in health services administration may start as department managers or in staff positions. The level of the starting position varies with the experience of the applicant and the size of the organization. Hospitals and other health facilities offer postgraduate residencies and fellowships, which are usually staff positions. Graduates from Master degree programs also take jobs in HMOs, large group medical practices, clinics, mental health facilities, multifacility nursing home corporations, and consulting firms.

Graduates with Bachelor degrees in health administration usually begin as administrative assistants or assistant department heads in larger hospitals, or as department heads or assistant administrators in small hospitals or nursing homes.

All states and the District of Columbia require nursing home administrators to have a Bachelor degree, pass a licensing examination, complete a state-approved training program, and pursue continuing education. Some states also require licenses for administrators in assisted-living facilities. A license is not required in other areas of medical and health services management.

Health services managers often are responsible for millions of dollars in facilities and equipment and hundreds of employees. In order to make effective decisions, they need to be open to different opinions and be good at analyzing contradictory information. They must understand finance and information systems and be able to interpret data. Motivating others to implement their decisions requires strong leadership abilities. Tact, diplomacy, flexibility, and communication skills are essential, because health services managers spend most of their time interacting with others.

Health services managers advance by moving into higher-paying positions with more responsibility, such as assistant or **associate administrator**, or by moving to larger facilities. Some experienced managers also may become consultants or professors of healthcare management.

Employment Trends

Employment of medical and health services managers is expected to grow 18% between 2008 and 2018, faster than the average for all occupations. Hospitals will continue to employ the most medical and health services managers over the 2008 to 2018 decade. However, the number of new jobs created is expected to increase at a slower rate in hospitals than in many other industries because of the growing use of clinics and other outpatient care sites. Despite relatively slow employment growth in hospitals, a large number of new jobs will be created because of the industry's large size.

Employment will grow fast in offices of health practitioners. Many services previously provided in hospitals will continue to shift to these settings, especially as medical technologies improve. Demand in medical group practice management will grow as medical group practices become larger and more complex.

Medical and health services managers also will be employed by healthcare management companies that provide management services to hospitals and other organizations, and to specific departments such as emergency, information management systems, managed care contract negotiations, and physician recruiting. As insurance companies and Medicare demand higher levels of accountability, medical and health services managers will be needed in all healthcare settings to improve the quality and efficiency of health care while controlling costs, and hospitals will continue to be the largest employers of medical and health services managers over the 2008 to 2018 decade.

Earnings

According to May 2008 data, median annual earnings of medical and health services managers were $80,240. The middle 50% earned between $62,170 and $104,120 per year. The lowest 10% earned less than $48,300, and the highest 10% earned more than $137,800 per year. Median annual earnings in the industries employing the largest number of medical and health services managers are shown in **Table 28-1**.

Earnings of health services managers vary by type and size of the facility, as well as by level of responsibility. For example, the Medical Group Management Association reported the following median salaries in 2008 for administrators by group practice size:

- Fewer than seven physicians: $82,423
- Seven to 25 physicians: $105,710
- More than 26 physicians: $119,000

TABLE 28-1   Median Annual Earnings in the Industries Employing the Largest Number of Medical and Health Service Managers

General medical and surgical hospitals	$78,660
Outpatient care centers	67,920
Offices of physicians	67,540
Nursing care facilities	66,730
Home healthcare services	66,720

Related Occupations

Health services managers have training or experience in both health care and management. Other occupations requiring knowledge of both fields are public health directors, social welfare administrators, directors of voluntary health agencies and health professional associations, and underwriters in health insurance companies.

Additional Information

General information about health administration is available from

- American College of Healthcare Executives, One North Franklin St., Suite 1700, Chicago, IL 60606. Internet: http://www.ache.org

Information about undergraduate and graduate academic programs in this field is available from

- Association of University Programs in Health Administration, 2000 14th St. North, Suite 780, Arlington, VA 22201. Internet: http://www.aupha.org

For a list of accredited graduate programs in health services administration, contact

- Commission on Accreditation of Health Care Management Educators, 2111 Wilson Blvd., Suite 700, Arlington, VA 22201. Internet: http://achca.org/joomla/

For information about career opportunities in long-term care administration, contact

- American College of Health Care Administrators, 1321 Duke St., Suite 400, Alexandria, VA 22314. Internet: http://achca.org/joomla/

For information about career opportunities in medical group practices and ambulatory care management, contact

- Medical Group Management Association, 104 Inverness Terrace East, Englewood, CO 80112. Internet: http://www.mgma.com

For information about healthcare office managers, contact

- Professional Association of Health Care Office Managers, 1576 Bella Cruz Dr., Suite 360, Lady Lake, FL 32159. Internet: http://www.pahcom.com

chapter twenty-nine

Federal and State Health Regulators*

*All information in this chapter was obtained from Bureau of Labor Statistics. U.S. Department of Labor. *Occupational Outlook Handbook 2010–2011 Edition*. 2010.

GOVERNMENT HEALTH AND SAFETY OFFICERS
SIGNIFICANT POINTS

- Government vigilance on environment, health, food in the market, food service, and general sanitation is constantly increasing, contributing to the importance of such fields.

- City, county, and state agencies are the major employers.

- Employment is expected to increase.

- Most jobs require a Bachelor degree, although some regulators learn the skill through on-the-job training.

Federal and state health regulators are responsible for controlling, preserving, or improving environmental conditions so that community health, safety, comfort, and well-being are maintained. **City, county, district, state, federal, and other laws** regulate sanitary standards for food and water supplies; garbage, waste, and sewage disposal; and housing maintenance. Health and safety officers **interpret and enforce** these laws. Within the field of **environmental health control**, they regulate hazardous substances and their disposal, and monitor water and air quality. New sanitary problems are created as the population increases and as more people move into the cities and suburbs of expanding metropolitan areas. With technical training and experience, regulators are equipped to recognize and anticipate **environmental hazards**. Their responsibilities entail calling these problems to the attention of local and other relevant governments, community leaders, civic groups, and the general public. They also recommend changes for solving the problems.

Work Description

Federal and state regulators, usually referred to as **inspectors** and compliance officers, help to keep workplaces safe, food healthy, and the environment clean. They also ensure that workers' rights are recognized in a variety of settings. They enforce rules on matters as diverse as health, safety, food quality, licensing, and finance. As the following occupations demonstrate, their duties vary widely, depending on their area of responsibility and level of experience.

Consumer safety inspectors and officers inspect food, feeds, pesticides, weights and measures, biological products, cosmetics, drugs, medical equipment, and radiation-emitting products. Working individually or in teams under a senior inspector, they check on firms that use, produce, handle, store, or market the products that they regulate. They ensure that standards are maintained and respond to consumer complaints by questioning employees, vendors, and others to obtain evidence. Inspectors look for inaccurate product labeling, inaccurate scales, and decomposition or chemical/bacteriological contamination that could result in a product becoming harmful to health. After completing their **inspection**, inspectors discuss their observations with plant managers or business owners to point out areas where corrective measures are needed. They write reports of their findings and compile evidence for use in court if legal action is required.

Occupational Safety and Health Administration (OSHA) inspectors serve the Department of Labor as expert consultants on the application of safety principles, practices, and techniques in the workplace. They conduct fact-finding **investigations** of workplaces to determine the existence of specific safety hazards. They may be assigned to conduct safety inspections and investigations, using any supplies, sampling and measuring devices, or other technical equipment required to complete their work. These inspectors attempt to prevent accidents by using their knowledge of engineering safety codes and standards, and they may order the suspension of activities that pose threats to workers.

Environmental health inspectors, also called sanitarians, work primarily for governments. The **U.S. Food and Drug Administration (FDA)** is responsible for the safety of both domestic and imported foods. Inspectors analyze substances to identify contamination or the presence of disease, and investigate sources of contamination to ensure that food, water, and air meet government standards. They certify the purity of food and beverages produced in dairies and processing plants, or served in restaurants, hospitals, and other institutions. Inspectors may find pollution sources through the collection and analysis of air, water, or waste samples. When they determine the nature and cause of pollution, they initiate action to stop it and force the firm or individual responsible for the pollutants to pay for their removal.

Food inspectors ensure that products are fit for human consumption in accordance with federal laws governing the wholesomeness and purity of meat, poultry, and egg products. The **U.S. Department of Agriculture's Food Safety and Inspection Service (FSIS)** is the governmental agency responsible for meat, poultry, and egg products. Its food inspectors visually examine livestock or poultry prior to slaughter, and conduct postmortem inspections to determine that the resulting food product is not contaminated and that sanitation procedures are maintained. Food processing inspectors specialize in processed meat and poultry products, and all other ingredients contained in the final products, including frozen dinners, canned goods, and cured and smoked products. They have the authority to shut a plant down if they encounter a problem that they are unable to resolve.

Work Environment

Inspection and compliance officers work with many different people and in a variety of environments. Their jobs often involve considerable fieldwork, and some inspectors travel frequently. When traveling, they are generally furnished with an automobile or are reimbursed for their travel expenses.

Inspectors may experience unpleasant, stressful, and dangerous working conditions. For example, federal food inspectors work in highly mechanized plant environments near operating machinery with moving parts, or with poultry or livestock in confined areas in extreme temperatures and on slippery floors. Their duties often require working with sharp knives, moderate lifting, and walking or standing for long periods. Many inspectors work long and often irregular hours. In addition, they may find themselves in adversarial roles when the organization or individual being inspected objects to the inspection process or its consequences.

Employment Opportunities

Environmental scientists and specialists held about 85,900 jobs in 2008. Federal, state, and local governments employ 44% of all environmental scientists and specialists. About 37% of environmental scientists were employed in state and local governments; 21% in management, scientific, and technical consulting services; 15% in architectural, engineering, and related services; and 7% in the federal government, primarily in the **Environmental Protection Agency (EPA)** and the **Department of Defense (DOD)**.

A wide range of agencies employs inspectors and compliance officers who work for the federal government. Some consumer safety inspectors, for example, work for the U.S. Food and Drug Administration, but the majority work for state governments. The U.S. Department of Agriculture employs most food inspectors and agricultural commodity graders. Other food inspectors are employed by the **National Oceanic and Atmospheric Administration** within the Department of Commerce and are responsible for the safety of fish and fish products. Many health inspectors work for state and local governments. The Departments of Treasury and Labor at the federal level are the primary employers of compliance inspectors, but some work for state and local governments. The Department of Defense employs the majority of quality assurance inspectors. The Environmental Protection Agency employs inspectors to verify compliance with air, water, and soil pollution control, and other laws. The U.S. Department of Labor and many state governments employ safety and health inspectors, equal opportunity officers, and mine safety and health inspectors. The U.S. Department of the Interior employs park rangers.

Many environmental scientists and specialists work in consulting. Consultants help businesses and government address issues related to underground tanks, land disposal areas, and other hazardous-waste-management facilities. Currently, environmental consulting is evolving from investigations to creating remediation and engineering solutions. At the same time, the regulatory climate is moving from a rigid structure to a more flexible risk-based approach. These factors, coupled with new federal and state initiatives that integrate environmental activities into the business process itself, will result in a greater focus on waste minimization, resource recovery, pollution prevention, and the consideration of environmental effects during product development. This shift in focus to preventive management will provide many new opportunities for environmental scientists in consulting roles.

Employment of environmental scientists and specialists is expected to increase by 28% between 2008 and 2018, much faster than the average for all occupations. Job growth should be strongest in private-sector consulting firms. Growth in employment will be spurred largely by the increasing demands placed on the environment by population growth and increasing awareness of the problems caused by environmental degradation. Further demand should result from the need to comply with complex environmental laws and regulations, particularly those regarding groundwater decontamination and clean air. Much job growth will result from a continued need to monitor the quality of the environment, to interpret the impact of human actions on terrestrial and aquatic ecosystems, and to develop strategies for restoring ecosystems. In addition, environmental scientists will be needed to help planners develop and construct buildings, transportation corridors, and utilities that protect water resources and reflect efficient and beneficial land use.

Employment of inspectors and compliance officers is seldom affected by general economic fluctuations. Federal, state, and local governments, which employ four-fifths of all inspectors, provide considerable job security.

Educational and Legal Requirements

Because of the diversity of the functions they perform, qualifications for inspector and compliance officer jobs vary widely. Requirements include a combination of education, experience, and passing scores on written examinations. Many employers, including the federal government, require college degrees for some positions. Experience in the area being investigated is also a prerequisite for many positions.

Environmental health inspectors or sanitarians, familiar to many health facility personnel, provide one example of the educational and other qualifications needed for work as an inspection and compliance officer. Entry-level environmental health inspectors may have completed a full 4-year course of study that meets all of the requirements for a Bachelor degree, and that included or was supplemented by at least 30 semester hours in a science or any combination of sciences directly related to environmental health—for example, sanitary science, public health, chemistry, microbiology, or any appropriate agricultural, biological, or physical science. Alternatively, sanitarians may have 4 years of specialized experience in inspectional, investigational, technical support, or other work that provides a fundamental understanding of environmental health principles, methods, and techniques equivalent to that which is gained through a 4-year college curriculum or some combination of education and experience as described above. Most environmental scientists need a Master degree in environmental science or a related science, such as a life science or chemistry, for jobs in the government. In most states, they are licensed by examining boards.

Personal qualifications that mark the true professional in any discipline may be applicable in this occupation as well. These characteristics include the ability to work effectively with people, a commitment to service, and true concern for public health and well-being. Prospective inspectors also should have a strong interest in science.

All inspectors and compliance officers are trained in the applicable laws or inspection procedures through some combination of classroom and on-the-job training. In general, people who want to enter this occupation should be responsible and like detailed work. Inspectors and compliance officers should be able to communicate well.

Federal government inspectors and compliance officers whose job performance is satisfactory can advance up their particular career ladder to a specified full-performance level. For positions above this level, usually supervisory positions, advancement is competitive and based on agency needs and individual merit. Advancement opportunities in state and local governments and the private sector are often similar to those found in the federal government.

Earnings

According to May 2008 information, the median annual salary of inspectors and compliance officers (other than construction inspectors) was $59,750. The middle half earned between $45,340 and $78,980. The lowest 10% earned less than $36,310, and the highest 10% earned more than $102,610. Inspectors and compliance officers employed by local governments had earnings of $60,030; those who worked for state governments earned a median annual salary of $56,480; and those in the federal government earned $93,700. According to the National Association of Colleges and Employers, beginning salary offers in July 2009 for graduates with Bachelor degrees in an environmental science averaged $39,160 a year. Beginning salaries were slightly higher in selected areas where the prevailing local pay level was higher. Average salaries for selected inspectors and compliance officers in the federal government in nonsupervisory, supervisory, and managerial positions in early 2006 are shown in **Table 29-1**.

Most inspectors and compliance officers work for federal, state, and local governments or in large private firms, most of which generally offer more generous benefits than do smaller firms.

Related Occupations

Inspectors and compliance officers ensure that laws and regulations are obeyed. Others who enforce laws and regulations include construction and

TABLE 29-1 Average Salaries for Selected Inspectors and Compliance Officers in the Federal Government in Nonsupervisory, Supervisory, and Managerial Positions, Early 2006

Environmental protection specialists	$68,280
Safety and occupational health managers	59,270
Agricultural commodity graders	44,141
Consumer safety inspectors	40,779
Food inspectors	39,864

building inspectors; fire marshals; federal, state, and local law enforcement professionals; correctional officers; fish and game wardens; aviation safety inspectors; equal opportunity specialists; mine safety and health inspectors; park rangers; and securities compliance examiners.

Additional Information

Information on obtaining a job with the federal government is available from the Office of Personnel Management through a telephone-based system. Consult a telephone directory under U.S. Government for a local number, or call (202) 606-2525 or (978) 461-8404 (TDD). Information is also available on the Internet at http://www.usajobs.opm.gov. Information regarding jobs in federal, state, and local governments, as well as in private industry, is available from each state's employment service.

ENVIRONMENTAL HEALTH TECHNICIANS AND AIDES

Environmental science and protection technicians perform laboratory and field tests to monitor environmental resources and determine the contaminants and sources of pollution in the environment. They may collect samples for testing or be involved in abating and controlling sources of environmental pollution. Some are responsible for waste management operations, the control and management of hazardous materials inventory, or general activities involving regulatory compliance. Many environmental science technicians employed at private consulting firms work directly under the supervision of an environmental scientist.

Employment Opportunities

A growing need exists for environmental health technicians and aides. Correspondingly, greater recognition exists that these paraprofessionals need a career ladder to advance to first-degree professional (Bachelor degree in science) and to postgraduate levels should they desire. Accredited community colleges, therefore, frequently offer a 2-year Associate of Science degree, which includes the necessary general education courses, and which allows students to transfer to a 4-year college or university to complete their training. Students interested in pursuing a course of study to become an environmental health technician or aide should contact local community or junior colleges for specifics.

Educational and Legal Requirements

There are many ways to qualify for a job as a science technician. Most employers prefer applicants who have at least 2 years of specialized postsecondary training or an Associate degree in applied science or science-related technology. Some science technicians have a Bachelor degree in the natural sciences, while others have no formal postsecondary education and learn their skills on the job. Some science technician specialties have higher education requirements. For example, biological technicians often need a Bachelor degree in biology or a closely related field. Forensic science positions also typically require a Bachelor degree, either in forensic science or another natural science. Knowledge and understanding of legal procedures also can be helpful. Chemical technician positions in research and development also often require a Bachelor degree, but most chemical process technicians have a 2-year degree instead, usually an Associate degree in process technology.

Earnings

Most occupational health and safety technicians work in large private firms or for federal, state, and local governments, most of which generally offer benefits more generous than those offered by smaller firms. Median annual salaries for technicians employed by local governments in 2008 were $45,320.

Additional Information

For general information on a variety of technology fields requiring an Associate degree, see the following:

- The Pathways to Technology website is a partnership of the American Association of Community Colleges, the National Science Foundation, and WGBH, Boston, MA. This site provides information about technology degree programs offered at community colleges. Internet: http://www.pathwaystotechnology.org

  For information about a career as a biological technician, contact

- Bio-Link, 1855 Folsom St., Suite 643, San Francisco, CA 94103. Internet: http://www.bio-link.org

  For information about a career as a chemical technician, contact

- American Chemical Society, Education Division, Career Publications, 1155 16th St. NW, Washington, DC 20036. Internet: http://www.acs.org

chapter thirty

Health Education*

*Information in this chapter was obtained from Bureau of Labor Statistics. U.S. Department of Labor. *Occupational Outlook Handbook 2010–2011 Edition*. 2010, and other cited sources.

HEALTH EDUCATION

SIGNIFICANT POINTS

- Fifty-one percent of health educators work in health care and social assistance, and an additional 23% work in government.

- A Bachelor degree is the minimum requirement for entry-level jobs, but a Master degree may be required for certain positions or for advancement.

- Faster-than-average job growth is expected.

HEALTH EDUCATORS IN SPECIALIZED SETTINGS

The health field offers a variety of career opportunities to persons interested in education—community health education, school health education, educational therapy, and **special education**. These professions and specialties within them are detailed in this chapter.

Health education is an expanding field that emphasizes the importance of preventive health care. As professionals, **health educators** use educational skills and a sound knowledge of public health to educate the public about health and disease and what can be done to maintain good health, prevent disease, or secure treatment.

While the health educator concentrates on the nonschool community, **school health educators** are concerned with the school environment. Their main concerns are classroom teaching and the factors that influence the knowledge, behavior, attitudes, and practices that affect the health of students. Educational therapy is another career area of major importance in the health field. **Educational therapists** work with individuals who live with **emotional disturbance** or physical, geriatric, or other disability in a variety of health and educational facilities and in private practice. Educational therapists combine both educational and therapeutic approaches in treating individuals of all ages with learning disabilities or learning problems. Examples of learning disability are attention deficit disorder, poor social skills, poor organizational or study skills, language processing problems, or visual processing problems.

Career opportunities are also available for teachers in special education. Special education teachers work with pupils who have **physical disabilities**, emotional disturbances, mental retardation, or specific **mental and intellectual gifts and talents**. They also work with pupils experiencing **cultural differences**. These types of pupils are found in school systems, institutions, hospitals, or rehabilitation centers, and, because of their unusual or extraordinary traits, they need the services that only special education can provide.

A significant branch of the health education field presents challenging career opportunities for work with individuals who are blind or have visual impairments. Professionals in this work provide essential services to persons with these conditions, enabling them to function successfully in a sighted world. The different types of specialists who work with those who are blind or have visual impairment include **orientation and mobility instructors**, vision rehabilitation therapists, and other specially trained teachers.

HEALTH EDUCATORS

Work Description

Health educators work in a variety of settings in public health departments, nonprofit organizations, private businesses, hospitals and clinics, schools, colleges and universities.

Health educators employed by state and local departments of public health administer state-mandated programs. They also develop educational materials for use by other public health officials. During a weather emergency, for example, a hurricane or tornado, health educators may be responsible for disseminating information to both the media and the public. Educators often serve as members of statewide councils or national committees on topics such as aging. As part of this work, they inform other professionals in changes to health policy.

In nonprofits, which may be referred to as community health organizations, health educators provide the public with information related to health and educate people about the resources available to help people in the community. While some organizations target a particular audience, others educate the community regarding one disease or health issue. Therefore, health educators may be limited in either the topics they cover, the populations they serve, or both. Work in this setting may include creating print-based material for distribution to the community, often in conjunction with organizing lectures, health screenings, and activities related to increasing health awareness. Health educators may also form and lead community coalitions to address public health issues ranging from water quality to the availability of healthy food or access to safe exercise areas. They can work to set policy that will improve public health. Examples include working to advance legislation for the prohibition of smoking in public areas and the limitation of junk food in vending machines in schools.

When working in private businesses, health educators create programs to inform employees and that fit into workers' schedules by arranging lunchtime speakers or daylong health screenings so that workers may come when attendance is convenient. Educators in these business settings must align their work with the overall goals of their employers.

Within medical care facilities, health educators tend to work one on one with patients and their families. Their goal in this setting is to educate individual patients on their diagnosis and how that may change or affect their lifestyle. This often includes explaining necessary procedures or surgeries, as well as how patients will need to change their lifestyles in order to manage their illness or return to full health. This may include directing patients to outside resources that may be useful in their transition, such as support groups, home health agencies, or social services. Health educators often work closely with physicians, nurses, and other staff to create educational programs or materials, such as brochures, websites, and classes. In some cases, health educators train hospital staff how to interact better with patients.

Health educators in schools are typically found in secondary schools, where they generally teach health class. They develop lesson plans that are relevant and age appropriate to their students. They may need to cover sensitive topics, like sexually transmitted diseases, alcohol, and drugs. They may be required to teach other subjects, such as science or physical education. Some develop the health education curriculum for the school or the entire school district.

Health educators in colleges and universities work primarily with the student population. Generally, they create programs on health topics that affect young adults, like sexual activity, smoking, and nutrition. They may need to alter their teaching methods to attract audiences to their events. For example, they might show a popular movie and follow it with a discussion, or hold programs in dormitories or cafeterias. They may teach courses for credit or give lectures on health-related topics. Often they train students to lead their own programs as peer educators.

From a broad perspective there are seven major areas of responsibility for **health education programs**. Individual health educators may have responsibilities in one or all areas depending on the work setting and qualifications. These include

1. Assess need for health education.
2. Plan health education.
3. Implement health education.
4. Evaluate the effectiveness of health education.
5. Manage health education programs.
6. Serve as a health education resource.
7. Advocate for public health and health education through policy.

The basic function of health educators is to provide people with the facts about health, the causes of disease, and methods of prevention so they will act for their own well-being and that of their families. The basic goals and duties of health educators are the same, but their jobs vary greatly depending on the type of organization in which they work.

Health educators attempt to prevent illnesses by informing and educating individuals and communities about health-related topics. They assess the needs of their audience, which includes determining which topics to cover and how best to present the information. For example, they may hold programs on self-examinations for breast cancer detection to women who are at higher risk, or may teach classes on the effects of binge drinking to college students. Health educators must take the cultural norms of their audience into account. Programs targeted at the elderly may need to be drastically different from those aimed at college students. After assessing their audiences' needs, health educators must decide how to meet those needs. They have many options to choose from when putting together programs. Health educators may organize a lecture, class, demonstration, or health screening, or they may create a video, pamphlet, or brochure. Often, planning a program requires working with others on a team or committee within a given organization.

Health educators also must consider the goals and objectives of their employers when planning a program. For example, many nonprofit organizations educate the public about a single disease or health issue, such as cardiovascular disease, and therefore limit their programs to topics related to that disease or issue. After planning their effort, health educators move on to implementing their proposed plan. They may obtain funding by applying for grants, writing curricula for classes, or creating written materials that would be made available to the public. In addition, implementing their programs may require dealing with basic logistics problems, such as finding speakers or locations for the planned event.

Generally, after a program is presented, health educators evaluate its success. This could include tracking the absentee rate of employees from work and students from school, surveying participants on their opinions about the program, or other methods of collecting evidence that suggests whether the programs were effective. Through evaluation, health educators can improve plans for the future by learning from mistakes and capitalizing on strengths. Although programming is a large part of their job, health educators also serve as a resource on health topics. They may locate services, reference material, and other resources useful to the community they serve, and refer individuals or groups to appropriate organizations or medical professionals.

Although programming is a large part of their job, health educators also serve as a resource on health topics. They may locate services, reference material, and other resources useful to the community they serve, and refer individuals or groups to appropriate organizations or medical professionals.

Health educators may work through a wide variety of intermediaries in the community—teachers, club leaders, health officers, public health nurses, trade-union program directors, scout leaders, and community group leaders. In this way, health educators can reach a much larger audience than they would otherwise. These various intermediaries have a personal relationship with those being educated and are therefore likely to have a significant influence on them.

Health educators also work with the mass media, including newspapers, magazines, radio and television programs, trade newspapers, and organizational newsletters. They prepare or direct the preparation of appropriate articles, features, and photographs for use by the media, or work directly with writers, editors, or program directors. As a result, the influence of community health educators is extended to vast audiences that could not be reached otherwise. Contact with the public through the media is admittedly less desirable than personal contact. However, in health education, as in other educational efforts, many methods are used to complement and reinforce each other for a cumulative effect. Educators have recognized that it is not enough just to point out the hazards of one practice or the advantages of another. There are many obstacles to perception and appropriate action, including emotional resistance, language barriers, or psychological blocks. Whatever the obstacles are, it is the job of the health educator to identify them and devise methods to overcome or sidestep them. Otherwise, health education will be ineffective or will not take place, because health education is meant to be more than information—it is meant to motivate effective action. To overcome resistance, health educators use various techniques of investigation—interviews, surveys, and community studies—together with insights gained from psychology, sociology, and anthropology. A basic tenet of health educators is that the individuals they are educating should be the ones to make final decisions about health practices. Nevertheless, educators accept responsibility for providing access to all sources of necessary information so that individuals can relate desirable health practices to their personal goals, aspirations, and values.

Health educators thus serve as psychological stage setters, stimulating people in the community to recognize health problems of which they may be unaware and to work for their solution. Such problems might be pollution of the environment, chronic disease, overpopulation, drug abuse, or any of hundreds of ills that plague today's society. Health educators know that constructive group action can often accomplish wonders. Even more important, when people work together to solve a problem of common concern, they are more likely to arrive at a solution that will work.

When a particular community interest group is ready to act, the health educator helps its members set up effective relationships with other interested groups in the community—schools, churches, health agencies, welfare organizations, and labor unions. The health educator might assist in organizing a conference, planning a neighborhood cleanup campaign, or developing a television series dramatizing poor health conditions in farm labor camps. Whatever the duties they may take on in any particular case, the aim of educators is always to encourage more effective individual and group action designed to maintain and improve the health of people throughout the community.

Sometimes the obstacles to health-promoting action lie not with the community, but with the people providing health services. Clinic hours may be arranged more for the convenience of the professionals working there than for the public. Clinic staff may be curt and impersonal in their treatment of the people they serve. Advice may be given in technical terms rather than in language that laypeople can easily understand. In these cases, the health educator can play an important role by helping other health personnel plan and deliver health care in ways that the community can and will utilize. Community health educators also often have the task of educating legislators and other policy makers in the importance of considering consumer interests while planning and funding health programs.

With major changes taking place in the delivery of health care at local, regional, and national levels, the participation of health educators in planning groups is increasingly in demand. By seeking the involvement of all interested persons, health educators work toward the solution of a particular problem through a variety of avenues. They help to define common goals and to stimulate and guide discussion to assist various groups in reaching their own decisions and determining how they will implement them. Whether helping a ghetto neighborhood plan its own health center, or helping representatives from state agencies agree on needed regional medical facilities, the health educator helps people to help themselves by bringing needs and resources together to create new partnerships for health.

Frequently, improving health care involves training for health workers who must keep abreast of new knowledge in their own professional disciplines through continuing education; for young people entering a new health career; for neighborhood health aides who help to improve health communications among the poor; and for ethnic group members and citizen volunteers who are ready to assume community leadership. Here again, the health educator can contribute to better health by helping to develop training programs, by suggesting creative methods, and even by training the trainers themselves to be better teachers.

Educational and Legal Requirements

Entry-level health educator positions generally require a Bachelor degree in health education, but some employers prefer a Bachelor degree and some related experience gained through an internship or volunteer work. A Master degree may be required for some positions and is usually required for advancement. In addition, some employers may require candidates to be Certified Health Education Specialists. More than 250 professional preparation programs in the United States offer formal degrees in school and community/public health education at the baccalaureate, master's, and doctoral levels.

Undergraduate programs teach students the theories of health education, and courses develop the skills necessary to implement health education programs. Courses in psychology, human development, and a foreign language are helpful, and experience gained through an internship or other volunteer opportunities can make graduates more appealing to employers.

A graduate degree is usually required to advance to jobs such as executive director, supervisor, or senior health educator. Work in these positions may require more time on planning and evaluating programs than on their implementation, and may require supervising other health educators who implement the programs. Health educators at this level may also work with other administrators of related programs.

Graduate health education programs are often offered under titles such as community health education, school health education, or health promotion, and lead to a Master of Arts, Master of Science, Master of Education, or a Master of Public Health degree. Many students pursue their Master degree in health education after majoring or working in another related field, such as nursing or psychology. A Master degree is required for most health educator positions in public health. Doctoral degrees are also offered in public health education. Many persons with doctoral degrees in this specialty will continue to be needed to meet the growing demand for research and evaluation skills in health education and for teaching in institutions of higher learning.

Health educators may choose to become a Certified Health Education Specialist (CHES) or become certified at the master's level (MCHES). These credentials are offered by the National Commission of Health Education Credentialing, Inc. The certification is awarded after successful completion of an examination in the basic areas of responsibility for a health educator. In addition, to maintain certification, health educators must complete 75 hours of approved continuing education courses or seminars over a 5-year period. Some employers may require and pay for educators to take continuing education courses to keep their skills up to date.

Health educators spend much of their time working with people and must be comfortable working with both individuals and groups. They need to be good communicators and be comfortable speaking in public as they may need to teach classes or give presentations. Health educators often work with diverse populations, so they must be sensitive to cultural differences and open to working with people of varied backgrounds. Health educators often create new programs or materials, so they should be creative and skilled writers. They must be able to play a variety of roles successfully and adjust to the demands of different situations. At times, these educators work behind the scenes to help others start and carry out projects in the public interest. Sometimes they need to help people caught in conflict understand one another's point of view, while they maintain the trust and goodwill of all parties concerned. At other times, educators must be people's advocates until the people come forward to speak for themselves.

SCHOOL HEALTH EDUCATORS

Work Description

School health educators help children and young people develop the knowledge, attitudes, and skills they need to live healthfully and safely. They cooperate closely in this task with the school's physician and nurse, as well as with the school's other teachers and service personnel. Usually, they also participate in community health activities as representatives of the school health education program.

Health education has a place all the way from nursery school and kindergarten through high school and on into college because it deals with day-to-day living. It is health education when 5-year-olds learn to eat new foods, and when high school seniors make a field survey of the health services available in their community.

Depending on the school system and on the school grades covered, health courses may include such subject matter as family life education, first aid, safety education, choice and use of health services and products, nutrition, personal hygiene, air and water pollution, alcohol and drug abuse, and community health. Health courses include the principles of mental health and good human relations, as well as marriage and family life. Comprehensive health education curricula include sex education where allowed; in some states, it is required.

School health educators may have even broader responsibilities as health coordinators. School health coordinators may work in a single school or in an entire school system; they furnish leadership in developing and maintaining an adequate, well-balanced health program and helping all groups interested in the health of schoolchildren work together effectively.

Educational and Legal Requirements

The school health educator needs 4 years of college education leading to a Bachelor degree, with a background in the biological, behavioral, and social sciences and health education. Increasingly, a Master degree is required.

The school health educator must meet the regular certification standards for teachers in the state. Generally, these call for 15 to 20 credits in professional courses in a school of education. These courses usually include educational philosophy, the techniques of teaching, child growth and development, and educational psychology. A period of internship may also be required. These standards vary from state to state, and the student is advised to check desired locations for requirements.

For the school health educator, the advanced degree is usually in the field of health education. A doctoral degree is often required for college teaching jobs. The school health educator should have an aptitude for scientific and social studies. In general, personal qualifications for this educational specialist are similar to those for a successful teacher in any field. It is important to like working with children and young people and to have patience, a sense of humor, good judgment, and emotional stability.

Employment Opportunities

Growth will result from the rising cost of health care and increased access as a result of healthcare reform. As healthcare costs continue to rise, insurance companies, employers, and governments are attempting to find ways to curb costs. One of the more cost-effective ways is to employ health educators to teach people how to live healthy lives and avoid costly treatments for illnesses. There are a number of illnesses, such as lung cancer, HIV, heart disease, and skin cancer that may be avoided with lifestyle changes. Health educators are necessary to help the public better understand the effects of their behavior on their health. Other illnesses, such as breast and testicular cancer, are best treated with early detection, so it is important for people to understand how to detect possible problems on their own. The need to provide the public with this kind of information will result in state and local governments, hospitals, and businesses employing a growing number of health educators.

The emphasis on health education has been coupled with a growing demand for qualified health educators. In the past, it was thought that anyone could do the job of a health educator and the duties were often given to nurses or other health professionals. However, in recent years, employers have recognized that those trained specifically in health education are better qualified to perform those duties. Therefore, demand for health professionals with a background specifically in health education has increased.

Employment Trends in Health Education

Employment of health educators is expected to grow by 18%, which is faster than the average for all occupations through 2018. Demand for health educators is expected to increase in most industries, but their employment may decrease in secondary schools. Many schools, facing budget cuts, ask teachers trained in other fields, such as science or physical education, to teach the subject of health education. Job prospects for health educators with Bachelor degrees will be favorable, but better for those who have acquired experience through internships or volunteer jobs. A graduate degree is preferred by employers in public health and for non-entry-level positions.

Earnings

Salaries for health educators will vary depending on the work setting. Those in school-affiliated roles receive salaries and benefits on the same scale as other teachers in their school system. Health educators working in industry and government usually receive higher salaries, commensurate with their education and experience. Those in college teaching receive the same range of pay as other teachers. Those in consultant roles usually set their own fees, based on their location and other factors. Median annual earnings of health educators were $44,000 in May 2008; the middle 50% earned between $33,170 and $60,810. The lowest 10% earned less than $26,210, and the highest 10% earned more than $78,260. Median annual earnings in the industries employing the largest numbers of health educators in May 2008 are shown in **Table 30-1**.

TABLE 30-1   **Median Annual Earnings in the Industries Employing the Largest Numbers of Health Educators, May 2006**

General medical and surgical hospitals	$40,890
State government	33,100
Local government	32,420
Outpatient care centers	27,530
Individual and family services	25,760

EDUCATIONAL THERAPISTS

Work Description

Educational therapy is designed to meet the needs of individuals through instruction in prescribed subjects, and through assessment, treatment, and rehabilitation to assist individuals in reaching their fullest mental and physical capacities. Educational therapists work with people of all ages including preschool, elementary, secondary and college students, as well as adults in nonacademic settings. Educational therapy is part of a prescribed treatment program for clients with learning disabilities or learning problems that may be secondary to physical disabilities or medical conditions, emotional disturbance, or impaired cognition. Learning disabilities can interfere with processing, comprehension, or memorizing information. It is used mainly with clients who, because of their disability, require alternative approaches to learning. As the name implies, educational therapy is a form of teaching. However, the purpose is not so much to give knowledge as it is to stimulate interest, confidence, and self-esteem to overcome learning difficulties to function more effectively in academic or work settings.

As a member of the rehabilitation team, the educational therapist evaluates the patient's learning ability and retention of previous learning experiences, interests, needs, and goals.

Using this information, the therapist devises a treatment plan that fits into the patient's total rehabilitation program. The therapist then starts group or individual training in elementary, secondary, commercial, or vocational subjects to meet the needs and goals of the patient. Subject areas include reading, writing, and math and other courses as determined appropriate for the individual client, such as study skills and test-taking skills. For adults, courses in basic living skills and driver education may be appropriate. The educational therapist adapts course content and teaching methods to the patient's particular disability and individual needs.

Educational therapists may administer tests and send results to school authorities or state departments of education for grading and certification of the patient's education level. They also report the client's progress to the school, family, or rehabilitation team. Educational therapists also refer patients to other medical services or community education services such as colleges, universities, and credit-by-exam programs.

Work Environment

Many educational therapists work in Veterans Administration (VA) facilities such as hospitals, centers, domiciles, and regional offices. They are also employed in private and state schools, federal prisons, the Job Corps, and adult learning centers. Therapists work under the direction of doctors in VA facilities, but independently in other types of facilities.

Educational therapists usually work from 8:00 a.m. to 4:30 p.m., 5 days a week. Their work setting is often unstructured, and therapists are often allowed to organize and conduct patient therapy independently, under the direction of the chief therapist. Clinics are often small, with a staff of three to five therapists who work closely with patients on a one-to-one basis. There are no unusual physical demands in this work, and therapists who have visual impairments, are partly or almost completely paralyzed, or use prosthetic devices can be successful if they have adapted to their disabilities.

Educational and Legal Requirements

Certain personal qualities are essential for success in educational therapy. Among these are sensitivity to underlying moods and emotions, strong motivation to help people with disabilities overcome their difficulties, and the ability to "reach" and communicate with troubled people. Before deciding on this field, a student should gain some volunteer experience in a community or institutional healthcare setting, with exposure to health and other rehabilitation problems.

After completing high school, a student interested in a career in educational therapy must enroll in a 4-year Bachelor of Arts or Bachelor of Sciences degree program. The degree can be in elementary, secondary, or special education; child development; speech and language; or psychological counseling. Courses include educational assessment, learning theory, learning disabilities, principles of educational therapy, and emotional and physical disabilities. In addition to a college degree, 2 to 7 months of clinical training are required, either as in-service training or at a training center affiliated with a professional school. While in clinical training, the student observes patient treatments, attends patient conferences, and receives training in all areas of educational therapy. The student works with clients under the guidance of therapists in various specialties and is evaluated for job performance, completion of clinical projects, and successful completion of a final examination. Several training institutions also offer postgraduate programs for qualified educational therapists.

Professional membership in the Association of Educational Therapists (AET) is open to educational therapists who have a Master degree or have met the course requirements, are engaged in educational therapy, have met the direct service delivery minimum of 1500 hours, and have completed their Board Certified Educational Therapist (BCET®) Supervised Hours. To become a Board Certified Educational Therapist, AET members must meet the following additional requirements to sit for the certification exam: Master degree, 1-year membership in the AET at the Professional level, and 1000 hours of professional practice. The AET requires 40 hours of continuing education every 2 years to maintain Professional and Board Certified Educational Therapist membership.

Employment Opportunities

As life expectancy increases, there should be a greater need for therapists in programs for the aging. Disabilities resulting from military service or trauma, or those caused by daily stress and poor living conditions should create a number of jobs for educational therapists. Qualified therapists can advance to supervisory positions; promotions are generally based on work experience and the completion of advanced education courses.

ORIENTATION AND MOBILITY INSTRUCTORS FOR PEOPLE WHO ARE BLIND OR HAVE VISUAL IMPAIRMENTS

Work Description

Orientation and mobility instructors are specialists who teach people with blindness or visual impairments to move about effectively, efficiently, and safely in familiar and unfamiliar environments. They work with people of differing ages and abilities, from young children to adults who have recently lost their sight. They also may work with persons who have multiple disabilities. Their objective is to help these individuals adjust personally and achieve maximum independence through specialized training. Orientation and mobility instructors evaluate their clients to determine their level of adjustment, degree of motivation, and the extent and safety of their indoor and outdoor mobility. Based on this information, they plan and provide individualized programs for instruction.

Most instructors work on a one-to-one basis and assist clients in making the maximum use of their remaining senses, primarily auditory (sound) and tactile (touch). They train clients to orient themselves to physical surroundings and use a variety of actual or simulated travel situations to develop the client's ability to travel alone, with or without a cane. Instructors train clients to use mobility devices and human or dog guides, electronic travel aids, or other adaptive mobility devices. Orientation and mobility instructors evaluate and prepare progress reports on each of their clients and work closely with other professionals such as physicians and social workers, as well as volunteers and families of clients. They work with others to develop community resources within their area of expertise and attend various professional seminars, workshops, and conferences to keep abreast of the latest methods, techniques, and travel aids.

Work Environment

Orientation and mobility instructors are employed in residential and public schools, rehabilitation centers, and public and private community-based agencies, hospitals, nursing homes, and homes of clients. Working conditions for instructors vary from one facility to another. They normally can expect to work a 40-hour week, with hours from 8:00 a.m. to 4:30 p.m., and occasionally are required to work at a specific location. Instructors may sometimes accompany their clients to recreational activities and social gatherings.

Educational and Legal Requirements

Persons considering a career in this area must enjoy working with people and have the capacity to learn from as well as teach clients. This work requires instructors to work closely with other professionals as part of a rehabilitation team, as well as with families, friends, and colleagues of clients. Orientation and mobility instructors should possess mature judgment, emotional and social maturity, adaptability, resourcefulness, and leadership potential.

The basic educational requirement for this work is a Bachelor degree, although a Master degree is preferable. If the Bachelor degree is not in the specific field and a higher degree is being sought, it is preferred that the Bachelor degree be in one of the behavioral sciences. Programs consist of combined academic and clinical training; upon completion of the training, graduates are required to serve an internship. In addition, students entering this field must have no less than 20/40 visual acuity in the better eye with best possible correction and a minimum 140-degree continuous field measured together.

The Academy for Certification of Vision Rehabilitation and Education Professionals provides certification for orientation and mobility instructors who meet specified education and experience standards. However, there are no nationwide uniform legal requirements for licensing, certification, or registration that serve as standards for employment. State or local licensing agencies should be contacted to determine relevant current standards.

Employment Opportunities

Employment prospects for qualified orientation and mobility instructors are quite favorable, and available openings far exceed the number of graduates entering the labor market each year.

Orientation and mobility instructors can advance to supervisory, managerial, and administrative positions in this field. Generally, advancement is based on work experience and expertise, and the completion of advanced education courses.

VISION REHABILITATION THERAPISTS

Work Description

Visual rehabilitation therapists are specialists who provide instruction and guidance to individuals who are blind or those who have visual impairments. They develop plans of instruction that enable their clients to carry out daily activities, develop independence, and achieve satisfactory ways of living. Visual rehabilitation therapists work with individuals or small groups in the home setting, as well as in healthcare facilities, such as rehabilitation centers, hospitals, nursing homes, retirement homes, or community centers. They must have a broad knowledge of many subjects, and some may specialize in a particular skill. For example, they help those who are newly blind or congenitally blind develop communication skills by providing instruction in the use of braille, large print, recorded materials, low-vision aids, and telephones. In addition, they teach nonverbal communication skills, such as facial expressions, hand movements, and head nods for use in communication with sighted persons.

Visual rehabilitation therapists provide instruction in personal and home management skills for normal living. These skills include personal hygiene and grooming, table etiquette, cooking, budget preparation, childcare, and minor home repairs. These teachers also help clients obtain specially designed equipment, such as braille clocks and watches, sewing aids, and various types of appliances.

Each client with whom the visual rehabilitation therapist works is unique. Beyond the obvious fact that they are adults with visual impairments, the most common attribute of clients is that they are individuals with their own needs and desires, levels of functioning, and goals. These differences must be noted and respected by the therapist, whose role is to help the client reach the level of functioning he or she wishes, rather than make the client fit a preconceived image.

Educational and Legal Requirements

Students considering this career area can expect to spend 4 to 6 years in preparation after completing high school. The minimum educational standard for entry into this field is a Bachelor degree from an accredited college; however, a Master degree in this specialization is preferable in most cases.

The Academy for Certification of Vision Rehabilitation and Education Professionals certifies visual rehabilitation therapists who meet specified education and experience requirements. However, there are no national legal standards concerning licensure, registration, certification, or continuing education. State or local licensing agencies should be contacted to obtain information specific to a particular locale.

Employment Opportunities

The need for qualified visual rehabilitation therapists is growing due to increases throughout the country in the number of persons experiencing blindness or visual impairment, particularly among senior citizens. There are currently 6.8 million Americans with visual impairments; one-third are 65 years and older, and the number of older adults with vision loss or impairment is expected to double by 2030. The elderly often do not receive the assistance needed to maintain independence with loss of vision. Each of these individuals will need the professional, specialized services that only a **rehabilitation teacher** can provide.

Qualified visual rehabilitation therapists can advance to supervisory or administrative positions in health agencies, or to teaching positions in colleges or universities. Generally, advancement in this field is governed by experience, skill level, and the completion of advanced education programs.

TEACHERS FOR PEOPLE WHO ARE BLIND OR HAVE VISUAL IMPAIRMENTS

Work Description

Teachers trained to teach students who are blind or have visual impairments provide specialized educational services to children in residential, public, or private schools. Residential schools are those in which children live and attend regular classes with other children who are also blind. Teachers in these schools usually concentrate their efforts on teaching a single subject, such as history or mathematics, but they may also be called on to give special education courses.

Resource programs differ from residential schools and programs by allowing students to attend regular public school classes. In these programs, a central location is provided for use by participating students from several school districts. Here, resource teachers provide instruction in special skills, such as braille or the use of recording devices. In addition, the teachers make certain that the students' assignments are up to date and that each student has required lessons in braille, large type, or recorded form. Besides working directly with their students, resource teachers coordinate their efforts with classroom teachers, school psychologists, and parents to ensure that educational objectives are being met.

An **itinerant program** is the third type of program employing teachers for students with blindness or visual impairments. In itinerant programs, teachers travel from school to school and meet with students on a regularly scheduled basis. In this way, students are able to attend classes at their regular neighborhood school and receive special instruction there, without needing to travel to a central school district location. Teachers in itinerant programs also act as consultants on special education to classroom teachers, parents, and school officials. It is important to note that teachers specializing in instruction of those with blindness or visual impairments, regardless of the type of program in which they work, may be called on to teach a wide range of regular school subjects along with special education courses.

Educational and Legal Requirements

Students considering this career area can expect to spend from 4 to 6 years in preparation after completing high school. The educational minimum for entry into this work is a Bachelor degree from an accredited college; however, a Master degree is preferred in most cases.

The Academy for Certification of Vision Rehabilitation and Education Professionals certifies teachers who meet specified education and experience requirements to become certified. In addition, these teachers must be certified or licensed by the department of education in the state in which they work. Because these requirements vary throughout the country, students considering this career should contact their local superintendent of schools or state department of education to obtain specific information.

Employment Opportunities

Employment prospects in this career area are favorable. As greater numbers of children with visual impairments require specialized education services, the demand for qualified teachers is expected to grow. Should they wish to do so, qualified teachers in this specialty can advance to supervisory and administrative positions or teach at the college level. Advancement is usually based on experience, skill level, and the completion of advanced education courses.

Related Occupations

Health education is a profession that bridges the gap between health information and health practices. It also seeks to encourage the responsibility of individuals for their own health and to work toward the national goal of optimal health for all. Other members of the healthcare team who engage in similar work include dietitians, nurses, physicians, physical therapists, occupational therapists, vocational rehabilitation counselors, and other related health professionals.

Additional Information

For further information, contact

- Academy of Certification of Vision Rehabilitation and Education Professionals, 3333 N. Campbell Ave., Suite 2, Tucson, AZ 85719. Internet: http://www.acvrep.org
- American Association for Health Education, 1900 Association Dr., Reston, VA 20191. Internet: http://www.aahperd.org/aahe
- American Counseling Association, 5999 Stevenson Ave., Alexandria, VA 22304. Internet: http://www.counseling.org
- American Foundation for the Blind, 2 Penn Plaza, Suite 1102, New York, NY 10121. Internet: http://www.afb.org
- American School Health Association, 7263 State Route 43, P.O. Box 708, Kent, OH 44240. Internet: http://www.ashaweb.org
- Association of Educational Therapists, 11300 W. Olympic Bend, Suite 600, Los Angeles, CA 90064. Internet: http://www.aetonline.org
- Association of Schools of Public Health, 1011 15th St. NW, Suite 910, Washington, DC 20005. Internet: http://www.asph.org
- Commission on Rehabilitation Counselor Certification, 1699 E. Woodfield Rd., Suite 300, Schaumburg, IL 60173. Internet: http://www.crc-certification.com
- National Commission for Health Education Credentialing, Inc., 1541 Alta Dr., Suite 303, Whitehall, PA 18052-5642. Internet: http://www.nchec.org
- National Rehabilitation Association, 633 S. Washington St., Alexandria, VA 22314. Internet: http://www.nationalrehab.org

- Online Resource for U.S. Disability Statistics: http://www.ilr.cornell.edu/edi/disabilitystatistics
- Online Tool for Career Exploration and Job Analysis: http://www.onetonline.org
- Society for Public Health Education, 750 First St. NE, Suite 910, Washington, DC 20002. Internet: http://www.sophe.org
- Video clip on the Health Education Specialist: http://www.sophe.org/healthedspecialist.cfm
- U.S. Department of Health and Human Services, HRSA, Bureau of Health Professions, 5600 Fishers Ln., Room 805, Rockville, MD 20857. Internet: http://www.hrsa.gov

chapter thirty-one

Nonclinical and Health-Related Professions*

*All information in this chapter, unless otherwise indicated, was obtained from Bureau of Labor Statistics. U.S. Department of Labor. *Occupational Outlook Handbook 2010–2011 Edition*. 2010.

HEALTH PROFESSIONS NOT INVOLVED IN THE CLINICAL CARE OF A PATIENT

The general public has a strong interest in health, medicine, and science and desires to learn more about them. People want to understand what is happening and how new developments will affect their lives and careers. Advanced communication technology has made delivery of this knowledge possible; the publishing and broadcast media provide both oral and written materials in these fields.

In addition, public and private organizations and agencies have a professional interest in keeping the public informed. They know that people who are informed about current developments and discoveries in health and medicine show more initiative in getting medical, dental, or preventive care for their families and themselves. These agencies and organizations also want to keep the public interested and involved in starting and supporting adequate healthcare facilities in the form of community hospitals, clinics, and mobile screening units.

In addition to the general public, other more specialized groups seek **health information**. These individuals include the various health professionals who require authoritative information to keep abreast of developments in their fields. There are many career opportunities in health information and communications; the following pages discuss the qualifications and duties of **biological photographers**, medical writers, science writers, technical writers, and medical illustrators.

Another important part of health information and communications is maintaining medical records and data for various health facilities. Typically, a health facility employs a staff consisting of a **medical record administrator**, **medical record technician**, **medical transcriptionist**, and other clerical personnel to handle all facets of medical information. They prepare medical reports; organize, analyze, and preserve the medical information of patients; and develop a variety of statistical reports. Maintaining this flow of health information is an extremely important function, because it is used in evaluating patient care, diagnosing and treating illness, and planning healthcare activities. Careers involving medical records and data are discussed in Chapter 27.

Library services in the health field occupy an important place in health information and communication activities. Year after year, a vast store of knowledge accumulates in many branches of medicine, in medical research, and in scientific research related to medicine. This knowledge is recorded in periodicals, textbooks, monographs, and other publications. These publications, coming from every part of the world, are collected in the medical library, where they are made available to health professionals.

Doctors, nurses, dentists, pharmacists, therapists of various kinds, technicians, and those studying for these health professions may come to the library for texts or monographs on a subject of special interest. They may search the journals for background material or for research reports on the latest developments in their fields. Research scientists and research students also use the medical and scientific journals; these are the main sources of information on what has been done and what is currently being done in their fields.

Libraries are maintained by almost all hospitals, schools, research institutions, and pharmaceutical houses, and by many other health organizations. They vary in size and function, but all serve to maintain information needed by their staffs, students, patients, or other interested persons. This is discussed in Chapter 27.

BIOLOGICAL PHOTOGRAPHERS
SIGNIFICANT POINTS

- Biological photographers should be skilled and creative.
- Responsibility includes, among others, the production of still and motion pictures in the medical and health fields.
- A successful biological photographer depends on job training and/or formal education.
- Some jobs require the ability to multitask and adjust to different environmental conditions.
- Some specialize in ophthalmic photography, photomicrography, cinematography, dental photography, or autopsy/specimen photography, among others.
- Job opportunities should be excellent.

Work Description

Biological photographers are scientific professionals responsible for the production of still and motion pictures of subjects for the health professions and natural sciences. These specialists apply a complete range of photographic skills creatively to complete a variety of assignments. Their role in health information and communications is very important. They prepare and produce motion pictures, videotapes, prints, and transparencies to document and record a broad spectrum of subjects and events used for education, patient records, and research, and as illustrations in publications. Photography is used to document the absence, presence, extent, and progress of a patient's disease or injury, and still or motion pictures are used to record and study surgical procedures. Furthermore, photographs of specimens can be magnified to serve as records or to illustrate medical conditions for use in classrooms, courtrooms, or research laboratories. Biological photographers also participate in the planning, coordination, production, and dissemination of educational programs encompassing both visual and auditory media, and they are key personnel in any project in which the recording of diagnosis, treatment, special technology, or any other aspect of health care is critical.

A biological photographer can specialize in one of several areas. **Ophthalmic photography**, for example, involves the use of specialized equipment and techniques to photograph disorders and injuries of the eye; **photomicrography** involves photographs taken through a microscope; and **cinematography** is the production of motion pictures. Other specializations include **dental photography**, which records dental techniques and procedures, and **autopsy/specimen photography**, in which postmortem or surgical specimens are documented.

Biological photographers are employed by many public and private hospitals; universities; medical schools; federal health organizations; research institutions; dental, veterinary, or natural science facilities; and some private medical and pharmaceutical suppliers. For the most part, they work regular hours, within normal hospital, office, or laboratory environments, and are not normally required to travel extensively. Occasionally, the physical conditions under which a biological photographer works change quite dramatically. For instance, he or she may spend some time working in close contact with patients, doctors, and staff members, along with some time in isolation working in the darkroom. Biological photographers may also come in contact with harmful chemicals, strong odors, and contagious diseases when carrying out assignments. The biological photographer must, therefore, have the ability to adapt to a wide range of tasks and environmental conditions in addition to being skilled and creative in this profession.

Educational and Legal Requirements

There are several ways to prepare for a career in biological photography. A number of colleges and universities offer full 4-year programs leading to a Bachelor degree in this field. Other educational institutions provide training in 2-year programs and grant a certificate or Associate degree. One of the accrediting agencies for these training programs is the Biological Photographic Association. Many individuals acquire skills in this work by successfully completing on-the-job or apprenticeship training programs, which may last up to 2 to 3 years.

Certification in this field is not mandatory, but those seeking certification can obtain the requirements through the Board of Registry of the BioCommunication Association. The prerequisites for certification are 2 years of satisfactory employment or training in an accredited school, plus successful completion of a three-part examination. Many employers determine general requisites before making final education or training arrangements for their employees.

Employment Opportunities

Growth in biological photography is quite rapid and is closely related to the entire healthcare industry, the growth of medical education, and the increased documentation requirements of government and independent agencies. Because photography occupies an increasingly significant place in scientific and medical research and education, opportunities are expected to be favorable for these specialized skills.

Advancement opportunities in this field, as in many other health career areas, depend on the individual system worked out by the employer.

Government agencies usually have career ladders with several steps, each of which represents an advancement opportunity. Private industry and education may have other opportunities. The biological photographer typically advances from photographic technician through photographer positions to department or service head. Possibilities also include general health facility administration or related positions in education for individuals with advanced degrees or experience.

Earnings

Earnings vary with education, experience, level of responsibility, performance, industry, amount of unionization, geographic area, specialized services rendered, and whether the practitioner is self-employed or part time. Using figures released by various agencies, both private and public, the range of salary for biological photographers was $29,000 to $39,000 in 2010.

Additional Information

For further information, contact

- BioCommunication Association, 220 Southwind Ln., Hillsborough, NC 27278. Internet: http://www.BCA.org

MEDICAL ILLUSTRATORS

SIGNIFICANT POINTS

- Medical illustrators are artists with an interest and a basic understanding of biological sciences and technology.
- They are sometimes known as paramedical artists.
- They provide a visual presentation of items of interest in various forums such as scientific publications or education programs based on science such as biology, medicine, and so on.
- They present information clearly and aesthetically.
- Job opportunities should be excellent for these specialized artists.

Work Description

Medical and scientific illustrators combine artistic skills with knowledge of the biological sciences. Medical illustrators draw illustrations of human anatomy and surgical procedures. Scientific illustrators draw illustrations of animals and plants. This artwork is used in medical and scientific publications and in audiovisual presentations for teaching purposes. Medical illustrators also work for lawyers, producing exhibits for court cases and doctors.

Medical illustrators can best be described as paramedical artists who illustrate medical or biological subjects using many types of visual presentations.

Historically, artists did detailed and complicated drawings of life systems because drawings were the only means available to capture and communicate the essence of scientific subjects. At one time, the illustrator's work was limited to drawings and charts for medical journals, textbooks, monographs, and similar publications. Later, additional technical training became necessary as a variety of graphic arts techniques began to be used to illustrate surgical procedures, anatomical and pathological specimens, clinical disorders, and microorganisms.

The health professions depend on the illustrator to produce visual presentations for their own use and for the public. Scientific illustrations are now widely used in general magazines, professional journals, textbooks, exhibits, and pamphlets. Medical education relies heavily on the work of medical illustrators, and with recent advancements in instructional technology using specially prepared audiovisual materials for teaching in the medical and health sciences, the medical illustrator's role of visual interpretation has expanded into a variety of new applications. For the most part, medical illustrators are employed by or do freelance work for hospitals, clinics, medical schools, public and private research institutes, large pharmaceutical firms, and medical publishing houses. Regardless of where medical illustrators are employed, their final illustrations must present information clearly and aesthetically.

Today's medical illustrators have broadened their scope and use drawings, models, photography, exhibits, and television to record facts and progress in many health fields, and they work with physicians, research scientists, educators, and authors. Illustrators tend to specialize along lines required by the employer. For example, a medical book publishing company may need illustrators with special photographic or illustration skills, and a museum may require an illustrator with a strong background in **medical sculpture**. Illustrators may also work with specialists in subjects such as anatomy, pathology, embryology, and ophthalmology.

Educational Requirements

Students intending to become medical illustrators should be science minded, with the scientist's capacity for accurate observation, and they must have the ability to visualize imaginatively and persevere. Medical illustrating is not a career for everyone interested in art. High school studies should include biology, other science courses, foreign languages, and courses in design. Students should document interest in various graphic art forms, still-life drawing in particular, and maintain a portfolio demonstrating ability in several media. Programs of education for medical illustrators require 6 to 7 years of college-level study beyond the high school level.

Earnings

Earnings vary with education, experience, level of responsibility, performance, industry, amount of unionization, geographic area, specialized services rendered, and whether the practitioner is self-employed or part time. Using figures released by various agencies, both private and public, the range of salary for medical illustrators was $33,000 to $61,000 in 2010.

Additional Information

For information on careers in medical illustration, contact

- The Association of Medical Illustrators, 201 E. Main St., Suite 1405, Lexington, KY 40507. Internet: http://www.ami.org
- Commission on Accreditation of Allied Health Education Programs, 1361 Park St., Clearwater, FL 33756. Internet: http://www.caahep.org

WRITERS: MEDICAL, SCIENCE, AND TECHNICAL
SIGNIFICANT POINTS

- They must have the ability to write in professional English.
- Most have a background in journalism.
- Skills are acquired through formal education and/or on-the-job training.
- They must be meticulous with details and accurate in the interpretation of information.
- Employment may be found in news media, hospitals, education institutes, industries, voluntary health programs, government agencies, and many others.
- There are excellent employment opportunities due to the Internet and an increase in careers in the health fields.

Individuals with good communication skills, a basic knowledge of life sciences, and an interest in health care or in medical research and development are finding career opportunities as medical writers in the mass media, the medical press, industry, hospitals, medical schools, and other settings. Technological, clinical, and sociological changes in the field of medicine and health are occurring at an unprecedented rate. As a result, both healthcare professionals and the general public represent vast audiences for medical news, information, and instructional material at virtually all levels of sophistication and in all media.

Work Description

In response to the public's keen interest in medicine and health, many newspapers, magazines, radio stations, and television stations employ trained journalists who function as science writers and specialize in interpreting scientific and technical developments for the general public. Their job is to acquaint the public with what is happening in the field of medicine: new treatments for cancer or heart disease, improved surgical techniques, research gains for the mentally ill, and changing concepts of health care.

Like other science writers in the mass media, medical writers not only report, but also interpret. Unlike sports writers, whose audience is already familiar with the subject, writers in the health field must explain new and complex developments in nontechnical terms that can be readily understood by a lay audience. Moreover, because of the critical nature of the subject, medical writers must be meticulously accurate and objective in presenting facts. The physicians, scientists, and health administrators to whom medical journalists look for information will hesitate to talk freely unless they know the writers are competent and trustworthy. Similarly, the confidence of the public depends on the writer's caution and integrity. Because these writers deal with experts from every branch of medicine and related disciplines, they must have at least a speaking acquaintance with the health sciences. Medical writers might interview neurosurgeons one day, pharmacologists the next, and biomedical engineers the next. They ask pertinent questions, weigh the value of the answers, and obtain additional supporting evidence. Finally, they present the information in such a way that it will not be misunderstood.

Other medical writers with training or experience in journalism—or in its "sister" discipline, public relations—are employed by hospitals, clinics, medical schools, voluntary health agencies, and medical societies as health information specialists. These communicators are responsible for keeping the public as well as their organization's personnel, clients, and supporters informed about the achievements, programs, and concerns of the organization. To generate and sustain good public relations, health information specialists may develop informational brochures, plan exhibits, publish "in-house" newsletters and magazines, and arrange for media coverage. To accomplish these tasks, health information specialists must have working knowledge of almost every medium of communication.

Medical writers sometimes function as technical writers specializing in reporting and writing about scientific and technical developments, primarily for users. In industry, and to a lesser extent in nonprofit medical research laboratories, there is growing demand for individuals who have a basic knowledge of electronics, biochemistry, or other technical subjects, as well as good communication skills and an interest in medicine and health. Developers and manufacturers of sophisticated diagnostic and treatment devices such as electrocardiographs, computerized imaging systems, heart-lung machines, and hemodialysis equipment employ medical writers in a variety of capacities. As in other settings, scientists, engineers, and health professionals working in industry rarely have the proficiency and time to meet all needs for scientific and technical information—hence the demand for medical communicators who can digest complex source material and write clearly and accurately for diverse audiences. Medical writers may produce promotional literature for health professionals and administrators or educational information for patients. Like other technical writers, they may prepare instruction manuals for operating and maintenance technicians, proposals, or reports for scientists and engineers, management, or a company's stockholders. With the increasing application of computers in medicine, some medical writers are now involved in the development of software. To become familiar with their subject, these writers may study technical books, journals, working papers, and mathematical data; interview scientific personnel; or tour laboratories, hospitals, and field stations. Often they simply work with the "raw material" provided by scientists, engineers, and health professionals.

Medical writers may find similar career opportunities in the pharmaceutical industry, which invests great amounts of money in the research and development of new drugs and new applications for existing drugs. Pharmaceutical companies have an ongoing need for individuals who can assist in documenting and reporting new discoveries and in promoting product lines. Pharmaceutical writers may prepare abstracts of journal articles, package inserts (descriptions of a drug's actions, indications, contraindications, and side effects), or reports of research findings. They may write market research reports or articles for in-house periodicals. Those with a **creative bent** may produce sales brochures, advertising copy, or other promotional material; scripts for educational films or closed-circuit broadcasts; or exhibits to be displayed at medical conferences. Like their counterparts in the medical equipment industry, pharmaceutical writers use all possible sources to become familiar with their subject.

Medical writers are employed by government agencies, companies that publish newspapers and magazines for health professionals, advertising agencies, film and art studios, and book publishing companies.

Within most settings there are opportunities for communicators at all levels of experience and expertise—and, quite often, for freelancers, who are hired for specific assignments as the need arises. Responsibilities in the field of medical writing span a wide range. At one end of the spectrum are such critical but relatively simple tasks as editing others' writing to ensure grammatical correctness and clarity of presentation, checking the accuracy of references, or proofreading. At the other end is such challenging and sophisticated work as writing books on medical subjects for laypersons, directing a corporate publications department, or designing and managing a new periodical.

Work Environment

In general, medical writers work in comfortable and well-lighted surroundings. They usually work a 40-hour week, but may be called on to put in additional hours to meet publication deadlines.

Educational Requirements

Medical writing is not a well-defined profession with a prescribed course of training and a standardized licensing or certification procedure. On the contrary, it is a field characterized by its practitioners' diversity of background, expertise, and professional responsibilities and activities. On-the-job training is the most common.

Physicians, allied health professionals, or scientists are often the writers of medical research reports, textbooks, and other highly technical materials.

The great majority of medical writers do not have advanced training in a healthcare discipline.

Although there are no uniform standards for entry into the field, a Bachelor degree from a 4-year college is generally considered a minimum requirement. To develop the background and skills essential to a medical writing career, students should take as many courses as possible in the life sciences and in English composition, journalism, or a related discipline. In addition, a few basic courses in electronics, electrical and mechanical engineering, or in basic physics can be useful. Although graduate education is not a formal requirement, more and more medical writing jobs are going to individuals with advanced degrees in scientific, medical, or communication specialties.

Perhaps more important than a specific educational background are personal characteristics such as the ability to think clearly and precisely, to pay close attention to detail, to handle the English language with ease, and to deal comfortably with a variety of people. It is interesting to point out that most medical or science writers in the printed news media learn their skills via "on-the-job" training. Most start out as reporters.

Employment Opportunities

Employment prospects in this field are favorable. Opportunities for qualified medical writers tend to grow in direct proportion to the accumulation of new data from basic research and clinical studies, the increasing sophistication of both experimental and clinical technology, the growing use of audio-visual teaching techniques, the increasing numbers of medical conferences and workshops, the growth of medical specialty journals and news publications for health professionals, the need for more frequent updating of medical textbooks, the greater use of computers in medicine, the creation of new abstracting and indexing services, and the mounting public interest in health-related information and issues. In this era of increasingly complex diagnostic techniques, constant therapeutic discoveries, growing interest in the prevention of disease and disability, and enormous expenditures on healthcare services and products, the need for well-trained and informed medical writers has never been greater. However, because many people are interested in this type of career, there may be heavy competition for jobs, especially in the mass media. Individuals considering a career in medical writing should carefully evaluate the labor market in the area in which they intend to work.

As in most professions, the skills helpful for entry may not be sufficient for advancement. For example, a recent college graduate with a major in biology, a minor in English, and perhaps some typing ability may find employment as an editorial assistant in a research laboratory or in a medical publishing house. To advance to a position such as director of communications for a research laboratory or series development editor for a medical publisher, the individual would have to acquire additional knowledge of medicine, become expert in many facets of communication, and develop whatever other skills may be required in a particular setting or particular medium. Skills necessary for advancement may be acquired through continuing education, practical experience, or both. In general, those who advance in this field are avid readers, careful researchers, meticulously accurate writers, flexible stylists who can adapt to the requirements of various media, and disciplined and dedicated workers who recognize the importance of deadlines.

Earnings

Earnings vary with education, experience, level of responsibility, performance, industry, amount of unionization, geographic area, specialized services rendered, and whether the practitioner is self-employed or part time.

Additional Information

For further information, contact

*   American Medical Writers Association, 30 West Gude Dr., Suite 525, Rockville, MD 20850. Internet: http://www.amwa.org
*   National Association of Science Writers, P.O. Box 7905, Berkeley, CA 94707. Internet: http://www.nasw.org

MEDICAL SECRETARIES

SIGNIFICANT POINTS

*   They perform similar duties as secretaries or administrative personnel in any modern office of a company, although their work is health oriented.
*   They are the backbone of the labor force in the office of a hospital, medical school, drug company, or similar industries.
*   Most employers require at least a high school diploma.
*   Employment opportunities are good, especially at the entry level.

Work Description and Environment

Medical secretaries work in private medical offices, hospitals, clinics, group practices, and other health facilities. Their responsibilities are limited to administrative and clerical duties, and they are not trained to assist physicians with clinical or laboratory tasks. Medical secretaries are primarily responsible for the orderly, efficient operation of the office. Typical duties include keeping individual medical records, taking simple medical histories, filling out insurance forms, and billing patients for medical services. They also schedule appointments for patients, arrange for patients to be hospitalized, handle telephone inquiries, and act as receptionists for incoming patients. Medical secretaries take dictation and type correspondence, reports, and manuscripts. They may also do bookkeeping, prepare financial records, and handle credit and collections for their employers.

Medical secretaries generally work in pleasant surroundings in modern medical offices. Their work is often performed under pressure and requires patience and tact at all times in dealing with patients.

Educational and Legal Requirements

Persons considering this career should be high school graduates or the equivalent, preferably with courses in English, biology, and typing. They should be familiar with or gain knowledge of computer word processing, spreadsheets, and database programs. A sound knowledge of spelling, punctuation, grammar, and vocabulary is also important. Accredited vocational schools and junior or community colleges offer 1- or 2-year programs in secretarial science, with a medical option. Graduates of 1-year programs receive certificates; those in 2-year programs are awarded the Associate in Applied Science degree. Although postsecondary education is not required for all beginning jobs in this field, it may be helpful in gaining initial employment and for job advancement.

In some cases, persons with secretarial experience in other fields prepare for this career by taking medical terminology and related courses as part of a continuing education program.

Employment Opportunities

Employment prospects for qualified medical secretaries are expected to be quite favorable. This outlook is based on increased public demand for health services; the expansion of medical facilities, **HMOs**, and group medical practices; and broader insurance coverage by government-sponsored and private health insurance plans. Qualified medical secretaries can advance to such positions as administrative assistant or office manager.

Earnings

Earnings vary with education, experience, level of responsibility, performance, industry, amount of unionization, geographic area, specialized services rendered, and whether the practitioner is self-employed or part time. Using figures released by various agencies, both private and public, the range of salary for medical secretaries was $30,000 to $40,000 in 2010.

Additional Information

For information on the latest trends in the profession and career development advice, contact

- International Association of Administrative Professionals, P.O. Box 20404, Kansas City, MO 64195-0404. Internet: http://www.iaap-hq.org
- Association of Executive and Administrative Professionals, 900 South Washington St., Suite G-13, Falls Church, VA 22046. Internet: http://www.theaeap.com

appendix A

Salaries for Health Professions

Profession	Salary
Animal care and service worker	$15,140–$31,590/year
Cardiovascular technologist and technician	$25,510–$74,760/year
Clinical laboratory technician	$23,480–$53,520/year
Clinical laboratory technologist	$36,180–$74,680/year
Dentist	$142,870/year
Dental assistant	$22,270–$46,150/year
Dental hygienist	$44,180–$91,470/year
Dental laboratory technician	$20,740–$58,140/year
Dietetic technician	$26,080 median/year
Dietitian	$31,460–$73,410/year
Emergency medical technician (paramedic)	$9.08–$23.77/hour
Healthcare worker	$30,590–$50,500/year
Health educator	$26,210–$78,260/year
Health information administrator	$60,730–$101,670/year
Health information technician	$20,440–$50,060/year
Health services manager	$48,300–$137,800/year
Home care aide	$7.81–$10.98/hour
Home health aide	$7.65–$13.93/hour
Human service worker	$25,260–$41,720/year
Inspector/compliance officer	$42,180–$77,210/year
Medical appliance technician	$21,720–$63,750/year
Medical assistant	$20,600–$39,570/year
Medical laboratory technician	$23,480–$53,520/year
Medical laboratory technologist	$36,180–$74,680/year
Medical librarian	$43,650–$82,110/year
Medical record technician	$20,440–$50,060/year
Medical transcriptionist	$10.76–$21.81/hour

Profession	Salary
Nuclear medicine technologist	$48,450–$87,700/year
Nurse, practical (LVN)	$28,260–$53,580/year
Nurse, registered	$43,410–$92,240/year
Nursing aide/orderly/attendant	$8.34–$15.97/hour
Nursing home administrator	$50,210–$79,270/year
Occupational therapist	$42,820–$98,310/year
Occupational therapy aide	$17,850–$46,910/year
Occupational therapy assistant	$31,150–$65,160/year
Ophthalmic laboratory technician	$18,080–$42,890/year
Optician, dispensing	$21,250–$50,580/year
Optometrist	$70,140–$179,205/year
Pharmacist	$77,390–$131,440/year
Pharmacy aide	$7.69–$14.26/hour
Pharmacy technician	$9.27–$18.98/hour
Physical therapist	$50,350–$104,350/year
Physical therapy aide	$17,270–$33,540/year
Physical therapy assistant	$28,580–$63,830/year
Physician	$186,044–$339,738/year
Physician assistant	$51,360–$110,240/year
Psychiatric aide	$8.35–$18.77/hour
Psychologist	$37,900–$106,840/year
Radiation therapist	$47,910–$104,350/year
Radiology technologist technician	$35,100–$74,970/year
Recreational therapist	$23,150–$60,280/year
Respiratory technician	$25,760–$55,430/year
Respiratory therapist	$37,920–$69,800/year
Social and human service assistant	$17,900–$43,510/year
Social assistant, except child day care	$9.41–$25.01/hour
Social worker	$25,870–$66,430/year
Sonographers, diagnostic, medical	$43,600–$83,950/year
Speech-language audiologist	$40,360–$98,880/year
Speech-language pathologist	$41,240–$99,220/year
Surgical technician	$27,510–$54,300/year
Veterinarian	$46,610–$143,660/year
Veterinarian technologist or technician	$19,770–$41,490/year

Notes: (1) Most data are from *Occupational Outlook Handbook 2010–2011*, U.S. Department of Labor. (2) Only salaries of major health professions are shown. Space limitation does not permit the listing of all health and health-related jobs. (3) Earnings vary with education, experience, level of responsibility, performance, industry, amount of unionization, geographic area, specialized services rendered, and whether the practitioner is self-employed or part-time. (4) No attempt is made to show variance by specialties. (5) Salaries shown are income averages and change rapidly over time. (6) For details, updates, and data on unlisted health professions, consult the Additional Information section for each profession in the chapters. Use the resources and Internet websites where applicable.

appendix B

Sources of Career Information

This appendix is provided for student use from the Occupational Outlook Handbook, 2010–2011 Edition. *Listed below are several places to begin collecting information on careers and job opportunities.*

Like any major decision, selecting a career involves a lot of fact finding. Fortunately, some of the best informational resources are easily accessible. You should assess career guidance materials carefully. Information that seems out of date or glamorizes an occupation—overstates its earnings or exaggerates the demand for workers, for example—should be evaluated with skepticism. Gathering as much information as possible will help you make a more informed decision.

PEOPLE YOU KNOW

One of the best resources can be your friends and family. They may answer some questions about a particular occupation or put you in touch with someone who has some experience in the field. This personal networking can be invaluable in evaluating an occupation or an employer. These people will be able to tell you about their specific duties and training, as well as what they did or did not like about a job. People who have worked in an occupation locally also may be able to give you a recommendation and get you in touch with specific employers.

EMPLOYERS

This is the primary source of information on specific jobs. Employers may post lists of job openings and application requirements, including the exact training and experience required, starting wages and benefits, and advancement opportunities and career paths.

INFORMATIONAL INTERVIEWS

People already working in a particular field often are willing to speak with people interested in joining their field. An informational interview will allow you to get good information from experts in a specific career without the pressure of a job interview. These interviews allow you to determine how a certain career may appeal to you while helping you build a network of personal contacts.

PROFESSIONAL SOCIETIES, TRADE GROUPS, AND LABOR UNIONS

These groups have information on an occupation or various related occupations with which they are associated or actively represent. This information may cover training requirements, earnings, and listings of local employers. These groups may train members or potential members themselves, or they may be able to put you in contact with organizations or individuals who perform such training. One valuable source for finding organizations associated with occupations is the *Encyclopedia of Associations*, an annual publication that lists trade associations, professional societies, labor unions, and other organizations.

GUIDANCE AND CAREER COUNSELORS

Counselors can help you make choices about which careers might suit you best. They can help you establish what occupations suit your skills by testing your aptitude for various types of work and determining your strengths and interests. Counselors can help you evaluate your options and search for a job in your field, or help you select a new field altogether. They can also help you determine which educational or training institutions best fit your goals, and then assist you in finding ways to finance them. Some counselors offer other services such as interview coaching, résumé building, and help in filling out various forms. Counselors in secondary schools and postsecondary institutions may arrange guest speakers, field trips, or job fairs.

You can find guidance and career counselors at many common institutions, including

- High school guidance offices
- College career planning and placement offices
- Placement offices in private vocational or technical schools and institutions
- Vocational rehabilitation agencies
- Counseling services offered by community organizations
- Private counseling agencies and private practices
- State employment service offices

When using a private counselor, check to see that the counselor is experienced. One way to do so is to ask people who have used the counselor's services in the past. The National Board of Certified Counselors and Affiliates is an institution that accredits career counselors. To verify the credentials of a career counselor and to find a career counselor in your area, contact

- National Board for Certified Counselor and Affiliates, 3 Terrace Way, Suite D, Greensboro, NC 27403-3660. Internet: http://www.nbcc.org/directory/FindCounselors.aspx

POSTSECONDARY INSTITUTIONS

Colleges, universities, and other postsecondary institutions typically put a lot of effort into helping place their graduates in good jobs, because the success of their graduates may indicate the quality of their institution and may affect the institution's ability to attract new students. Postsecondary institutions commonly have career centers with libraries of information on different careers, listings of related jobs, and alumni contacts in various professions. Career centers frequently employ career counselors who generally provide their services only to their students and alumni. Career centers can help you build your résumé; find internships and co-ops, which can lead to full-time positions; and tailor your course selection or program to make you a more attractive job applicant.

LOCAL LIBRARIES

Libraries can be an invaluable source of information. Because most areas have libraries, they can be a convenient place to look for information. Also, many libraries provide access to the Internet and e-mail. Libraries may have information on job openings, locally and nationally; potential contacts within occupations or industries; colleges and financial aid; vocational training; individual businesses or careers; and writing résumés. Libraries frequently have subscriptions to various trade magazines that can provide information on occupations and industries. Your local library also may have video materials. These sources often have references to organizations that can provide additional information about training and employment opportunities. If you need help getting started or finding a resource, ask your librarian for assistance.

INTERNET RESOURCES

A wide variety of career information is easily accessible on the Internet. Many online resources include job listings, résumé posting services, and information on job fairs, training, and local wages. Many of the resources listed elsewhere in this section have Internet sites that include valuable information on potential careers. No single source contains all information on an occupation, field, or employer; therefore, you will likely need to use a variety of sources.

When using Internet resources, be sure that the organization is a credible, established source of information on the particular occupation.

Individual companies may include job listings on their websites, and may include information about required credentials, wages and benefits, and the job's location. Contact information, such as whom to call or where to send a résumé, is usually included.

Some sources exist primarily as Web services. These services often have information on specific jobs and can greatly aid in the job-hunting process. Some commercial sites offer these services, as do federal, state, and some local governments. *Career OneStop*, a joint program by the Department of Labor and the states as well as local agencies, provides these services free of charge.

Online Sources from the Department of Labor

A major portion of the U.S. Department of Labor's Labor Market Information System is the *Career OneStop* site. This site includes links to the following:

- State job banks allow you to search over a million job openings listed with state employment agencies.
- *America's Career InfoNet* provides data on employment growth and wages by occupation; the knowledge, skills, and abilities required by an occupation; and links to employers.
- *America's Service Locator* is a comprehensive database of career centers and information on unemployment benefits, job training, youth programs, seminars, educational opportunities, and disabled or older worker programs.

Career OneStop, along with the National Toll-Free Jobs Helpline (877-USA-JOBS) and the local One-Stop Career Centers in each state, combine to provide a wide range of workforce assistance and resources:

- Career OneStop. Internet: http://www.careeronestop.org

Use the O*NET numbers at the start of each Handbook statement to find more information on specific occupations:

- O*NET Online. Internet: http://www.onetcenter.org/

The Department of Labor's Bureau of Labor Statistics publishes a wide range of labor market information, from regional wages for specific occupations to statistics on national, state, and area employment:

- Bureau of Labor Statistics. Internet: http://www.bls.gov

Although the *Handbook* discusses careers from an occupational perspective, a companion publication—*Career Guide to Industries*—discusses careers from an industry perspective:

- *Career Guide to Industries.* Internet: http://www.bls.gov/oco/cg/

  For information on occupational wages, see

- Wage Data. Internet: http://www.bls.gov/bls/blswage.htm

  For information on training, workers' rights, and job listings, see

- Employment and Training Administration. Internet: http://www.doleta. gov/jobseekers

Organizations for Specific Groups

Some organizations provide information designed to help specific groups of people. Consult directories in your library's reference center or a career guidance office for information on additional organizations associated with specific groups.

Disabled Workers

Information on employment opportunities, transportation, and other considerations for people with a wide variety of disabilities is available from

- National Organization on Disability, 1625 K St. NW, Suite 850, Washington, DC 20006. Telephone: (202) 293-5960. Internet: http://www.nod.org/

  For information on making accommodations in the workplace for people with disabilities, contact

- Job Accommodation Network (JAN), P.O. Box 6080, Morgantown, WV 26506. Internet: http://www.jan.wvu.edu

  A comprehensive federal website of disability-related resources is accessible at

- Internet: http://www.disability.gov

Blind Workers

Information on the free national reference and referral service for the blind can be obtained by contacting

- National Federation of the Blind, 200 East Wells St., at Jernigan Place, Baltimore, MD 21230. Telephone: (410) 659-9314. Fax: (410) 685-5653. Internet: http://www.nfb.org

Older Workers

- National Council on the Aging, 1901 L St. NW, 4th Floor, Washington, DC 20036. Telephone: (202) 479-1200. Internet: http://www.ncoa.org
- National Caucus and Center on Black Aged, Inc., Senior Employment Programs, 1220 L St. NW, Suite 800, Washington, DC 20005. Telephone: (202) 637-8400. Fax: (202) 347-0895. Internet: http://www.ncba-aged.org

Veterans

Contact the nearest regional office of the U.S. Department of Labor's Veterans Employment and Training Service or

- Credentialing Opportunities Online (COOL), which explains how military personnel can meet civilian certification and license requirements related to their Military Occupational Specialty (MOS). Internet: http://www.cool.army.mil

Women

- Department of Labor, Women's Bureau, 200 Constitution Ave. NW, Washington, DC 20210. Telephone: (800) 827-5335. Internet: http://www.dol.gov/wb

Federal laws, executive orders, and selected federal grant programs bar discrimination in employment based on race, color, religion, sex, national origin, age, and handicap. Information on how to file a charge of discrimination is available from U.S. Equal Employment Opportunity Commission offices around the country. Their addresses and telephone numbers are listed in telephone directories under U.S. Government, EEOC. Telephone: (800) 669-4000. TTY: (800) 669-6820. Internet: http://www.eeoc.gov.

Office of Personnel Management

Information on obtaining civilian positions within the federal government is available from the U.S. Office of Personnel Management through USA-Jobs, the federal government's official employment information system. This resource for locating and applying for job opportunities can be accessed through the Internet or through an interactive voice response telephone system at (703) 724-1850 or TDD (978) 461-8404.

- USA Jobs: http://www.usajobs.opm.gov

Military

The military employs and has information on hundreds of occupations. Information is available on tuition assistance programs, which provide money for school and educational debt repayments. Your local military recruiting office can provide information on military service. Also see the *Handbook* statement on Job Opportunities in the Armed Forces. You can find more information on careers in the military at

• Today's Military. Internet: http://www.todaysmilitary.com

appendix C

How to Create an Effective Résumé

All information in this appendix was modified from *Training Manual and Supplements*, Transition Assistance Program, U.S. Department of Labor Veterans' Employment and Training Service, September 2007, available at http://www.dol.gov. This discussion offers examples of résumé preparation. The final version of any individual résumé will depend on the job seeker's career plans and choices.

PURPOSE OF A RÉSUMÉ

- Marketing tool—sells YOU!
- Summarizes how your skills and abilities can contribute to the work of a company or other employer
- Helps you land a job interview
- Serves as an employer screening tool

To write the most effective résumé, you need to determine the career field that interests you and research the following:

- The career field you would like to pursue
- Where the jobs are and who is hiring
- What qualifications and credentials you need to attain
- How best to market your qualifications

RÉSUMÉ FORMATS

The four major résumé formats to choose from are
1. Chronological (see **Figure C-1**)
2. Functional (see **Figure C-2**)
3. Combination (see **Figure C-3**)
4. Targeted

Chronological Format

- Focuses on your work history with most recent position first
- Allows potential employers to follow your career history and career progression easily

Functional Format

- Focuses on your skills and experience; skills are grouped into functional areas
- Used most often when changing careers or to address employment gaps

Combination Format

- Combines the chronological and functional résumé formats
- Highlights skills while providing the chronological work history that some employers prefer

Targeted Format

- Customized to a specific job
- Written specifically to the employer's needs

The résumé's Objective Statement is important and must refer specifically to the position sought. The résumé will then be directed to the appropriate company personnel. There are other more specialized résumé formats, but they will not be discussed here.

RÉSUMÉ COMPARISON

One can evaluate the appropriateness of each of the four types of résumé formats by studying the comparison chart in **Figure C-4**. Only a few of the many aspects of preparing a suitable résumé are discussed here. For more details, major reference sources are

- The original U.S. Department of Labor document mentioned at the beginning of this appendix.
- The career development centers located in most educational institutions, including high schools, colleges, and universities.
- Public library resources devoted to jobs and careers.

Ben Turner

2345 Brook Avenue, Englewood, CO 12345

(123) 456-7890

ben.turner@email.com

OBJECTIVE

Seeking a position as an armed security guard for Pinkerton Services

SUMMARY OF QUALIFICATIONS

Active U.S. government security clearance

Bilingual—fluent in both English and Spanish

Superior performance award for past 4 years in security management

Able to make difficult decisions in stressful situations

EXPERIENCE

19XX–20XX **Security Specialist** U.S. Marine Corps

Supervised $100 million of highly sensitive equipment—efforts led to zero loss in a 3-year period.

Implemented new system security plan that led to increased lockdown protection for brig personnel.

Provided leadership, instruction, and supervision of 25 personnel—efforts resulted in a 30% decrease in staff turnover and a 10% increase in promotions.

Expertly managed investigative reports—recognized as NCO of the Quarter for efficiency and accuracy of written instructions and documents.

Proven ability to communicate effectively in diverse environments—efficiently managed a diverse workforce and inmate population resulting in a 10% decrease in inmate violence.

19XX–19XX **Warehouse Supervisor** Micro Chemical, Inc., Denver, CO

Supervised a crew of 15 in daily operations, including evaluation and discipline—efforts led to a company-record promotion rate for staff and a 10% decrease in staff turnover.

Monitored complex cataloging and ordering systems, implemented a fast-track procurement system for office supplies resulting in a 20% decrease in supply turnaround.

Helped develop and implement an effective security system—efforts led to $24K savings annually by reducing pilferage and damage.

Proficient at using Windows Vista, Microsoft Office, and PeopleSoft Databases.

19XX–19XX **Security Guard** Mayfield Malls, Denver, CO

Coordinated work assignments, evaluated performance, and disciplined a four-member security team—recognized as "Security Supervisor of the Quarter" for boosting morale and encouraging an innovative and safe working environment.

Investigated security and safety violations and wrote detailed incident reports—led to Mayfield Mall being recognized as the "Safest Shopping Facility in the Mountain States."

Helped diffuse conflicts in a public environment with regard to everyone's safety—consistently recognized through customer feedback for excellent customer relations.

EDUCATION

U.S. Marine Corps Specialized Training: Explosives, Firearms, Leadership, Diversity, Communication

Metro State College 42 Semester Units in Administration of Justice, Denver, CO

FIGURE C-1 Sample chronological résumé.

Ben Turner

2345 Brook Avenue, Englewood, CO 12345

(123) 456-7890

ben.turner@email.com

OBJECTIVE

Seeking a position as an armed security guard for Pinkerton Services

SUMMARY OF QUALIFICATIONS

Active U.S. government security clearance

Bilingual—fluent in both English and Spanish

Superior performance award for past 4 years in security management

Able to make difficult decisions in stressful situations

EXPERIENCE

Security

- Supervised $100 million of highly sensitive equipment—efforts led to zero loss in a 3-year period.
- Implemented new system security plan that led to increased lockdown protection for brig personnel.
- Monitored restricted personnel in a correctional facility ensuring they remained in detention.
- Helped develop and implement an effective security system—efforts led to $24K savings annually by reducing pilferage and damage.

Investigation

- Investigated security and safety violations and wrote detailed incident reports—led to Mayfield Mall being recognized as the "Safest Shopping Facility in the Mountain States."
- Expertly managed investigative reports—recognized as NCO of the Quarter for efficiency and accuracy of written instructions and documents.

Communication

- Proven ability to communicate effectively in diverse environments—efficiently managed a diverse workforce and inmate population resulting in a 10% decrease in inmate violence.
- Helped diffuse conflicts in a public environment with regard to everyone's safety—consistently recognized through customer feedback for excellent customer relations.
- Proficient at using Windows Vista, Microsoft Office, and PeopleSoft Databases.

Supervision

- Provided leadership, instruction, and supervision of 25 personnel—efforts resulted in a 30% decrease in staff turnover and a 10% increase in promotions.
- Supervised a crew of 15 in daily operations, including evaluation and discipline—efforts led to a company-record promotion rate for staff and a 10% decrease in staff turnover.

EMPLOYMENT HISTORY

Security Specialist U.S. Marine Corps

Warehouse Supervisor Micro Chemical, Inc. Denver, CO

Security Guard Mayfield Malls, Denver, CO

EDUCATION

U.S. Marine Corps Specialized Training: Explosives, Firearms, Leadership, Diversity, and Communication

Metro State College 42 Semester units in Administration of Justice, Denver, CO

FIGURE C-2   Sample functional résumé.

Ben Turner

2345 Brook Avenue, Englewood, CO 12345

(123) 456-7890

ben.turner@email.com

OBJECTIVE

Seeking a position as an armed security guard for Pinkerton Services

SUMMARY OF QUALIFICATIONS

- Active U.S. government security clearance
- Bilingual—fluent in both English and Spanish
- Superior performance award for past 4 years in security management
- Able to make difficult decisions in stressful situations

EXPERIENCE

Security

- Supervised $100 million of highly sensitive equipment—efforts led to zero loss in a 3-year period.
- Implemented new system security plan that led to increased lockdown protection for brig personnel.
- Monitored restricted personnel in a correctional facility ensuring they remained in detention.
- Helped develop and implement an effective security system—efforts led to $24K savings annually by reducing pilferage and damage.

Investigation

- Investigated security and safety violations and wrote detailed incident reports—led to Mayfield Mall being recognized as the "Safest Shopping Facility in the Mountain States."
- Expertly managed investigative reports—recognized as NCO of the Quarter for efficiency and accuracy of written instructions and documents.

Communication

- Proven ability to communicate effectively in diverse environments—efficiently managed a diverse workforce and inmate population resulting in a 10% decrease in inmate violence.
- Helped diffuse conflicts in a public environment with regard to everyone's safety—consistently recognized through customer feedback for excellent customer relations.
- Proficient at using Windows Vista, Microsoft Office, and PeopleSoft Databases.

Supervision

- Provided leadership, instruction, and supervision of 25 personnel—efforts resulted in a 30% decrease in staff turnover and a 10% increase in promotions.
- Supervised a crew of 15 in daily operations, including evaluation and discipline—efforts led to a company-record promotion rate for staff and a 10% decrease in staff turnover.

EMPLOYMENT HISTORY

- 19XX–20XX Security Specialist, U.S. Marine Corps
- 19XX–19XX Warehouseman Supervisor, Micro Chemical, Inc., Denver, CO
- 19XX–19XX Security Guard, Mayfield Malls, Denver, CO

EDUCATION

- **U.S. Marine Corps** Specialized Training: Explosives, Firearms, Leadership, Diversity, and Communication
- **Metro State College** 42 Semester units in Administration of Justice, Denver, CO

FIGURE C-3   Sample combination résumé.

Resume Format	Advantages	Disadvantages	Best Used By
Chronological	• Widely used format • Logical flow, easy to read • Showcases growth in skills and responsibility • Easy to prepare	• Emphasizes gaps in employment • Not suitable if you have no work history • Highlights frequent job changes • Emphasizes employment but not skill development • Emphasizes lack of related experience and career changes	• Individuals with steady work record
Functional	• Emphasizes skills rather than employment • Organizes a variety of experience (paid and unpaid work, other activities) • Disguises gaps in work record or a series of short-term jobs	• Viewed with suspicion by employers due to lack of information about specific employers and dates	• Individuals who have developed skills from other than documented employment and who may be changing careers • Individuals with no previous employment • Individuals with gaps in employment • Frequent job changers
Combination	• Highlights most relevant skills and accomplishments • De-emphasizes employment history in less relevant jobs • Combines skills developed in a variety of jobs or other activities • Minimizes drawbacks such as employment gaps and absence of directly related experience	• Confusing if not well organized • De-emphasizes job tasks, responsibilities • Requires more effort and creativity to prepare	• Career changers or those in transition • Individuals reentering the job market after some absence • Individuals who have grown in skills and responsibility • Individuals pursuing the same or similar work as they have had in the past
Targeted (should be used in all resumes)	• Personalized to company/position • Shows research • More impressive to employer • Written specifically to employer's needs	• Time consuming to prepare • Confusing if not well organized • Should be revised for each employer	• Everyone—because any of the other formats can be made into a targeted resume

FIGURE C-4 Resume comparison chart.

appendix D

References

America's Health Responders. U.S. Public Health Service Commissioned Corps. U.S. Department of Health and Human Services. Internet: http://www.usphs.gov

ASPH Policy Brief. Confronting the Public Health Workforce Crisis. Executive Summary. Association of Schools of Public Health. Washington, DC; 2008.

Barely Hanging On: Middle-Class and Uninsured. A State-by-State Analysis. Robert Wood Johnson Foundation/State Health Access Data Assistance Center. Minneapolis, MN; 2010.

Bredesen P. *Fresh Medicine. How to Fix Reform and Build a Sustainable Health Care System.* New York, NY: Atlantic Monthly Press; 2010.

Centers for Medicare and Medicaid Services. *Real Choice Systems Change.* Community and Long-Term Supports. 2010. Internet: http://www.cms.gov/CommunityServices/30_RCSC.asp

Clinical Integration—The Key to Real Reform. TrendWatch. American Hospital Association. 2010.

Cohen RA, Martinez ME, Ward BW. *Health Insurance Coverage: Early Release of Estimates from the National Health Interview Survey, 2009.* National Center for Health Statistics. June 2010. Internet: http://www.cdc.gov/nchs/nhis.htm

County Health Rankings. Mobilizing Action Toward Community Health, Robert Wood Johnson Foundation and University of Wisconsin Population Health Institute. 2010. Internet: http://www.countyhealthrankings.org/about-project

Department of Labor. Bureau of Labor Statistics. *Employment Projections.* Data released February 2010. Internet: http://www.bls.gov/bls/employment.htm

Dill MJ, Salsberg ES. *The Complexities of Physician Supply and Demand: Projections Through 2025.* Center for Workforce Studies. Washington, DC: Association of American Medical Colleges; 2008.

Education Therapy Defined. Association of Educational Therapists. 2009. Internet: http://www.aetonline.org/about/defined.php

Erickson W, Lee C, von Schrader S. *Disability Statistics from the 2008 American Community Survey (ACS).* March 17, 2010. Ithaca, NY: Cornell University Rehabilitation Research and Training Center on Disability Demographics and Statistics (StatsRRTC). Internet: http://www.disabilitystatistics.org

Federal Health Insurance Reforms 2010. Health Insurance. Health Resources and Research. National Conference of State Legislators. Washington, DC; 2010. Internet: http://www.ncsl.org/Default.aspx?TabID=160

Haddock CC, McLean RA, Chapman RC. *Careers in Healthcare Management. How to Find Your Path and Follow It.* Chicago, IL: Health Administration Press; 2002.

Health Care. Health Care Reform. Internet: http://www.whitehouse.gov/issues/health-care

Health Education Specialist. Promoting a Healthy World. Society for Public Health Education; 2010. Internet: http://www.sophe.org/healthedspecialist.cfm

Health Educator Job Analysis 2010 Update. Role and Responsibilities of Health Education. American Association for Health Education, National Commission for Health Education. Credentialing and Society for Public Health Education; 2010.

Health Reform Details. Putting Americans in Control of their Health Care. The Administration. The White House; 2010. Internet: http://www.whitehouse.gov/health-caremeeting/proposal/titlevii

Health Reform in Action. Health Care. Issues. The White House; 2010. Internet: http://www.whitehouse.gov/healthreform

Hoffman C, Schwartz K, Howard J, Tolbert J, Cook A, Lawton E. *The Uninsured. A Primer. Key Facts About Americans Without Health Insurance.* Kaiser Family Foundation's Commission on Medicaid and the Uninsured and the Urban Institute. Kaiser Family Foundation. Report #7451-05. Washington, DC; 2009.

Immigrants' Health Coverage and Health Reform: Key Questions and Answers. Focus on Health Reform. Publication no. 7982. Menlo Park, CA: Kaiser Family Foundation; 2009.

Klein RJ. *Healthy People 2010. Progress Review Focus Area 18. Mental Health and Mental Disorders.* Health Promotion Statistics Branch. National Center for Health Statistics; 2007.

Morrisey MA. *Health Insurance.* Chicago, IL: Health Administration Press; 2007.

National Summary of New Health Reform Law. Focus on Health Reform. Publication no. 8061. Menlo Park, CA: The Henry J. Kaiser Family Foundation; 2010.

Summary Report for 29-1122.01—Low Vision Therapists, Orientation and Mobility Specialists, and Vision Rehabilitation Therapists. O*NetOnline. 2010. Internet: http://www.onetonline.org/link/summary/29-1122.01

U.S. Department of Health and Human Services. *Find Insurance Options.* Washington, DC; 2010. Internet: http://www.healthcare.gov/index.html

Workforce 2015: Strategy Trumps Shortage. American Hospital Association's 2009 Long-Range Policy Committee. American Hospital Association; 2010.

glossary

accredited record technician (ART) A medical record technician that has completed a 2-year program and passed a written exam.

acute infectious disease An illness with sudden onset that has a intense but short effect on the body.

ADA American Dental Association.

adaptive equipment Special equipment designed to facilitate everyday functioning for patients.

ADHA American Dental Hygienists Association.

AND Nurse associate degree in nursing.

advanced life support units Carry tools and equipment similar to what is found in a hospital.

advanced practice nurse (APN) Specialty that requires at least a master's degree.

advanced practice nursing Requires education beyond a bachelor's degree and specific experience and skills. Examples are oncology clinical nurse specialist, nurse midwife, and nurse practitioner.

aerosol liquid Medications suspended in a gas that forms a mist the patient inhales.

Affordable Care Act (ACA) Healthcare reform legislation signed into law by President Barack Obama in March 2010.

allergists Treat conditions and illnesses caused by allergies or related to the immune system.

allopathic System of medical practice that aims to combat disease by use of remedies producing effects different from or incompatible with those produced by the disease being treated.

Alzheimer's disease A degenerative brain disease of unknown cause that is the most common form of dementia, which usually starts in late middle age or in old age as a memory loss for recent events spreading to memories for more distant events and progressing over the course of five to ten years to a profound intellectual decline characterized by dementia and personal help-lessness.

ambulatory care Care that is provided outside of institutional settings.

ambulatory monitoring Used to monitor brain activity over a 24-hour period.

American Dietetic Association (ADA) Committed to improving the nation's health and advancing the profession of dietetics through research, education, and advocacy.

American Health Insurance Exchange Part of the healthcare reform legis-lation of 2010. Exchanges will be established by states to serve as clearing-houses for federally subsidized health insurance for uninsured individuals and small businesses.

American Medical Association (AMA) Helps doctors help patients by unit-ing physicians nationwide to work on the most important professional and public health issues.

American Physical Therapy Association (APTA) A national professional organization whose goal is to foster advancements in physical therapy prac-tice, research, and education.

American Registry of Diagnostic Medical Sonographers (ARDMS) Certify the skills and knowledge of sonographers through credentialing, including registration.

American Registry of Radiologic Technologists (ARRT) Promotes high standards of patient care by recognizing qualified individuals in medical imaging, interventional procedures, and radiation therapy.

anesthesiologist Uses drugs and gases to render patients unconscious during surgery.

animal and human health Control of diseases transmissible from animals to humans.

animal technician Conducts clinical work in a private practice under the supervision of a licensed veterinarian.

apprenticeship program Combination of on-the-job training and related instruction where workers learn the aspects of a specific occupation.

Area Health Education Centers (AHECs) Academic and community part-nerships that provide health career recruitment programs for K–12 students and increase access to health care in medically underserved areas.

art therapy Uses the concept of art as a device for nonverbal expression and communication.

arterial blood Sample blood sample taken from an artery instead of a vein.

artifact An electrocardiographic wave that arises from sources other than the heart or brain.

assessments Determine the needs of a specific population.

assistant administrator Manage the day to day responsibilities in large companies or facilities.

assisted living care Provides assistance with daily living activities.

assistive devices Medical equipment designed to help patients with disabilities perform everyday tasks and activities. Also known as protective or preventive devices including tape, bandages, and braces that athletes or their trainers use to protective, prevent, or avoid injuries during a sport or other form of training that involves the human body.

associate administrator Manages the day to day responsibilities in large companies or facilities.

audiologist Works with people who have hearing, balance, and related ear problems.

autopsy/specimen photography Postmortem or surgical specimens are documented.

behavior therapists Professionals who help individuals to modify their behavior in an aspect of their life. As an example, a behavior therapist may be asked to modify the eating behavior of an obese person.

biological photographer Scientific professionals responsible for the production of still and motion pictures of subjects for the health professions and natural sciences.

biological sciences The study of the branch of knowledge that deals with living organisms and vital processes.

blood pH A measure of the acidity or alkalinity level of the blood.

blood bank Technology the collection and preparation of blood products for transfusion.

Blue Cross Blue Shield Collectively, provides healthcare coverage for more than 100 million people or one-in-three Americans.

board examination Standardized licensing examinations for a specific area a medical practice.

bone injuries Injuries to body bones most common among athletes in certain sports, for example, injury to wrist bones among tennis players.

brain wave Mapping computer generated images of brain functions.

BSN Nurse bachelor's of science degree in nursing.

budget The amount of money that is available for, required for, or assigned to a particular purpose.

business dietitian Works as a professional resource for corporations in product development, food styling, and menu design; as the sales professional or purchasing agent representing food, equipment, or nutrition product accounts; and as a food, nutrition, or marketing expert in public relations and media.

calibration The standardization of a measuring instrument by finding the deviation from a standard to determine the proper correction factors.

capitation Paying the physician a fixed amount per person per unit of time without regard to the volume of services provided.

cardiologist physicians Physicians who study the heart and its functions in health and disease.

cardiology technologist Assists physicians in diagnosing and treating heart and blood vessel ailments.

cardiopulmonary diseases Disease of the heart and/or lungs.

career alteration Due to new technology additional training of healthcare providers that is needed when a new machine or technique is introduced.

catastrophic health care Designed for healthy individuals not requiring regular doctor visits. Coverage is limited to the cost of major hospital and medical expenses associated with an unexpected accident or illness.

Centers for Medicare & Medicaid Services (CMS) Strives to ensure effective, up-to-date healthcare coverage and to promote quality care for beneficiaries.

centrifuge machine Using centrifugal force for separating substances of different densities.

Certificate of Clinical Competence in Audiology (CCC-A) Issued to individuals who present evidence of their ability to provide independent clinical services to patients diagnosed with auditory disorders.

Certificate of Clinical Competence in Speech-Language Pathology (CCC-SLP) Issued to individuals who present evidence of their ability to provide independent clinical services to patients diagnosed with speech or language disorders.

certified nurse midwife Provides primary care to women, including gynecological exams, family planning advice, prenatal care, assistance in labor and delivery, and neonatal care.

certified registered nurse anesthetists Provide anesthetics to patients in every practice setting, and for every type of surgery or procedure.

Certified Respiratory Therapist (CRT) Credential to those who graduate from entry-level or advanced programs accredited by CoARC and who also pass an exam.

chest physiotherapy Treatment prescribed after surgery to help return the patient's lungs to their normal level of functioning and prevent the lungs from becoming congested.

chief executive officer (CEO) Provides overall management direction to an organization.

child or adult protective services Social workers investigate reports of abuse and neglect and intervene if necessary.

child welfare/family services social worker Provides social services and assistance to improve the social and psychological functioning of children and their families and to maximize the well-being of families and the academic functioning of children.

Children's Health Insurance Program (CHIP) Healthcare insurance for children from families with incomes too high for the child to be eligible for Medicaid but too low to afford the cost of premiums for private health insurance.

chronic illness A disease that is long in duration, reoccurs frequently, and progresses slowly.

cinematography Production of motion pictures.

city, county, district, state, and federal laws Regulate sanitary standards for food and water supplies; garbage, waste, and sewage disposal; as well as housing maintenance.

clinical chemistry The chemical analysis of body fluids.

clinical dietitian Provides nutritional services for patients in hospitals, nursing homes, clinics, or doctors' offices.

clinical laboratory (medical) technician Performs laboratory testing in conjunction with pathologists.

clinical laboratory (medical) technologist A mid-level laboratory supervisor who generally has an associate degree and performs a range of routine tests and laboratory procedures.

clinical nurse specialist Provides direct patient care and expert consultations in one of many nursing specialties.

clinical psychologist Specializes in the assessment and treatment of persons with mental and emotional problems and illnesses.

clinical social worker Makes recommendations to courts, prepares presentencing assessments, and provides services to prison inmates.

CNAs Certified nurse assistants.

code A system of symbols used to represent assigned meanings.

cognitive skills Competent use of one's intellectual activity (as thinking, reasoning, remembering, imagining, or learning words).

Committee on Accreditation for Respiratory Care (CoARC) Promotes quality respiratory therapy education through accreditation services.

communication disorders Disruption in the regular or normal functions of communication.

communication skills A set of skills that enables a person to convey information so it is received and understood.

community dietitian Counsels individuals and groups on sound nutrition practices to prevent disease and to promote good health.

community-based care Delivery of health care in outpatient clinics, surgical centers, or the home instead of in hospitals, nursing homes, or rehabilitation centers.

companion animal medicine Encompasses the prevention, diagnosis, and treatment of pet diseases.

compounding The actual mixing of ingredients to form powders, tablets, capsules, ointments, and solutions.

computerized tomography (CT) Radiography where a three-dimensional image of a body structure is constructed by computer from a series of plane cross-sectional images made along an axis.

consultant dietitian Works under contract with healthcare facilities or in their own private practices.

consultant Gives professional advice or services.

consumer safety Inspectors and officers inspect food, feeds, pesticides, weights and measures, biological products, cosmetics, drugs, medical equipment, and radiation-emitting products.

continuing care Facilities that allow residents to move from independent living, to assisted living, to a skilled nursing facility as their needs change.

contrast medium A solution of iodine or barium sulfate that is introduced into the body to contrast an internal part with its surrounding tissue in radiographic visualization.

corrective lens Lens that is worn in front of the eye to correct problems with vision.

corrective therapy Used to treat patients by applying medically prescribed physical exercises and activities that strengthen and coordinate body functions and prevent muscular deterioration caused by inactivity due to illness.

cost of training Physician's training is costly, according to the Association of American Medical Colleges; more than 80 percent of medical school graduates were in debt for educational expenses.

counseling psychologist Helps normal or moderately maladjusted persons, either individually or in groups, to gain self-understanding, recognize problems, and develop methods of coping with their difficulties.

criminal justice social worker Makes recommendations to courts, prepares presentencing assessments, and provides services to prison inmates.

CT technologist A radiographer who specializes in computed tomography.

cultural difference The customary beliefs, values, and traits of a racial, religious, or social group that distinguishes one from another.

cytotechnologist Screens human cell samples under a microscope for early signs of cancer.

cytotechnology The study of human body cells.

DO Doctor of Osteopathic Medicine.

dance therapy Used with individuals who have emotional and physical impairments as a tool to further emotional and physical integration and well-being.

DAT Dental Admissions Test.

defibrillator An electronic device used to restore a heart by applying an electric shock to it.

demographics The dynamic balance of a population.

dental assistant Assists dentists by performing a variety of patient care, office, and laboratory duties.

dental hygienist Cleans teeth, provides other preventive dental care, and teaches patients how to practice good oral hygiene.

dental photography Records dental techniques and procedures.

Department of Defense (DOD) Branch of the U.S. government that provides health care for active and retired members of the military service and their families in clinics, rehabilitation centers, and hospitals.

Department of Health and Human Services (DHHS) The U.S. government's principal agency for protecting the health of all Americans and providing essential human services, especially for those who are least able to help themselves.

dermatologist Treats infections, growths, and injuries related to the skin.

developmental disability A term used in the United States and Canada to describe lifelong disabilities attributable to mental and/or physical impairments manifested prior to age 18.

developmental psychologist Specializes in investigating the development of individuals from prenatal origins through old age.

diagnosis and treatment Identifying and caring for a disease.

diagnosis and treatment plan Identification of a disease and the detailed program of action for treating the patient.

diagnosis-related groupings (DRGs) A set of payment categories that are used to classify patients for the purpose of hospital reimbursement with a fixed fee regardless of the actual cost and that are based on the diagnosis, surgical procedure used, age of patient, and expected length of stay.

diagnostic imaging The use of an image of a part of the body by radiographic techniques to aid in a diagnosis.

diagnostic medical sonography Uses sound waves to generate an image for the assessment and diagnosis of various medical conditions.

diagnostic-related groups (DRGs) A set of payment categories that are used to classify patients for the purpose of hospital reimbursement with a fixed fee regardless of the actual cost and that are based on the diagnosis, surgical procedure used, age of patient, and expected length of stay.

dietetic assistant Under direct supervision from a food service manager, dietetic technician, or dietitian, works in preparation and serving areas of hospitals and other healthcare facilities.

dietetic technician, registered (DTR) Works as a member of the food service, management, and healthcare team either independently or in consultation with a registered dietitian.

diploma nurse A nurse who has received a diploma administered in a hospital.

dispensing Opticians fit and adjust eyeglasses and may in some states fit contact lenses according to prescriptions written by ophthalmologists or optometrists, but they do not examine eyes or prescribe treatment.

Doctor of Optometry Degree that requires the completion of a four-year program at an accredited optometry school, preceded by at least three years of preoptometric study at an accredited college or university.

documentation official Paper relied on as the basis, proof, or support of something.

dosimetrist A technician who calculates the dose of radiation that will be used for treatment.

Early Retiree Reinsurance Part of the healthcare reform legislation of 2010 for employers providing health insurance coverage for retirees 55 years and older who are not eligible for Medicare.

echocardiograph (EKG) An instrument for recording the changes of electrical potential occurring during the heartbeat that is used to diagnosis abnormalities of the heart.

echocardiographer Technologist who uses ultrasound to examine the heart chambers, valves, and vessels.

educational psychologist Designs, develops, and evaluates materials and procedures to resolve problems in educational and training programs.

educational therapist Evaluates the patient's learning ability and retention of previous learning experiences, interests, needs, and goals.

educator dietitian Teaches the science of nutrition and food service systems management in colleges, universities, and hospitals; conducts nutrition and food service systems research; and authors articles and books on nutrition and food service systems.

electrocardiograph (EKG/ECG) technician Cardiovascular technicians who specialize in EKGs, stress testing, and Holter monitor procedures.

electroencephalography Procedure that measures the electrical activity of the brain.

electroneurodiagnostic technologist (EEG technologist) A technician who operates selectroencephalographs to measure the electrical activity of the brain.

electronic health records (EHRs) Individual patient medical records stored in a computer database for easy access by physicians and other healthcare workers regardless of the setting—clinic, hospital, nursing home, or emergency care center.

emergency department Provides more advanced care in emergency situations.

emergency equipment Under medical emergency, equipment such as heart defibrillator, intravenous accessory, oxygen supply, and so on.

emergency medical services A network of services coordinated to provide aid and medical assistance from primary response to definitive care, involving personnel trained in the rescue, stabilization, transportation, and advanced treatment of traumatic or medical emergencies.

emergency medical technician-paramedics (EMT-Paramedics) Provide emergency care and, when necessary, transport the patient to a hospital.

emergency medicine A medical specialty in which physicians care for patients with acute illnesses or injuries that require immediate medical attention.

emergency medicine physicians In this field work specifically in emergency rooms, where they treat acute illnesses and emergency situations.

emergency skills Skills applicable to a medical emergency including, but not limited to emergency care (health care at the basic life support level), for example, spinal immobilization, administration of oxygen, and control of bleeding.

emotional disorders Competent use of one's intellectual activity (as thinking, reasoning, remembering, imagining, or learning words).

emotional disturbance A condition with the inability to learn, inability to build or maintain interpersonal relationships, display of inappropriate behaviors, and tendency to develop physical symptoms or fears associated with personal or school problems that adversely affects a child's educational performance.

emotional stress Feeling of being suddenly overwhelmed by the tasks of your everyday life.

EMT-Basic An EMT trained at this level is prepared to care for patients at the scene of an accident and while transporting patients by ambulance to the hospital under medical direction.

EMT-Intermediate An EMT at this level has more advanced training and can provide the most extensive pre-hospital care; however, what they are permitted to do varies by state.

endodontics Root canal therapy.

engineering psychologist Deals with the design and use of the systems and environments in which people live and work.

environmental factors Determinants of disease that are found in an individual surrounding area.

environmental hazards Sources of danger in the area that surrounds you.

environmental health control Regulation of hazardous substances and their disposal and monitoring of water and air quality.

Environmental Protection Agency (EPA) Branch of the U.S. government that develops policies to protect the safety of air, soil, and water. The EPA monitors compliance by industry and provides technical assistance in times of weather and other emergencies.

epidemic An outbreak of disease in a certain geographic area in greater numbers than usual; the most common cause of an epidemic in the United States is influenza (flu).

evoked potential studies Aid in the evaluation of the visual, auditory, and other sensory systems of the body.

executive health services (generalist, clinical) Responsible for planning, directing, coordinating, and supervising the delivery of health care. Generalists manage an entire facility or system and specialists manage clinical departments such as nursing, laboratory, or rehabilitation services.

exercise programs A regimen of exercises designed to achieve certain goals in physical and mental health. For example, walk 1 hour a day, 15 minutes each time. The components of the program vary: age, gender, height, weight, residence, home equipment, and so on.

expanded medical technology Excessive cost and new skills associated with the advances in healthcare technology.

experimental psychologist Designs, conducts, and analyzes experiments to develop knowledge regarding human and animal behavior.

family practice A medical practice that provides health care regardless of age or sex while placing emphasis on the family unit.

family practitioner Delivers comprehensive, primary healthcare services for all family members.

family services Child and family services is a government and/or nonprofit organization designed to better the well-being of individuals who come from unfortunate situations, environmental or biological.

federal and state health regulators Responsible for controlling, preserving, or improving environmental conditions so community health, safety, comfort, and well-being are maintained.

federally funded primary care centers Provide preventive, medical, dental, and mental health services to uninsured low income, minority, and homeless individuals in both urban and rural underserved areas.

fee-for-service payment Payment to a healthcare provider for each medical service rendered to a patient.

financial viability Ability to work, function, and develop on a financial level.

first aid training and accessories Training to learn about first aid to apply to a person in need, for example, to use accessories such as a bandage and antibiotic creams for a bleeding finger.

first responder This term has many meanings. In general, it refers to the first "certified" person at an accident scene—for example, an emergency medical technician, a police officer, or a firefighter—who arrives at the scene of a disaster, accident, or life-threatening medical situation. The first responder's duties include providing medical assistance and calling other emergency caregivers to the scene.

fissure sealants Sometimes known as pits sealants. In dentistry, one method of preventing cavities from developing in the pits and fissures identified in or near teeth is to seal them off with a special varnish called a pit and fissure sealant.

fluoroscopy An instrument used in medical diagnosis for observing the internal structure of opaque objects by casting a shadow of the object upon a fluorescent screen.

food animal veterinarian Specializes in the health care of cattle, poultry, swine, fish, and sheep.

food inspectors Ensure products are fit for human consumption in accordance with federal laws governing the wholesomeness and purity of meat, poultry, and egg products.

food safety inspections Viewing the food supply closely in critical appraisal.

frail elderly Physically weak patients of advanced age.

franchise license Granted to an individual or group to market a company's goods or services.

fringe benefits An employment benefit that has a monetary value but does not affect basic wage rates.

functional independence The degree to which a patient can function on their own.

gamma scintillation Camera scanner used to take pictures of the radioisotopes as they pass through the patient's body.

Geriatric Academic Career Awards (GACA) Grants awarded to accredited medical schools for training academic geriatricians and interdisciplinary teams of health professionals.

geriatrics Branch of medicine that deals with the problems and diseases of old age and aging people.

gerontology The scientific study of the biological, psychological, and sociological phenomena associated with old age and aging.

gerontology social worker Specializes in services to the aged.

geropsychologist Deals with the special problems faced by the elderly.

globalization Ease of access to travel and transportation of food products. Increases exposure to communicable diseases and food-borne illness, and adds to challenges in tracking the origin of disease or food-borne illness.

governing board leadership Group of persons having authority in managerial, supervisory, investigatory, or advisory powers.

grammatical patterns Proper use of words and their meanings.

groom Care for horses in stables.

groomer Animal caretaker who specializes in grooming or maintaining a pet's appearance.

group insurance Insurance available to members of a group through an employer, credit union, or professional or trade group.

group practice Physicians who often work as part of a team coordinating care for a population of patients providing backup coverage and allowing for more time off.

gynecologist Involved in the health care and maintenance of the reproductive system of women.

gynecology The branch of medicine dealing with health care for women, especially the diagnosis and treatment of disorders affecting the female reproductive organs.

hardship waiver Part of 2010 healthcare reform legislation that exempts individuals from purchasing health insurance because of financial hardship.

health and visual sciences Studied during an optometry program; courses in pharmacology, optics, vision science, biochemistry, and systemic diseases are included.

Health Care and Education Reconciliation Act of 2010 Modification of the original Patient Protection and Affordable Care Act with the addition of student loan reform.

healthcare facilities One of a variety of settings where a patient can receive care.

healthcare financing To furnish with necessary funds needed to pay for health care.

healthcare reform Federal legislation in 2010 designed to expand healthcare coverage while controlling healthcare costs and improving healthcare delivery systems.

healthcare social worker Helps patients and their families cope with chronic, acute, or terminal illness and handles problems that may stand in the way of recovery or rehabilitation.

healthcare workers Employees or volunteers in a healthcare facility who may include, but are not limited to, physicians, nurses, aides, dental workers, technicians, workers in laboratories and morgues, emergency medical service personnel, part-time personnel, and temporary staff (such as students) not employed by the healthcare facility.

healthcare workforce All professional and nonprofessional workers in all healthcare settings—hospitals, clinics, nursing homes, laboratories—that provide health care to individuals.

health education programs Programs designed to educate communities about health-related topics.

health educator Provides people with the facts about health, the causes of disease, and methods of prevention so they will act for their own well-being and that of their families.

health information Basic data (e.g., age, gender, height, weight), clinical conditions (e.g., diabetes, asthma), and many other health data about patients and their family health histories.

health information administrator Directs and controls the activities of the medical record department.

health information personnel Administrators, technicians, transcriptionists, and medical librarians that work together to manage an information system that meets medical, administrative, ethical, and legal requirements.

health information technician Organizes and evaluates medical records for completeness and accuracy.

health literacy The ability of an individual to obtain, process, and understand health information and services needed to make appropriate health decisions.

health maintenance organization (HMO) Provides basic and supplemental health maintenance and treatment services to enrollees who pay a fixed fee.

health outcome Health status of an individual or community as a result of preventive public health programs or medical intervention.

Health Professional Shortage Area (HPSA) The Health Resources and Services Administration Shortage Designation Branch of the U.S. Department of Health and Human Services. Develops and uses criteria to identify the medically underserved with lack of access to primary care, dental, or mental health providers or groups who face economic, cultural, or linguistic barriers to health care.

health professions Involving patient care, a variety of healthcare careers that focus on providing direct care to the patient.

health promotion and illness prevention services Help clients reduce the risk of illness, maintain optimal function, and follow healthy lifestyles through a wide variety of assistance and activities.

health psychologist Promotes good health through health maintenance counseling programs designed to help people achieve health-oriented goals, such as to stop smoking or lose weight.

Health Savings Account (HSA) A form of nontaxable savings that can be used to pay for medical care, often used by individuals in combination with high deductible health plans (HDHPs).

health team A variety of health personnel, each with a specialized function, designed in accordance with the needs of the client and his or her family.

Healthy People 2020 Public health goals and objectives for achieving optimal health for all who live in the United States. Four major categories are general health, health-related quality of life and well-being, determinants of health, and disparities in access to health care. The goals are based on four previous decade-long Healthy People initiatives.

hearing impairment An inability to hear speech and other sounds clearly, an inability to understand and use speech in communication, or the inability to hear speech and other sounds loudly enough.

hematology The study of blood cells.

high deductible health plan (HDHP) A health insurance plan that requires individuals to pay a set amount of healthcare costs at the beginning of each calendar year before the health plan covers the costs. Usually premiums are lower than traditional health plans.

high risk pools Government-subsidized group health insurance offered at the state level for individuals who are not eligible to purchase private insurance because of preexisting health conditions.

histology technician Cuts and stains tissue specimens for microscopic examination by pathologists and phlebotomists and draws and tests blood.

histology The study of human tissue.

Holter monitoring A portable device that makes a continuous record of electrical activity of the heart in order to detect episodes of abnormal heart rhythms.

home health agency (HHA) Provides part-time nursing and medical care in patients' homes.

home health aides Most are direct care workers and work with patients who need long-term care. They do many things. They often help patients to eat, dress, and bathe. They also answer calls for help, deliver messages, serve meals, make beds, and tidy up rooms. They take body temperature, pick up prescriptions, and collect urine samples. For all intents and purposes, terms such as *health aides, home care aides, home health aides, nursing aides, personal aides,* and similar terminologies are treated interchangeably. However, depending on the agency that provides such care, the wage per hour and components of specific tasks expected will be clearly defined for a variety of reasons.

home health care competent Use of one's intellectual activity (as thinking, reasoning, remembering, imagining, or learning words).

home health nurse Provides at-home nursing care for patients, often as follow-up care after discharge from a hospital or from a rehabilitation, long-term care, or skilled nursing facility.

horticultural therapy Uses gardening activities as the primary treatment method to bring about beneficial change is an individual with a physical, mental, or social handicap.

hospice Helps manage pain and other symptoms associated with dying when conventional treatment is no longer of value.

hospital nurse Provides bedside care to patients admitted to a hospital.

human service workers and assistant Helps social workers, healthcare workers, and other professionals to provide services to people.

immunology The study of the human immune system.

industrial psychologist Uses scientific techniques to deal with problems of motivation and morale in the work setting.

infectious disease Caused by pathogenic viruses or bacteria and transmitted by person-to-person contact or through a vector such as an infected mosquito in the case of West Nile virus.

inspection View closely in critical appraisal.

inspector Ensures products are fit for human consumption in accordance with federal laws governing the wholesomeness and purity of meat, poultry, and egg products.

insurance claims Submitted to insurance companies to request compensation for medical expenses.

intermediate care facility (ICF) Provides personal care and social services.

internal medicine The branch of medicine that deals with the diagnosis and (nonsurgical) treatment of diseases of the internal organs (especially in adults).

internist Physician who specializes in internal medicine deal with the internal organs of the body.

internship Supervised, practical experience.

interpretation and enforcement Explanation in understandable terms; to carry out effectively.

investigations To study by close examination.

itinerant program Program where teachers travel from school to school and meet with students on a regularly scheduled basis.

keeper Prepares the diets and clean the enclosures of animals who are living in a zoo.

laboratory technician Dental, medical, and ophthalmic technicians who produce a variety of medical devices to help patients see clearly, chew and speak well, or walk better.

language disorder An inability to use the symbols of language through appropriate grammatical patterns and the correct use of speech sounds.

laser surgery Corrective eye surgery.

licensed practical nurse (LPN) Care for people who are sick, injured, convalescent, or disabled under the direction of physicians and registered nurses.

licensure Having a license granted by official or legal authority to perform medical acts and procedures not permitted by persons without such a license.

life expectancy Represents the average number of years of life that could be expected if current death rates were to remain constant; used as a gauge of the overall health of a population.

lifestyle Behaviors that impact the incidence and development of disease, for example, diet, physical activity, sexual activity, and the use of alcohol, illegal drugs, and cigarettes.

lifetime limits Dollar limits imposed by a group health insurance plan for the cost of all health care or a specific diagnosis for an individual over his or her lifetime. The healthcare reform legislation of 2010 eliminated lifetime limits.

livestock Health general condition of the animals kept or raised for food consumption.

longevity The length of human life; longevity usually refers to living past the estimated life expectancy or the average age of death.

long-term health care (LTC) The help needed by people of any age who are unable to care for themselves because of physical and/or mental impairment.

lung capacity The volume and flow of air during inhalation and exhalation.

MD Doctor of Medicine.

magnetic resonance imaging (MRI) Technologist radiographers that specialize in magnetic resonance imaging.

magnetic resonance scanner/imaging (MRI) A noninvasive diagnostic technique that is based on nuclear magnetic resonance of atoms within the body induced by the application of radio waves to produce computerized images of internal body tissues.

maldistribution of health personnel Occurs when new health workers are finding it difficult to obtain jobs, while in other places communities cannot find enough workers to fill existing healthcare jobs.

managed care organization (MCO) Company offering healthcare plans with cost controls using managed care.

management dietitian Responsible for large-scale food services in such places as hospitals, company cafeterias, prisons, schools, and colleges and universities.

manual arts therapy Uses mechanical, technical, and industrial activities that are vocationally significant to assist patients in their recovery and in maintaining, improving, or developing work skills.

manual dexterity The ability to quickly make coordinated movements of the hands and arms.

marine research The study of sea life.

marketing Promoting, selling, and distributing a product or service.

Meals on Wheels Supplies one hot meal a day to people cannot or do not leave their homes.

medical (health science) librarian Provides quick and efficient access to large volumes of information and materials to keep professional staff and personnel abreast of developments, new procedures and techniques, and other relevant data.

medical and scientific illustrator Draws illustrations of human anatomy and surgical procedures.

medical assistants Medical assistants perform administrative and clinical tasks to keep the offices of physicians, podiatrists, chiropractors, and other health practitioners running smoothly.

medical billing The process of submitting and following up on claims to insurance companies in order to receive payment for services rendered by a healthcare provider.

medical home The primary source of ongoing preventive care or disease management for an individual or family.

medical record administrator Supervises a medical transcriptionist to organize medical records.

medical record technician Works with a medical transcriptionist.

medical regimen Provide healthcare services on a recurring basis to patients with chronic physical or mental disorders, often in long-term care.

medical secretary Responsible for the orderly, efficient operation of the office.

medical transcriptionist (MT) An allied health profession that deals in the process of transcription or converting voice-recorded reports as dictated by physicians and/or other healthcare professionals into text format.

medical transcriptionist Translates and edits recorded dictation by physicians and other healthcare providers regarding patient assessment and treatment.

medical, science, and technical writer Reports and interprets scientific and technical developments for the general public.

Medicare and Medicaid Provide health care to those who cannot afford it; government insurance programs designed to pay for the treatment of disease and medically diagnosed conditions.

Medicare reimbursement Repayment from Medicare for out of pocket medical expenses.

medication profile A computerized record of the customer's drug therapy.

mental and intellectual Gifts and talents outstanding abilities that allow a person to be capable of mental and intellectual high performance.

mental health A state of emotional and psychological well-being in which an individual is able to use his or her cognitive and emotional capabilities, to function in society, and to meet the ordinary demands of everyday life.

mental health assistants Also known as psychiatric aides or psychiatric nursing assistants, they provide routine care for mentally impaired or emotionally disturbed patients. They work under the supervision of a mental health team that may include psychiatrists, psychologists, and social workers.

mental health services Staff devoted to diagnosing and treating patients with mental or emotional illnesses.

mental health social worker Assesses and treats individuals with mental illness or substance abuse problems, including abuse of alcohol, tobacco, or other drugs.

microbiology The study of bacteria and other microorganisms.

middle-level health workers Skills beyond those of a registered nurse and short those of a licensed physician.

multidisciplinary team Medical group comprised of several different specialties that evaluate the patient in terms of their individual specialties and work together to develop goals that meet the patient's needs.

muscle injuries Any muscle in the body may be damaged or injured. The various types of muscle injuries are categorized as strains, bruises (contusions), detached injuries (avulsions), and exercise-induced injury or delayed-onset soreness. The thigh and back muscles are most commonly injured.

music therapy Music is used within a therapeutic relationship to address the physical, psychological, cognitive, and social needs of individuals.

National Association of Free Clinics A nonprofit organization in the United States that supports local and regional organizations and volunteers that provides medical, dental, pharmacy, and behavioral health care to the economically disadvantaged who also are uninsured.

National Athletic Trainers' Association A national association that distributes information about athletic trainers in education, services, and counseling and represents their interests in employment, accomplishments, and similar attributes.

National Collegiate Athletic Association Division Represents the interests of college athletes only.

National Conference of State Legislation (NCSL) An organization that serves state legislators and staff of the each of the 50 states by advocating for state governments before the U.S. Congress and other federal agencies. NCSL also provides a forum for exchanging ideas as well as technical assistance.

National Institute of Environmental Health Sciences (NIEHS) One of the institutes of the National Institutes of Health that evaluates environmental factors, such as pollution, that impact the development and progression of human disease.

National Institute of National Oceanic and Atmospheric Administration (NOAA) Understand and predict changes in Earth's environment and conserve and manage coastal and marine resources to meet our Nation's economic, social, and environmental needs.

National Registry of Emergency Medical Technicians (NREMT) Certifies emergency medical service providers at five levels: First Responder; EMT-Basic; EMT-Intermediate, which has two levels called 1985 and 1999; and Paramedic.

NCLEX National Council Licensure Examination.

negotiation To work with another and arrive at a settlement.

neurology/neurophysiology Branch of medicine concerned especially with the structure, functions, and diseases of the nervous system.

neuropsychologist Studies the relationship between the brain and behavior.

nuclear medicine Branch of radiology that uses radionuclides in the diagnosis and treatment of disease.

nuclear medicine technologist Operates imaging devices to perform tests that require the use of radionuclides for diagnosis.

nurse practitioners (NPs) Advanced practice registered nurses (APRNs) with a master's or a doctoral degree. Further specializations in APRN include the certified registered nurse anesthetist (CRNA), CNM, and CNS. All nurse practitioners are registered nurses who have completed extensive additional education, training, examinations, and certifications, and have a dramatically expanded scope of practice over the traditional RN role.

nursing aides *See* Home health aides.

nursing care The care provided by a skilled nurse pertaining to professional treatment for illness or injury.

nursing care facilities According to the U.S. Census Bureau, they comprise establishments primarily engaged in providing inpatient nursing and rehabilitative services. The care is generally provided for an extended period of time to individuals requiring nursing care. These establishments have a permanent core staff of registered or licensed practical nurses who, along with other staff, provide nursing and continuous personal care services. Illustrative examples: convalescent homes or convalescent hospitals (except psychiatric), nursing homes, homes for the elderly with nursing care, rest homes with nursing care, and inpatient care hospices.

nursing home nurses They manage nursing care for residents with conditions ranging from a fracture to Alzheimer's disease. Although they often spend much of their time on administrative and supervisory tasks, RNs also assess residents' health conditions, develop treatment plans, supervise licensed practical nurses and nursing aides, and perform difficult procedures such as starting intravenous fluids.

nutrition support Pharmacists help determine and prepare the drugs needed for nutrition.

nutritionist Professional trained in applying the principles of nutrition to food selection and meal preparation.

obstetricians Work with women throughout their pregnancies, deliver infants, and care for the mothers after the delivery.

Occupational Safety and Health Administration (OSHA) Expert consultants on the application of safety principles, practices, and techniques in the workplace.

occupational social worker Helps employees cope with job-related pressures or personal problems that affect the quality of their work.

occupational therapist, registered (OTR) Credential awarded to those who graduate from an accredited educational program and pass a national certification examination.

occupational therapy Therapy for those recuperating from illness that encourages rehabilitation by performing the activities of daily life.

occupational therapy aide/assistant Medical group comprised of several different specialties that evaluate the patient in terms of their individual specialties and work together to develop goals that meet the patient's needs.

ocular disease Eye disease, which must be treated by an optometrist.

operating room Area designed for surgery.

ophthalmic laboratory technicians Grind and create lenses for glasses based on orders from dispensing opticians.

ophthalmic photography Involves the use of specialized equipment and techniques to photograph disorders and injuries of the eye.

ophthalmologist Physician who specializes in medical diagnosis and treatment of vision disorders, especially diseases and injuries to the eye.

optics Coursework that must be completed by those who wish to work in the field of optometry.

optometrist Provides vision care to patients.

oral pathology Diseases of the mouth.

oral surgery Operate on the mouth and jaws.

orderlies Attendants in a hospital responsible for the nonmedical care of patients and the maintenance of order and cleanliness.

organization and coordination Arrange and pull together several independent aspects into a whole.

orientation and mobility instructor Specialist who teaches people with blindness or visual impairments to move about effectively, efficiently, and safely in familiar and unfamiliar environments.

orthodontics The largest group of dental specialists, work to straighten teeth.

orthopedists They are medical specialists in correcting deformities of the skeletal system (especially in children).

otolaryngologist Specialist in the treatment of conditions or diseases of the ear, nose, and throat.

outpatient care Sometimes referred to as ambulatory care, it describes medical care or treatment that does not require an overnight stay in a hospital or medical facility. Outpatient care may be administered in a medical office or a hospital.

oxygen/oxygen mixture Treatment of gases to help patients suffering from breathing disorders.

passive exercise Exercises during which the therapist stretches and manipulates a patient's extremities according to the patient's tolerance.

pathologists Study the characteristics, causes, and progression of diseases.

Patient Bill of Rights Adopted by the American Hospital Association in 1972 to ensure the rights and responsibilities of hospitalized patients and their families to make decisions about treatment and other care.

pediatricians Care for children from birth to adolescence.

pediatrics Doctors who work in this field care for infants, children, and young adults.

pedodontics Dentistry for children.

perceptual skills Awareness of the elements of environment through physical sensation.

periodontics Specialize in treating the gums.

personal and home care aides *See* Home health aides.

personnel psychologist Applies his professional knowledge and skills to the hiring, assignment, and promotion of employees to increase productivity and job satisfaction.

pharmaceutical chemistry Physical and chemical properties of drugs and dosage forms.

pharmaceuticals Medicinal drugs.

pharmacotherapists Specialize in drug therapy and work closely with physicians.

pharmacy aides/assistant Often a clerk or cashier who primarily answers telephones, handles money, stocks shelves, and performs other clerical duties.

pharmacy technicians Help licensed pharmacists provide medication and other healthcare products to patients.

philosophy Most basic beliefs, concepts, and attitudes of an individual or group.

photomicrography Involves photographs taken through a microscope.

physical and mental disabilities Impaired of the body or mind that substantially limits activity.

physical disability Its definition varies, depending on whether it is a medical, legal, cultural, or other issue. For most of us, the definition is simple. A blind man has a physical disability. However, if this physical disability has something to do with insurance or payment of any form, the question of simultaneous mental disability becomes a medical or legal issue.

physical therapist Provides services that help restore function, improve mobility, relieve pain, and prevent or limit permanent physical disabilities.

physical therapist aide Helps make therapy sessions productive, under the direct supervision of a physical therapist or physical therapist assistant.

physical therapist assistant Under the direction and supervision of physical therapists, they provide part of a patient's treatment.

physical therapy The treatment of disease, injury, or deformity by physical methods such as massage, heat treatment, and exercise rather than by drugs or surgery.

physician assistant May practice preventive, diagnostic, and therapeutic medicine under the supervision of a physician or surgeon. Responsibilities may include taking a medical history, conducting a physical exam, and ordering and interpreting lab tests and X-rays required for making a diagnosis.

physician/veterinarian teams Research ways to prevent and treat various human health problems and determine the effects of drug therapies, antibiotics, or new surgical techniques by testing them on animals.

policies Acceptable procedures of a governmental body.

positron emission scanners/tomography (PET) Nuclear medicine imaging technique that produces a three-dimensional image of body processes.

preexisting medical condition Term used by the health insurance industry to describe potential subscribers who have a medical condition such as diabetes or heart disease. The healthcare reform legislation of 2010 makes it possible for those with preexisting conditions to purchase insurance through federal high-risk pools when denied coverage by private insurance carriers.

preferred provider organization (PPO) Comprises groups of physicians or a hospital that provides companies with comprehensive health services at a discount.

prevention of work-related injuries One common injury at work is carpal tunnel syndrome. The person develops a painful wrist because of the malfunction of certain nerves. It is common among workers who make repetitive motions with their hands, for example, assembly-line workers and grocery packers. There are preventive measures including rotating job types and using specialized bandages.

prevention Taking advanced measures against disease.

preventive medicine/occupational medicine physician In this field, may work as health officers in infectious disease control or in treatment of illnesses associated with industry.

primary care Focuses on prevention, early detection and treatment, and overall responsibility for individual patients.

primary care physician Involved with the care of the total patient and is prepared educationally to handle most types of illnesses.

primary health care Includes family practice physicians, physicians in general pediatric practice, or those in general internal medicine practice and focuses on prevention, early detection and treatment, and overall responsibility for individual patients.

private hospital Funded and operated by private corporations, religious organizations, or medical groups instead of government funds.

private insurance Health insurance provided through an employer or purchased by an individual through another group such as a professional organization.

The risk of high healthcare cost is pooled among a large number of people, which keeps the cost of premiums affordable.

professional certification Granted by health professionals' national organizations to ensure health professionals meet established levels of competency.

professional registration The listing of certified health professionals on an official roster kept by a state agency or health professionals' organization; some health professionals' organizations use the term "registration" interchangeably with "certification."

Program of All-Inclusive Care for the Elderly (PACE) Provides comprehensive preventive, primary, acute, and long-term care services so older individuals with chronic care needs can continue living in their local community.

programs course Constituting an area of specialization.

proprietary hospital Operated for the financial benefit of the persons, partnerships, or corporations that own them.

proprietary nursing homes Nursing home that operates as a for profit entity.

prosthodontics Make artificial teeth or dentures.

psychiatric aide Works as part of a team to care for mentally impaired or emotionally disturbed individuals

psychiatric or mental health technician Works as part of a team to provide care and treatment of emotionally or mentally disabled patients.

psychiatrist Helps patients recover their mental health.

psychiatry The branch of medicine that deals with the diagnosis, treatment, and prevention of mental and emotional disorders.

psychological treatment Alteration in an individual's interpersonal environment intended to have the effect of alleviating symptoms of mental or emotional disturbance.

psychometric psychologist Directly measures human behavior, primarily through the use of tests.

public health dentistry Community dental health.

public health Focuses on the protection and improvement of community health.

Public Health Service (PHS) Group of eight agencies that focus on making laws, allocating funds, and doing investigative work to protect the health of all Americans.

public hospital Hospital owned by local, state, or federal agencies.

radiation therapy Treatment of disease by radiation.

radiologic technician/radiographer/X-ray technician Takes X-rays and administers nonradioactive materials into patients' bloodstreams for diagnostic purposes.

radiologist Physician who specializes in the interpretation of radiographs.

radiologist Diagnoses and treats illness by the use of X-rays and radioactive materials.

radionuclides Unstable atoms that emit radiation spontaneously.

radiopharmaceutical Radioactive drug.

radiopharmacist/nuclear pharmacist Applies the principles and practices of pharmacy and radiochemistry to produce radioactive drugs that are used for diagnosis and therapy.

recreational sports Those activities where the primary purpose of the activity is participation, with the related goals of improved physical fitness, fun, and social involvement often prominent. Recreational sports are usually perceived as being less stressful, both physically and mentally, on the participants. This contrasts with competitive sports where the participants have a goal of winning.

recreational therapy Uses medically approved activities such as sports, games, and field trips, to treat or maintain the physical, mental, and emotional well-being of patients.

registered nurse (RN) Regardless of specialty or work setting, treats patients, educates patients and the public about various medical conditions, and provides advice and emotional support to patients' family members.

Registered Respiratory Therapist (RRT) Credential awarded to CRTs who have graduated from advanced programs and pass two separate examinations.

registration The listing of certified health professionals on an official roster kept by a state agency or health professionals' organization.

regulatory medicine Focuses on the control/elimination of certain diseases, and protection of the public from animal diseases.

rehabilitation The restoration of a person to normal or near normal function after a physical or mental illness, including chemical addiction.

rehabilitation center credential Awarded to those who graduate from an accredited educational program and pass a national certification examination.

rehabilitation counselor A professional who counsels a person how to restore to good health or useful life.

rehabilitation psychologist Work with disabled persons, either individually or in groups, to assess the degree of disability and develop ways to correct or compensate for these impairments.

rehabilitation teacher A specialist who provides instruction and guidance to individuals who are blind or those who have visual impairments.

rehabilitative services Help people with disabilities achieve employment and independent living.

reimbursement To make a return payment to.

repetitive stress injuries (RSIs) RSIs are injuries that happen when too much stress is placed on a part of the body, resulting in inflammation (pain and swelling), muscle strain, or tissue damage. This stress generally occurs from repeating the same movements over and over again. RSIs are common work-related injuries, often affecting people who spend a lot of time using computer keyboards.

research Collecting of information about a particular subject.

research dietitians Employed in academic medical centers or educational institutions, although some work in community health programs.

school health educator Helps children and young people develop the knowledge, attitudes, and skills they need to live healthfully and safely.

school psychologist Concerned with developing effective programs for improving the intellectual, social, and emotional development of children in an educational system or school.

school social worker Serves as the link between students' families and the school, working with parents, guardians, teachers, and other school officials to ensure students reach their academic and personal potential.

self-directed services Provides for people with disabilities to allow them freedom, authority, support, and responsibility within an assisted environment.

shelter care Provides the basics—food, shelter, clothing, companionship—to long-term care recipients that have no major physical problems that require nursing care.

side effects A secondary and usually adverse effect.

skilled nursing facility (SNF) A nursing home that provides the level of care closest to hospital care.

sleep study Records the physical changes that occur in the body while the patient is sleeping.

Small Business Options Program Exchange (SHOP) Part of the 2010 health-care reform legislation in which small businesses with up to 100 employees can purchase qualified coverage for employees through SHOP exchanges established at the state or regional level.

social work administrator Performs overall management tasks in hospital, clinic, or other setting that offers social worker services.

social work planners and policy makers Develop programs to address such issues as child abuse, homelessness, substance abuse, poverty, and violence.

socioeconomic status (SES) Position or rank based on a combination of social and economic factors.

solo practitioner Physician who works in an independent setting instead of a group practice.

sonographer/ultrasound technologist Operates which collects reflected echoes and forms an image that may be videotaped, transmitted, or photographed for interpretation and diagnosis by a physician.

space research Study of the region beyond the earth's atmosphere.

special education teacher Works with pupils who have physical disabilities, emotional disturbances, mental retardation, or specific mental and intellectual gifts and talents.

spectator sports Sports that attract more people as spectators than as participants.

speech disorder Identified by an individual's difficulty in producing speech sounds, controlling voice production, and maintaining speech rhythm.

speech pathologists and audiologists Speech pathologists specialize in identifying and treating speech problems such as stuttering. Audiologists specialize in clinical disorders of hearing.

speech-language pathologist Assesses, diagnoses, treats, and helps to prevent disorders related to speech, language, cognitive-communication, voice, swallowing, and fluency.

sport centers Area or locations in a private (e.g., spa, fitness) or public (e.g., stadium, school) environment where specific sports take place, for example, a football stadium, a tennis court, or a spa center.

sports equipment Refers to equipment used in a sport, for example, shoes for basketball players and helmets for football players.

sports medicine A branch of medicine concerned with the effects of exercise and sports on the human body, including the treatment of injuries.

sports medicine Specialty concerned with the prevention and treatment of injuries and disorders that are related to participation in sports.

standards for pure food from animal sources Measure of quality established to ensure safe food production from animal sources.

statistics Collection of quantitative data.

strategic planning A careful, well-thought method of establishing goals, policies, and procedures.

stress testing Monitors the heart's performance while the patient is walking on a treadmill, gradually increasing the treadmill's speed to observe the effect of increased exertion on the heart.

surgeon Operates so as to treat disease, repair injury, correct deformities, and improve the general health of the patient.

surgery The branch of medicine that deals with the diagnosis and treatment of injury, deformity, and disease by manual and instrumental means.

surgical technologist Assists in surgical operations under the supervision of surgeons, registered nurses, or other surgical personnel.

symptoms and response Evidence of disease and the bodies reaction to a course of treatment.

teachers of those who are blind or have visual impairment Provide specialized educational services to children in residential, public, or private schools.

teaching credentials A U.S. teaching credential is a basic multiple- or single-subject credential obtained upon completion of a bachelor's degree and prescribed professional education requirements. Teaching credentials are required in the United States in order to qualify to teach public school as well as many other types of instruction. Requirements vary from state to state.

technology Tools and systems used to deliver health care including computerized medical records, automated laboratory analysis, surgical robotics, and sophisticated diagnostic imaging—computerized axial tomography (CAT) and magnetic resonance imaging (MRI). Advances in technology contribute to the high cost of health care in the United States.

telecommunications Communication at a distance.

telemedicine Practice of medicine when the doctor and patient are widely separated using two-way voice and visual communication.

The Health Care and Education Reconciliation Act Modification of the original Patient Protection and Affordable Care Act with the addition of student loan reform.

third-party payer Payment for medical services that comes from elsewhere then the patient generally government programs and private health insurance.

third-party reimbursement Reimbursement for services rendered by a provider to a person in which an entity other than the receiver of the service is responsible for the payment. For a doctor, a patient, and an insurance company in the healthcare system, the insurance company is the third-party reimbursing the doctor's fee.

toxicology Measure of quality established to ensure safe food production from animal sources.

transmissible diseases Illnesses and infections easily based from one to another.

trauma center A hospital unit specializing in the treatment of patients with acute and life-threatening traumatic injuries.

tumor registrar Compile and maintain records of patients who have cancer to provide information to physicians and for research studies.

U.S. Department of Agriculture's Food Safety and Inspection Service (FSIS) The public health agency in the U.S. Department of Agriculture responsible for ensuring that the nation's commercial supply of meat, poultry, and egg products is safe, wholesome, and correctly labeled and packaged.

U.S. Food and Drug Administration (FDA) Responsible for protecting the public health by assuring the safety, efficacy, and security of human and veterinary drugs, biological products, medical devices, our nation's food supply, cosmetics, and products that emit radiation.

ultrasound machine An electronic device that uses vibrations of the same physical nature as sound to form a two-dimensional image used for the examination and measurement of internal body structures.

ventilator A machine that pumps air into the lungs.

veterinarian Cares for the health of pets, livestock, and animals in zoos, racetracks, and laboratories.

veterinary assistant An animal caretaker in an animal hospital or clinic.

video display terminals A computer output surface and projecting mechanism that shows text and graphic images to the user.

vision therapy Treatment for those with vision issues.

voluntary nursing Homes nursing home that operates as a for profit entity.

volunteer EMT Depending on the legal requirements of a state, this term refers to "volunteer first aid, rescue, and ambulance squad," which provides emergency medical services without receiving payment for those services. In this country the oldest and traditional volunteer emergency medical technician is a voluntary firefighter. To protect such persons or representatives from liability, many states standardize this term.

wellness and health promotion Wellness is generally used to mean a healthy balance of the mind, body, and spirit that results in an overall feeling of well-being. Health promotion refers to the improvement of health or wellness. For example, stopping smoking is one means to promote one's health and wellness.

World Health Organization (WHO) The directing and coordinating authority for health within the United Nations system; responsible for providing leadership on global health matters, shaping the health research agenda, setting norms and standards, articulating evidence-based policy options, providing technical support to countries, and monitoring and assessing health trends.

Index

A

Note: Page numbers referencing tables are italicized.

Photo Credits

Openers: Chapter 1 © Photos.com; **Chapter 2** © James Steidl/ShutterStock, Inc.; **Chapter 3** © Frank Anusewicz/ShutterStock, Inc.; **Chapter 4** © Photos.com; **Chapter 5** © Andy Dean/Fotolia.com; **Chapter 6** © visi.stock/Shutter Stock, Inc.; **Chapter 7** © Monkey Business Images/ShutterStock, Inc.; **Chapter 8** © Serghei Starus/ShutterStock, Inc.; **Chapter 9** © Kurhan/Shut terStock, Inc.; **Chapter 10** © Corbis/age fotostock; **Chapter 11** Courtesy of USDA; **Chapter 12** © LiquidLibrary; **Chapter 13** © Photos.com; **Chapter 14** © Paul Matthew Photography/ShutterStock, Inc.; **Chapter 16** © Photos.com; **Chapter 17** © Lisa F. Young/ShutterStock, Inc.; **Chapter 18** © iStockphoto/Thinkstock; **Chapter 19** © CARDOSO/age fotostock; **Chapter 20** © Evok20/ShutterStock, Inc.; **Chapter 21** © Marcus Miranda/ShutterStock, Inc.; **Chapter 22** © Ian Wyatt/Photodisc/Getty Images; **Chapter 23** © Jupiterimages/Brand X/Alamy Images; **Chapter 24** © iStockphoto/Thinkstock; **Chapter 25** © Alexander Raths/ShutterStock, Inc.; **Chapter 26** © Photodisc; **Chapter 27** © gilles lougassi/Fotolia.com; **Chapter 28** © Hannah Gleghorn/ShutterStock, Inc.; **Chapter 29** Courtesy of James Gathany/CDC; **Chapter 30** © Photos.com; **Chapter 31** © Miodrag Gajic/ShutterStock, Inc.

Unless otherwise indicated, all photographs and illustrations are under copyright of Jones & Bartlett Learning.

Some images in this book feature models. These models do not necessarily endorse, represent, or participate in the activities represented in the images.